Shojo Beat

ORESAMA TEACHER

eternal relation

Vol. **11**

Story & Art by

Izumi Tsubaki

ORESAMA TEACHER

Volume 11
CONTENTS

Chapter 58------------------------3

Chapter 59------------------------33

Chapter 60------------------------65

Chapter 61------------------------95

Chapter 62------------------------126

Chapter 63------------------------159

End Notes------------------------191

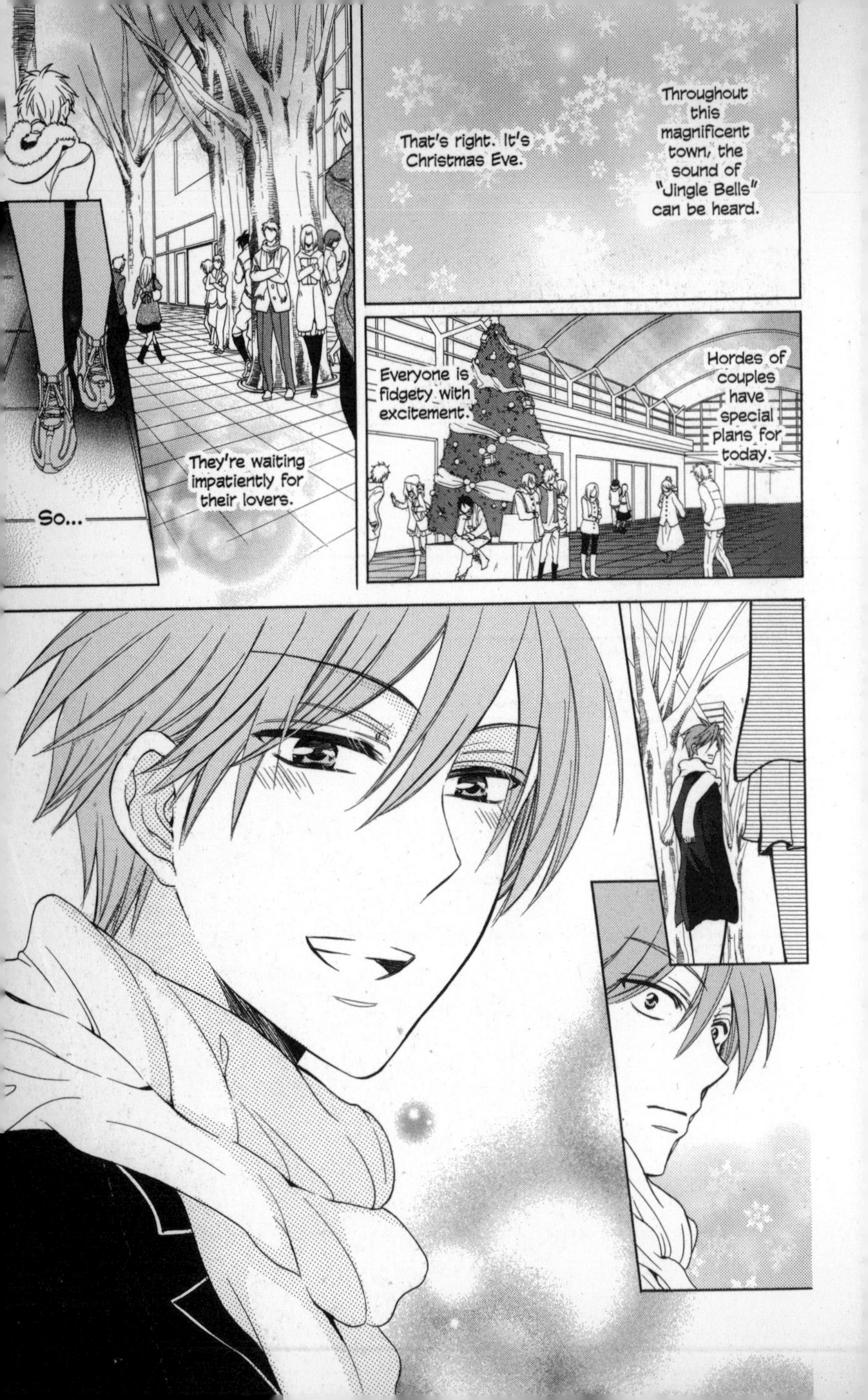
Throughout this magnificent town, the sound of "Jingle Bells" can be heard.
That's right. It's Christmas Eve.
Hordes of couples have special plans for today.
Everyone is fidgety with excitement.
They're waiting impatiently for their lovers.
So...

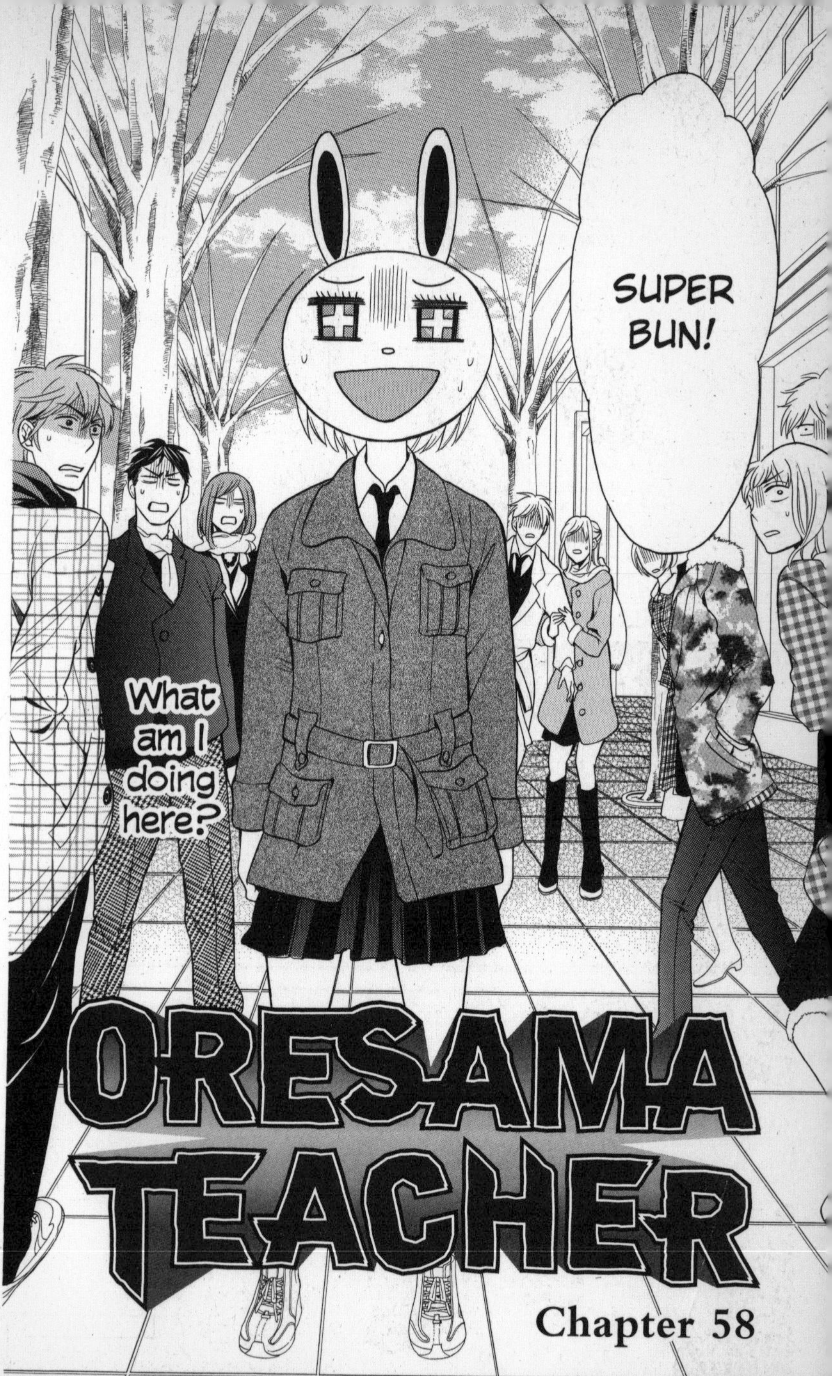
SUPER BUN!
What am I doing here?
ORESAMA TEACHER
Chapter 58

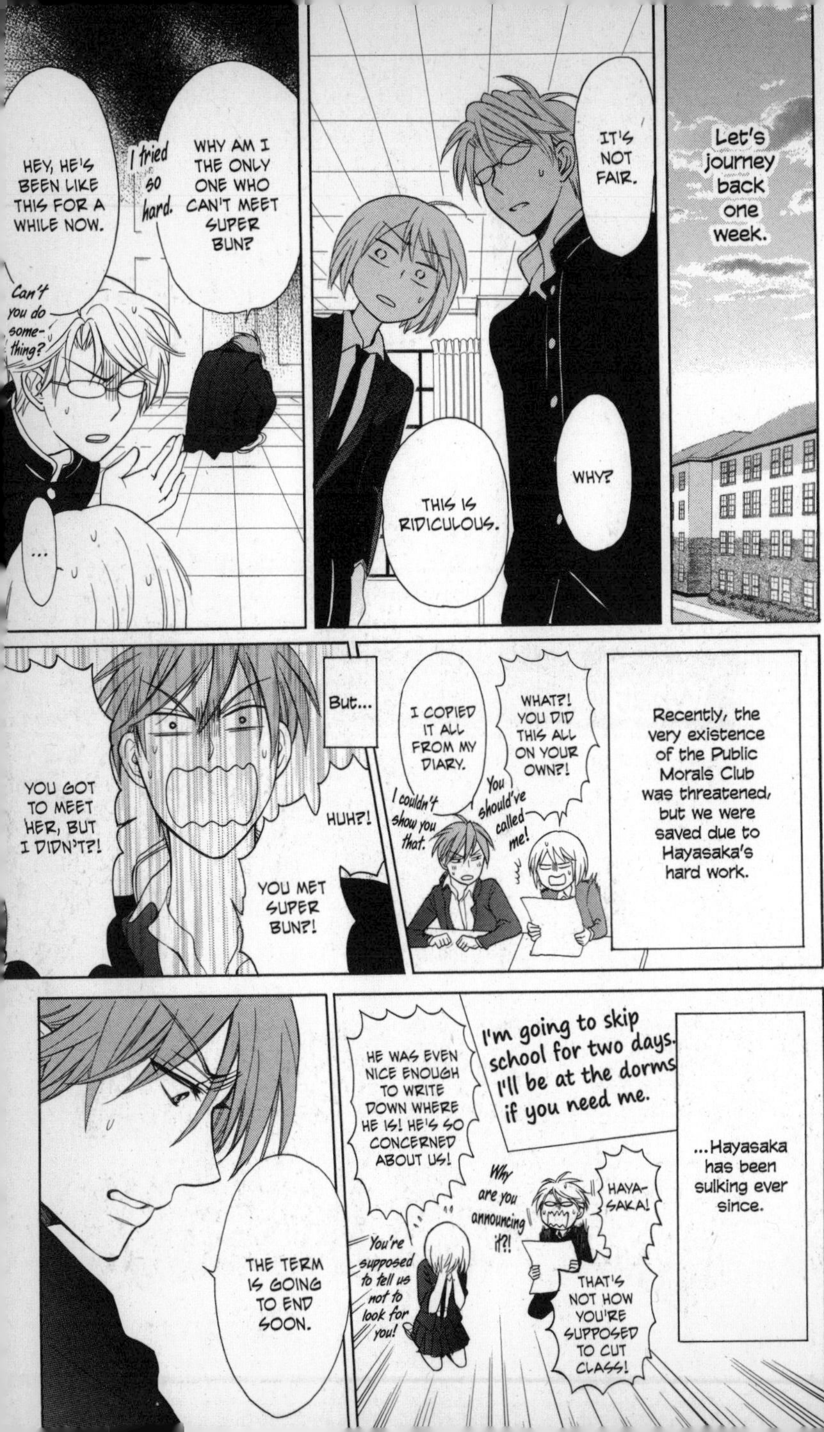

Let's journey back one week.
IT'S NOT FAIR.
WHY?
THIS IS RIDICULOUS.
WHY AM I THE ONLY ONE WHO CAN'T MEET SUPER BUN?
I tried so hard.
HEY, HE'S BEEN LIKE THIS FOR A WHILE NOW.
Can't you do some-thing?
...
Recently, the very existence of the Public Morals Club was threatened, but we were saved due to Hayasaka's hard work.
WHAT?! YOU DID THIS ALL ON YOUR OWN?!
You should've called me!
I COPIED IT ALL FROM MY DIARY.
I couldn't show you that.
But...
HUH?!
YOU MET SUPER BUN?!
YOU GOT TO MEET HER, BUT I DIDN'T?!
...Hayasaka has been sulking ever since.
I'm going to skip school for two days. I'll be at the dorms if you need me.
HAYA-SAKA!
THAT'S NOT HOW YOU'RE SUPPOSED TO CUT CLASS!
Why are you announcing it?!
HE WAS EVEN NICE ENOUGH TO WRITE DOWN WHERE HE IS! HE'S SO CONCERNED ABOUT US!
You're supposed to tell us not to look for you!
THE TERM IS GOING TO END SOON.

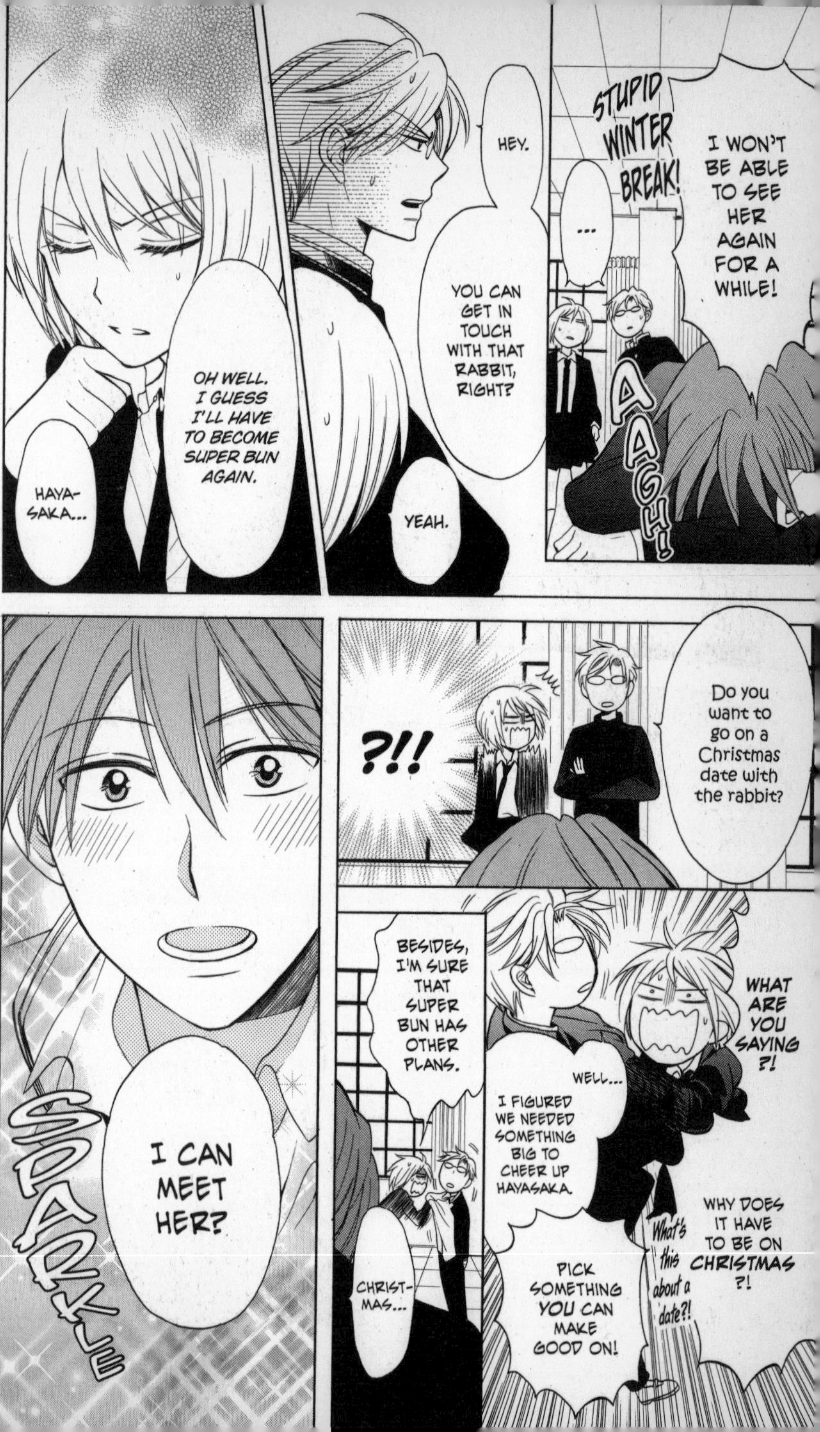
I WON'T BE ABLE TO SEE HER AGAIN FOR A WHILE!
STUPID WINTER BREAK!
AAGH!
...
HEY.
YOU CAN GET IN TOUCH WITH THAT RABBIT, RIGHT?
YEAH.
OH WELL. I GUESS I'LL HAVE TO BECOME SUPER BUN AGAIN.
HAYA-SAKA...
Do you want to go on a Christmas date with the rabbit?
?!!
WHAT ARE YOU SAYING?!
BESIDES, I'M SURE THAT SUPER BUN HAS OTHER PLANS.
WELL...
I FIGURED WE NEEDED SOMETHING BIG TO CHEER UP HAYASAKA.
WHY DOES IT HAVE TO BE ON CHRISTMAS?!
What's this about a date?!
PICK SOMETHING YOU CAN MAKE GOOD ON!
CHRIST-MAS...
I CAN MEET HER?
SPARKLE

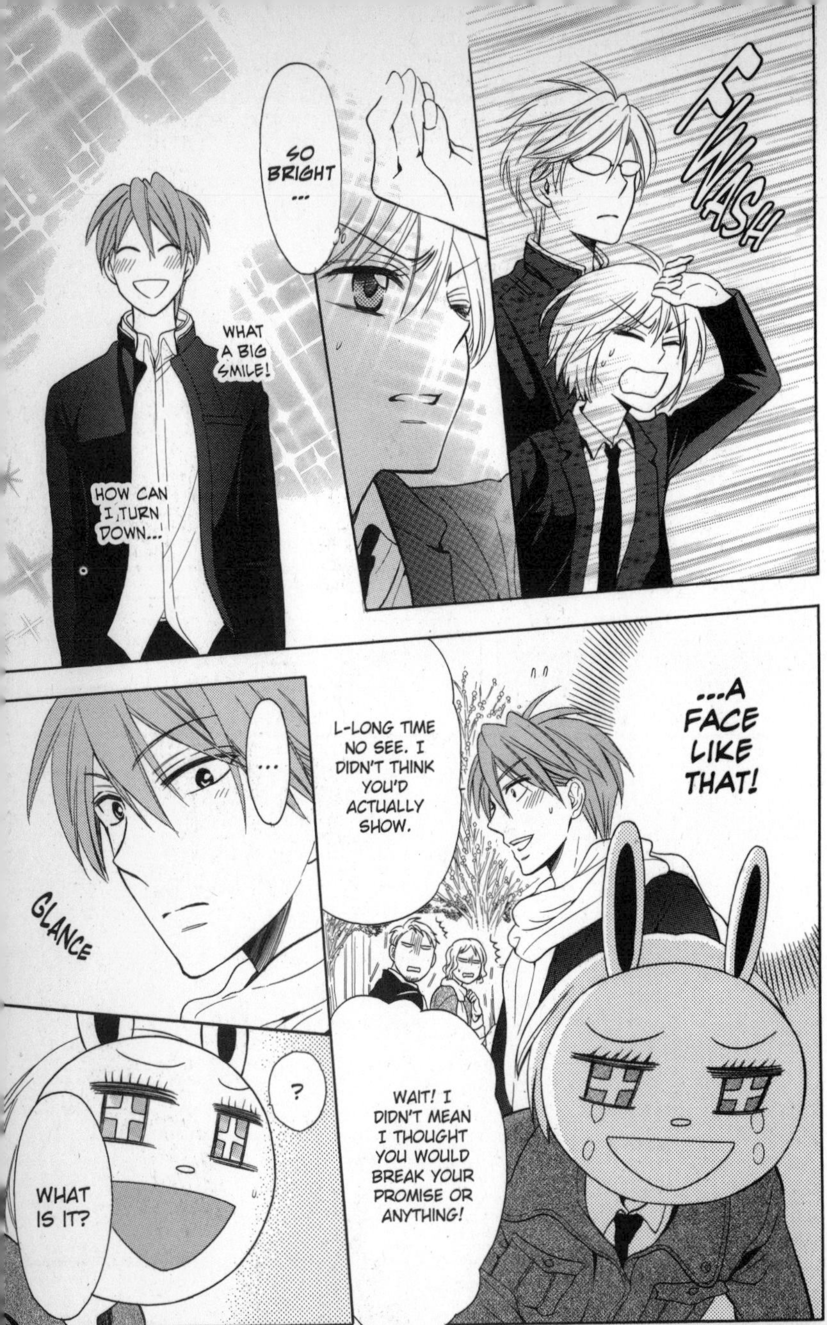
FWASH
SO BRIGHT ...
WHAT A BIG SMILE!
HOW CAN I TURN DOWN...!
...A FACE LIKE THAT!
L-LONG TIME NO SEE. I DIDN'T THINK YOU'D ACTUALLY SHOW.
...
GLANCE
WAIT! I DIDN'T MEAN I THOUGHT YOU WOULD BREAK YOUR PROMISE OR ANYTHING!
?
WHAT IS IT?

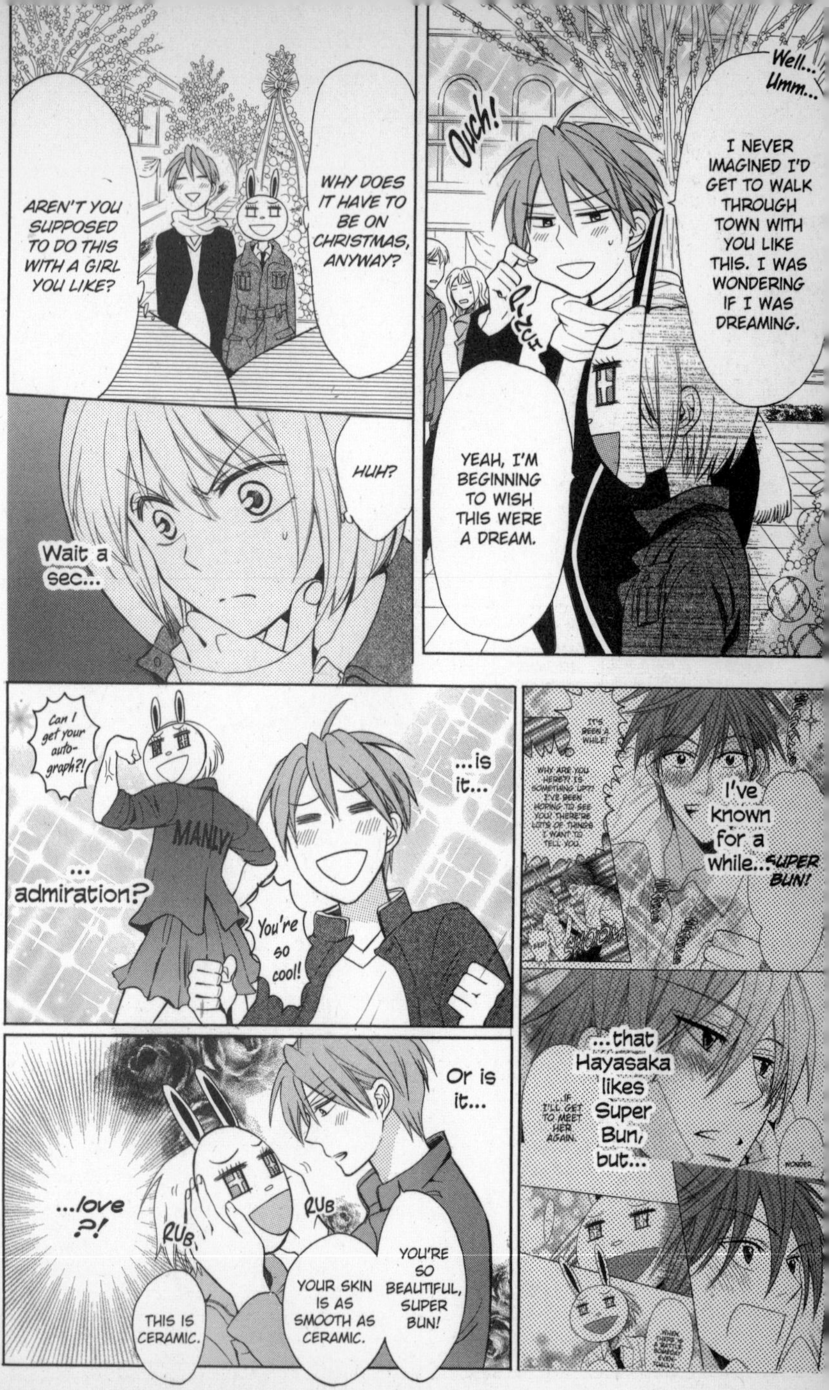
Well... Umm...
I NEVER IMAGINED I'D GET TO WALK THROUGH TOWN WITH YOU LIKE THIS. I WAS WONDERING IF I WAS DREAMING.
Ouch!
YEAH, I'M BEGINNING TO WISH THIS WERE A DREAM.
WHY DOES IT HAVE TO BE ON CHRISTMAS, ANYWAY?
AREN'T YOU SUPPOSED TO DO THIS WITH A GIRL YOU LIKE?
HUH?
Wait a sec...
IT'S BEEN A WHILE!
WHY ARE YOU HERE?! IS SOMETHING UP?! I'VE BEEN HOPING TO SEE YOU! THERE'RE LOTS OF THINGS I WANT TO TELL YOU.
I've known for a while...
SUPER BUN!
SHOOM
...that Hayasaka likes Super Bun, but...
I WONDER
...IF I'LL GET TO MEET HER AGAIN.
...is it...
Can I get your autograph?!
MANLY
... admiration?
You're so cool!
Or is it...
...love ?!
RUB
RUB
YOU'RE SO BEAUTIFUL, SUPER BUN!
YOUR SKIN IS AS SMOOTH AS CERAMIC.
THIS IS CERAMIC.

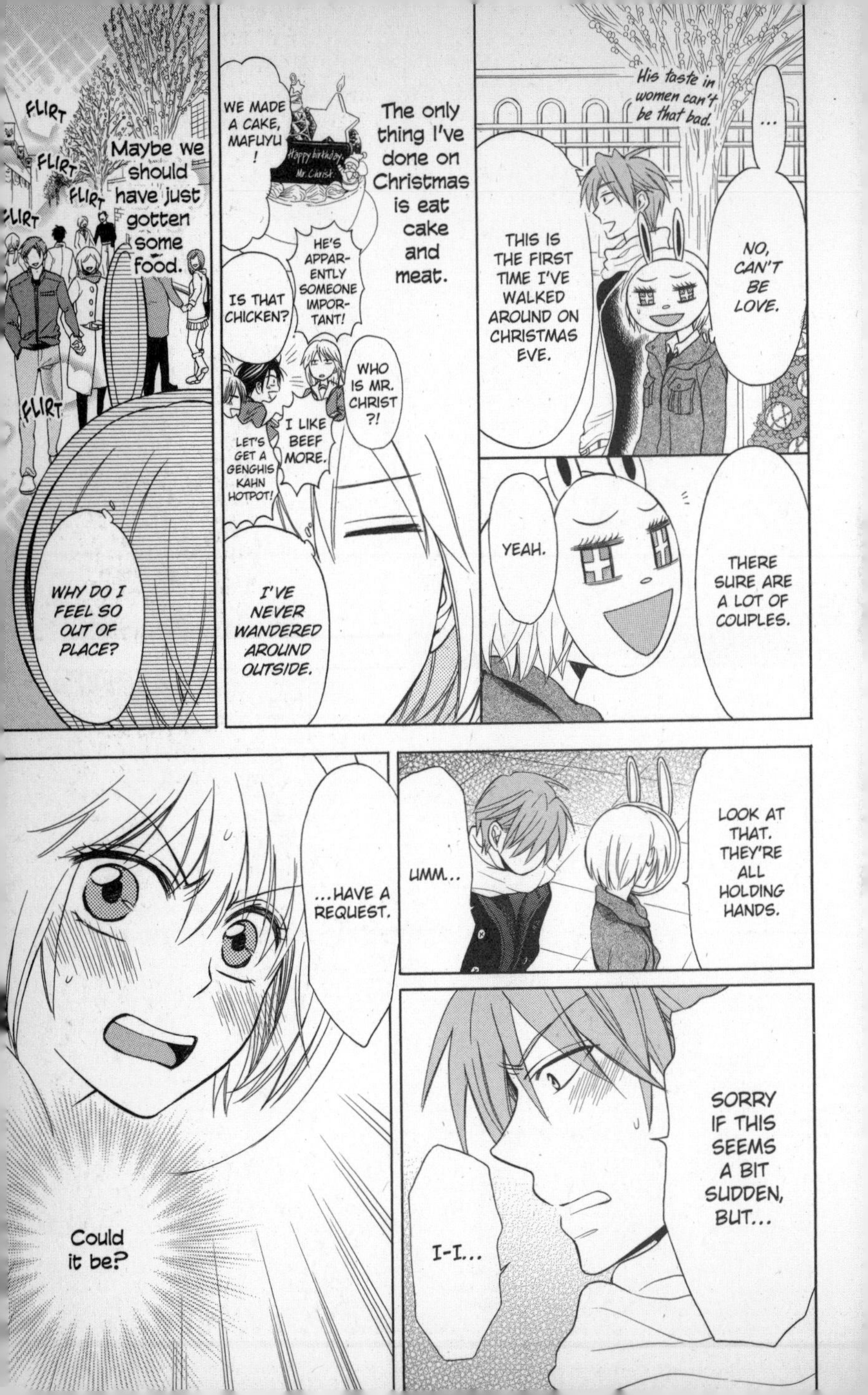
His taste in women can't be that bad.
...
NO, CAN'T BE LOVE.
THIS IS THE FIRST TIME I'VE WALKED AROUND ON CHRISTMAS EVE.
THERE SURE ARE A LOT OF COUPLES.
YEAH.
The only thing I've done on Christmas is eat cake and meat.
WE MADE A CAKE, MAFUYU!
Happy birthday, Mr. Christ.
HE'S APPARENTLY SOMEONE IMPORTANT!
IS THAT CHICKEN?
WHO IS MR. CHRIST?!
I LIKE BEEF MORE.
LET'S GET A GENGHIS KAHN HOTPOT!
I'VE NEVER WANDERED AROUND OUTSIDE.
Maybe we should have just gotten some food.
FLIRT
FLIRT
FLIRT
FLIRT
FLIRT
WHY DO I FEEL SO OUT OF PLACE?
LOOK AT THAT. THEY'RE ALL HOLDING HANDS.
UMM...
SORRY IF THIS SEEMS A BIT SUDDEN, BUT...
I-I...
...HAVE A REQUEST.
Could it be?

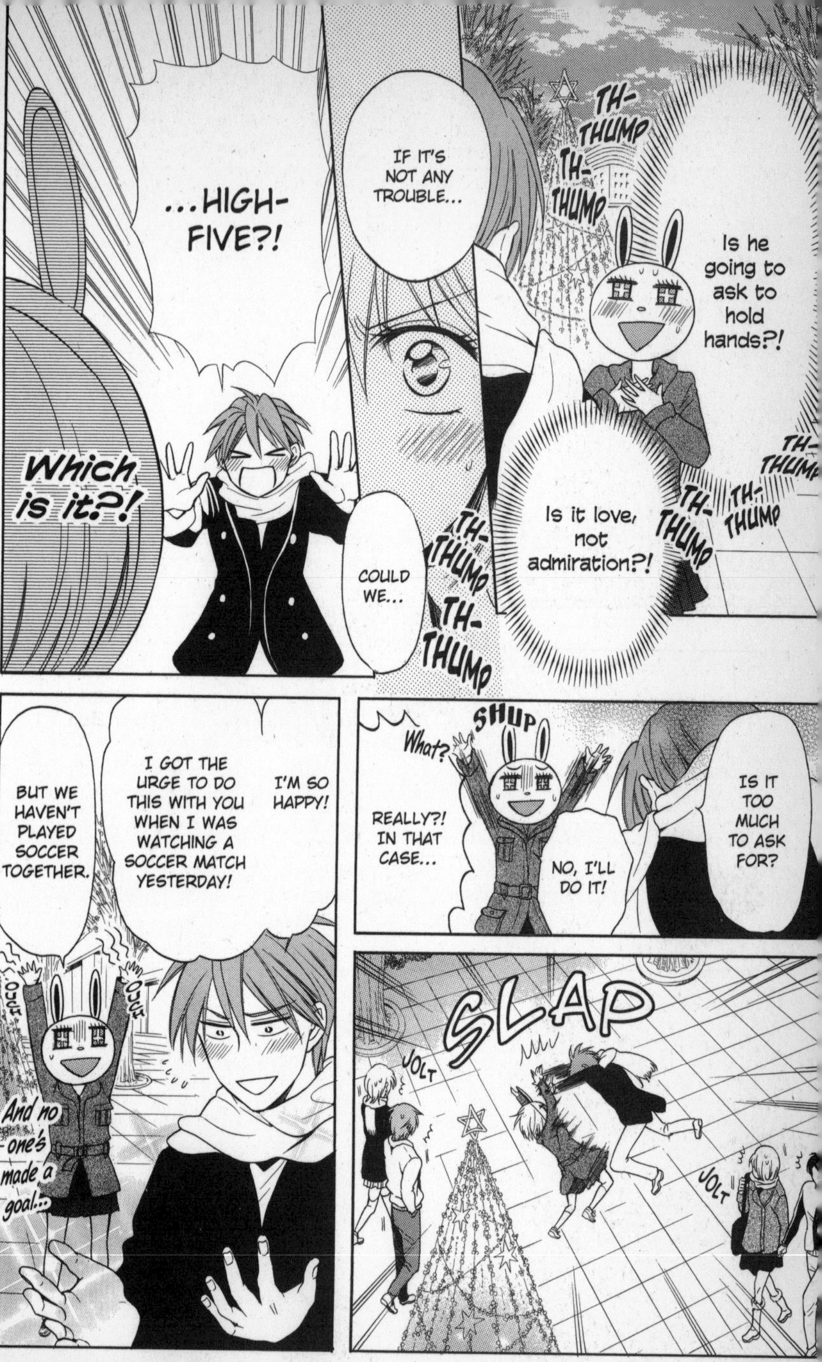
TH-THUMP
TH-THUMP
Is he going to ask to hold hands?!
TH-THUMP
TH-THUMP
TH-THUMP
Is it love, not admiration?!
IF IT'S NOT ANY TROUBLE...
TH-THUMP
TH-THUMP
COULD WE...
...HIGH-FIVE?!
Which is it?!
IS IT TOO MUCH TO ASK FOR?
NO, I'LL DO IT!
SHUP
What?
REALLY?! IN THAT CASE...
SLAP
JOLT
JOLT
I'M SO HAPPY!
I GOT THE URGE TO DO THIS WITH YOU WHEN I WAS WATCHING A SOCCER MATCH YESTERDAY!
BUT WE HAVEN'T PLAYED SOCCER TOGETHER.
OUCH
OUCH
And no one's made a goal...

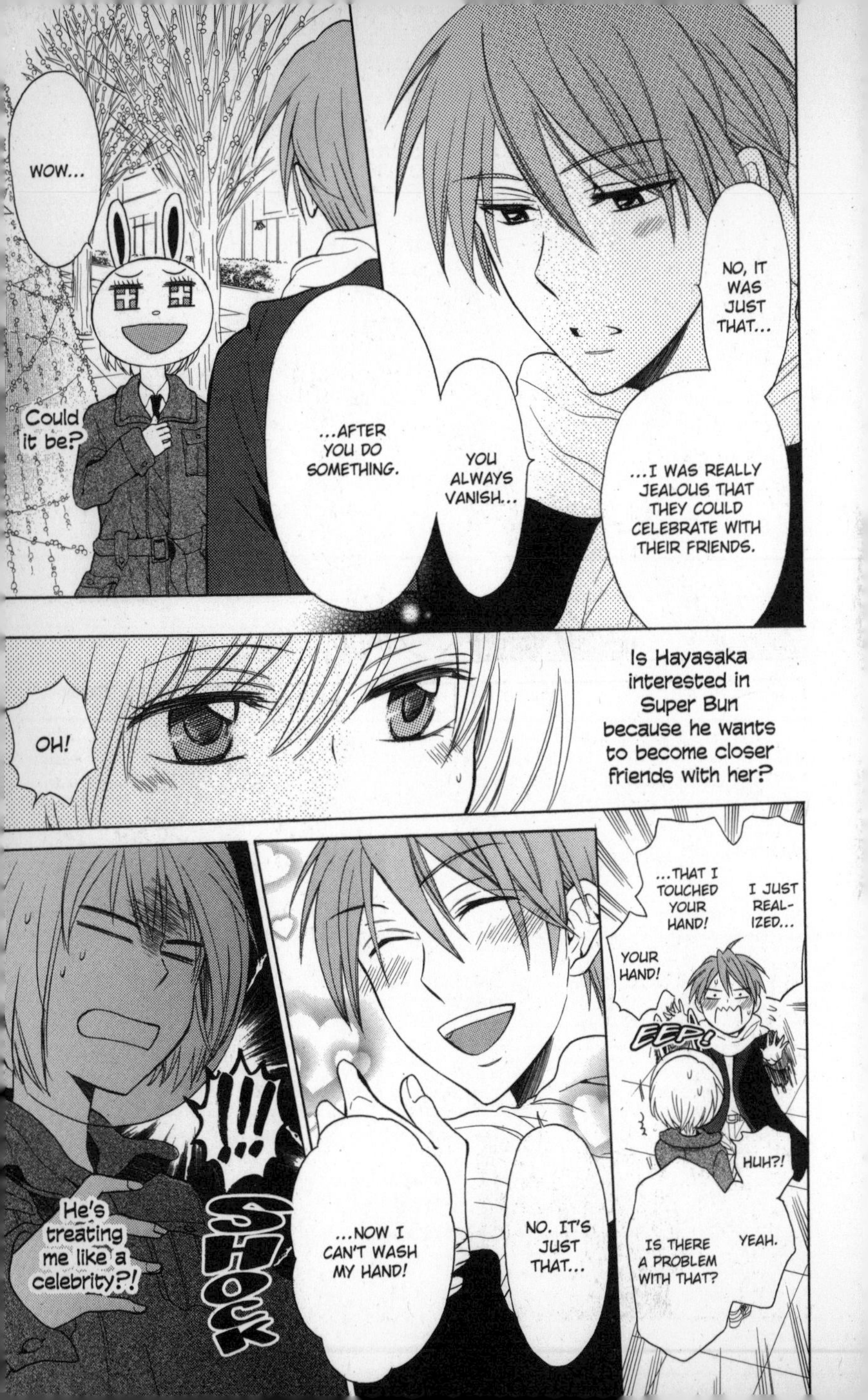
NO, IT WAS JUST THAT...
...I WAS REALLY JEALOUS THAT THEY COULD CELEBRATE WITH THEIR FRIENDS.
YOU ALWAYS VANISH...
...AFTER YOU DO SOMETHING.
WOW...
Could it be?
Is Hayasaka interested in Super Bun because he wants to become closer friends with her?
OH!
I JUST REAL-IZED...
...THAT I TOUCHED YOUR HAND!
YOUR HAND!
EEP!
HUH?!
YEAH.
IS THERE A PROBLEM WITH THAT?
NO. IT'S JUST THAT...
...NOW I CAN'T WASH MY HAND!
!!!
SHOCK
He's treating me like a celebrity?!

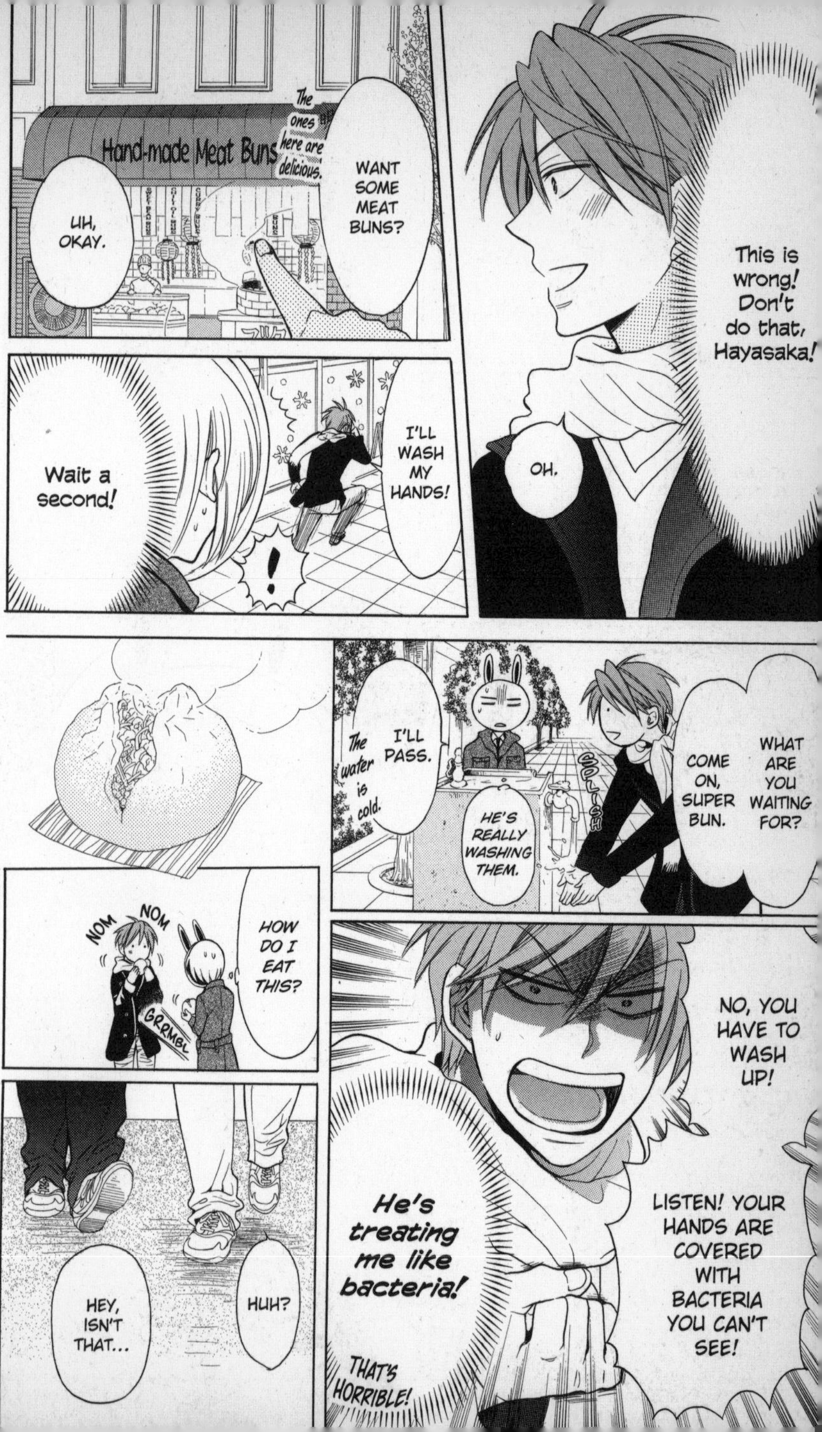
This is wrong! Don't do that, Hayasaka!
OH.
Hand-made Meat Buns
The ones here are delicious.
WANT SOME MEAT BUNS?
UH, OKAY.
I'LL WASH MY HANDS!
!
Wait a second!
WHAT ARE YOU WAITING FOR?
COME ON, SUPER BUN.
SPLISH
HE'S REALLY WASHING THEM.
I'LL PASS.
The water is cold.
NO, YOU HAVE TO WASH UP!
LISTEN! YOUR HANDS ARE COVERED WITH BACTERIA YOU CAN'T SEE!
He's treating me like bacteria!
THAT'S HORRIBLE!
HOW DO I EAT THIS?
NOM NOM
GRRMBL
HUH?
HEY, ISN'T THAT...

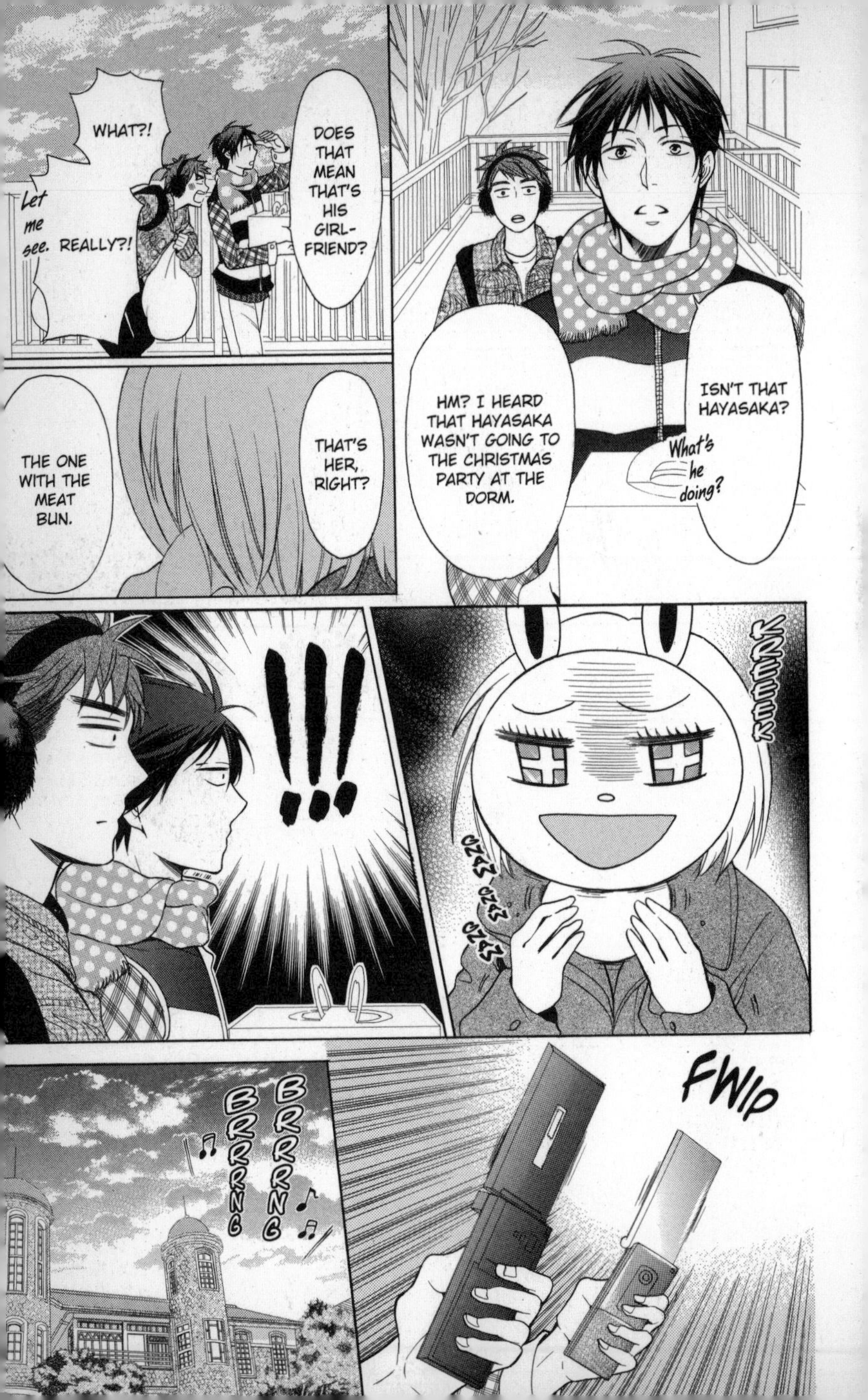
ISN'T THAT HAYASAKA?
What's he doing?
HM? I HEARD THAT HAYASAKA WASN'T GOING TO THE CHRISTMAS PARTY AT THE DORM.
DOES THAT MEAN THAT'S HIS GIRL-FRIEND?
WHAT?!
REALLY?!
Let me see.
THAT'S HER, RIGHT?
THE ONE WITH THE MEAT BUN.
KREEEK
GNAW GNAW GNAW
!!!
FWIP
BRRRRNG BRRRRNG

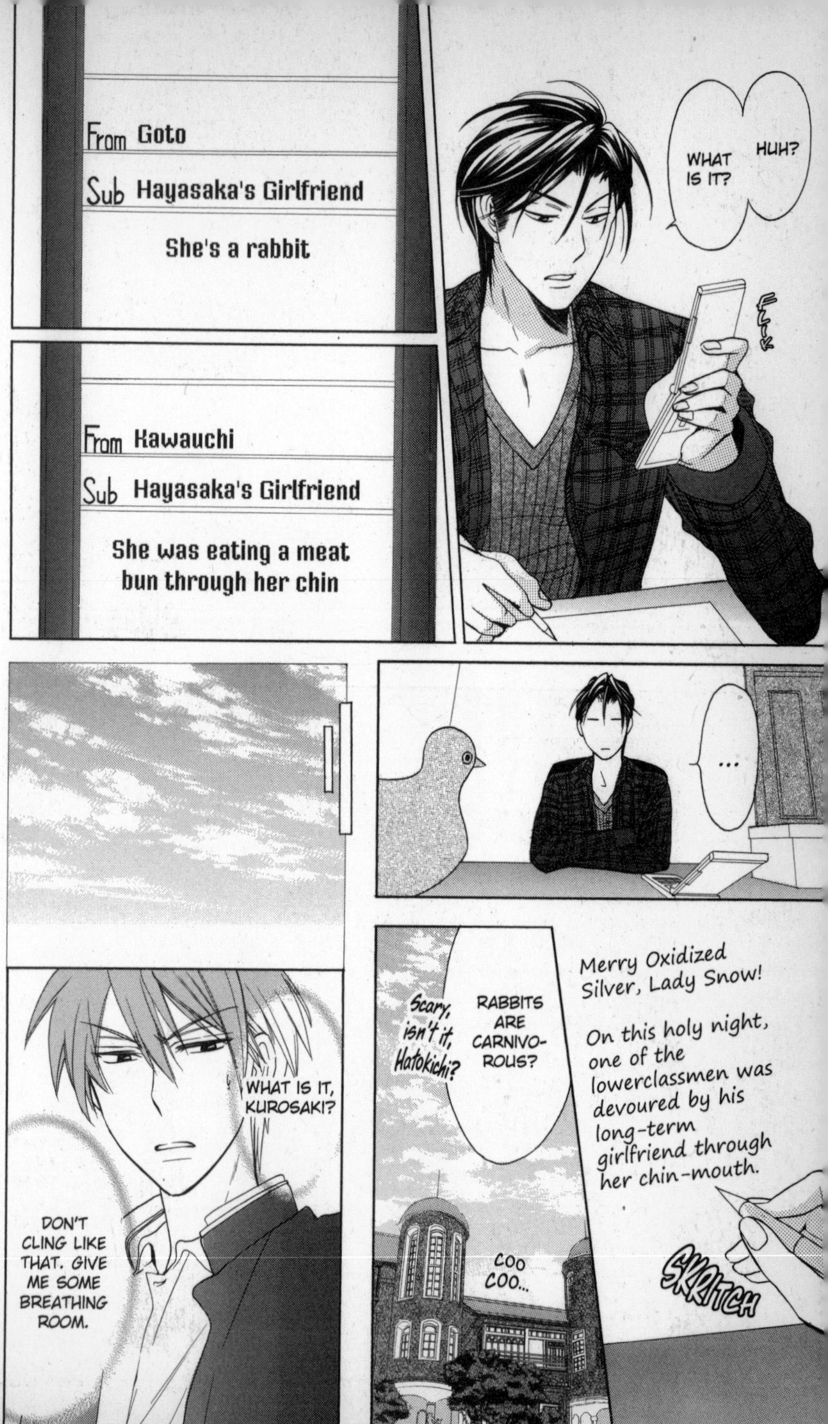
HUH?
WHAT IS IT?
FLIK
From Goto
Sub Hayasaka's Girlfriend
She's a rabbit
From Kawauchi
Sub Hayasaka's Girlfriend
She was eating a meat bun through her chin
...
Merry Oxidized Silver, Lady Snow!
On this holy night, one of the lowerclassmen was devoured by his long-term girlfriend through her chin-mouth.
RABBITS ARE CARNIVOROUS?
Scary, isn't it, Hatokichi?
COO COO...
SKRITCH
WHAT IS IT, KUROSAKI?
DON'T CLING LIKE THAT. GIVE ME SOME BREATHING ROOM.

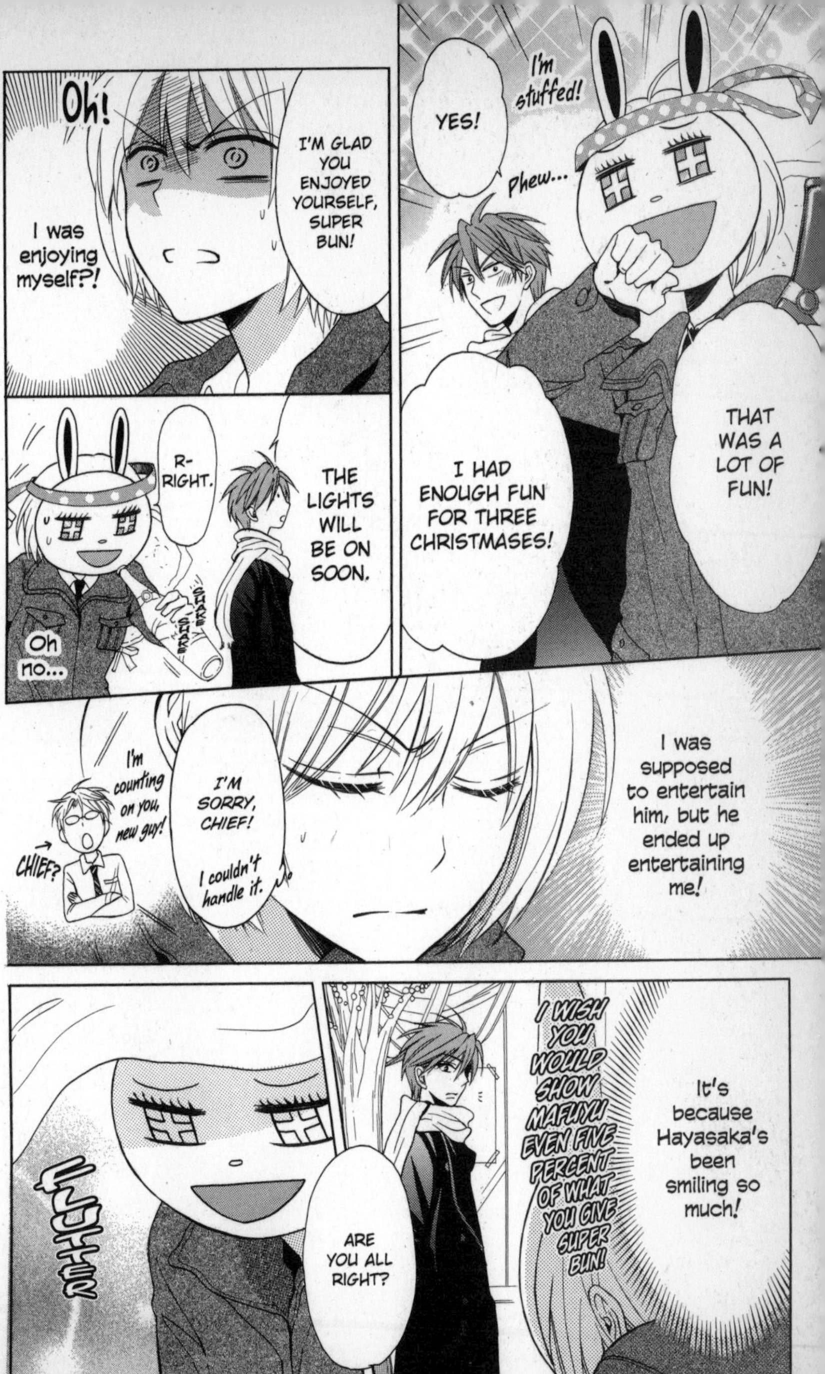
I'm stuffed!
YES!
Phew...
THAT WAS A LOT OF FUN!
I HAD ENOUGH FUN FOR THREE CHRISTMASES!
Oh!
I'M GLAD YOU ENJOYED YOURSELF, SUPER BUN!
I was enjoying myself?!
THE LIGHTS WILL BE ON SOON.
R-RIGHT.
SHAKE SHAKE
Oh no...
I was supposed to entertain him, but he ended up entertaining me!
I'M SORRY, CHIEF!
I couldn't handle it.
I'm counting on you, new guy!
CHIEF?
It's because Hayasaka's been smiling so much!
I WISH YOU WOULD SHOW MAFUYU EVEN FIVE PERCENT OF WHAT YOU GIVE SUPER BUN!
ARE YOU ALL RIGHT?
FLUTTER

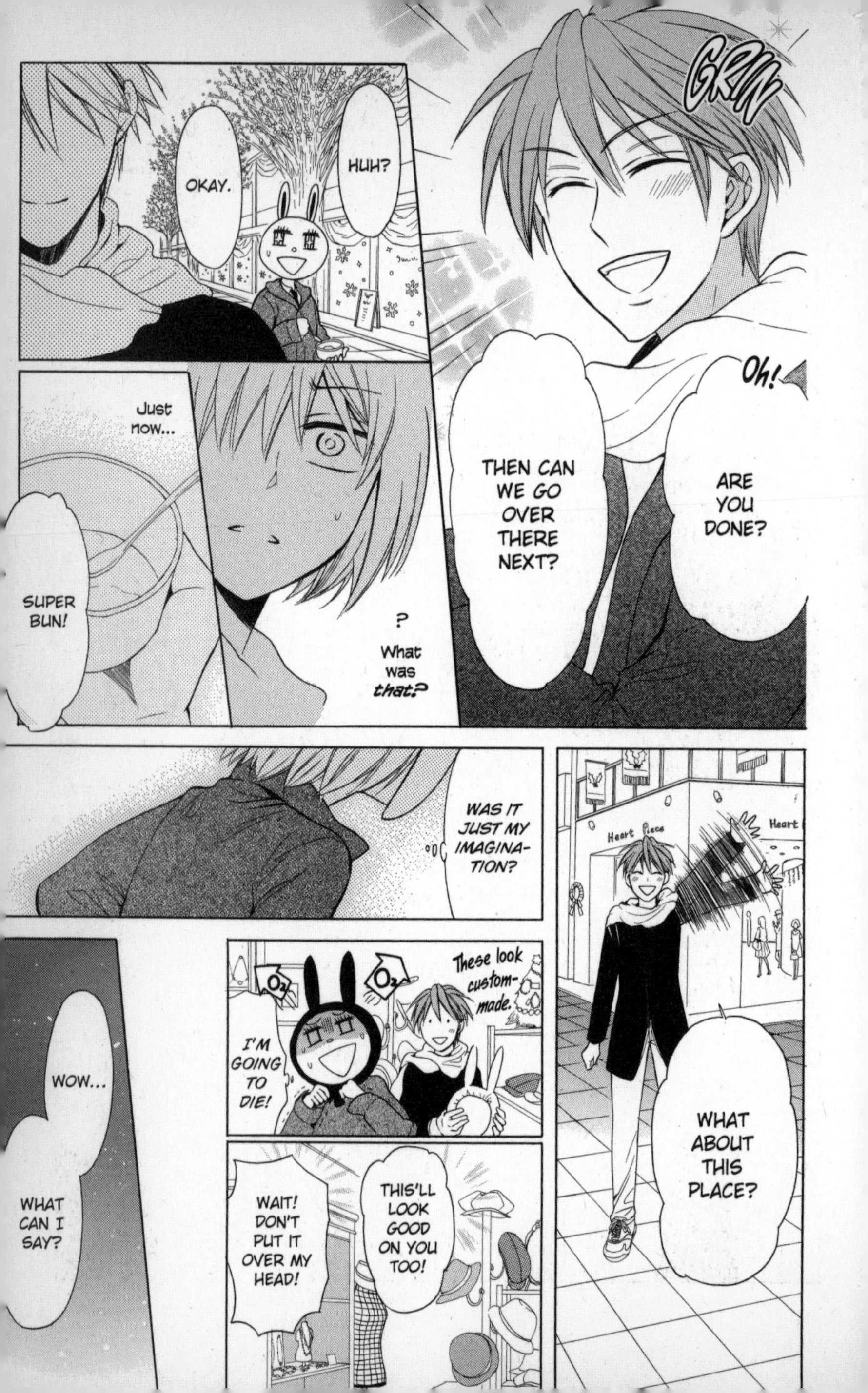
GRIN
Oh!
ARE YOU DONE?
THEN CAN WE GO OVER THERE NEXT?
HUH?
OKAY.
Just now...
?
What was *that?*
SUPER BUN!
Heart Piece
Heart
WHAT ABOUT THIS PLACE?
WAS IT JUST MY IMAGINATION?
These look custom-made.
O_2
O_2
I'M GOING TO DIE!
THIS'LL LOOK GOOD ON YOU TOO!
WAIT! DON'T PUT IT OVER MY HEAD!
WOW...
WHAT CAN I SAY?

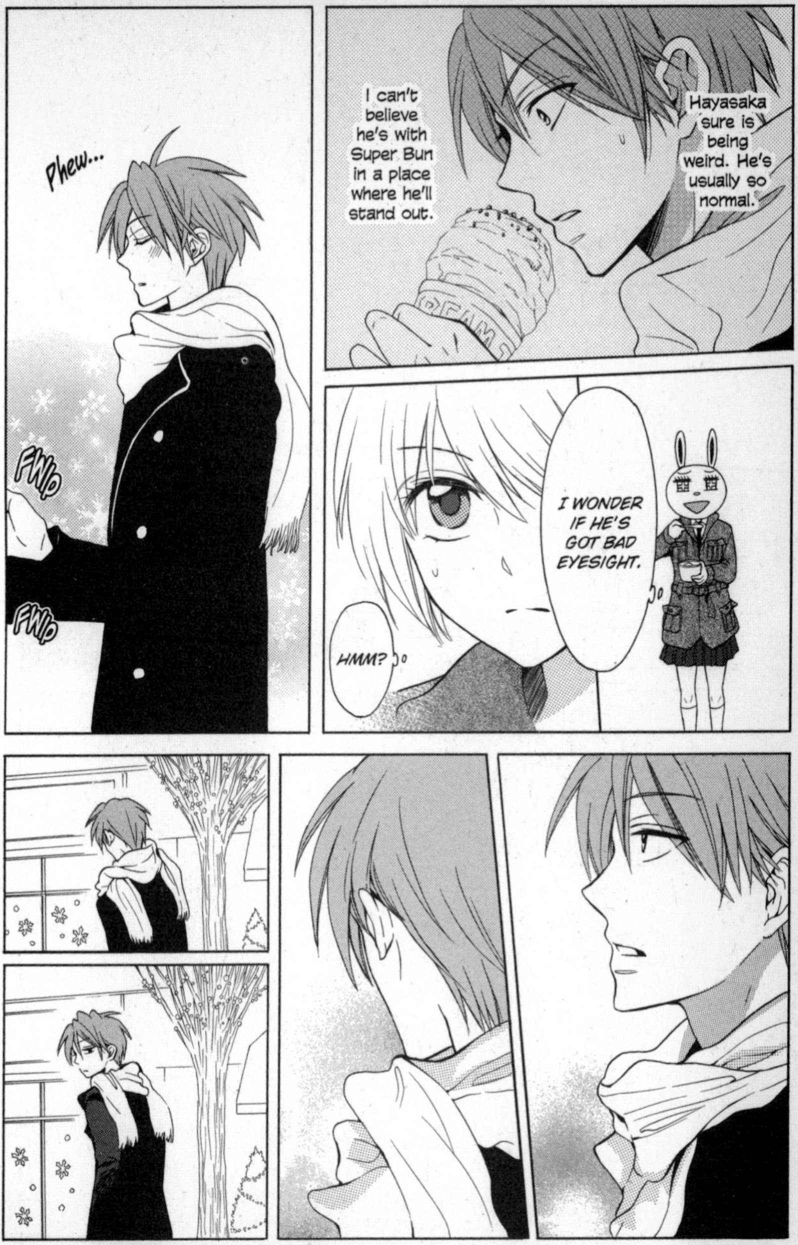
Hayasaka sure is being weird. He's usually so normal.
I can't believe he's with Super Bun in a place where he'll stand out.
I WONDER IF HE'S GOT BAD EYESIGHT.
HMM?
Phew...
FWIP
FWIP

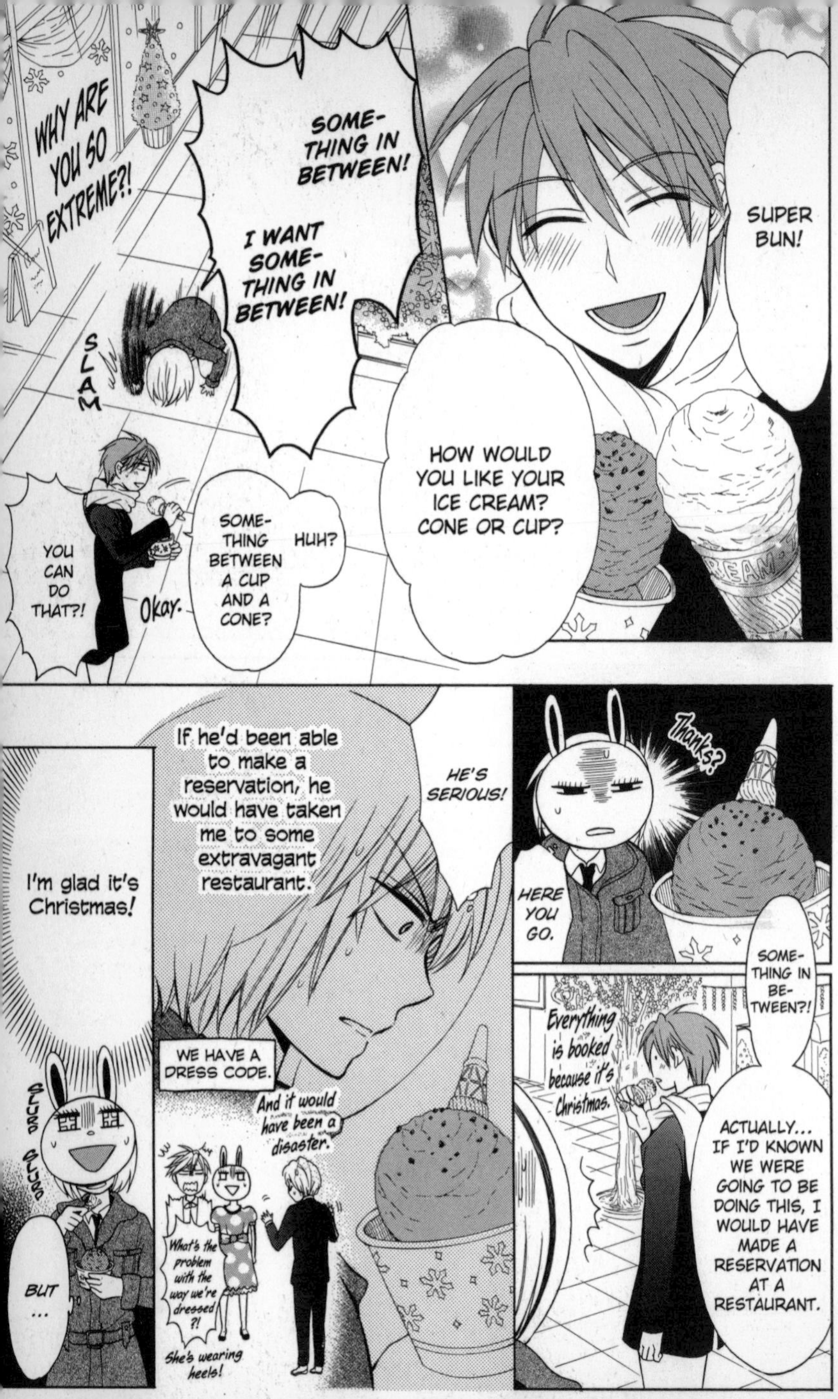
SUPER BUN!
HOW WOULD YOU LIKE YOUR ICE CREAM? CONE OR CUP?
SOME-THING IN BETWEEN!
I WANT SOME-THING IN BETWEEN!
WHY ARE YOU SO EXTREME?!
SLAM
HUH?
SOME-THING BETWEEN A CUP AND A CONE?
Okay.
YOU CAN DO THAT?!
Thanks?
HERE YOU GO.
SOME-THING IN BE-TWEEN?!
ACTUALLY... IF I'D KNOWN WE WERE GOING TO BE DOING THIS, I WOULD HAVE MADE A RESERVATION AT A RESTAURANT.
Everything is booked because it's Christmas.
HE'S SERIOUS!
If he'd been able to make a reservation, he would have taken me to some extravagant restaurant.
WE HAVE A DRESS CODE.
And it would have been a disaster.
What's the problem with the way we're dressed?!
She's wearing heels!
I'm glad it's Christmas!
SLURP SLURP
BUT ...

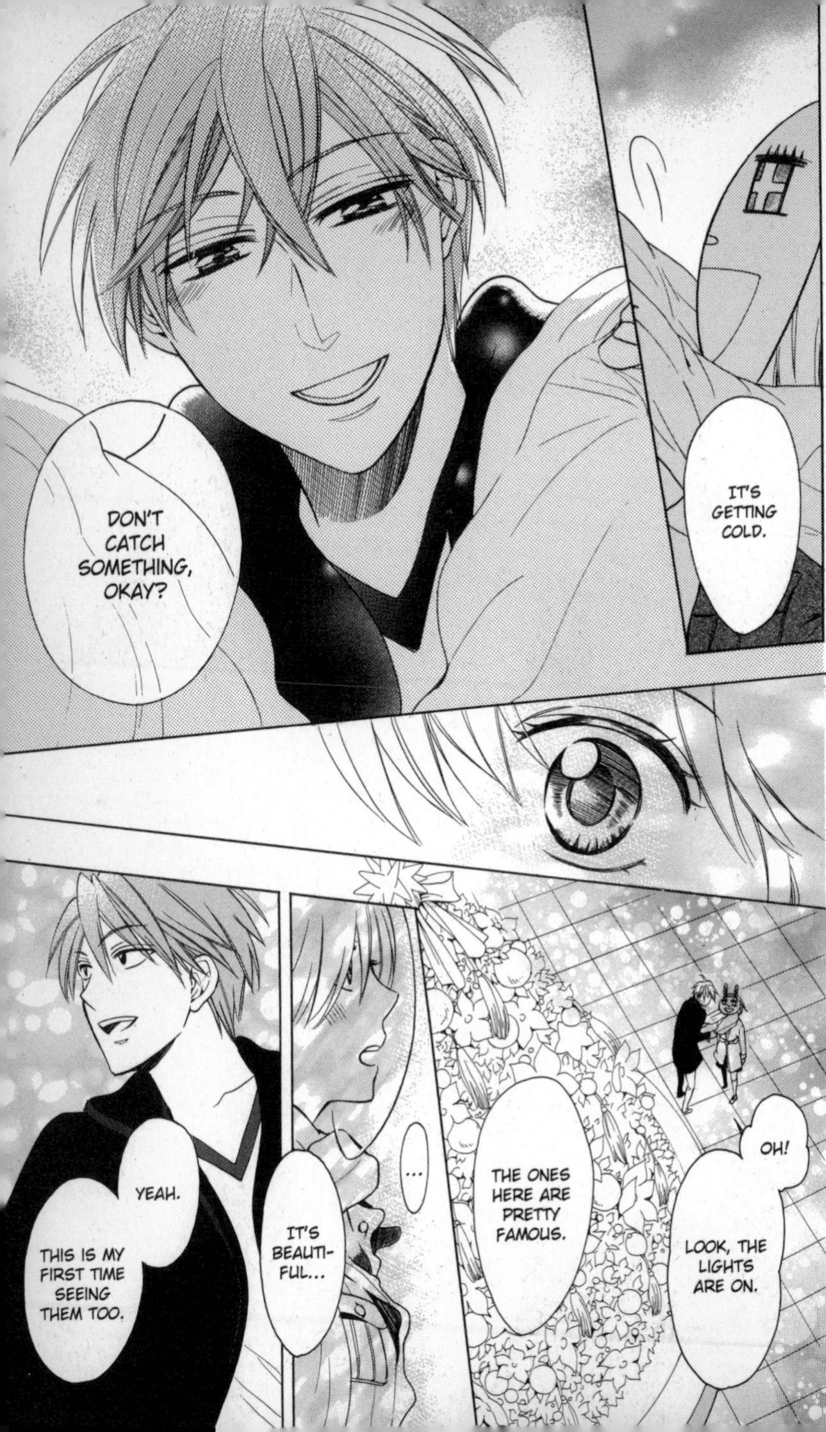
IT'S GETTING COLD.
DON'T CATCH SOMETHING, OKAY?
OH!
LOOK, THE LIGHTS ARE ON.
THE ONES HERE ARE PRETTY FAMOUS.
...
IT'S BEAUTI-FUL...
YEAH.
THIS IS MY FIRST TIME SEEING THEM TOO.

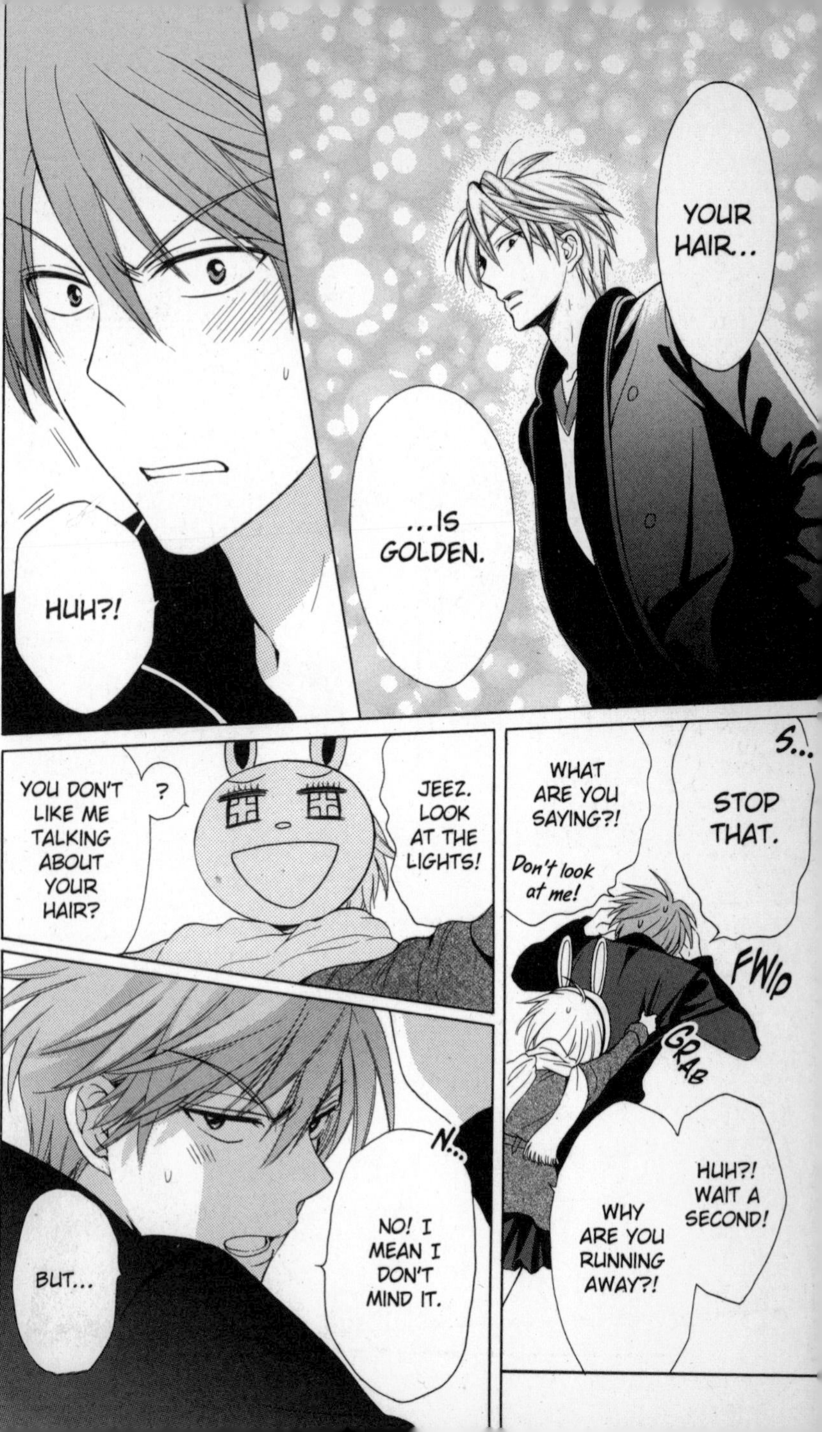
YOUR HAIR...
...IS GOLDEN.
HUH?!
S...
STOP THAT.
WHAT ARE YOU SAYING?!
Don't look at me!
FWIP
GRAB
HUH?! WAIT A SECOND!
WHY ARE YOU RUNNING AWAY?!
JEEZ. LOOK AT THE LIGHTS!
?
YOU DON'T LIKE ME TALKING ABOUT YOUR HAIR?
N...
NO! I MEAN I DON'T MIND IT.
BUT...

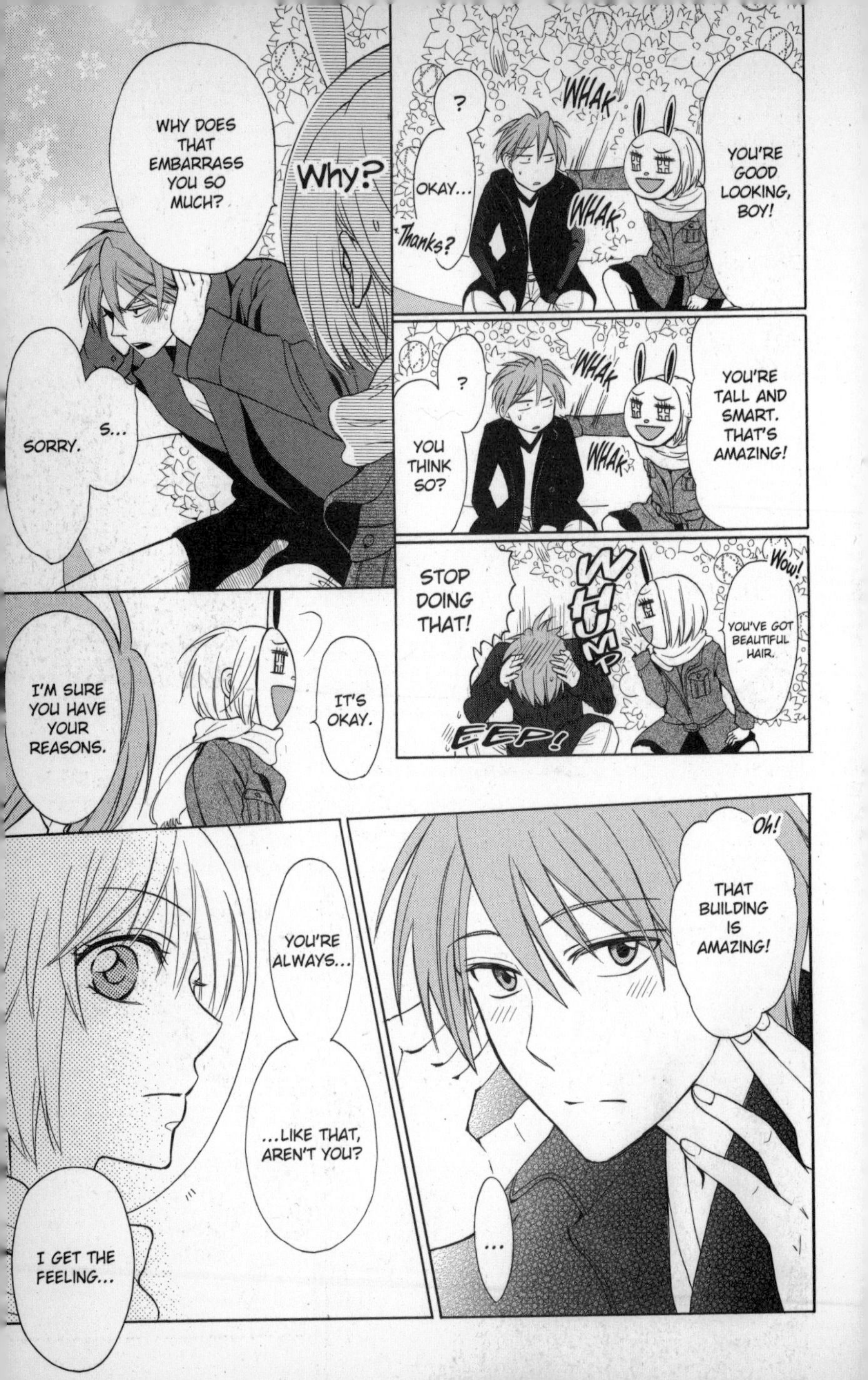

YOU'RE GOOD LOOKING, BOY!
WHAK
WHAK
?
OKAY...
Thanks?
YOU'RE TALL AND SMART. THAT'S AMAZING!
WHAK
WHAK
?
YOU THINK SO?
Wow!
YOU'VE GOT BEAUTIFUL HAIR.
WHUMP
STOP DOING THAT!
EEP!
WHY DOES THAT EMBARRASS YOU SO MUCH?
Why?
S... SORRY.
IT'S OKAY.
I'M SURE YOU HAVE YOUR REASONS.
Oh!
THAT BUILDING IS AMAZING!
...
YOU'RE ALWAYS...
...LIKE THAT, AREN'T YOU?
I GET THE FEELING...

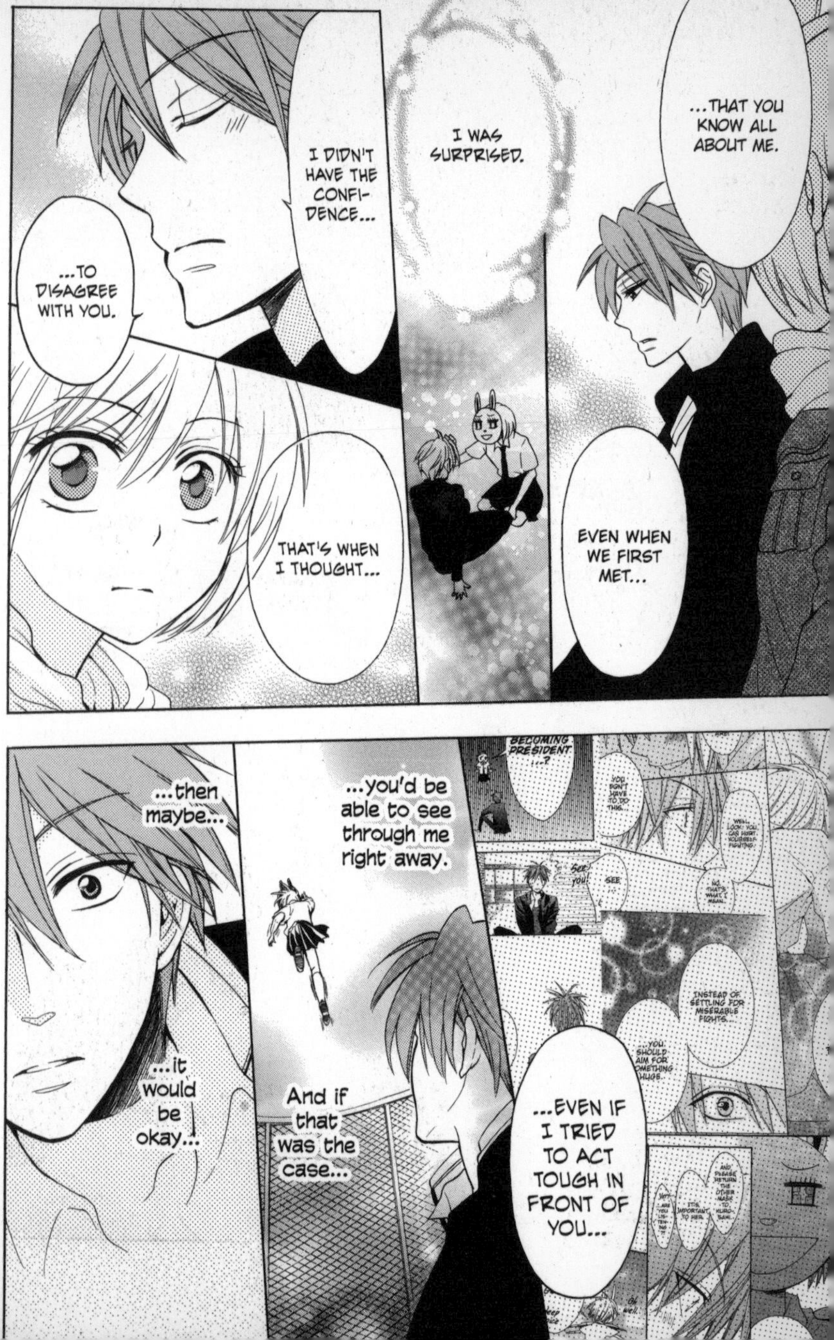
...THAT YOU KNOW ALL ABOUT ME.
EVEN WHEN WE FIRST MET...
I WAS SURPRISED.
I DIDN'T HAVE THE CONFI-DENCE...
...TO DISAGREE WITH YOU.
THAT'S WHEN I THOUGHT...
WELL, LOOK: YOU CAN HURT YOURSELF FIGHTING.
NO, THAT'S WHAT I MEAN...
YOU DIDN'T HAVE TO DO THIS...
BECOMING PRESIDENT...?
SEE...
See you!
INSTEAD OF SETTLING FOR MISERABLE FIGHTS...
...YOU SHOULD AIM FOR SOMETHING HUGE.
AND PLEASE RETURN THE OTHER MASK TO KURO-SAN...
IT'S IMPORTANT TO HER.
...ARE YOU LIS-TEN-ING?!
Oh well.
...EVEN IF I TRIED TO ACT TOUGH IN FRONT OF YOU...
...you'd be able to see through me right away.
And if that was the case...
...then maybe...
...it would be okay...

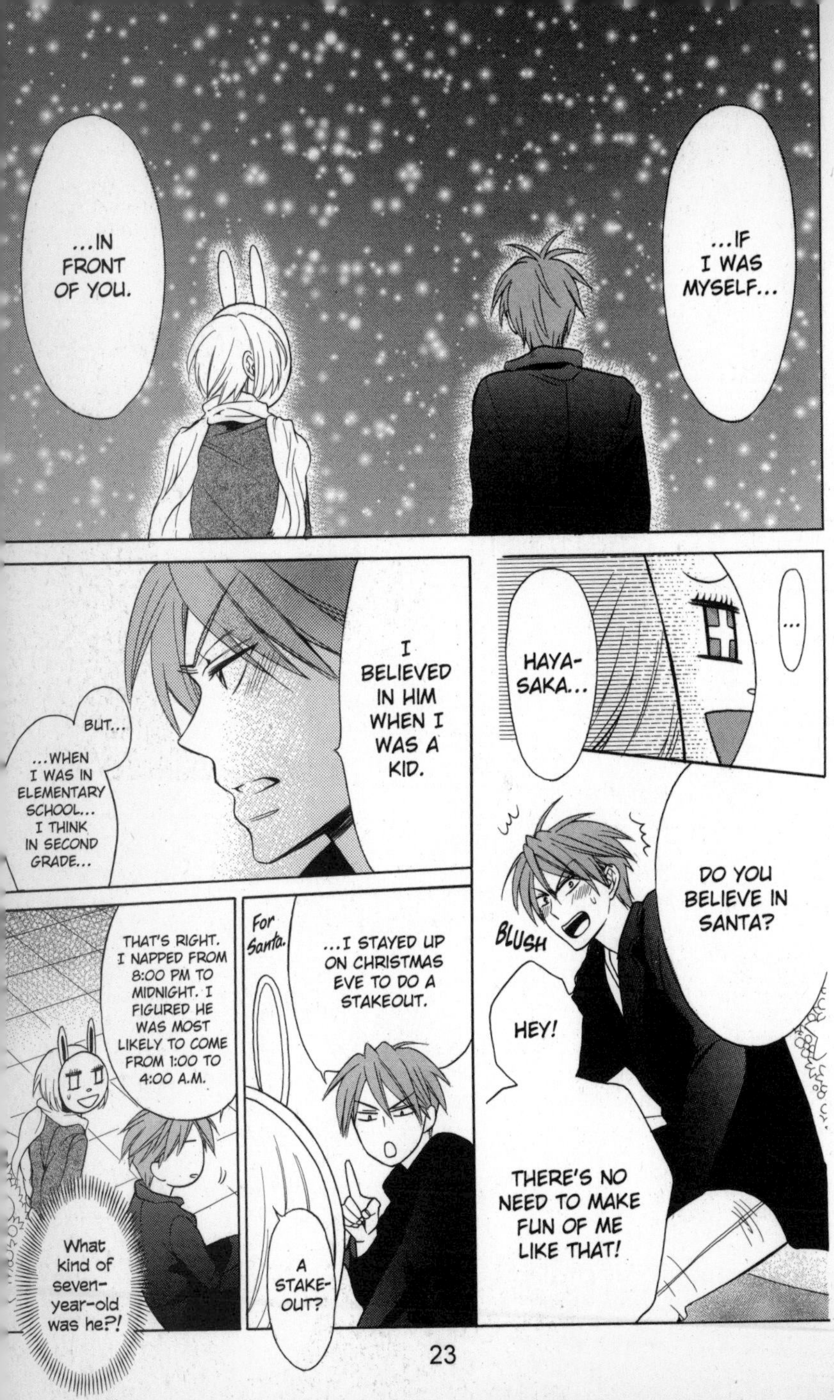
...IF I WAS MYSELF...
...IN FRONT OF YOU.
...
HAYA-SAKA...
DO YOU BELIEVE IN SANTA?
BLUSH
HEY!
THERE'S NO NEED TO MAKE FUN OF ME LIKE THAT!
I BELIEVED IN HIM WHEN I WAS A KID.
BUT...
...WHEN I WAS IN ELEMENTARY SCHOOL... I THINK IN SECOND GRADE...
...I STAYED UP ON CHRISTMAS EVE TO DO A STAKEOUT.
For Santa.
A STAKE-OUT?
THAT'S RIGHT. I NAPPED FROM 8:00 PM TO MIDNIGHT. I FIGURED HE WAS MOST LIKELY TO COME FROM 1:00 TO 4:00 A.M.
What kind of seven-year-old was he?!

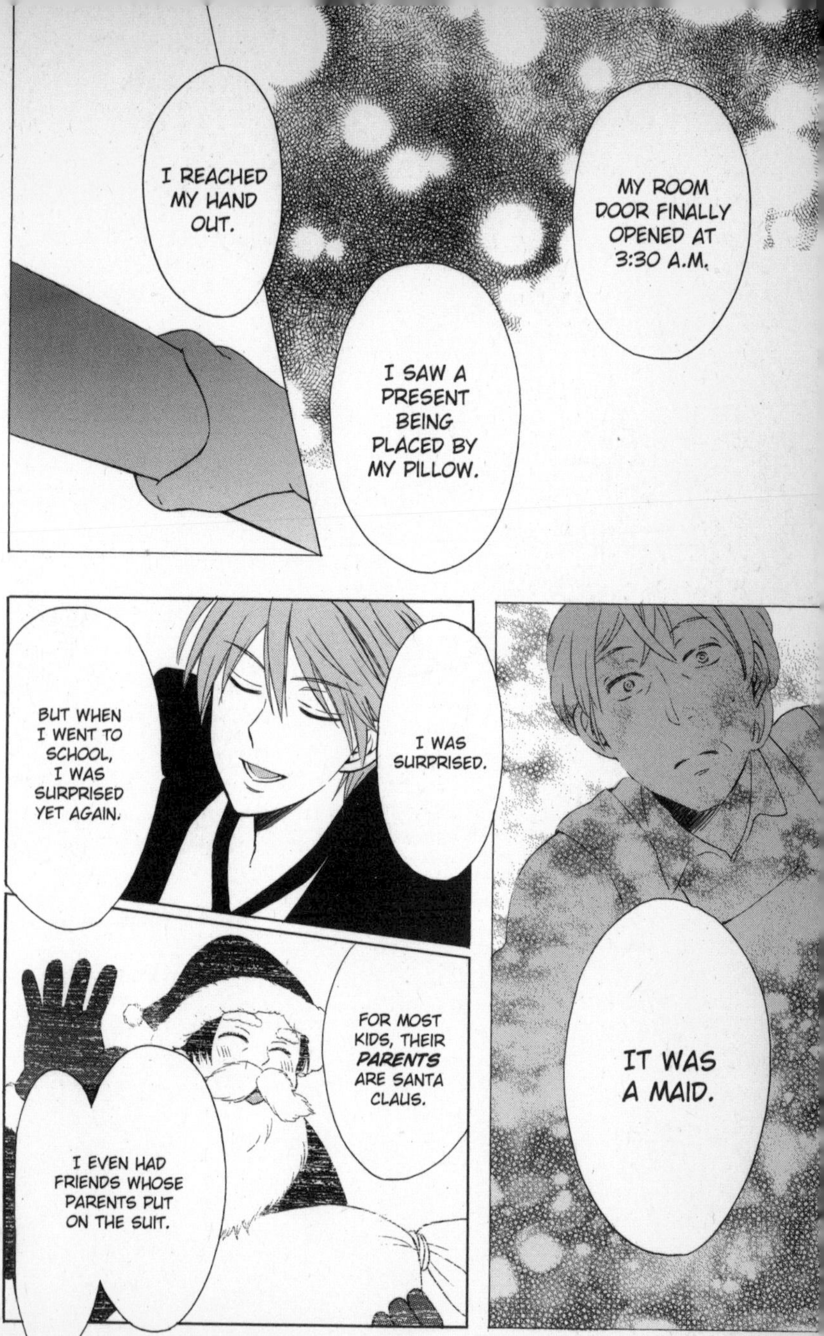
MY ROOM DOOR FINALLY OPENED AT 3:30 A.M.
I SAW A PRESENT BEING PLACED BY MY PILLOW.
I REACHED MY HAND OUT.
IT WAS A MAID.
I WAS SURPRISED.
BUT WHEN I WENT TO SCHOOL, I WAS SURPRISED YET AGAIN.
FOR MOST KIDS, THEIR ***PARENTS*** ARE SANTA CLAUS.
I EVEN HAD FRIENDS WHOSE PARENTS PUT ON THE SUIT.

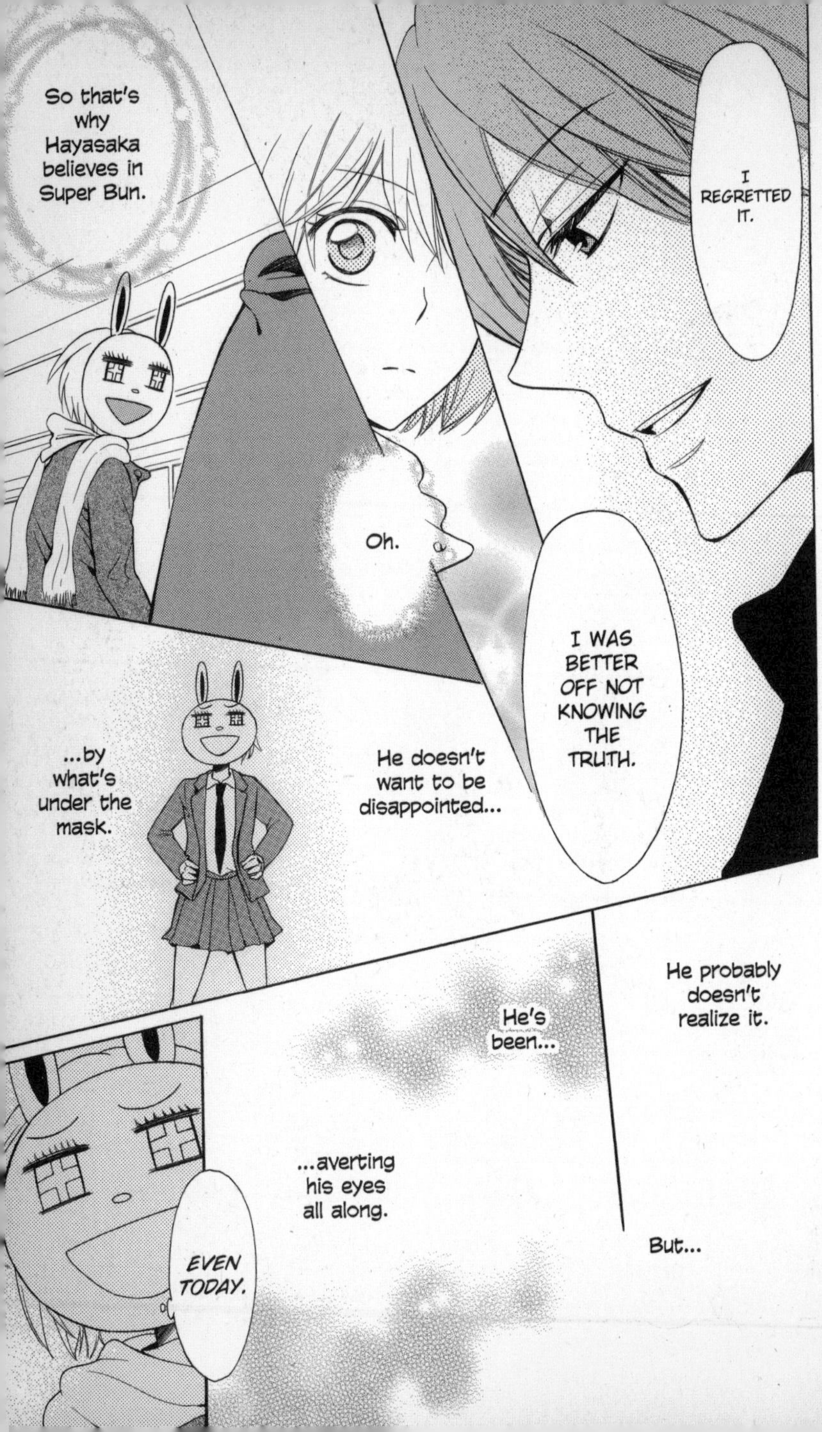
I REGRETTED IT.
I WAS BETTER OFF NOT KNOWING THE TRUTH.
Oh.
So that's why Hayasaka believes in Super Bun.
He doesn't want to be disappointed...
...by what's under the mask.
He probably doesn't realize it.
But...
He's been...
...averting his eyes all along.
EVEN TODAY.

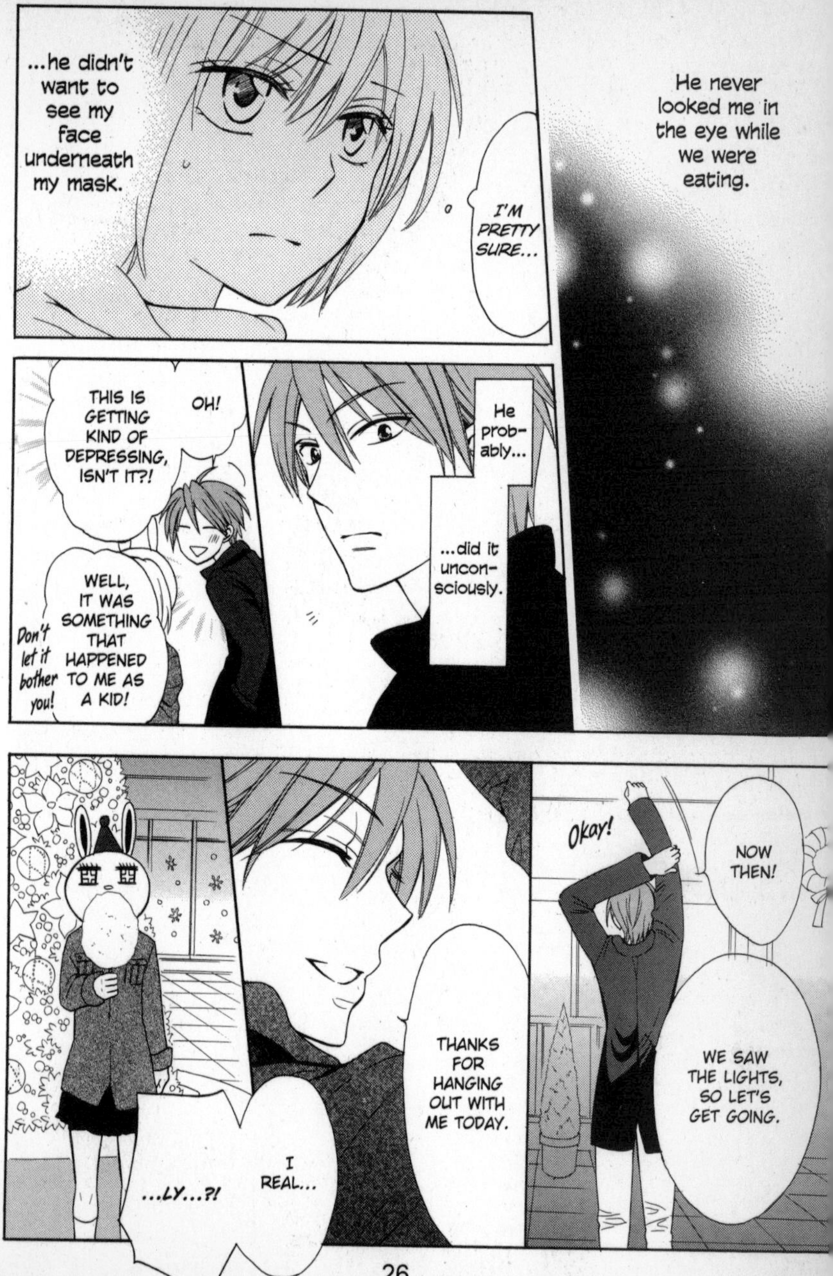
He never looked me in the eye while we were eating.
I'M PRETTY SURE...
...he didn't want to see my face underneath my mask.
He probably...
...did it unconsciously.
OH!
THIS IS GETTING KIND OF DEPRESSING, ISN'T IT?!
WELL, IT WAS SOMETHING THAT HAPPENED TO ME AS A KID!
Don't let it bother you!
NOW THEN!
Okay!
WE SAW THE LIGHTS, SO LET'S GET GOING.
THANKS FOR HANGING OUT WITH ME TODAY.
I REAL...
...LY...?!

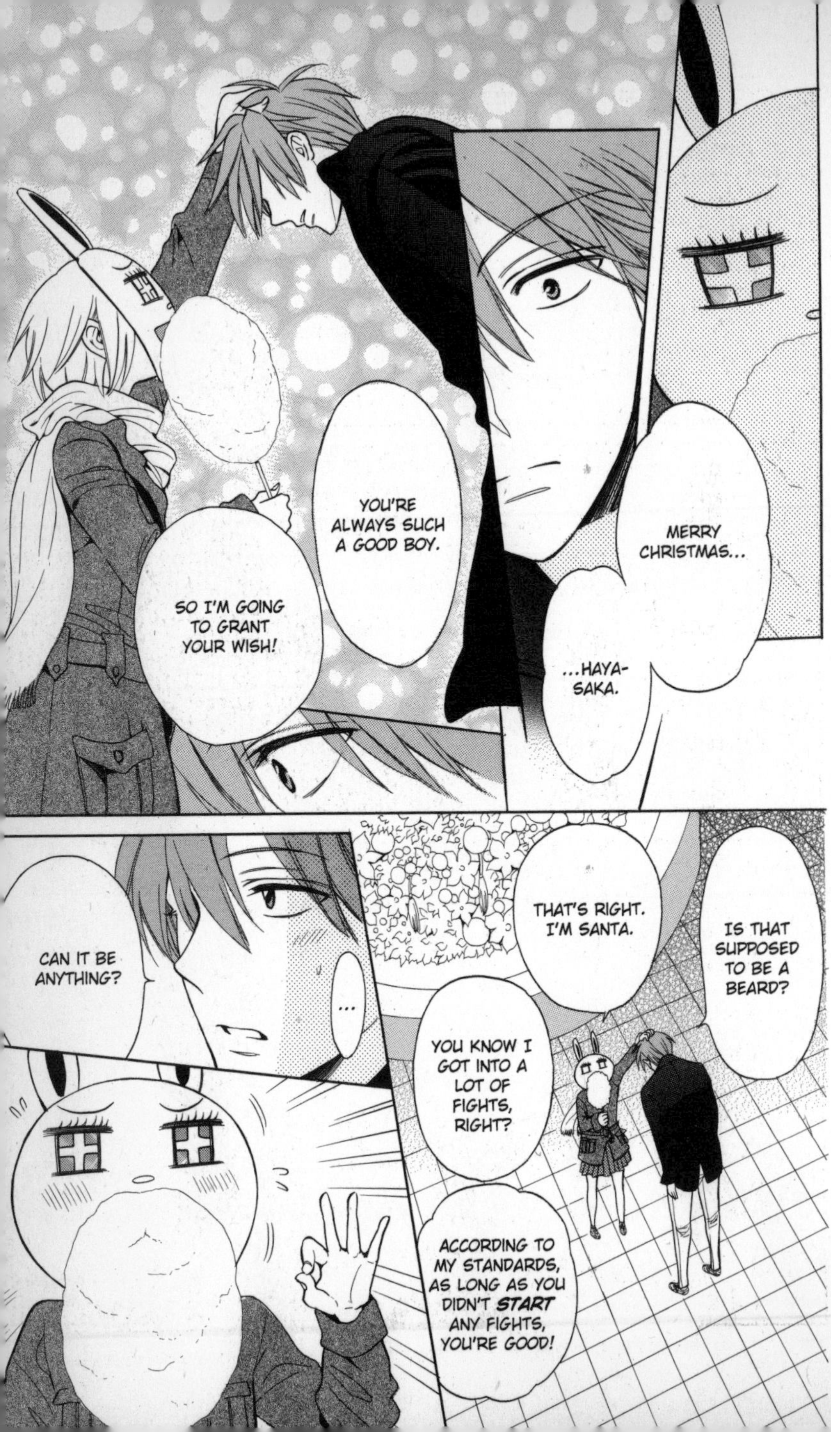
MERRY CHRISTMAS...
...HAYA-SAKA.
YOU'RE ALWAYS SUCH A GOOD BOY.
SO I'M GOING TO GRANT YOUR WISH!
IS THAT SUPPOSED TO BE A BEARD?
THAT'S RIGHT. I'M SANTA.
YOU KNOW I GOT INTO A LOT OF FIGHTS, RIGHT?
ACCORDING TO MY STANDARDS, AS LONG AS YOU DIDN'T *START* ANY FIGHTS, YOU'RE GOOD!
...
CAN IT BE ANYTHING?

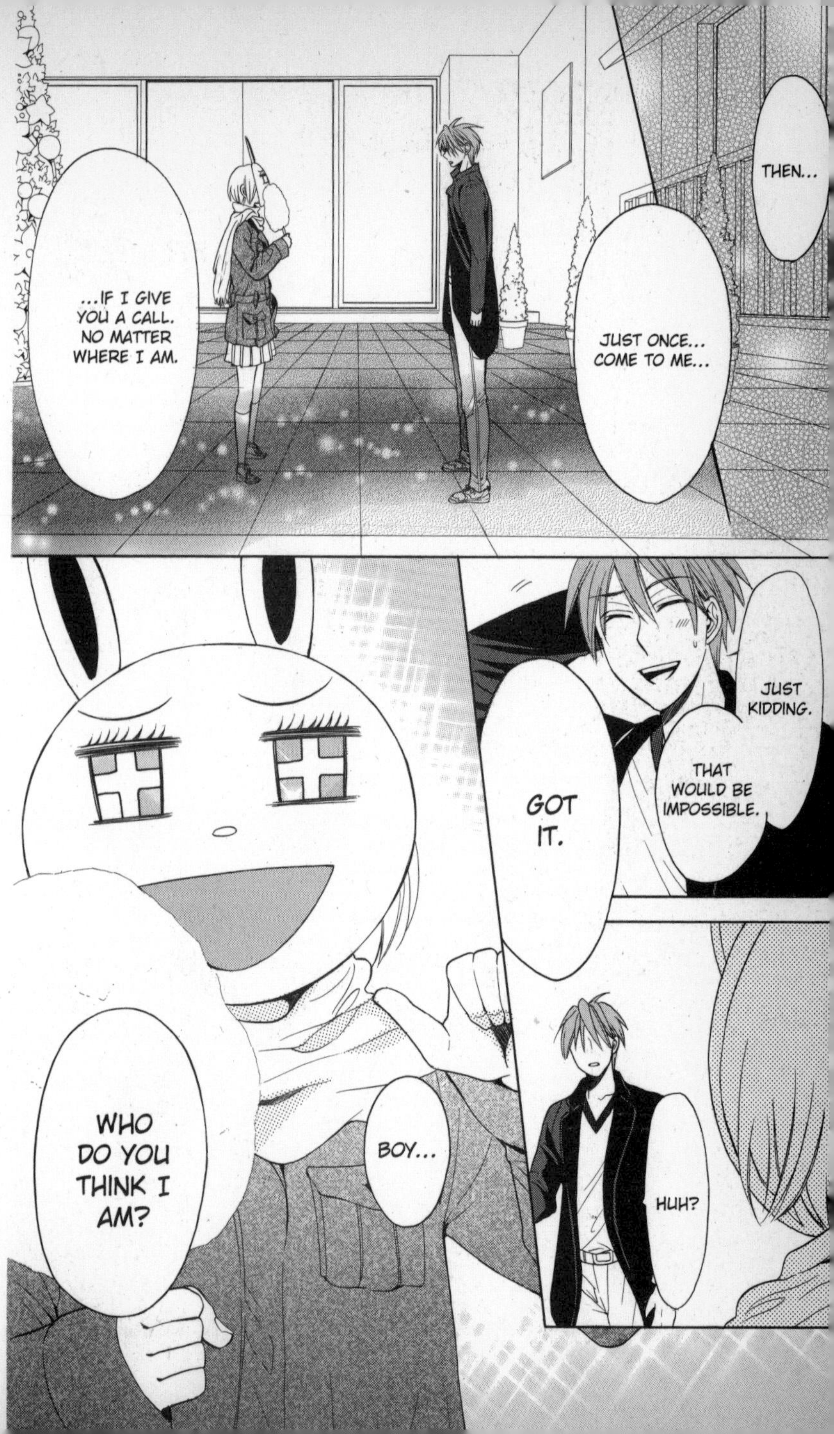
THEN...
JUST ONCE... COME TO ME...
...IF I GIVE YOU A CALL. NO MATTER WHERE I AM.
JUST KIDDING.
THAT WOULD BE IMPOSSIBLE.
GOT IT.
HUH?
BOY...
WHO DO YOU THINK I AM?

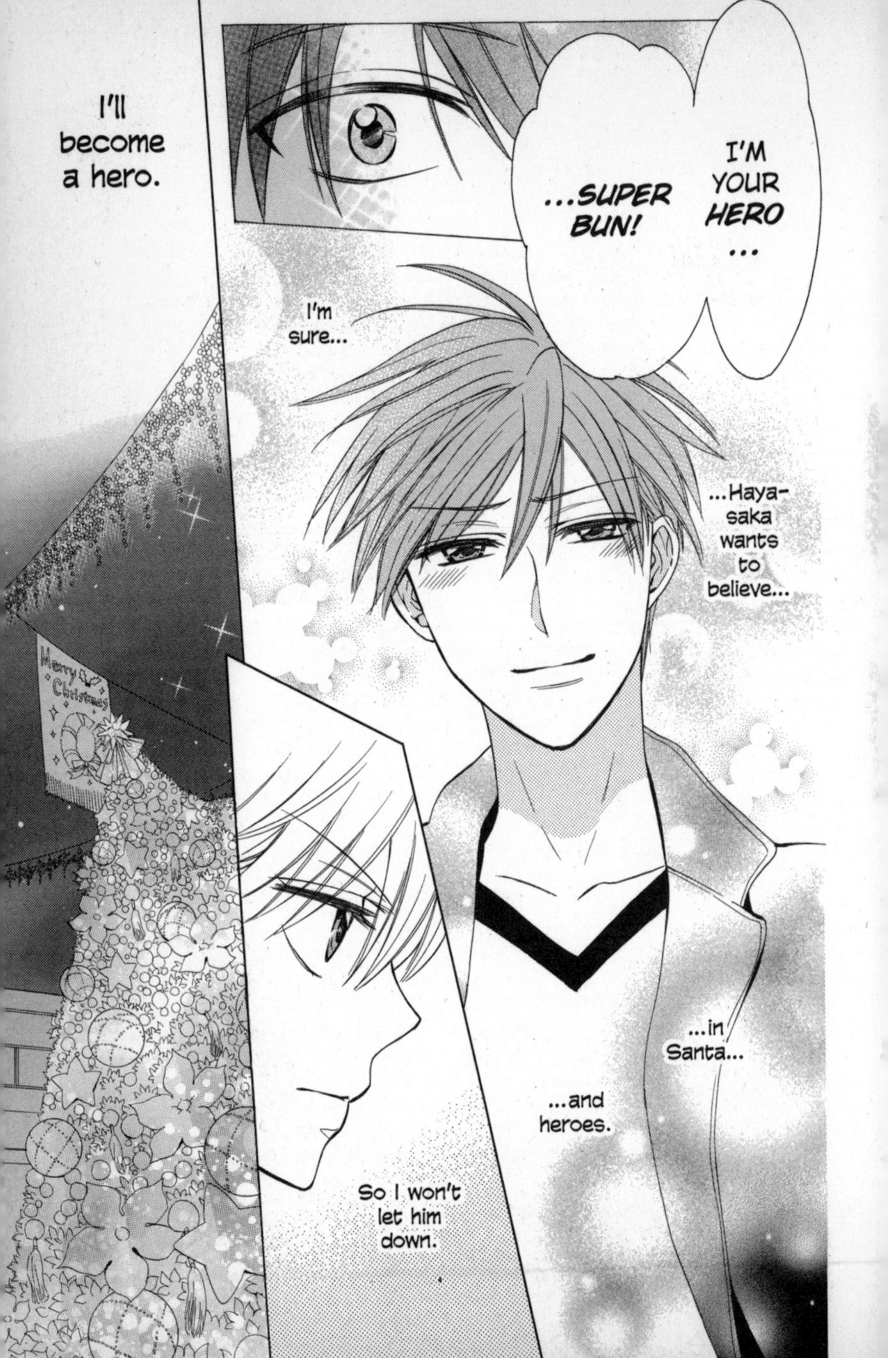
I'M YOUR HERO ...
...SUPER BUN!
I'm sure...
...Haya-saka wants to believe...
...in Santa...
...and heroes.
So I won't let him down.
I'll become a hero.
Merry Christmas

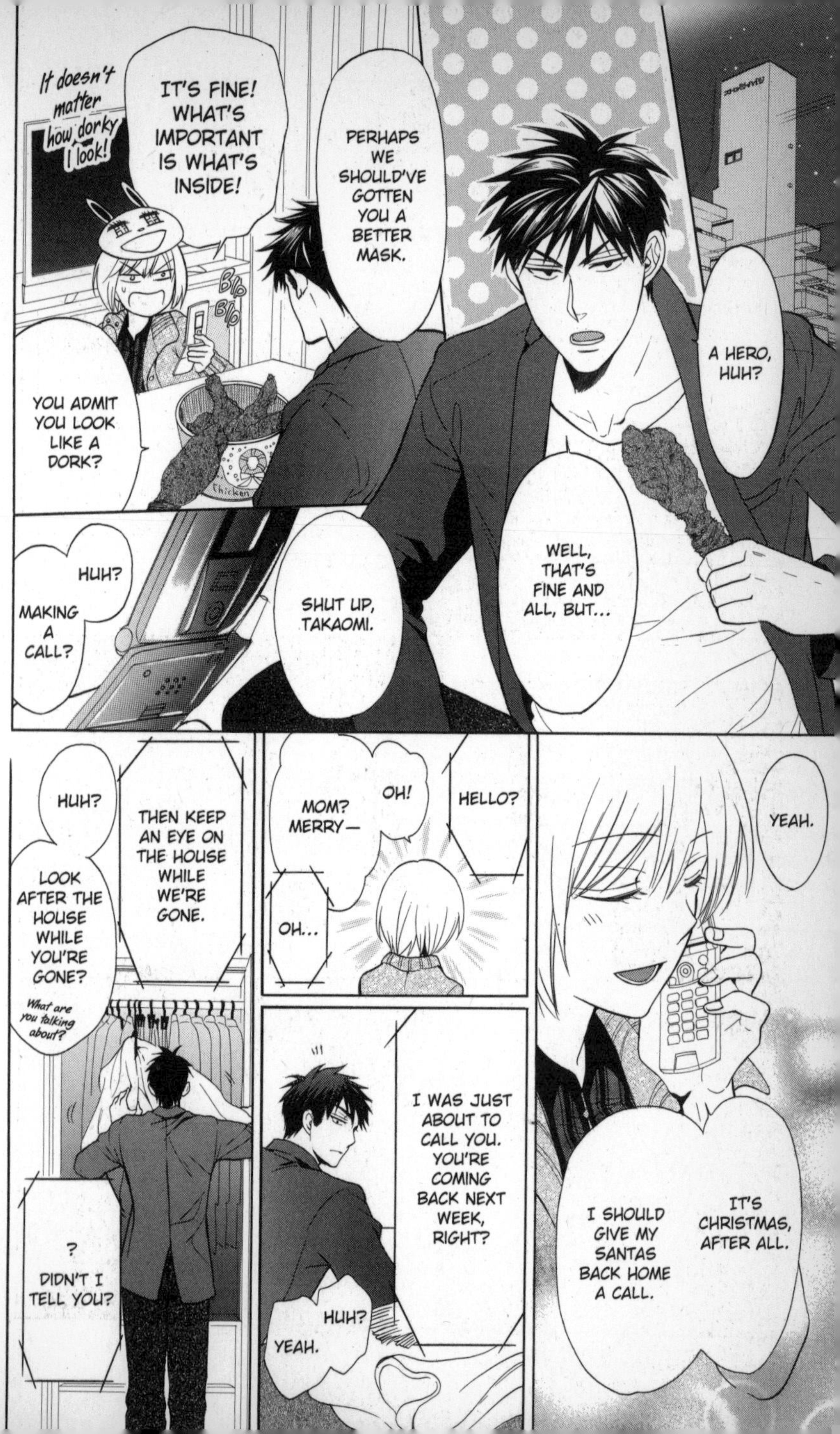
A HERO, HUH?
PERHAPS WE SHOULD'VE GOTTEN YOU A BETTER MASK.
IT'S FINE! WHAT'S IMPORTANT IS WHAT'S INSIDE!
It doesn't matter how dorky I look!
BIP BIP
YOU ADMIT YOU LOOK LIKE A DORK?
WELL, THAT'S FINE AND ALL, BUT...
SHUT UP, TAKAOMI.
HUH?
MAKING A CALL?
YEAH.
IT'S CHRISTMAS, AFTER ALL.
I SHOULD GIVE MY SANTAS BACK HOME A CALL.
HELLO?
OH!
MOM? MERRY—
OH...
I WAS JUST ABOUT TO CALL YOU. YOU'RE COMING BACK NEXT WEEK, RIGHT?
HUH?
YEAH.
THEN KEEP AN EYE ON THE HOUSE WHILE WE'RE GONE.
HUH?
LOOK AFTER THE HOUSE WHILE YOU'RE GONE?
What are you talking about?
?
DIDN'T I TELL YOU?

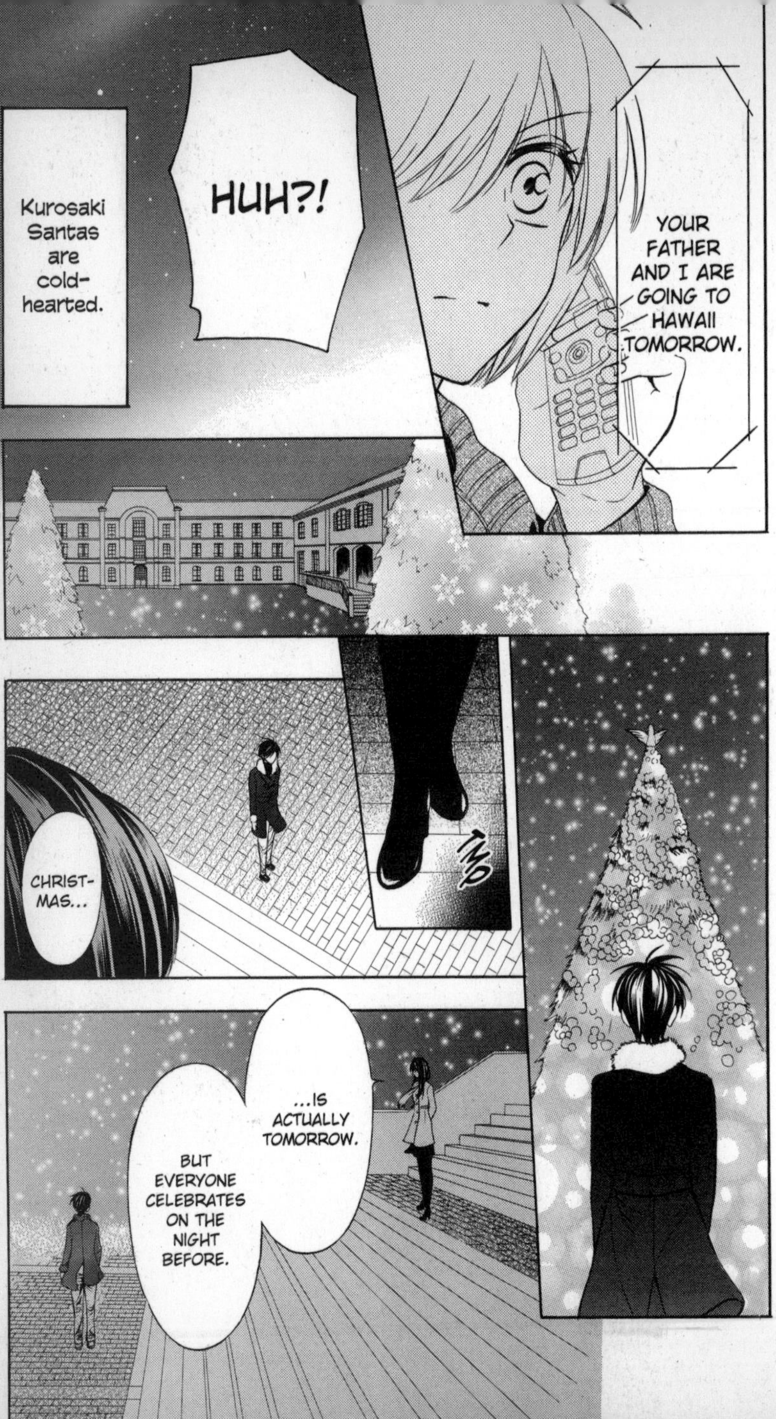
YOUR FATHER AND I ARE GOING TO HAWAII TOMORROW.
HUH?!
Kurosaki Santas are cold-hearted.
TMP
CHRIST-MAS...
...IS ACTUALLY TOMORROW.
BUT EVERYONE CELEBRATES ON THE NIGHT BEFORE.

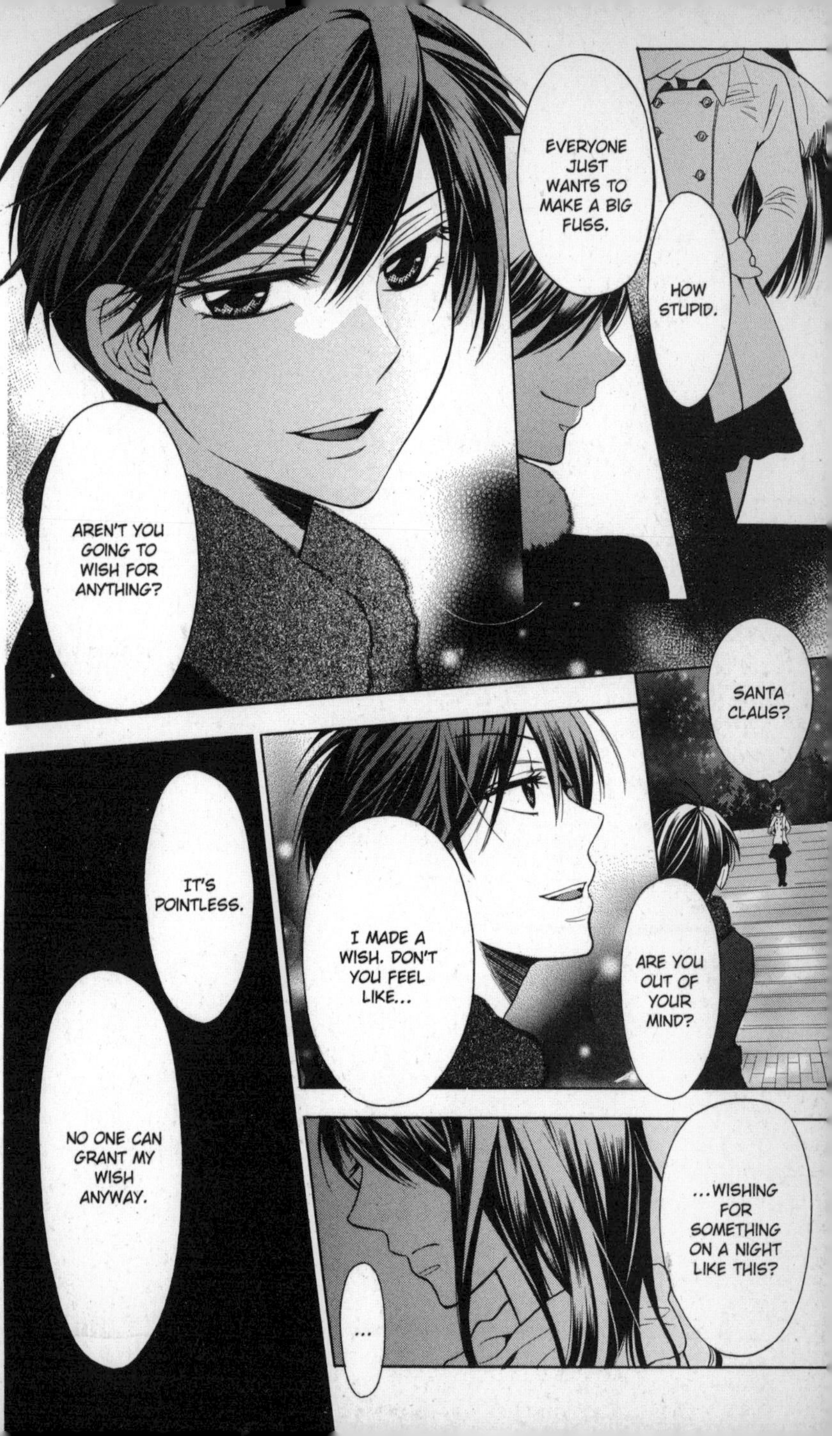
EVERYONE JUST WANTS TO MAKE A BIG FUSS.
HOW STUPID.
AREN'T YOU GOING TO WISH FOR ANYTHING?
SANTA CLAUS?
ARE YOU OUT OF YOUR MIND?
I MADE A WISH. DON'T YOU FEEL LIKE...
...WISHING FOR SOMETHING ON A NIGHT LIKE THIS?
...
IT'S POINTLESS.
NO ONE CAN GRANT MY WISH ANYWAY.

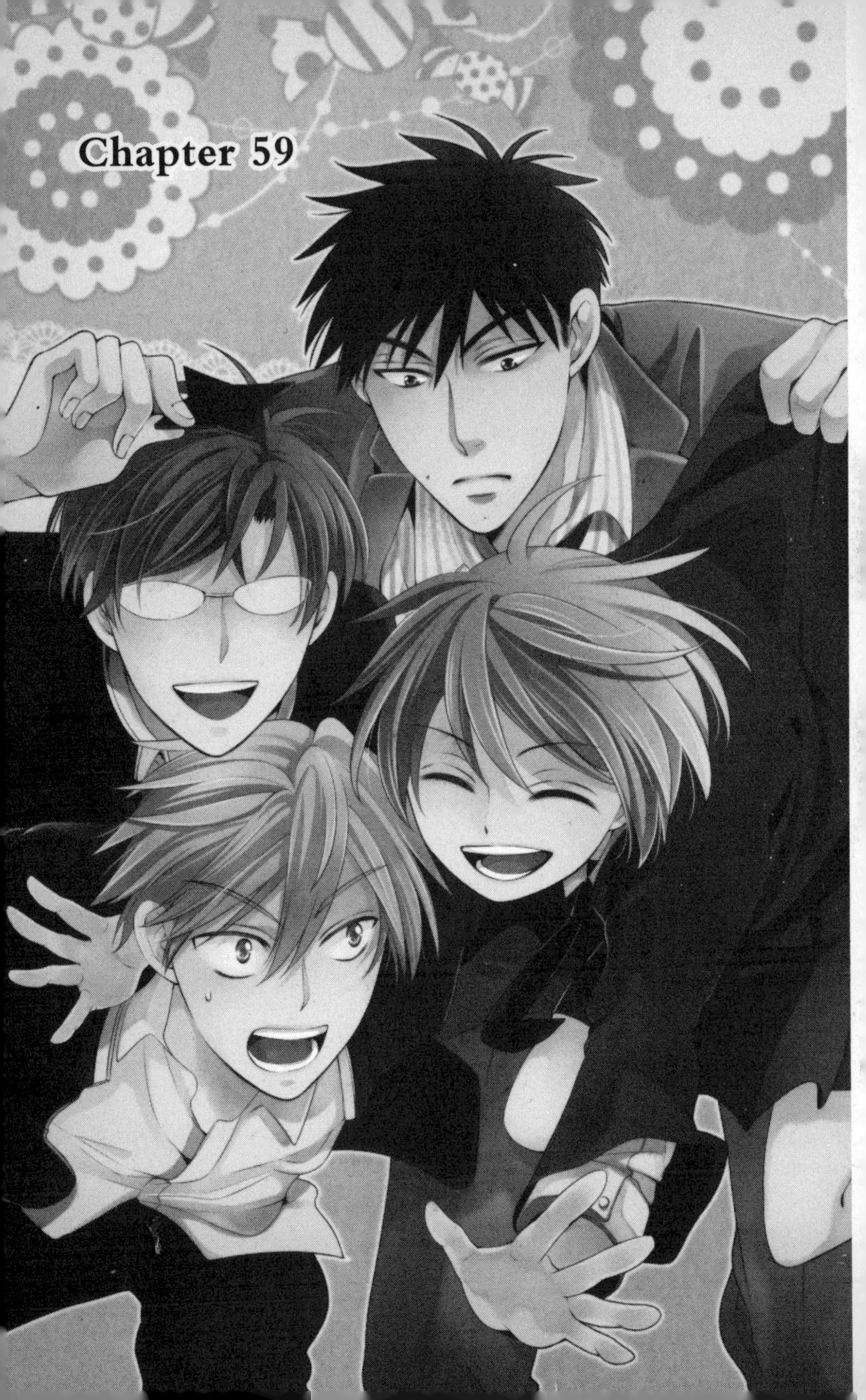
Chapter 59

A HOLY NIGHT AT THE BOYS' DORM PART 1

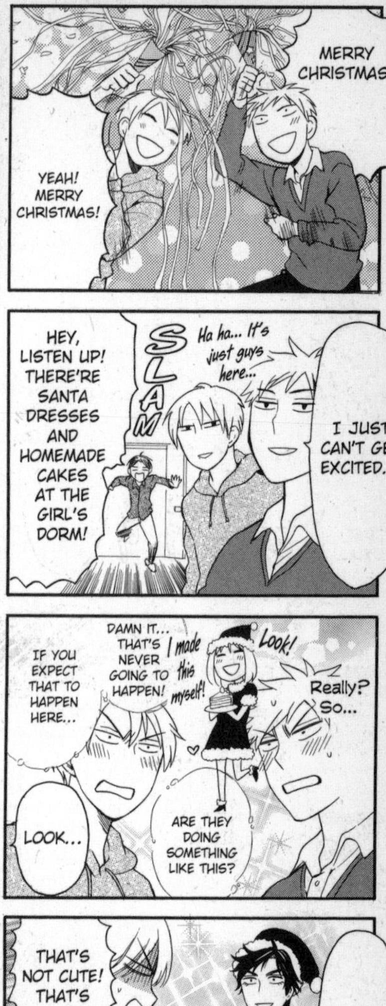
MERRY CHRISTMAS!
YEAH! MERRY CHRISTMAS!
I JUST CAN'T GET EXCITED...
Ha ha... It's just guys here...
SLAM
HEY, LISTEN UP! THERE'RE SANTA DRESSES AND HOMEMADE CAKES AT THE GIRL'S DORM!
Look!
I made this myself!
Really? So...
DAMN IT... THAT'S NEVER GOING TO HAPPEN!
IF YOU EXPECT THAT TO HAPPEN HERE...
ARE THEY DOING SOMETHING LIKE THIS?
LOOK...
I MADE THIS MYSELF.
THAT'S NOT CUTE! THAT'S NOT CUTE AT ALL!
AND WHAT IS THAT?! IT'S RIDICULOUSLY AMAZING!
It looks delicious!

A HOLY NIGHT AT THE BOY'S DORM PART 2

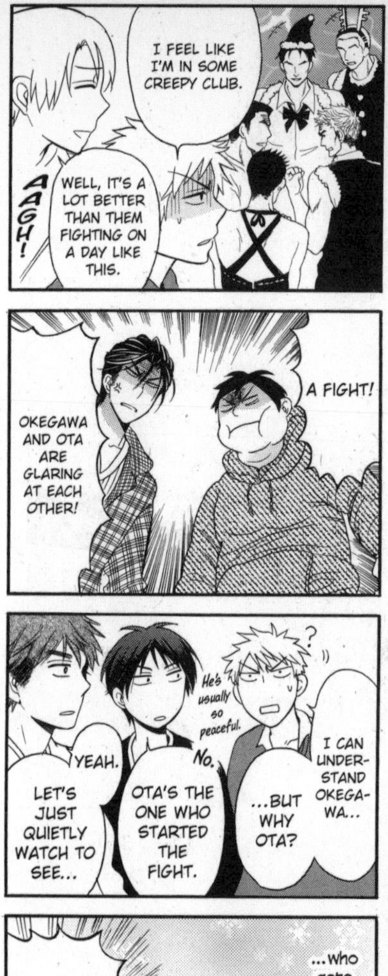
I FEEL LIKE I'M IN SOME CREEPY CLUB.
WELL, IT'S A LOT BETTER THAN THEM FIGHTING ON A DAY LIKE THIS.
AAGH!
A FIGHT!
OKEGAWA AND OTA ARE GLARING AT EACH OTHER!
?
He's usually so peaceful.
I CAN UNDERSTAND OKEGAWA...
...BUT WHY OTA?
No.
OTA'S THE ONE WHO STARTED THE FIGHT.
YEAH.
LET'S JUST QUIETLY WATCH TO SEE...
...who gets the last slice of cake.
JUST BUY ANOTHER ONE!

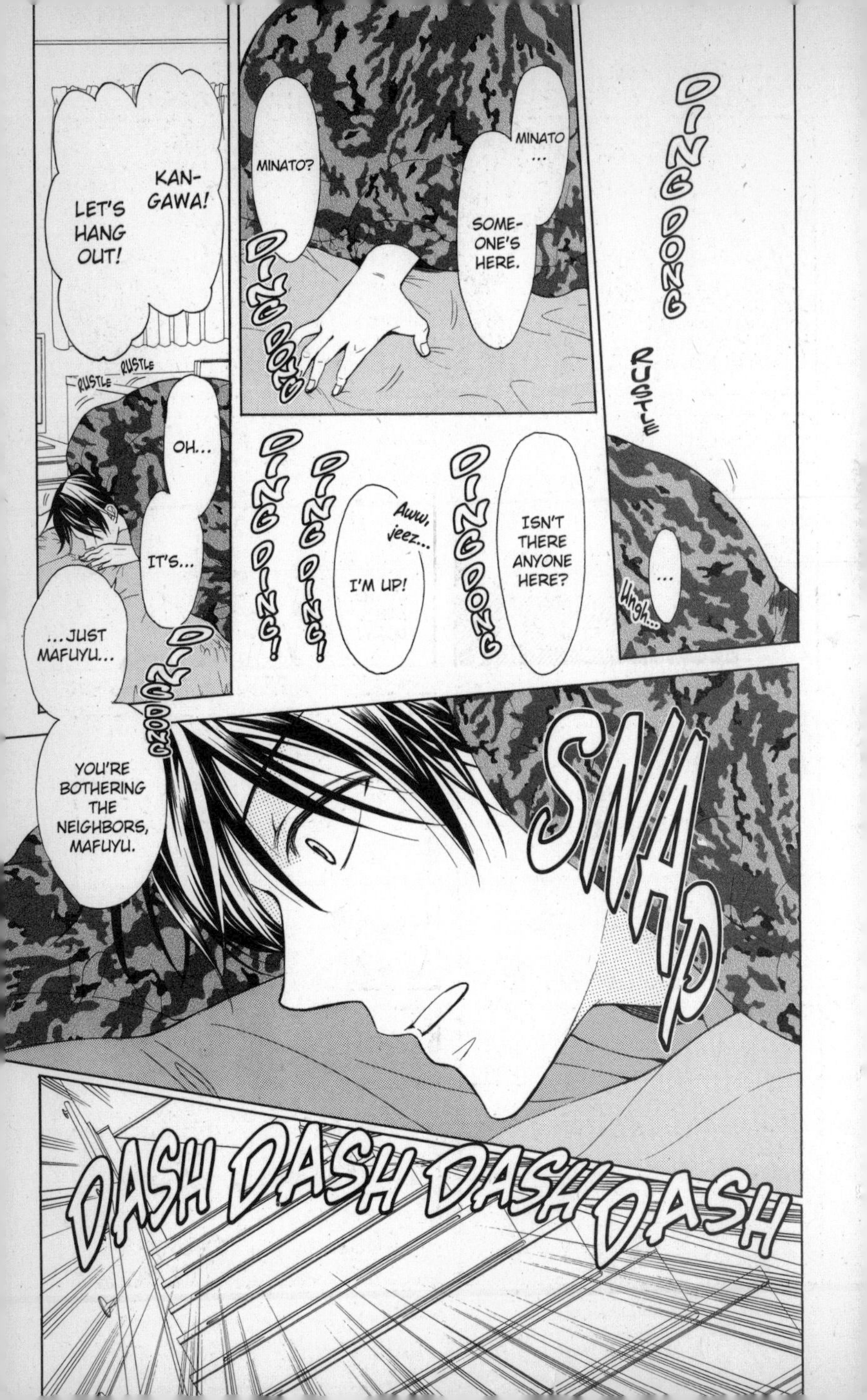
DING DONG
RUSTLE
...
Unngh...
MINATO... SOMEONE'S HERE.
MINATO?
DING DONG
DING DONG
ISN'T THERE ANYONE HERE?
Aww, jeez... I'M UP!
DING DING!
DING DING!
KAN-GAWA! LET'S HANG OUT!
RUSTLE RUSTLE
OH... IT'S... ...JUST MAFUYU...
DING DONG
YOU'RE BOTHERING THE NEIGHBORS, MAFUYU.
SNAP
DASH DASH DASH DASH

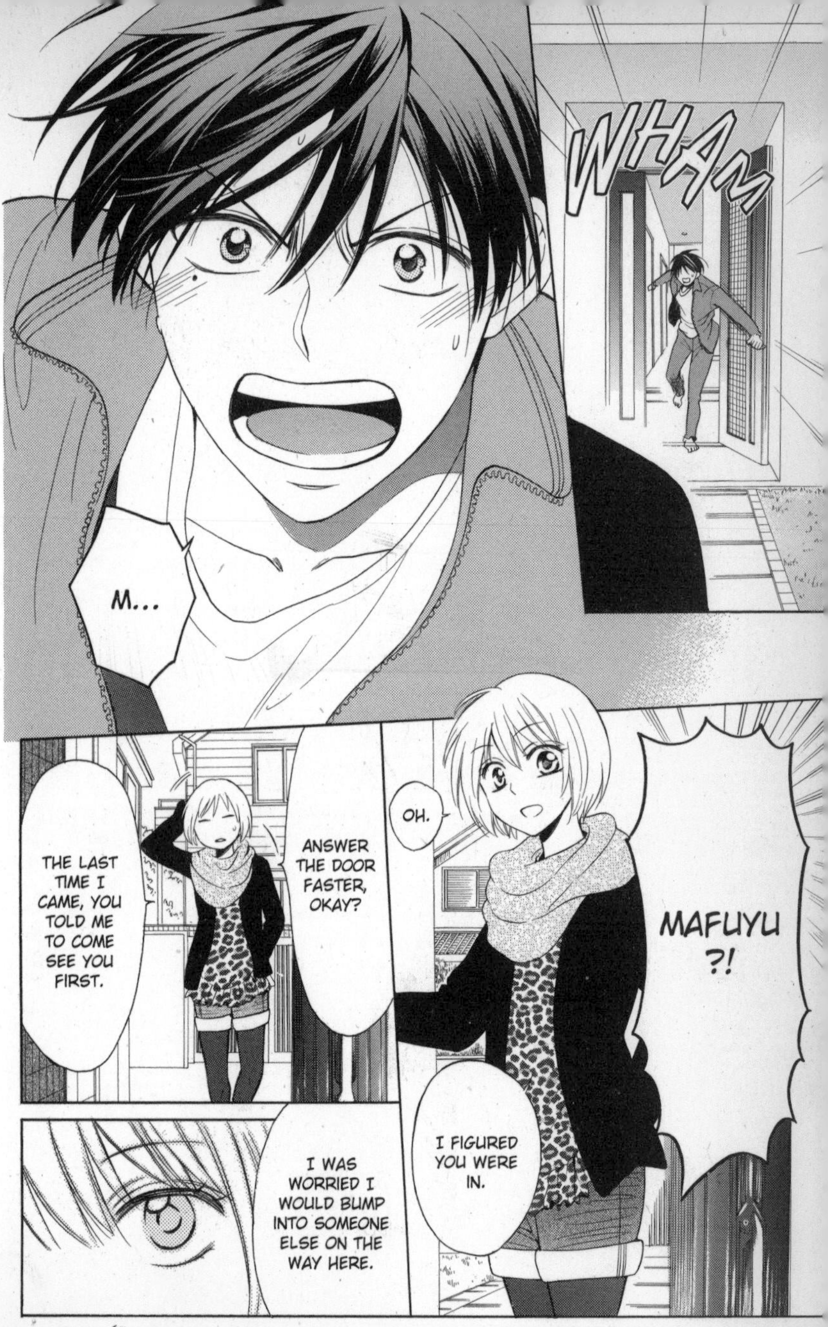
WHAM
M...
MAFUYU ?!
OH.
I FIGURED YOU WERE IN.
ANSWER THE DOOR FASTER, OKAY?
THE LAST TIME I CAME, YOU TOLD ME TO COME SEE YOU FIRST.
I WAS WORRIED I WOULD BUMP INTO SOMEONE ELSE ON THE WAY HERE.

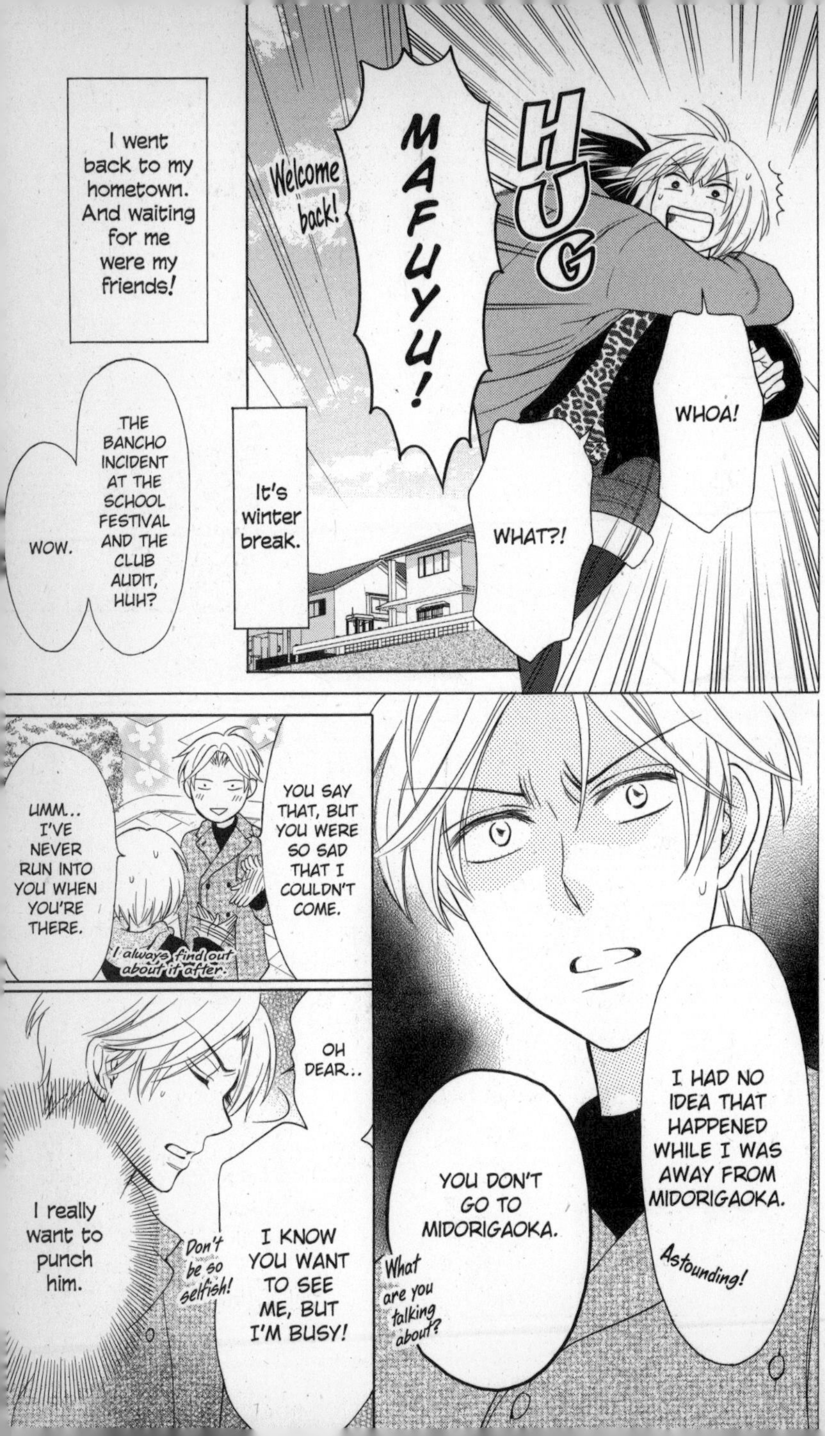

HUG
MAFUYU!
Welcome back!
WHOA!
WHAT?!
It's winter break.
I went back to my hometown. And waiting for me were my friends!
THE BANCHO INCIDENT AT THE SCHOOL FESTIVAL AND THE CLUB AUDIT, HUH?
WOW.
I HAD NO IDEA THAT HAPPENED WHILE I WAS AWAY FROM MIDORIGAOKA.
Astounding!
YOU DON'T GO TO MIDORIGAOKA.
What are you talking about?
YOU SAY THAT, BUT YOU WERE SO SAD THAT I COULDN'T COME.
UMM.. I'VE NEVER RUN INTO YOU WHEN YOU'RE THERE.
I always find out about it after.
OH DEAR..
I KNOW YOU WANT TO SEE ME, BUT I'M BUSY!
Don't be so selfish!
I really want to punch him.

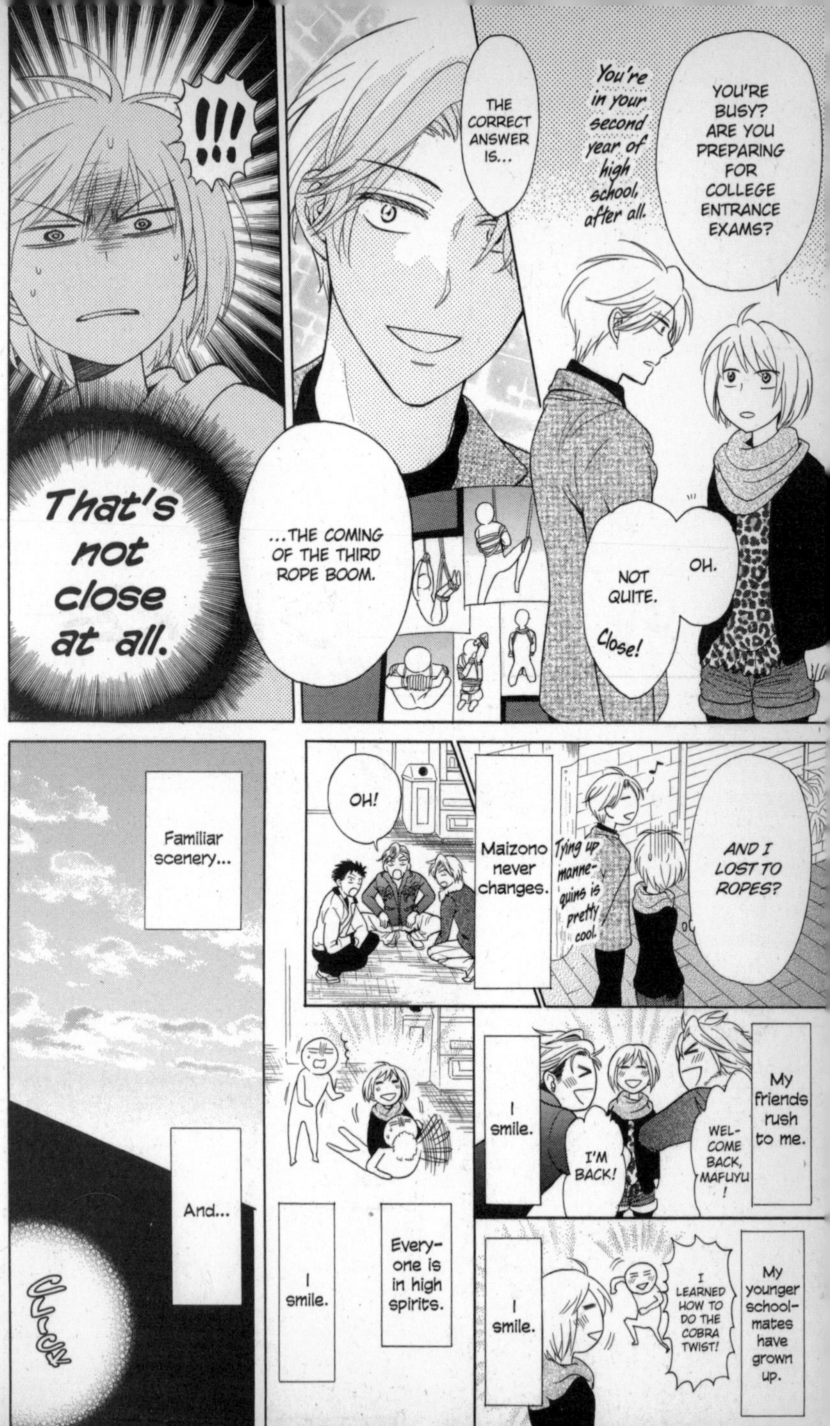
YOU'RE BUSY? ARE YOU PREPARING FOR COLLEGE ENTRANCE EXAMS?
You're in your second year of high school, after all.
OH.
NOT QUITE.
Close!
THE CORRECT ANSWER IS...
...THE COMING OF THE THIRD ROPE BOOM.
!!!
That's not close at all.
AND I LOST TO ROPES?
Tying up manne-quins is pretty cool.
Maizono never changes.
OH!
My friends rush to me.
WEL-COME BACK, MAFUYU!
I'M BACK!
I smile.
My younger school-mates have grown up.
I LEARNED HOW TO DO THE COBRA TWIST!
I smile.
Every-one is in high spirits.
I smile.
Familiar scenery...
And...
CLICK

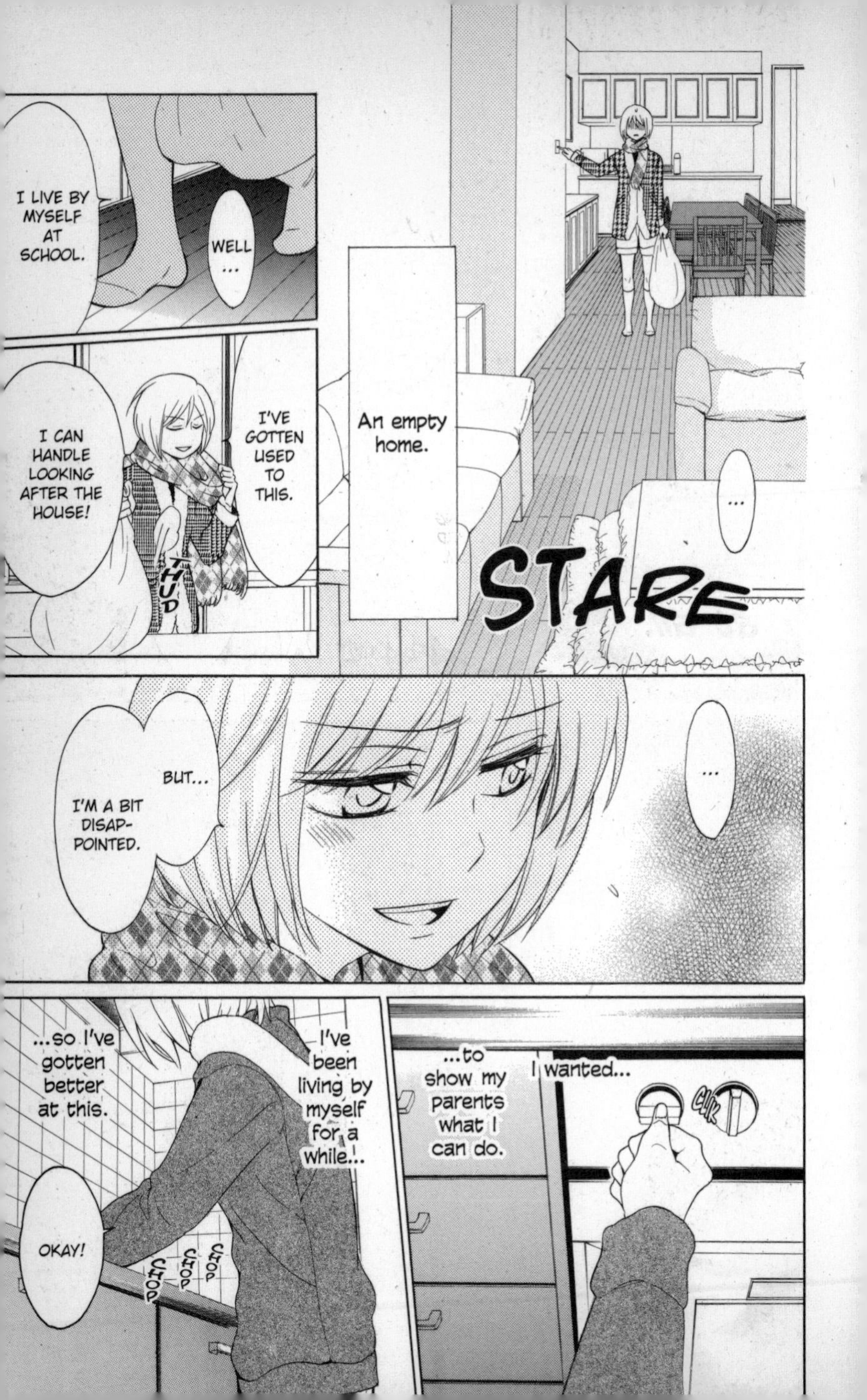
An empty home.
...
STARE
WELL ...
I LIVE BY MYSELF AT SCHOOL.
I'VE GOTTEN USED TO THIS.
I CAN HANDLE LOOKING AFTER THE HOUSE!
THUD
...
BUT...
I'M A BIT DISAP-POINTED.
I wanted...
...to show my parents what I can do.
CLIK
I've been living by myself for a while..!
...so I've gotten better at this.
OKAY!
CHOP CHOP CHOP

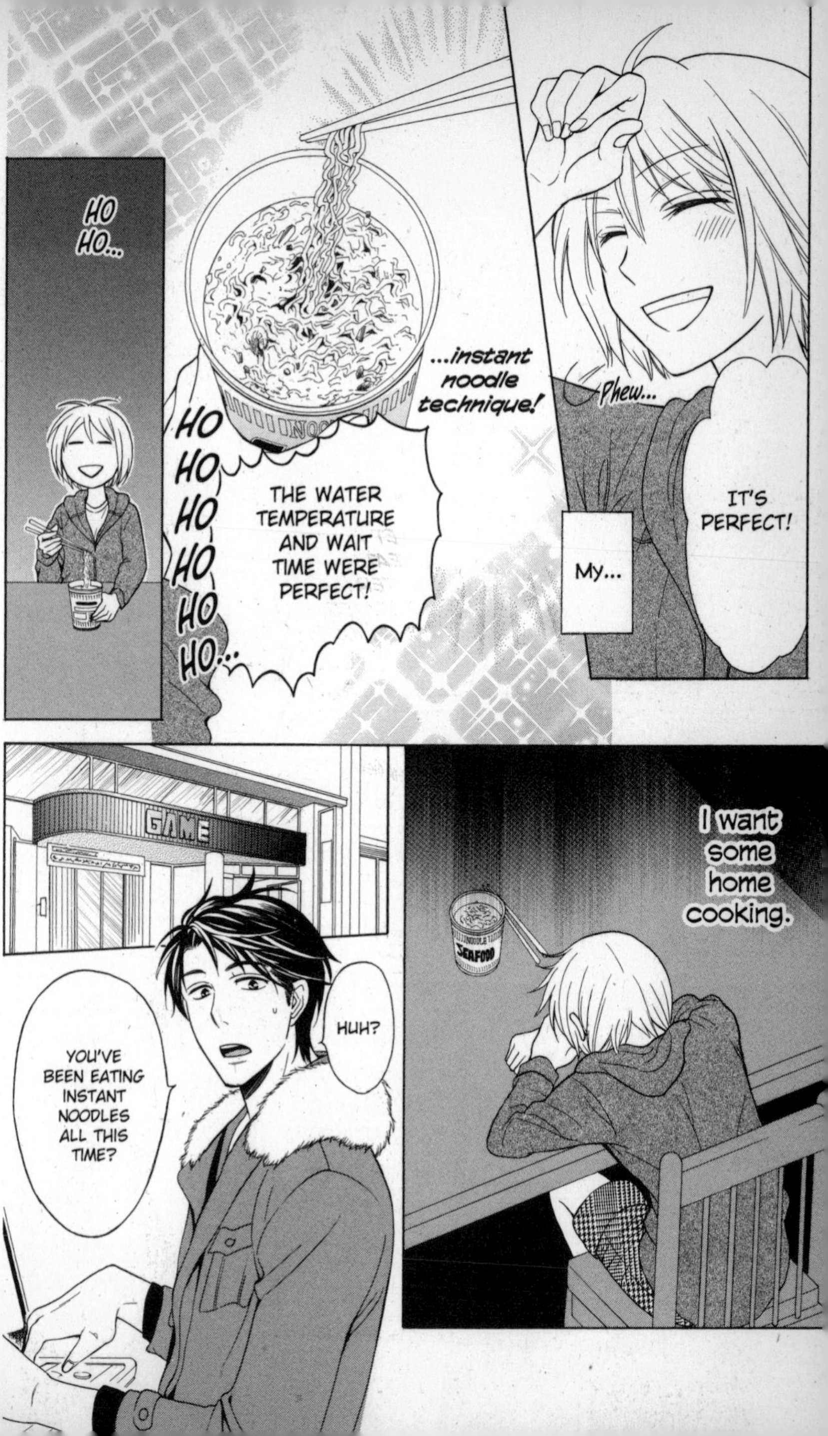
Phew...
IT'S PERFECT!
My...
...instant noodle technique!
THE WATER TEMPERATURE AND WAIT TIME WERE PERFECT!
HO HO HO HO HO HO...
HO HO...
I want some home cooking.
NOODLE
SEAFOOD
GAME
HUH?
YOU'VE BEEN EATING INSTANT NOODLES ALL THIS TIME?

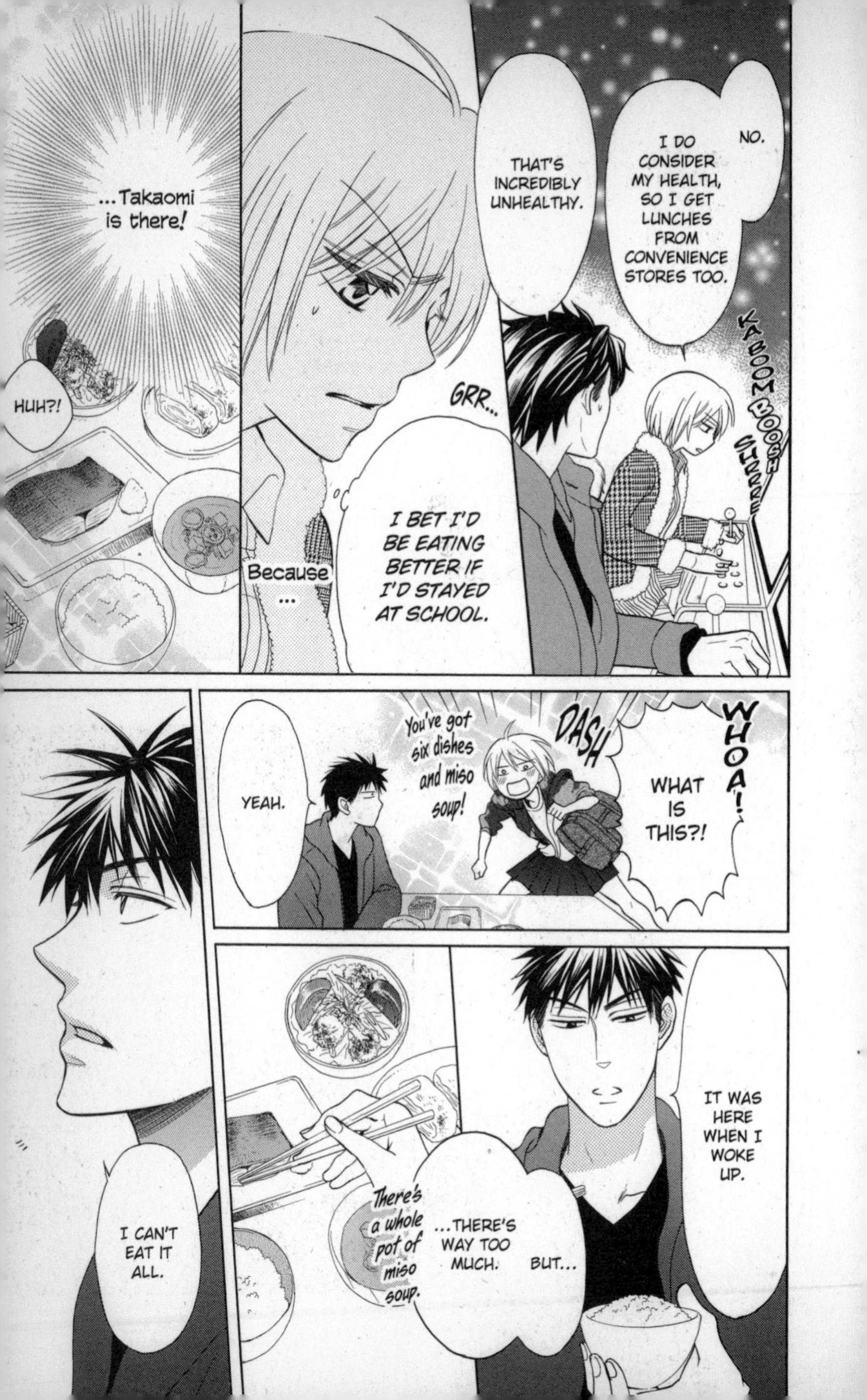
NO.
I DO CONSIDER MY HEALTH, SO I GET LUNCHES FROM CONVENIENCE STORES TOO.
THAT'S INCREDIBLY UNHEALTHY.
KABOOM BOOSH
SHRRRE
GRR...
I BET I'D BE EATING BETTER IF I'D STAYED AT SCHOOL.
Because ...
...Takaomi is there!
HUH?!
WHOA!
WHAT IS THIS?!
DASH
You've got six dishes and miso soup!
YEAH.
IT WAS HERE WHEN I WOKE UP.
BUT...
...THERE'S WAY TOO MUCH.
There's a whole pot of miso soup.
I CAN'T EAT IT ALL.

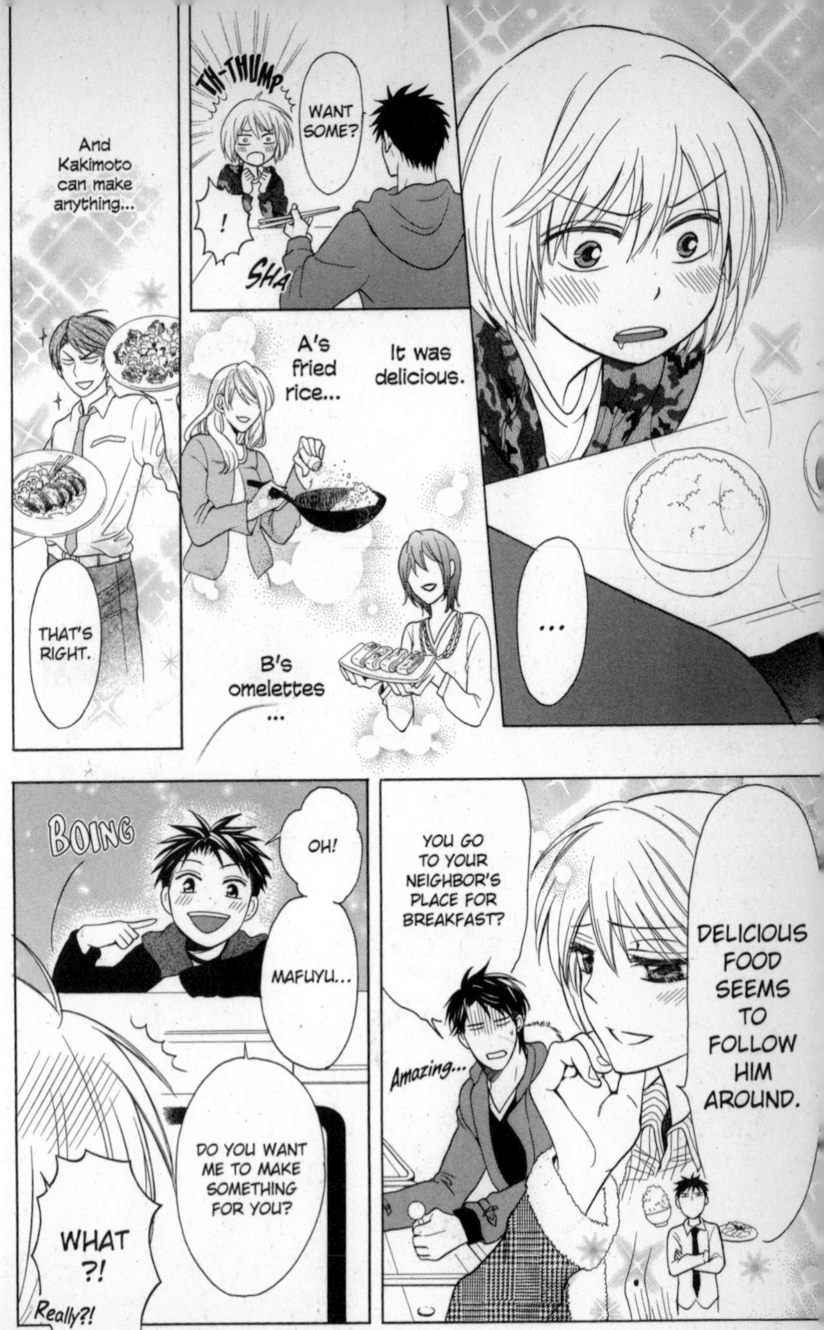
...
TH-THUMP
WANT SOME?
!
SHA
It was delicious.
A's fried rice...
B's omelettes ...
And Kakimoto can make anything...
THAT'S RIGHT.
DELICIOUS FOOD SEEMS TO FOLLOW HIM AROUND.
YOU GO TO YOUR NEIGHBOR'S PLACE FOR BREAKFAST?
Amazing...
OH!
BOING
MAFUYU...
DO YOU WANT ME TO MAKE SOMETHING FOR YOU?
WHAT ?!
Really?!

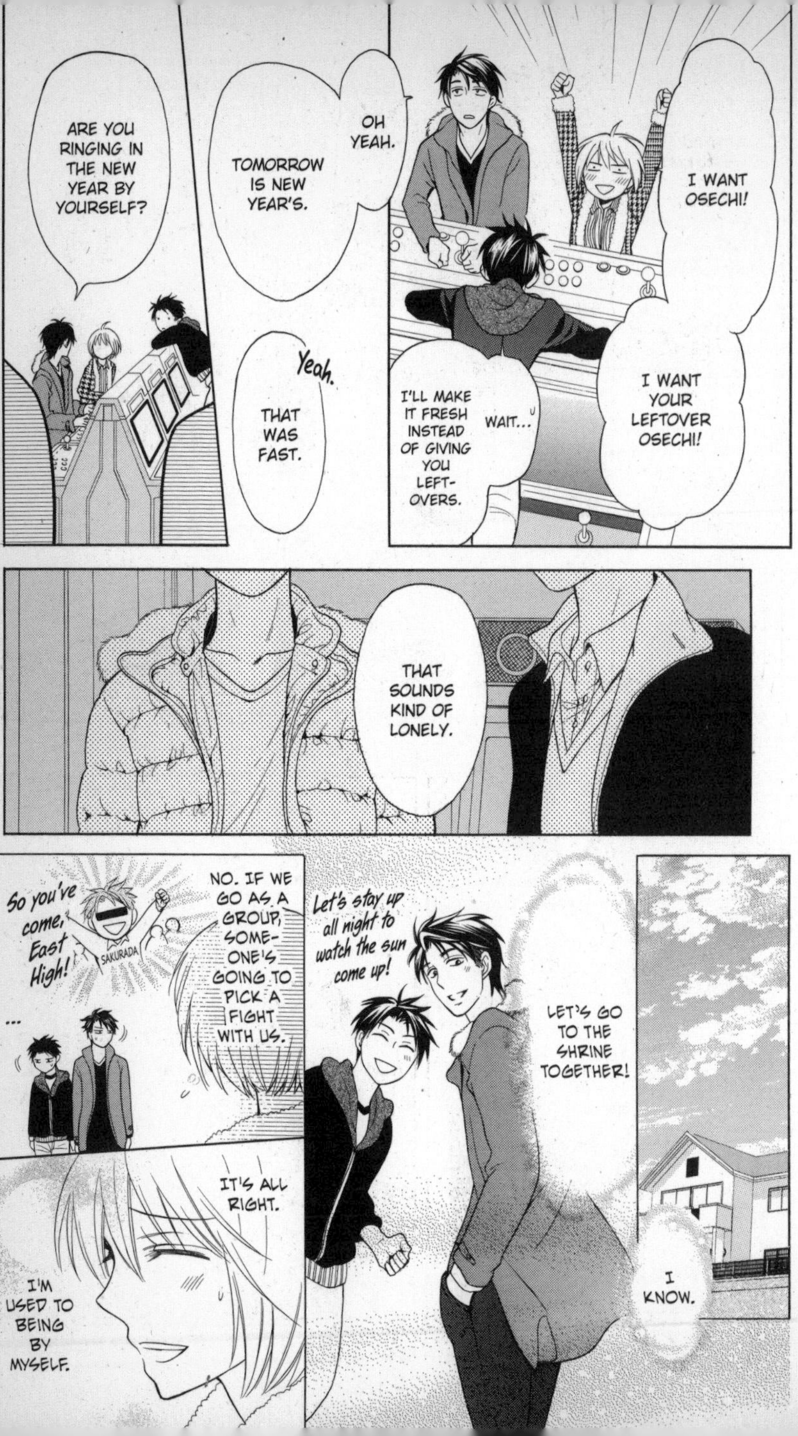

I WANT OSECHI!
I WANT YOUR LEFTOVER OSECHI!
WAIT...
I'LL MAKE IT FRESH INSTEAD OF GIVING YOU LEFT-OVERS.
OH YEAH.
TOMORROW IS NEW YEAR'S.
Yeah.
THAT WAS FAST.
ARE YOU RINGING IN THE NEW YEAR BY YOURSELF?
THAT SOUNDS KIND OF LONELY.
LET'S GO TO THE SHRINE TOGETHER!
I KNOW.
Let's stay up all night to watch the sun come up!
NO. IF WE GO AS A GROUP, SOME-ONE'S GOING TO PICK A FIGHT WITH US.
So you've come, East High!
SAKURADA
...
IT'S ALL RIGHT.
I'M USED TO BEING BY MYSELF.

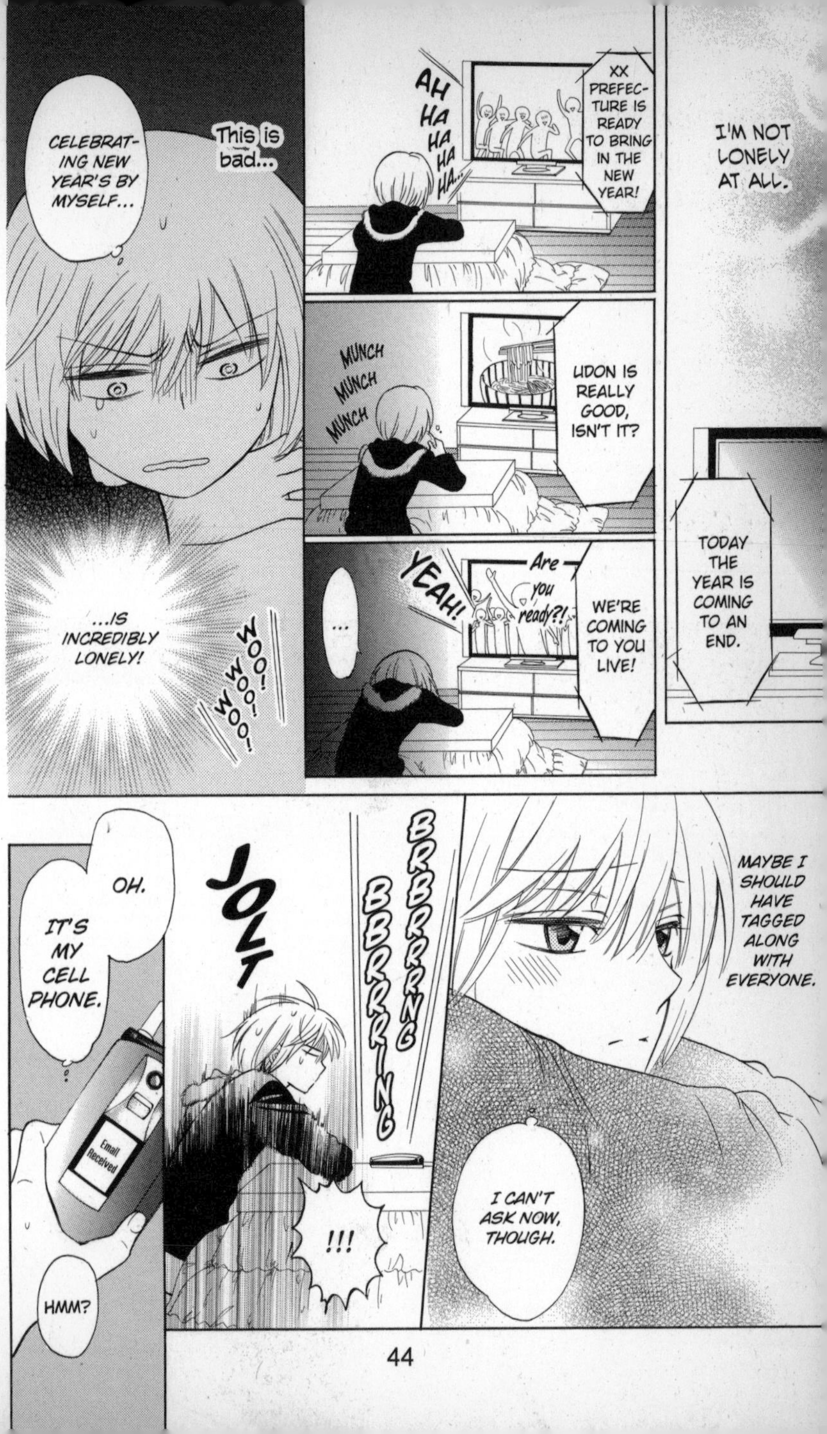
I'M NOT LONELY AT ALL.
TODAY THE YEAR IS COMING TO AN END.
XX PREFECTURE IS READY TO BRING IN THE NEW YEAR!
AH HA HA HA HA...
UDON IS REALLY GOOD, ISN'T IT?
MUNCH MUNCH MUNCH
WE'RE COMING TO YOU LIVE!
Are you ready?!
YEAH!
...
This is bad...
CELEBRATING NEW YEAR'S BY MYSELF...
...IS INCREDIBLY LONELY!
WOO! WOO! WOO!
MAYBE I SHOULD HAVE TAGGED ALONG WITH EVERYONE.
I CAN'T ASK NOW, THOUGH.
BRBRRRRNG BBRRRRING
JOLT
!!!
OH.
IT'S MY CELL PHONE.
Email Received
HMM?

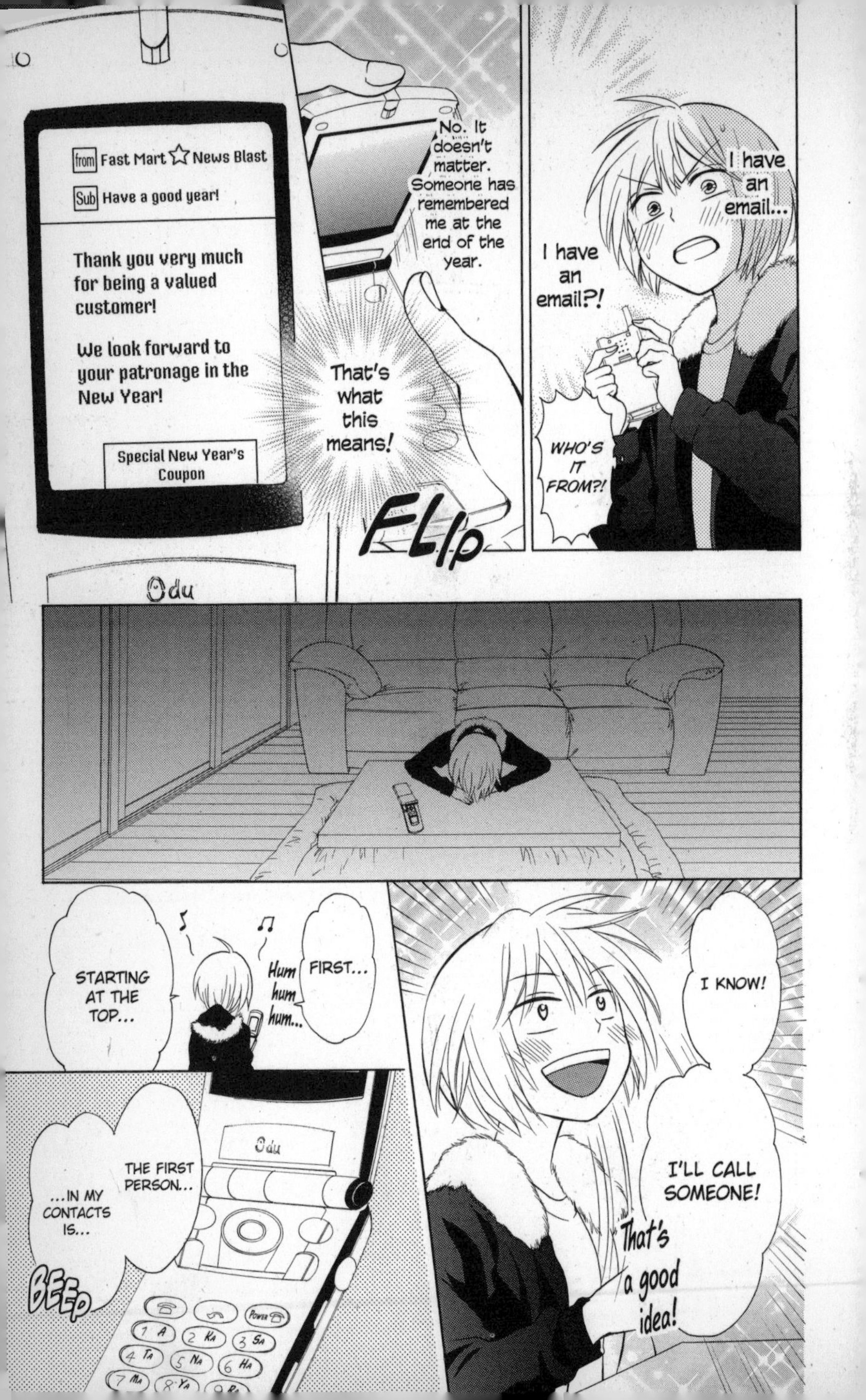
I have an email...
I have an email?!
WHO'S IT FROM?!
No. It doesn't matter. Someone has remembered me at the end of the year.
from Fast Mart ☆ News Blast
Sub Have a good year!
Thank you very much for being a valued customer!
We look forward to your patronage in the New Year!
Special New Year's Coupon
That's what this means!
FLIp
Odu
I KNOW!
I'LL CALL SOMEONE!
That's a good idea!
FIRST...
Hum hum hum...
STARTING AT THE TOP...
Odu
THE FIRST PERSON...
...IN MY CONTACTS IS...
BEEp

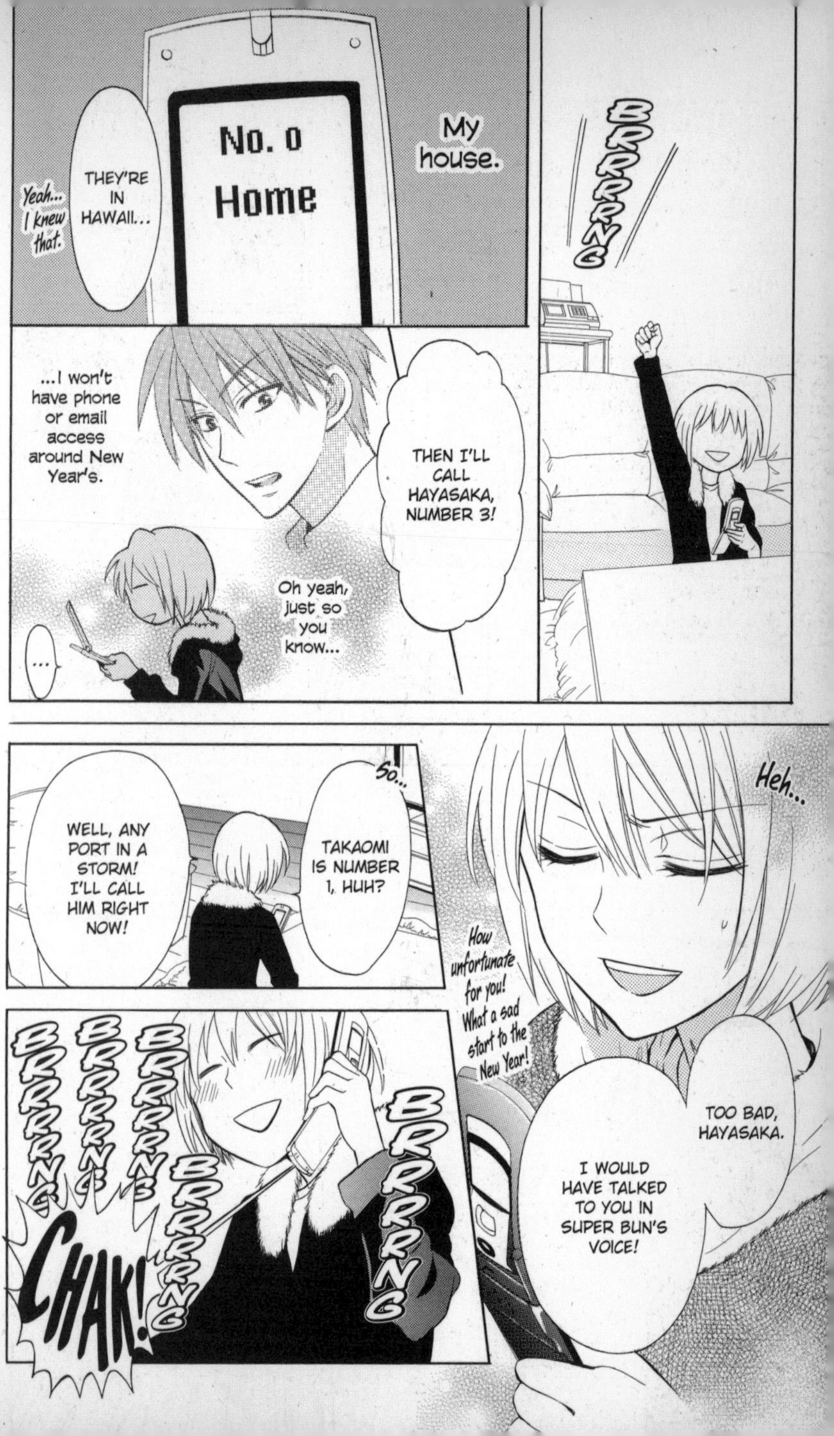
BRRRRNG
My house.
No. 0
Home
THEY'RE IN HAWAII...
Yeah... I knew that.
THEN I'LL CALL HAYASAKA, NUMBER 3!
Oh yeah, just so you know...
...I won't have phone or email access around New Year's.
...
Heh...
How unfortunate for you! What a sad start to the New Year!
TOO BAD, HAYASAKA.
I WOULD HAVE TALKED TO YOU IN SUPER BUN'S VOICE!
So...
TAKAOMI IS NUMBER 1, HUH?
WELL, ANY PORT IN A STORM! I'LL CALL HIM RIGHT NOW!
BRRRRNG
BRRRRNG
BRRRRNG
BRRRRNG
BRRRRNG
CHAK!

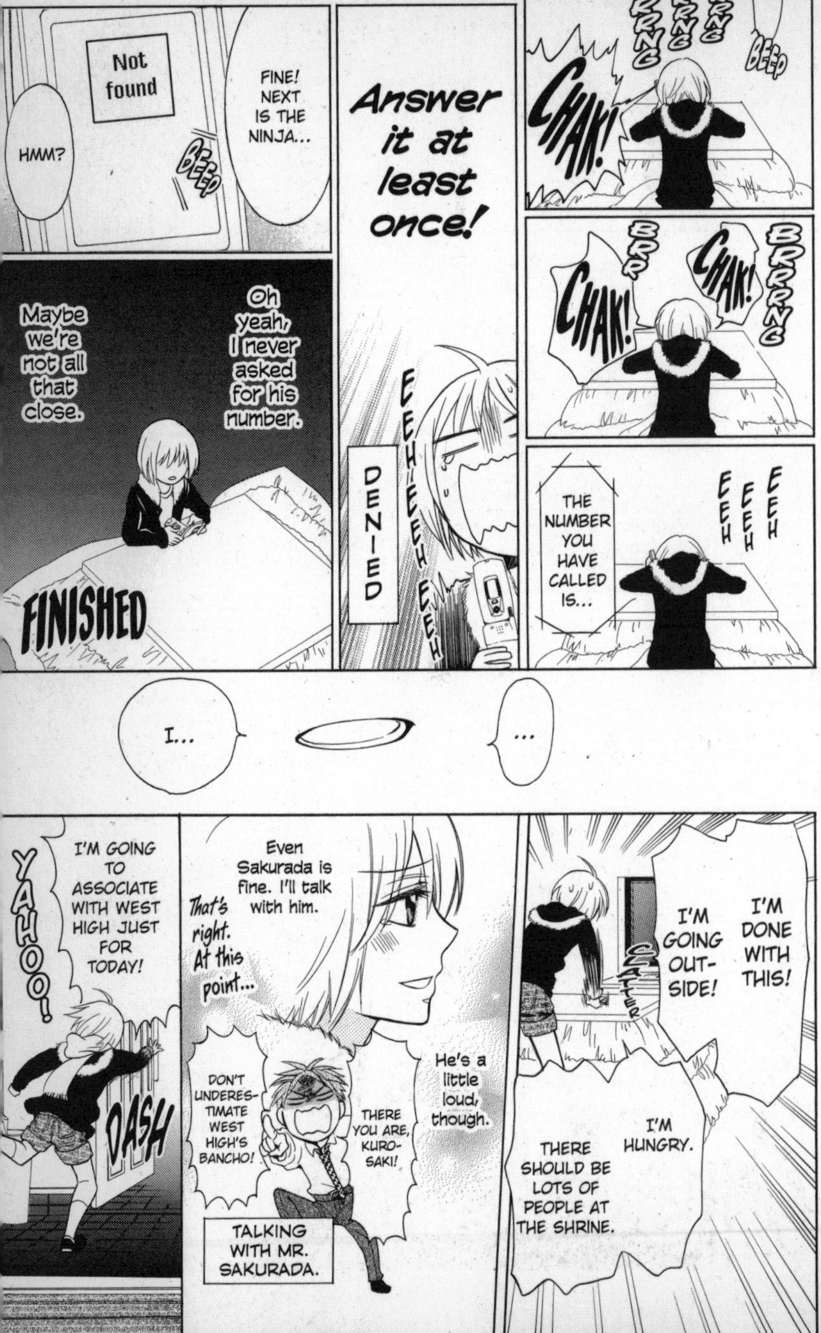
...
BRRRNG BRRRNG BRRRNG
BEEP
CHAK!
BRRRNG
CHAK!
BRR
CHAK!
THE NUMBER YOU HAVE CALLED IS...
EEH EEH EEH
Answer it at least once!
EEHIEEEEH EEH
DENIED
FINE! NEXT IS THE NINJA...
BEEP
Not found
HMM?
Oh yeah, I never asked for his number.
Maybe we're not all that close.
FINISHED
...
I...
I'M DONE WITH THIS!
I'M GOING OUT-SIDE!
CLATTER
I'M HUNGRY.
THERE SHOULD BE LOTS OF PEOPLE AT THE SHRINE.
Even Sakurada is fine. I'll talk with him.
That's right. At this point...
He's a little loud, though.
THERE YOU ARE, KURO-SAKI!
DON'T UNDERES-TIMATE WEST HIGH'S BANCHO!
TALKING WITH MR. SAKURADA.
I'M GOING TO ASSOCIATE WITH WEST HIGH JUST FOR TODAY!
YAHOO!
DASH

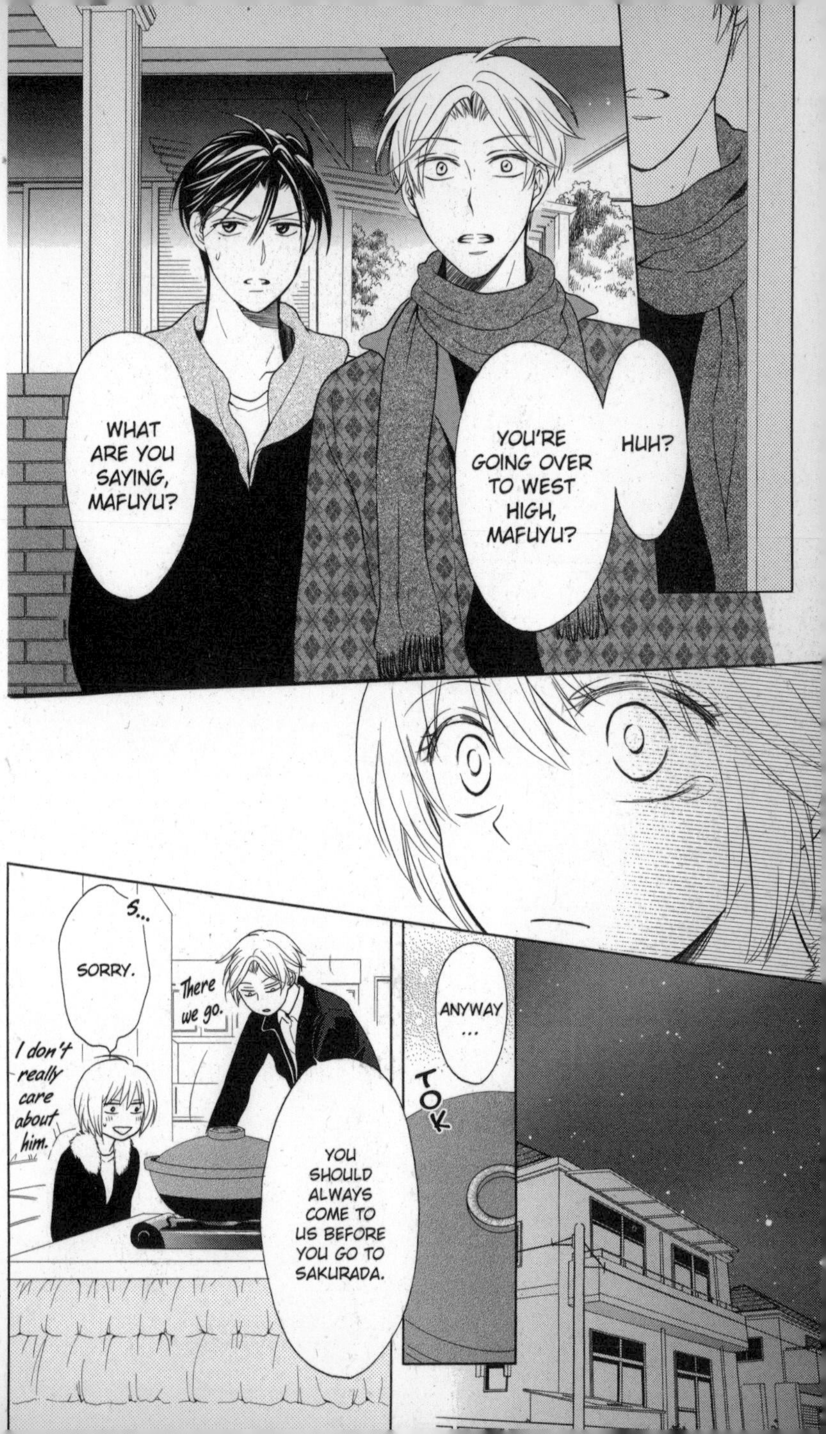
HUH?
YOU'RE GOING OVER TO WEST HIGH, MAFUYU?
WHAT ARE YOU SAYING, MAFUYU?
ANYWAY ...
TOK
YOU SHOULD ALWAYS COME TO US BEFORE YOU GO TO SAKURADA.
There we go.
S... SORRY.
I don't really care about him.

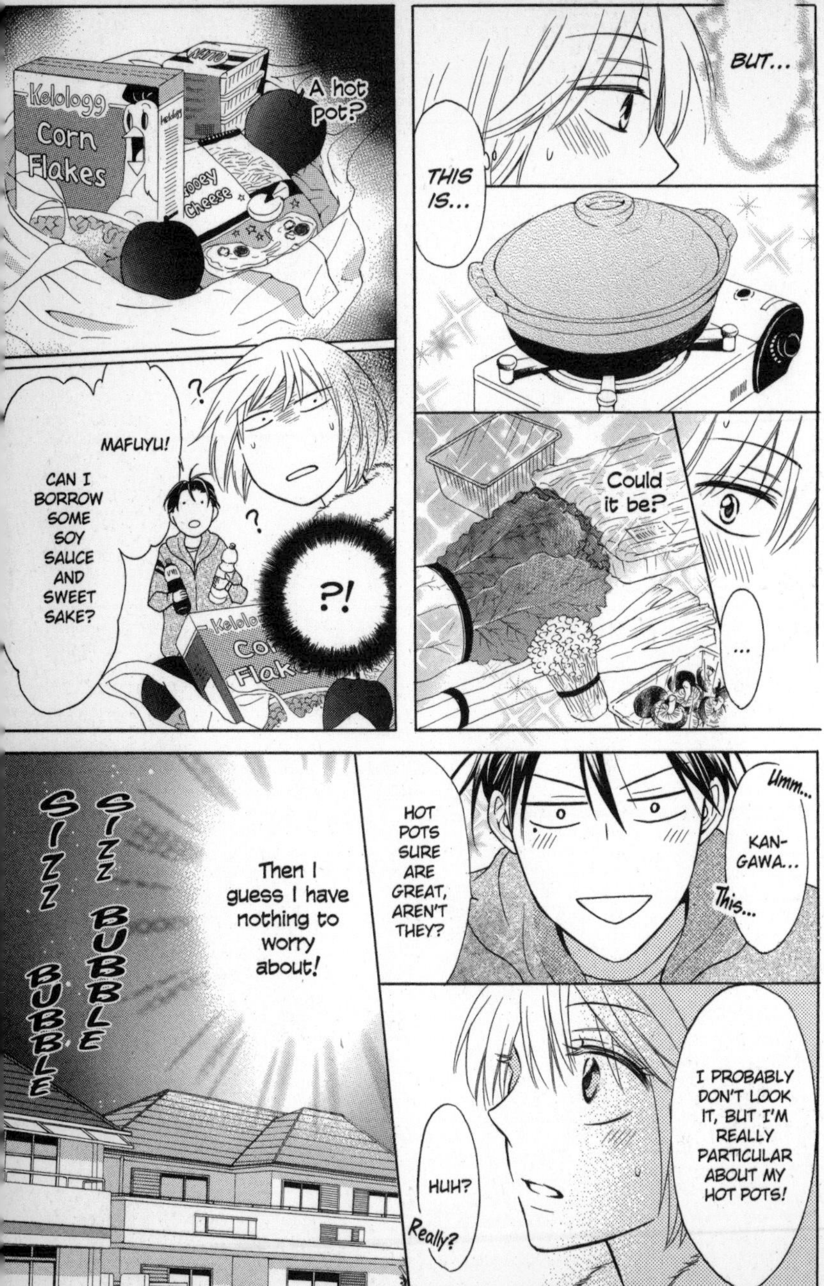
BUT...
THIS IS...
Kelologg
Corn Flakes
Gooey Cheese
A hot pot?
Could it be?
...
MAFUYU!
CAN I BORROW SOME SOY SAUCE AND SWEET SAKE?
?!
Kelologg
Umm...
KAN-GAWA...
This...
HOT POTS SURE ARE GREAT, AREN'T THEY?
I PROBABLY DON'T LOOK IT, BUT I'M REALLY PARTICULAR ABOUT MY HOT POTS!
HUH?
Really?
Then I guess I have nothing to worry about!
SIZZ SIZZ
BUBBLE BUBBLE

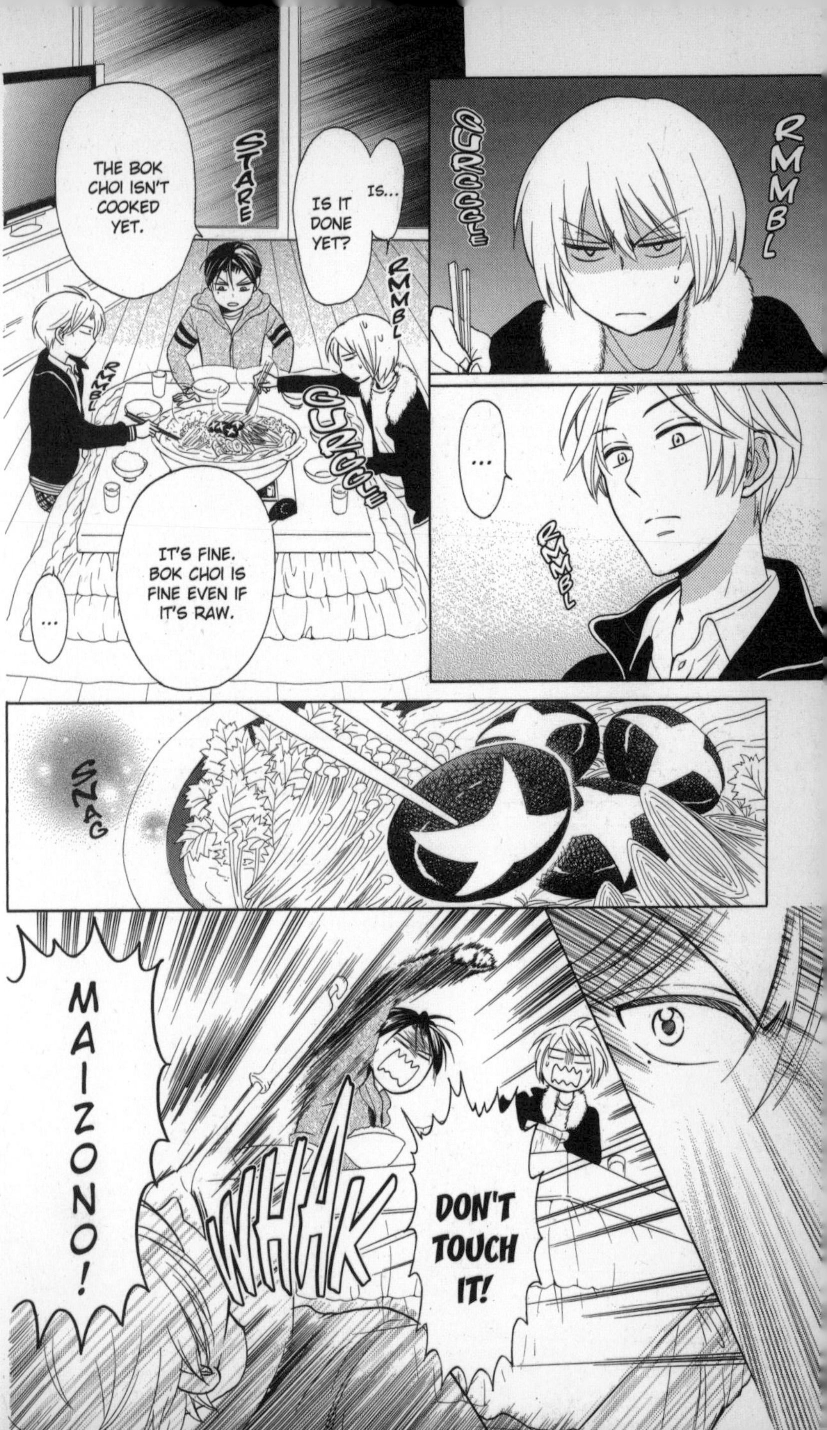
RMMBL
GURGGGLE
...
RMMBL
IS... IS IT DONE YET?
STARE
THE BOK CHOI ISN'T COOKED YET.
RMMBL
GURGGLE
RMMBL
IT'S FINE. BOK CHOI IS FINE EVEN IF IT'S RAW.
...
SNAG
DON'T TOUCH IT!
WHAK
MAIZONO!

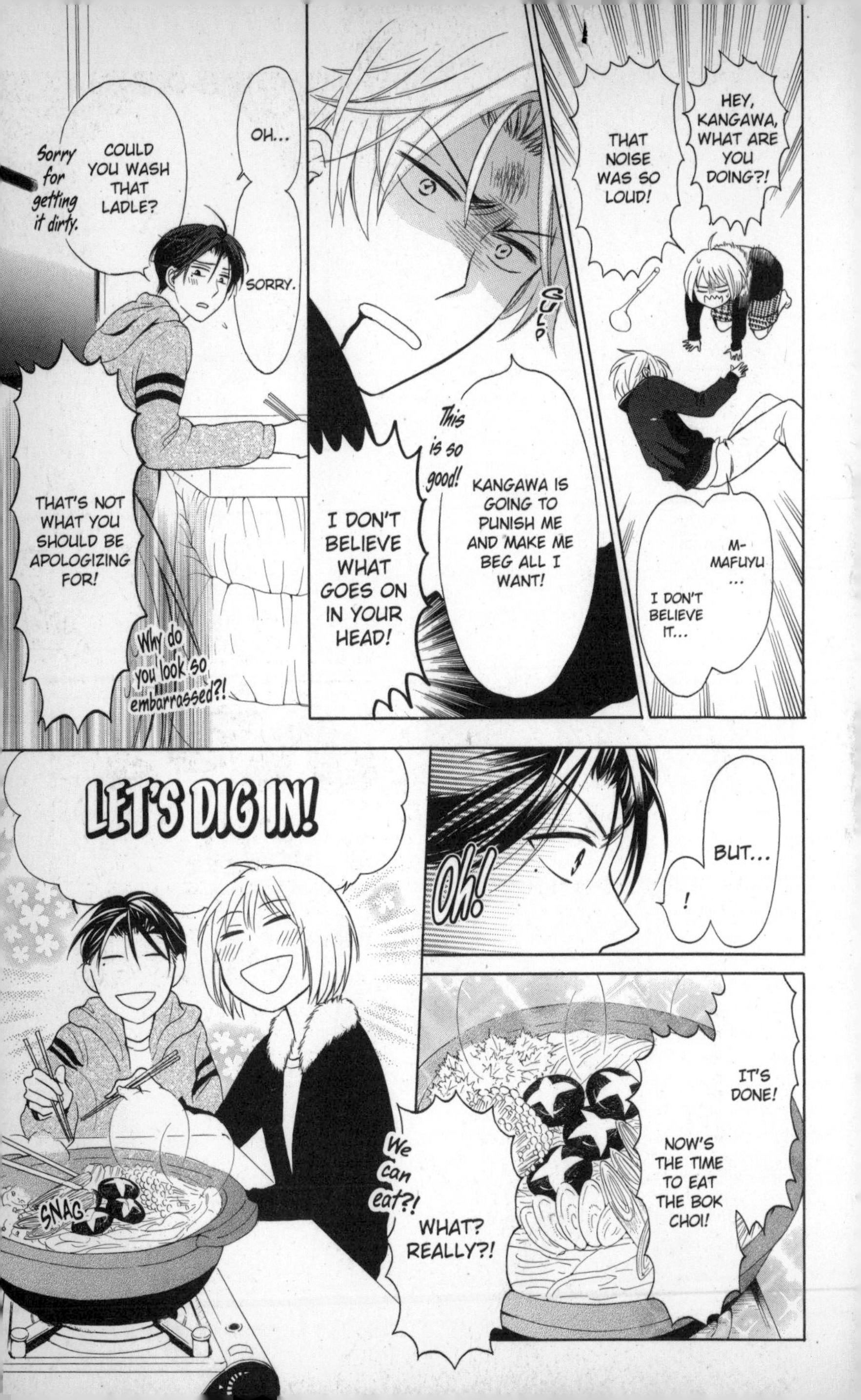
HEY, KANGAWA, WHAT ARE YOU DOING?!
THAT NOISE WAS SO LOUD!
M-MAFUYU...
I DON'T BELIEVE IT...
GULP
KANGAWA IS GOING TO PUNISH ME AND MAKE ME BEG ALL I WANT!
This is so good!
I DON'T BELIEVE WHAT GOES ON IN YOUR HEAD!
OH...
COULD YOU WASH THAT LADLE?
Sorry for getting it dirty.
SORRY.
THAT'S NOT WHAT YOU SHOULD BE APOLOGIZING FOR!
Why do you look so embarrassed?!
BUT...
!
Oh!
IT'S DONE!
NOW'S THE TIME TO EAT THE BOK CHOI!
WHAT? REALLY?!
We can eat?!
LET'S DIG IN!
SNAG

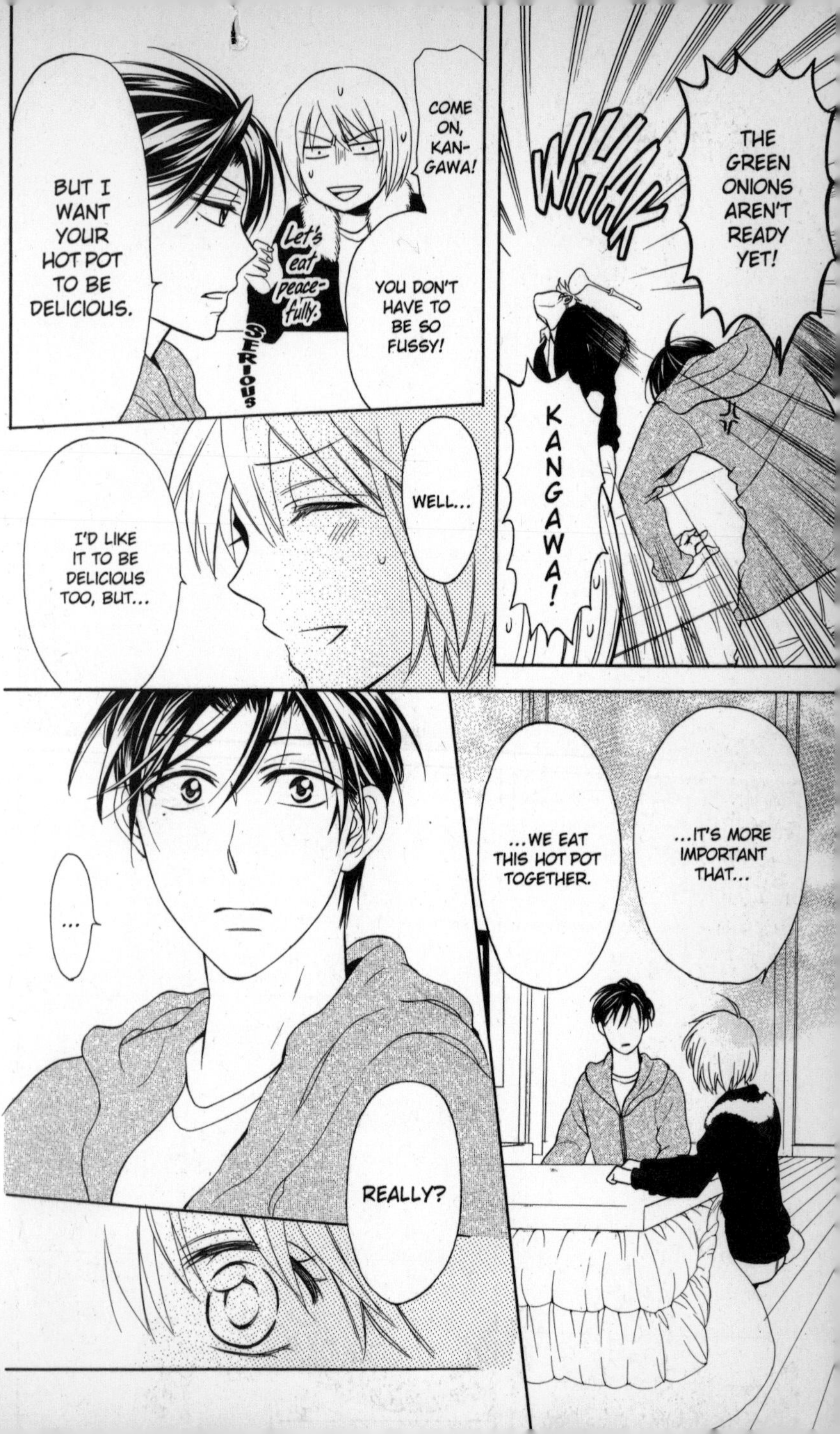
WHAK
THE GREEN ONIONS AREN'T READY YET!
KANGAWA!
COME ON, KAN-GAWA!
YOU DON'T HAVE TO BE SO FUSSY!
Let's eat peace-fully.
SERIOUS
BUT I WANT YOUR HOT POT TO BE DELICIOUS.
WELL...
I'D LIKE IT TO BE DELICIOUS TOO, BUT...
...IT'S MORE IMPORTANT THAT...
...WE EAT THIS HOT POT TOGETHER.
...
REALLY?

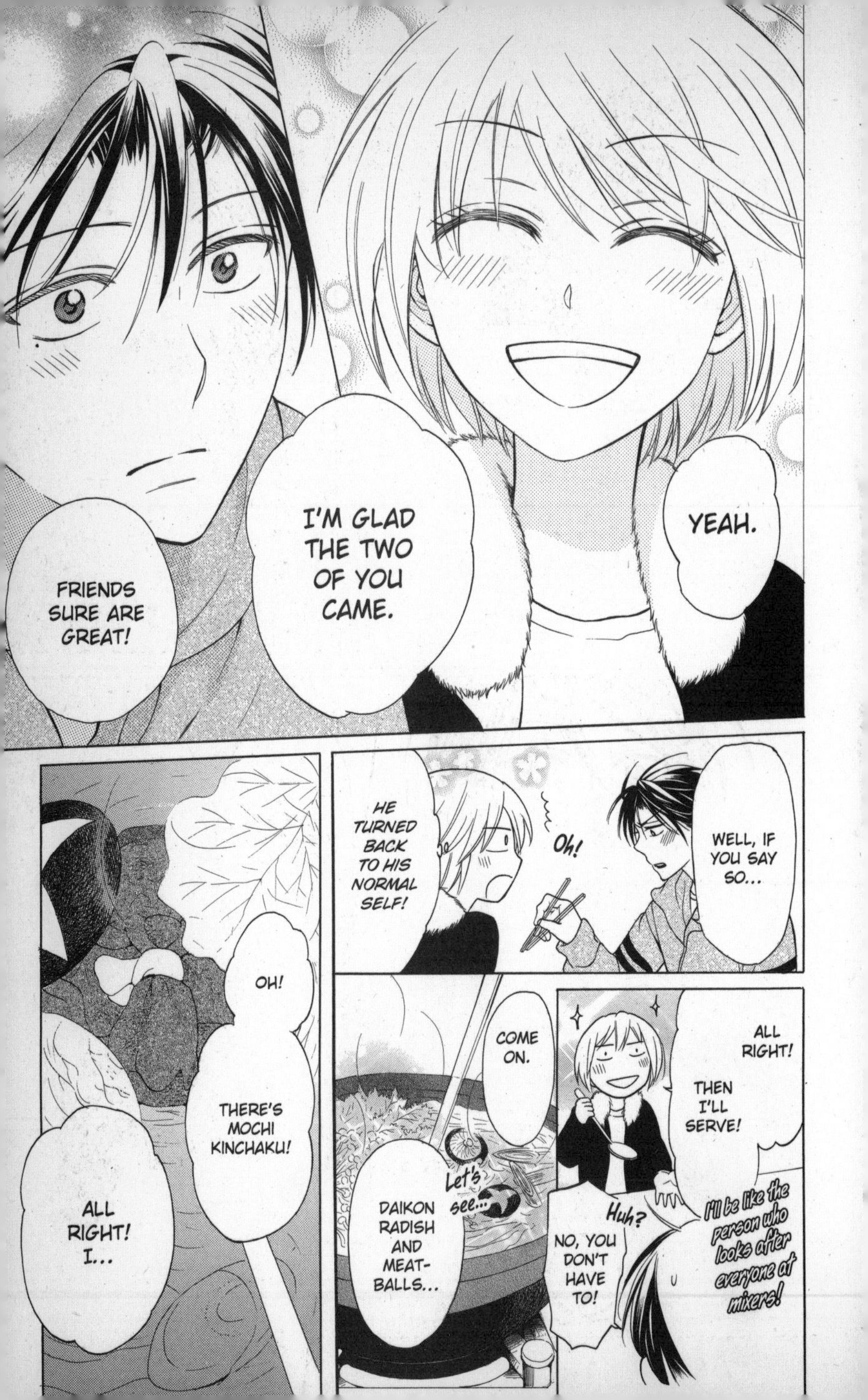
YEAH.
I'M GLAD THE TWO OF YOU CAME.
FRIENDS SURE ARE GREAT!
WELL, IF YOU SAY SO...
Oh!
HE TURNED BACK TO HIS NORMAL SELF!
ALL RIGHT! THEN I'LL SERVE!
I'll be like the person who looks after everyone at mixers!
COME ON.
Huh?
NO, YOU DON'T HAVE TO!
Let's see...
DAIKON RADISH AND MEAT-BALLS...
OH!
THERE'S MOCHI KINCHAKU!
ALL RIGHT! I...

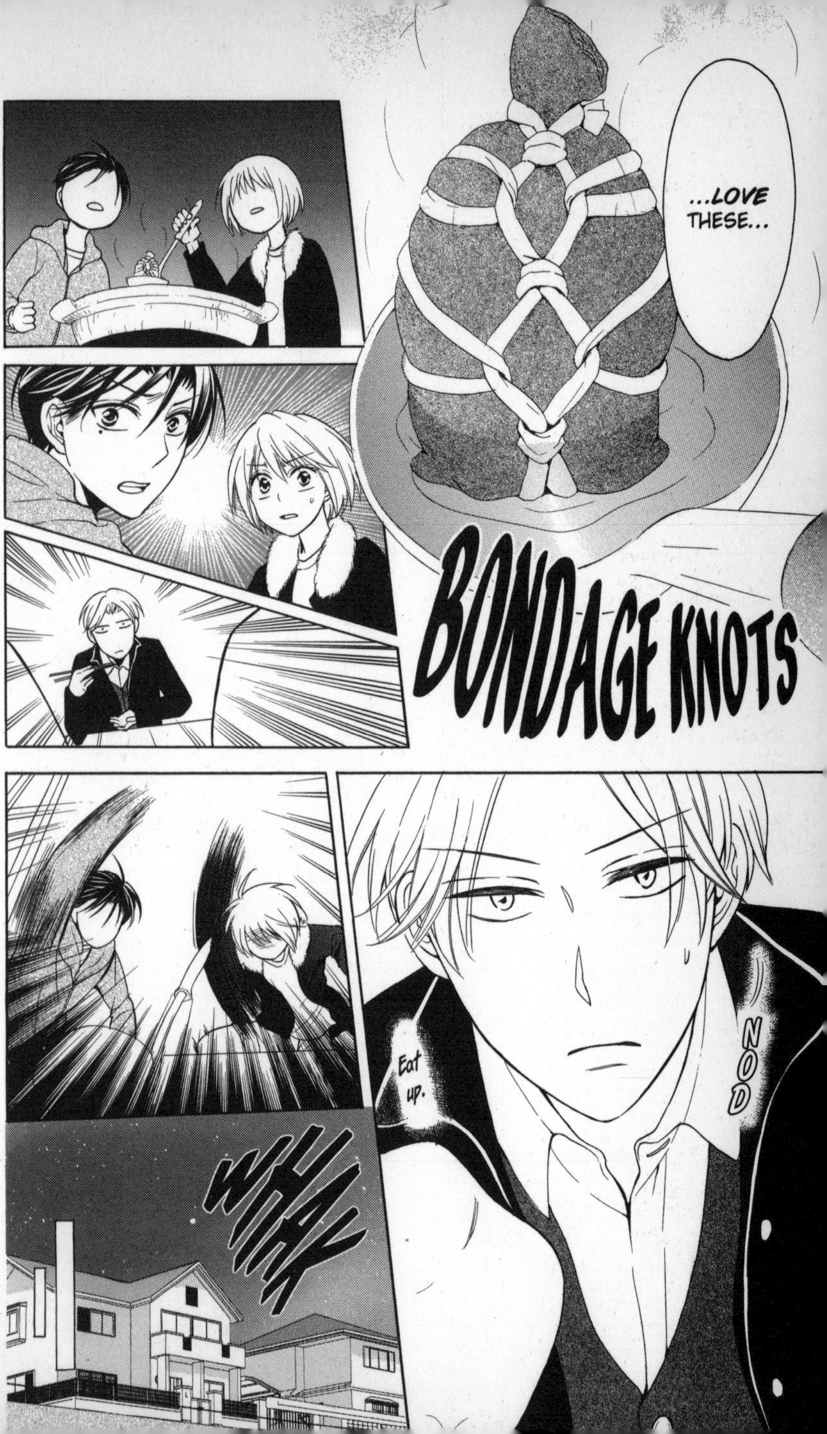
...LOVE THESE...
BONDAGE KNOTS
NOD
Eat up.
WHAM

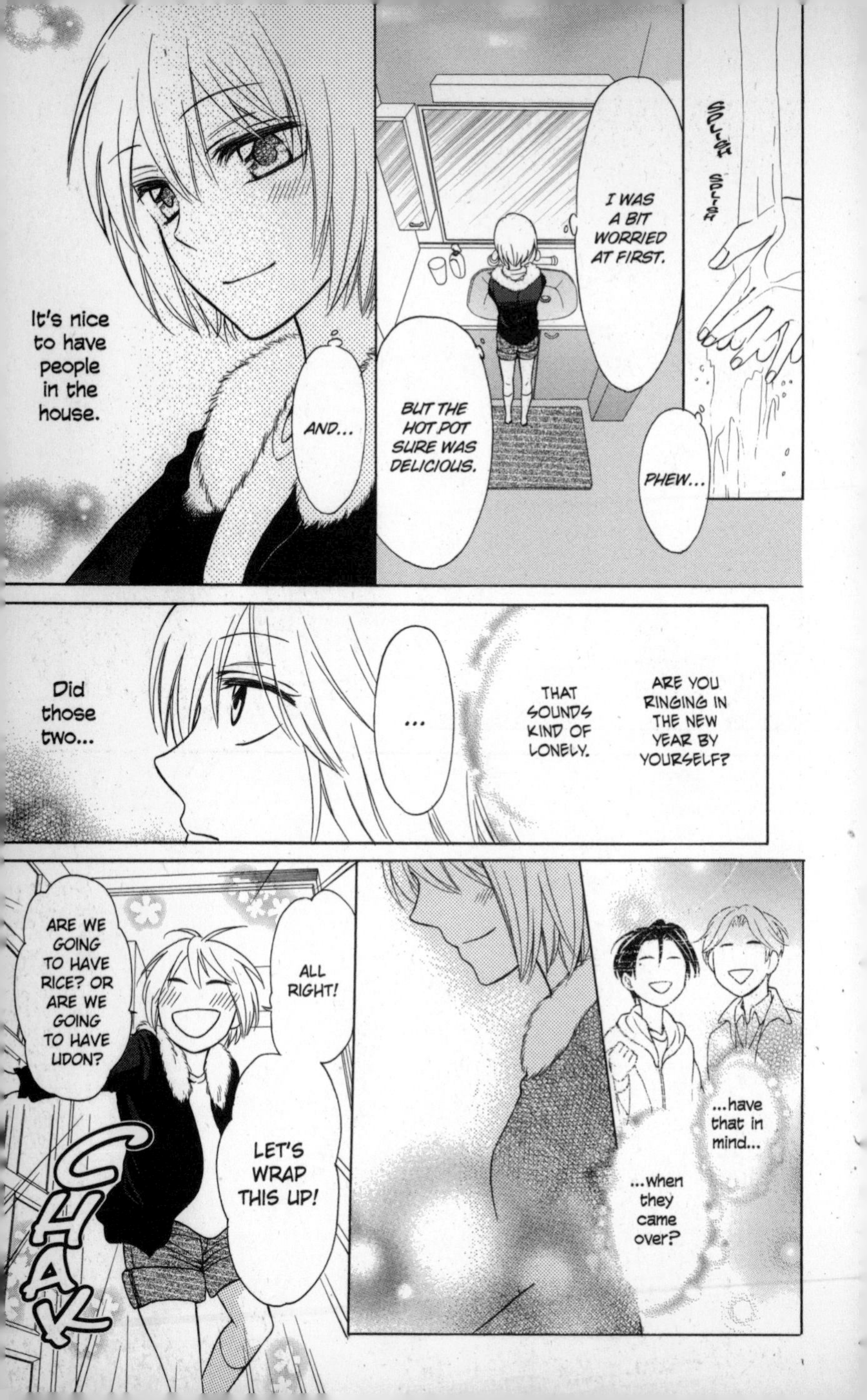
SPLISH SPLISH
I WAS A BIT WORRIED AT FIRST.
PHEW...
BUT THE HOT POT SURE WAS DELICIOUS.
AND...
It's nice to have people in the house.
ARE YOU RINGING IN THE NEW YEAR BY YOURSELF?
THAT SOUNDS KIND OF LONELY.
...
Did those two...
...have that in mind...
...when they came over?
ALL RIGHT!
ARE WE GOING TO HAVE RICE? OR ARE WE GOING TO HAVE UDON?
LET'S WRAP THIS UP!
CHAK

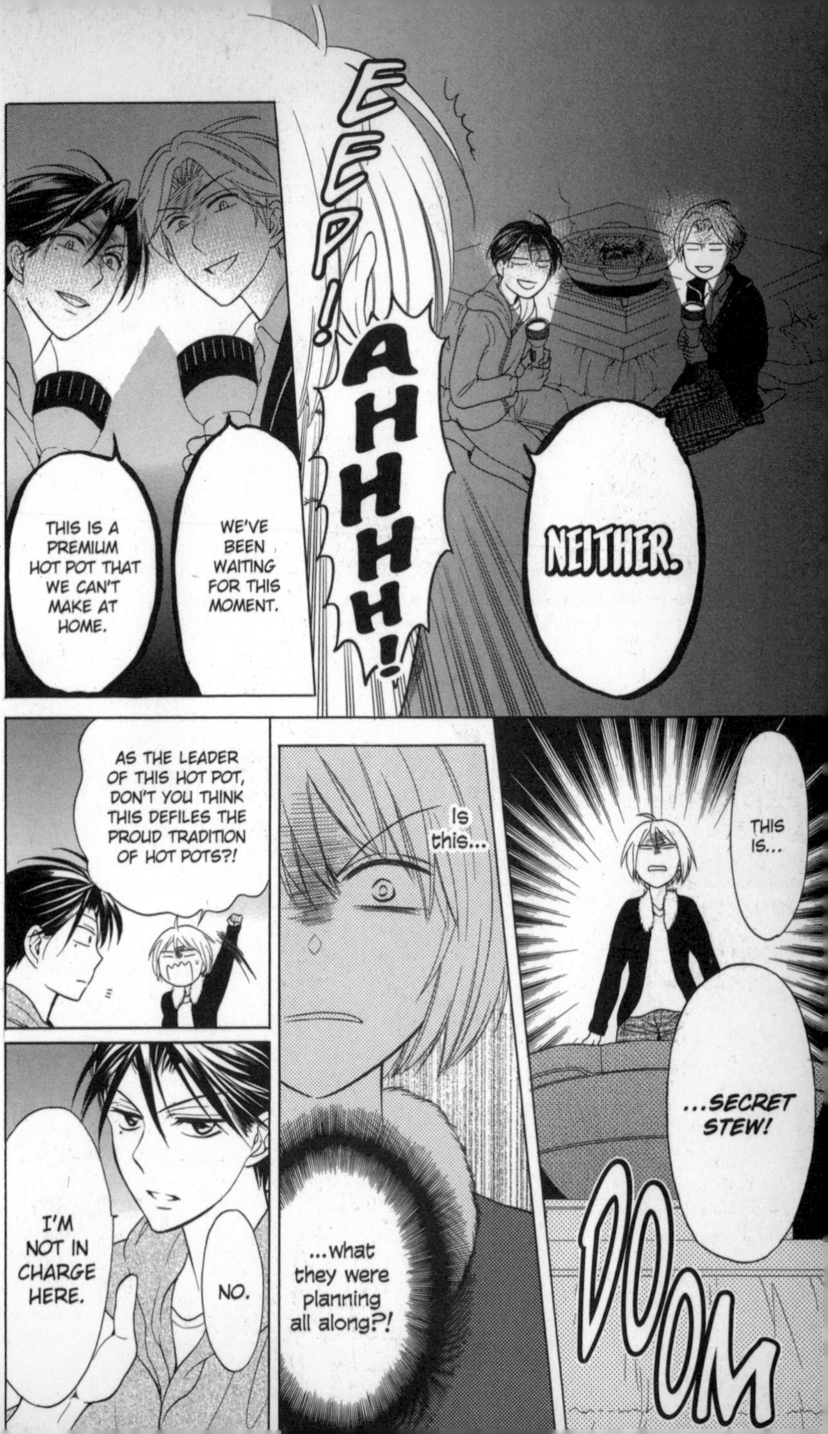
NEITHER.
EEP!
AHHHH!
WE'VE BEEN WAITING FOR THIS MOMENT.
THIS IS A PREMIUM HOT POT THAT WE CAN'T MAKE AT HOME.
THIS IS...
...SECRET STEW!
DOOM
Is this...
...what they were planning all along?!
AS THE LEADER OF THIS HOT POT, DON'T YOU THINK THIS DEFILES THE PROUD TRADITION OF HOT POTS?!
NO.
I'M NOT IN CHARGE HERE.

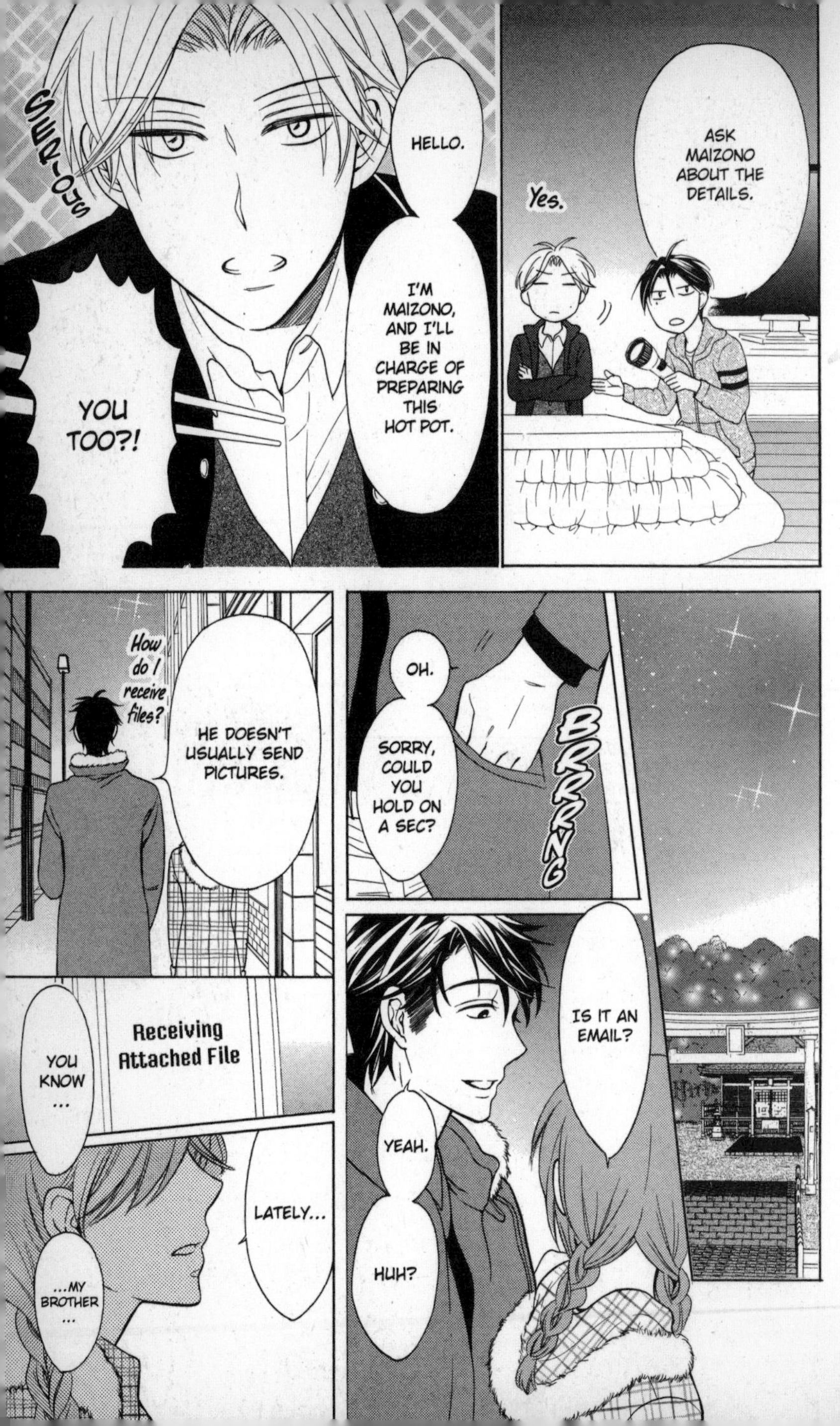
ASK MAIZONO ABOUT THE DETAILS.
Yes.
HELLO.
I'M MAIZONO, AND I'LL BE IN CHARGE OF PREPARING THIS HOT POT.
SERIOUS
YOU TOO?!
OH.
SORRY, COULD YOU HOLD ON A SEC?
BRRRNG
How do I receive files?
HE DOESN'T USUALLY SEND PICTURES.
IS IT AN EMAIL?
YEAH.
HUH?
Receiving Attached File
YOU KNOW...
LATELY...
...MY BROTHER...

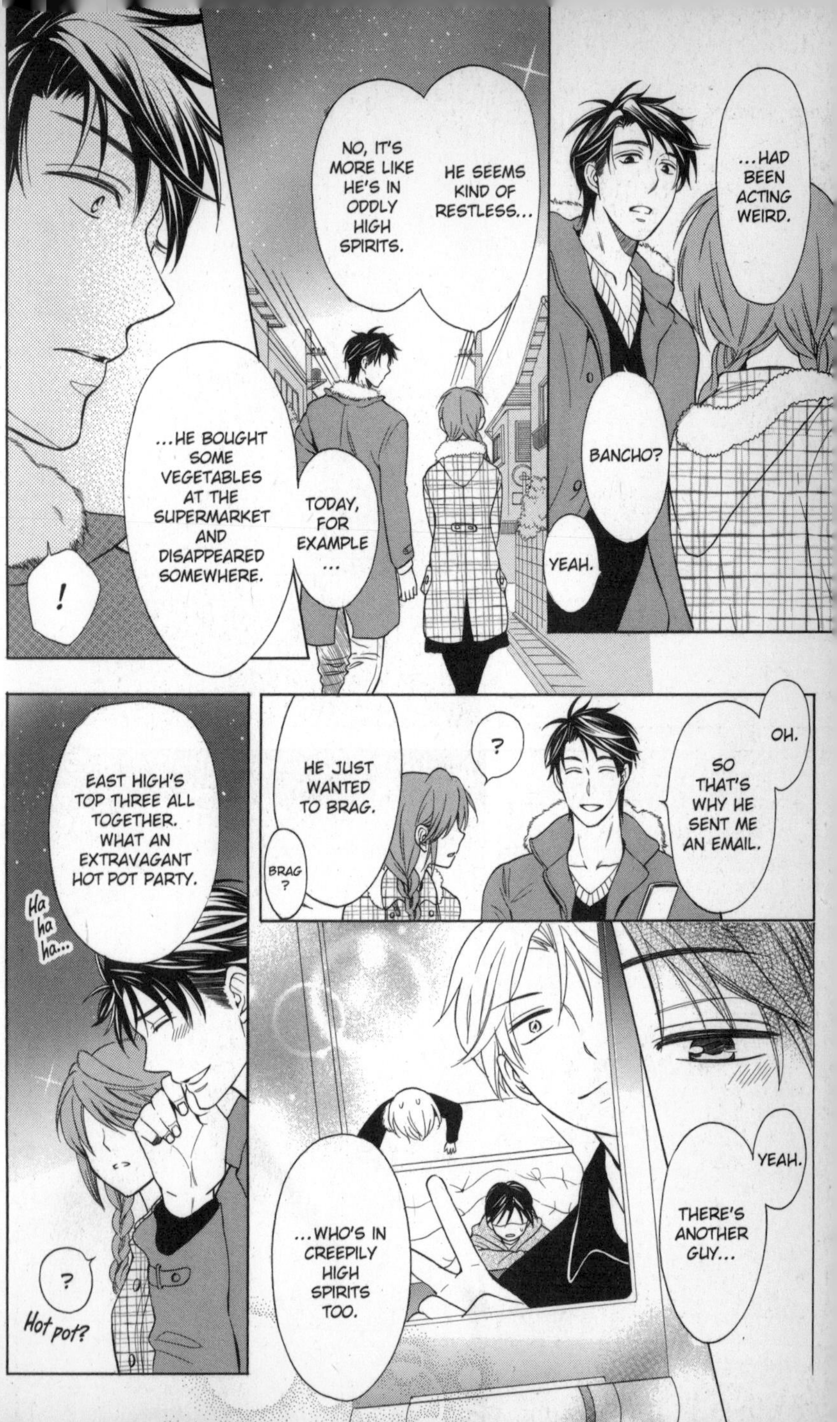
...HAD BEEN ACTING WEIRD.
BANCHO?
YEAH.
HE SEEMS KIND OF RESTLESS...
NO, IT'S MORE LIKE HE'S IN ODDLY HIGH SPIRITS.
TODAY, FOR EXAMPLE...
...HE BOUGHT SOME VEGETABLES AT THE SUPERMARKET AND DISAPPEARED SOMEWHERE.
!
OH. SO THAT'S WHY HE SENT ME AN EMAIL.
?
HE JUST WANTED TO BRAG.
BRAG?
YEAH. THERE'S ANOTHER GUY...
...WHO'S IN CREEPILY HIGH SPIRITS TOO.
EAST HIGH'S TOP THREE ALL TOGETHER. WHAT AN EXTRAVAGANT HOT POT PARTY.
Ha ha ha...
?
Hot pot?

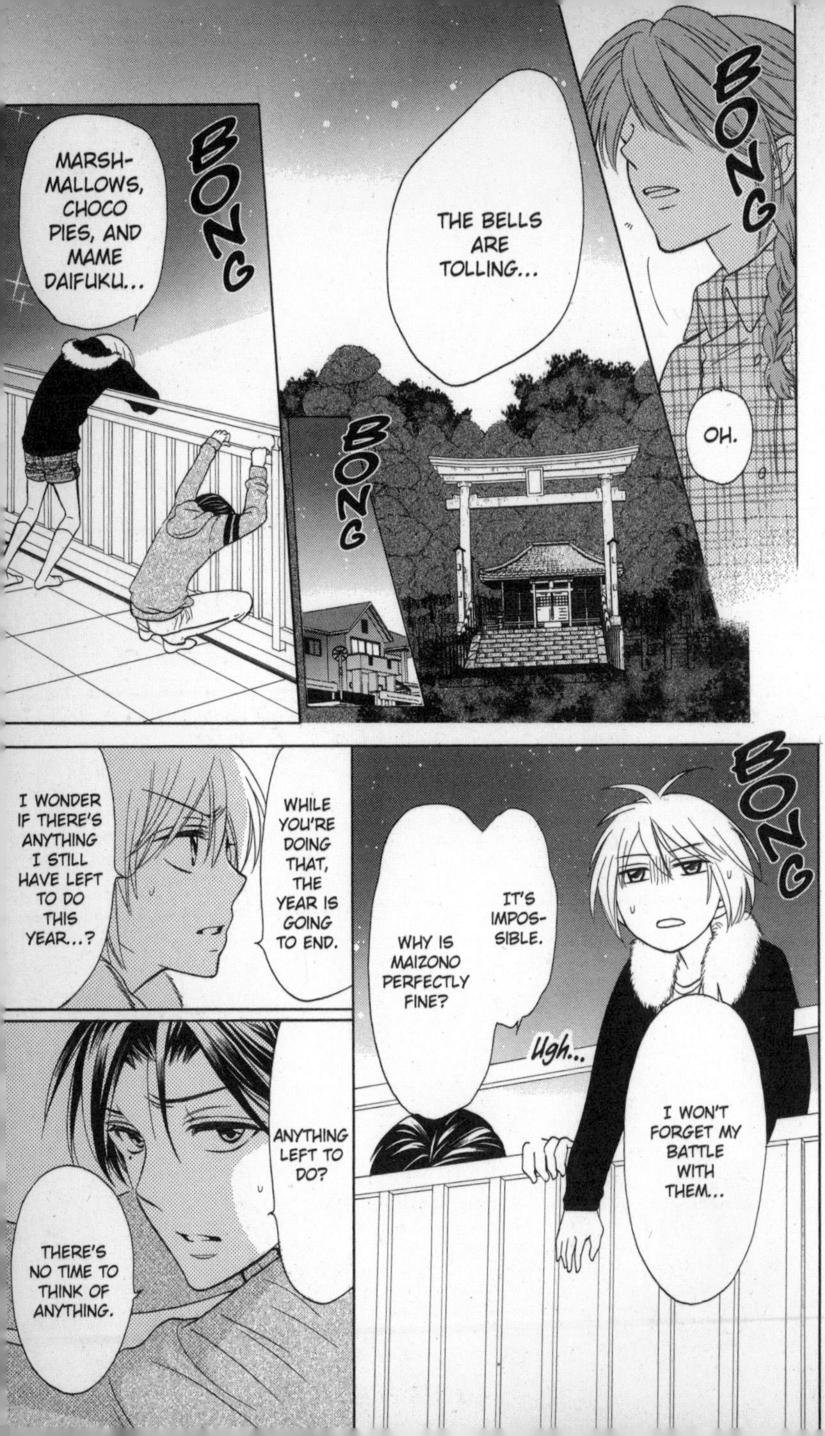
BONG BONG
THE BELLS ARE TOLLING...
OH.
BONG
BONG
MARSH-MALLOWS, CHOCO PIES, AND MAME DAIFUKU...
BONG
IT'S IMPOSSIBLE.
WHY IS MAIZONO PERFECTLY FINE?
Ugh...
I WON'T FORGET MY BATTLE WITH THEM...
WHILE YOU'RE DOING THAT, THE YEAR IS GOING TO END.
I WONDER IF THERE'S ANYTHING I STILL HAVE LEFT TO DO THIS YEAR...?
ANYTHING LEFT TO DO?
THERE'S NO TIME TO THINK OF ANYTHING.

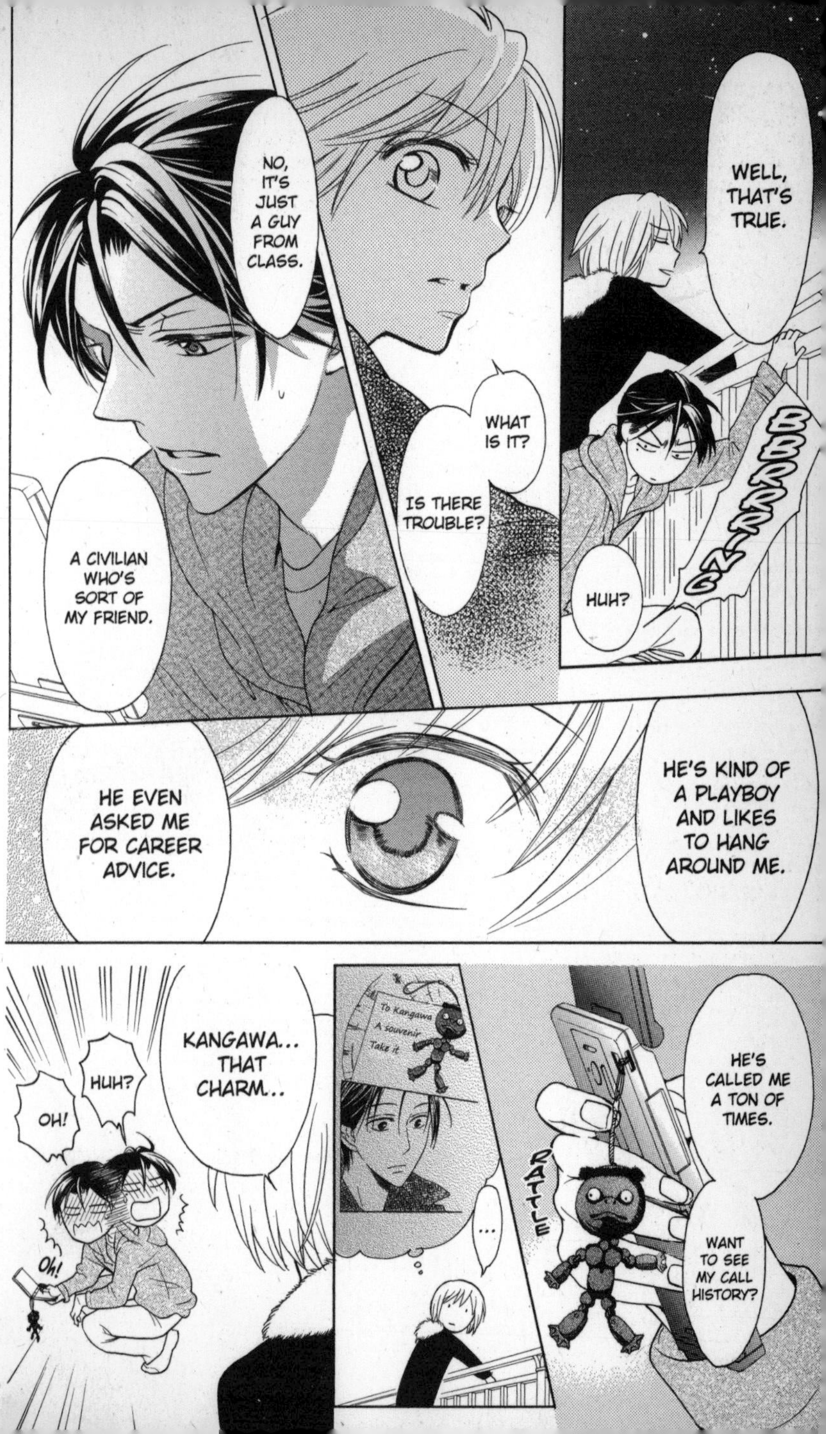
WELL, THAT'S TRUE.
BBRRRING
HUH?
WHAT IS IT?
IS THERE TROUBLE?
NO, IT'S JUST A GUY FROM CLASS.
A CIVILIAN WHO'S SORT OF MY FRIEND.
HE'S KIND OF A PLAYBOY AND LIKES TO HANG AROUND ME.
HE EVEN ASKED ME FOR CAREER ADVICE.
HE'S CALLED ME A TON OF TIMES.
RATTLE
WANT TO SEE MY CALL HISTORY?
To Kangawa
A souvenir
Take it
...
KANGAWA... THAT CHARM...
HUH?
OH!
OH!

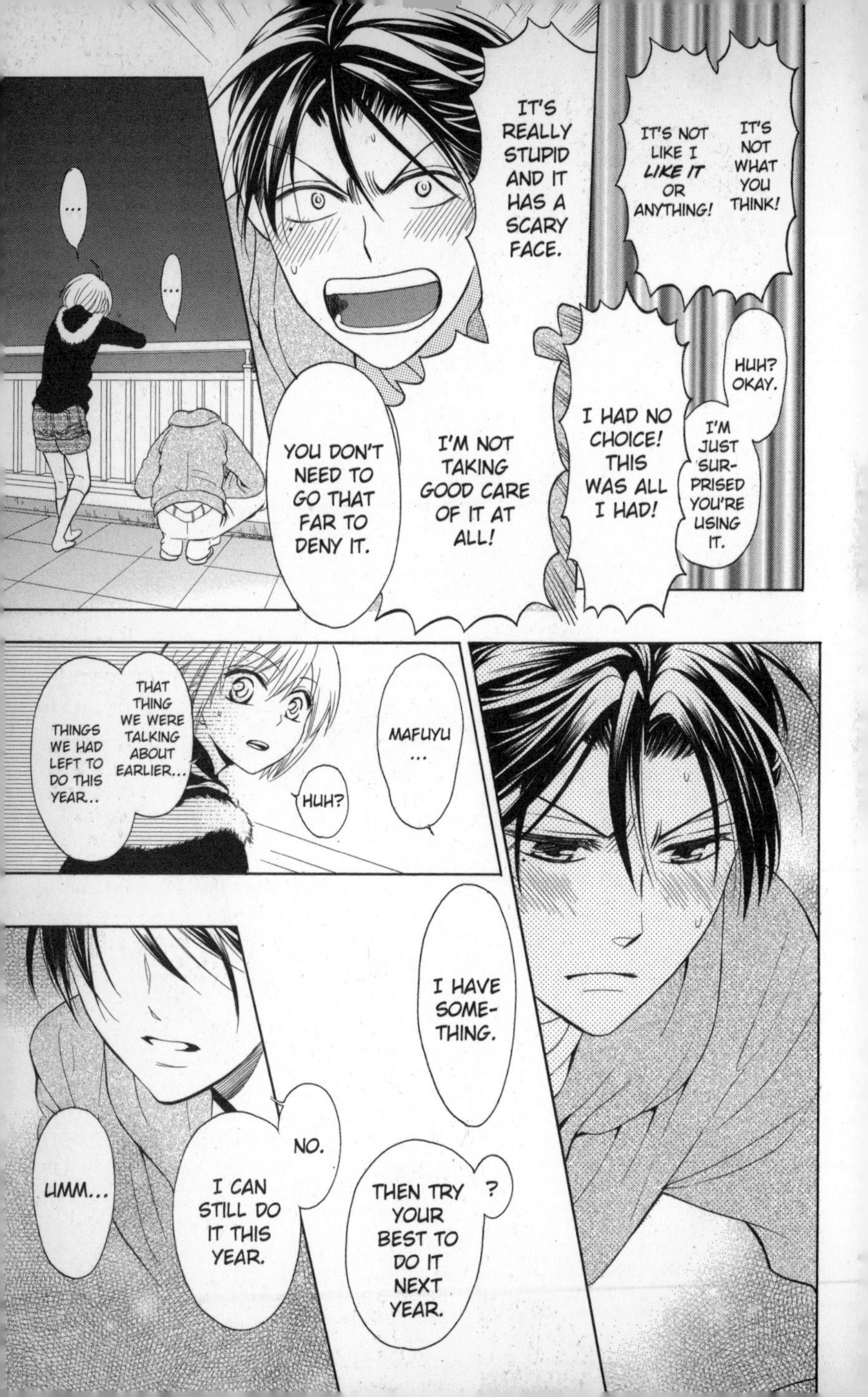
IT'S NOT WHAT YOU THINK!
IT'S NOT LIKE I *LIKE IT* OR ANYTHING!
IT'S REALLY STUPID AND IT HAS A SCARY FACE.
HUH? OKAY.
I'M JUST SUR-PRISED YOU'RE USING IT.
I HAD NO CHOICE! THIS WAS ALL I HAD!
I'M NOT TAKING GOOD CARE OF IT AT ALL!
YOU DON'T NEED TO GO THAT FAR TO DENY IT.
...
...
MAFUYU...
HUH?
THAT THING WE WERE TALKING ABOUT EARLIER...
THINGS WE HAD LEFT TO DO THIS YEAR...
I HAVE SOME-THING.
?
THEN TRY YOUR BEST TO DO IT NEXT YEAR.
NO.
I CAN STILL DO IT THIS YEAR.
UMM...

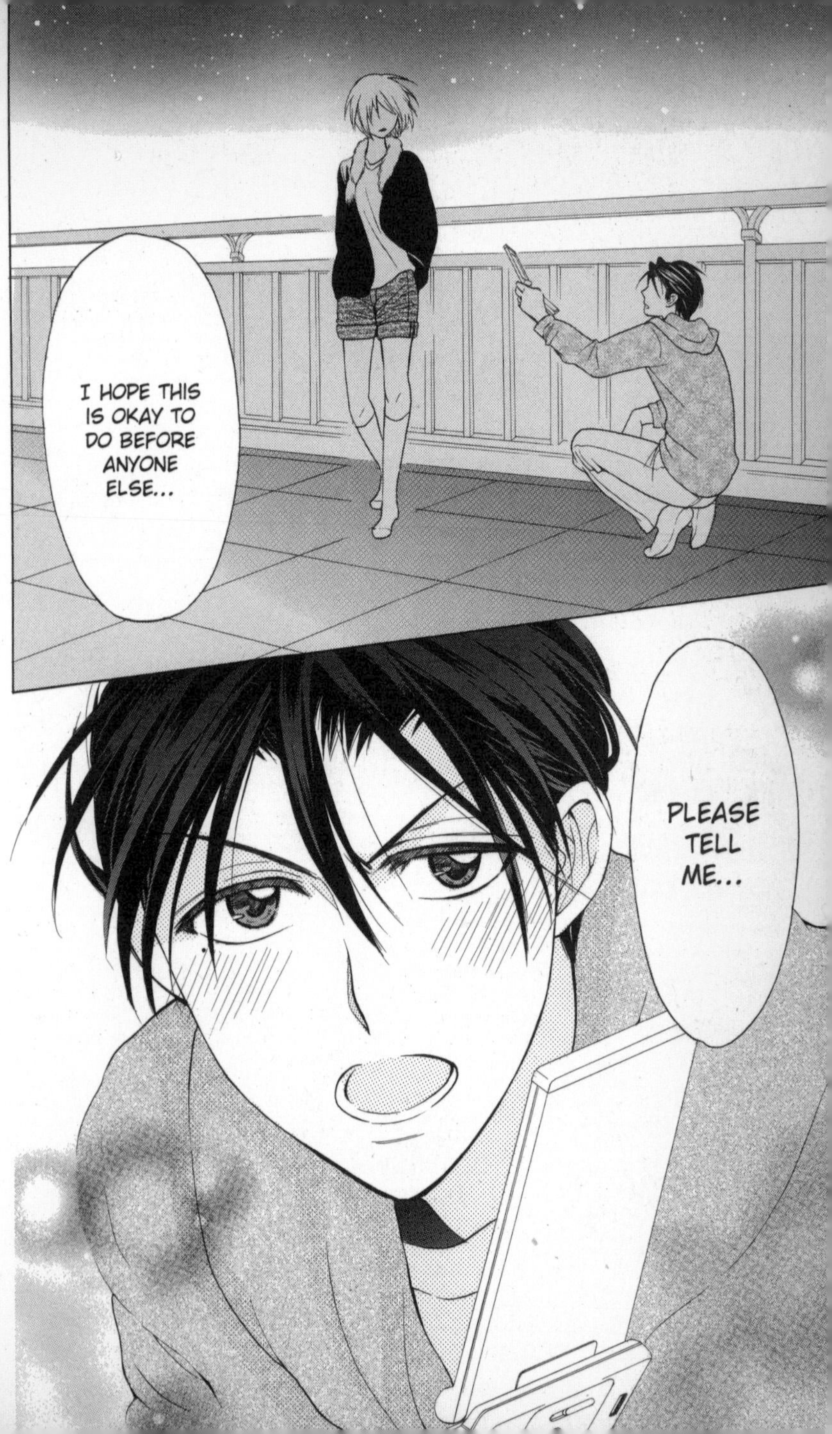
I HOPE THIS IS OKAY TO DO BEFORE ANYONE ELSE...
PLEASE TELL ME...

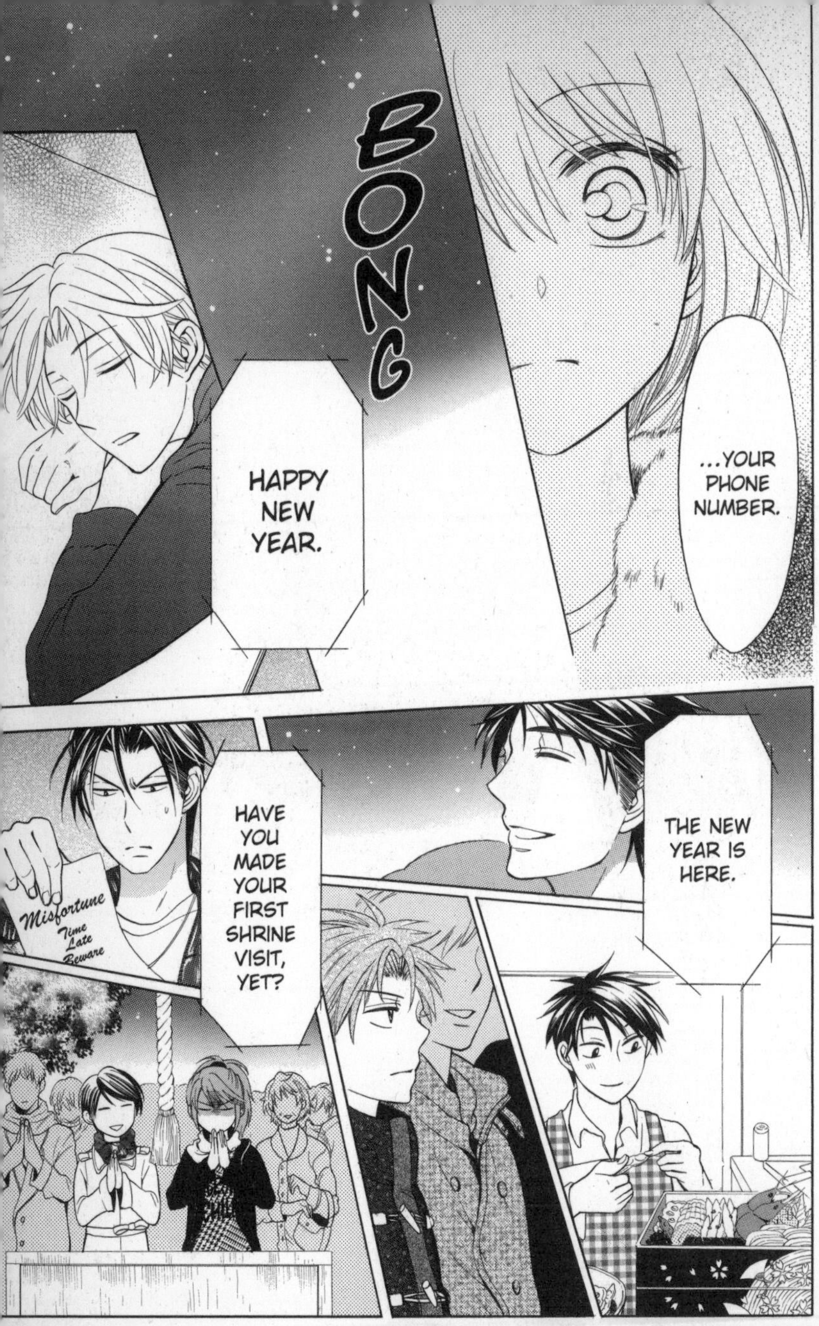
...YOUR PHONE NUMBER.
BONG
HAPPY NEW YEAR.
THE NEW YEAR IS HERE.
HAVE YOU MADE YOUR FIRST SHRINE VISIT, YET?
Misfortune
Time Late Beware

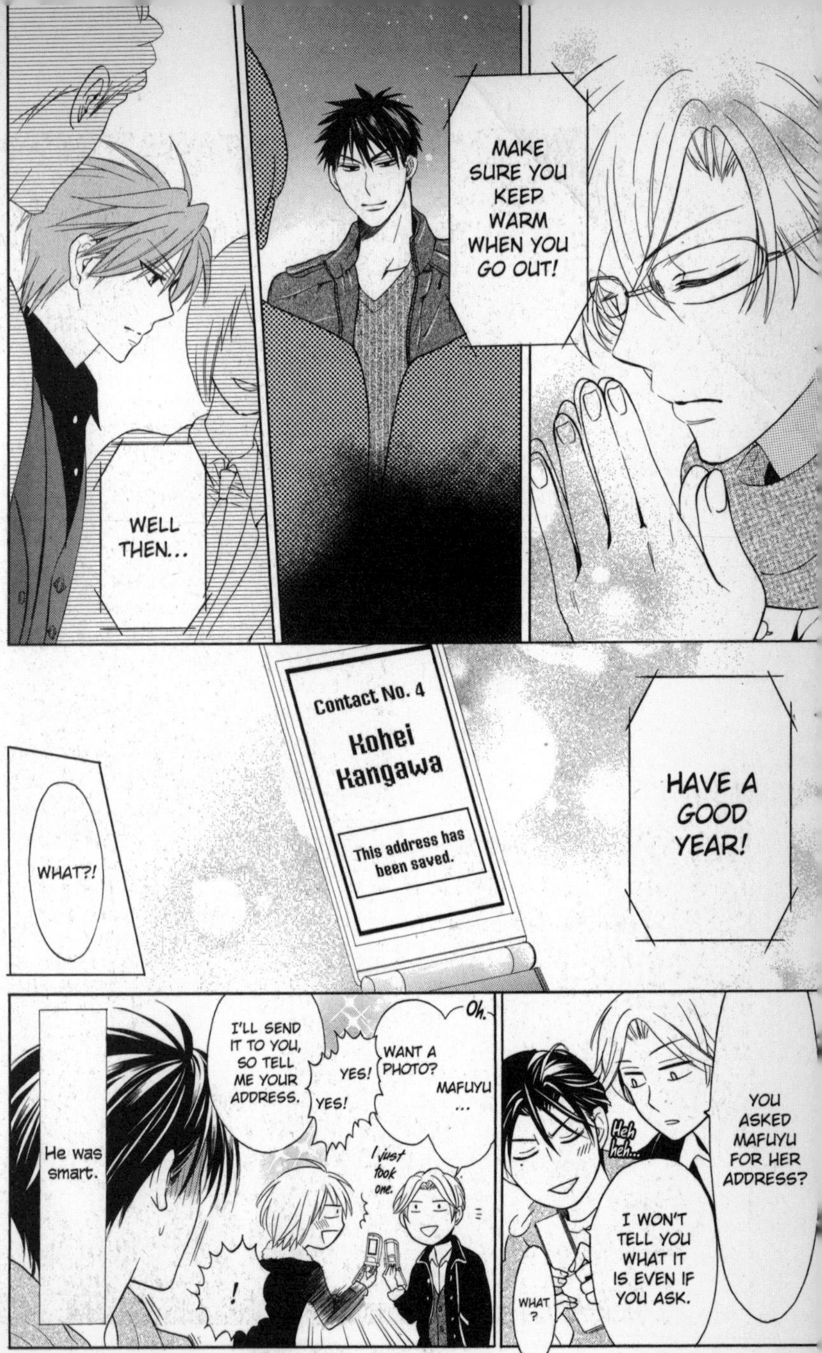
MAKE SURE YOU KEEP WARM WHEN YOU GO OUT!
WELL THEN...
HAVE A GOOD YEAR!
Contact No. 4
Kohei Kangawa
This address has been saved.
WHAT?!
YOU ASKED MAFUYU FOR HER ADDRESS?
Heh heh...
I WON'T TELL YOU WHAT IT IS EVEN IF YOU ASK.
WHAT?
Oh.
WANT A PHOTO?
MAFUYU...
I just took one.
I'LL SEND IT TO YOU, SO TELL ME YOUR ADDRESS.
YES!
YES!
!
He was smart.

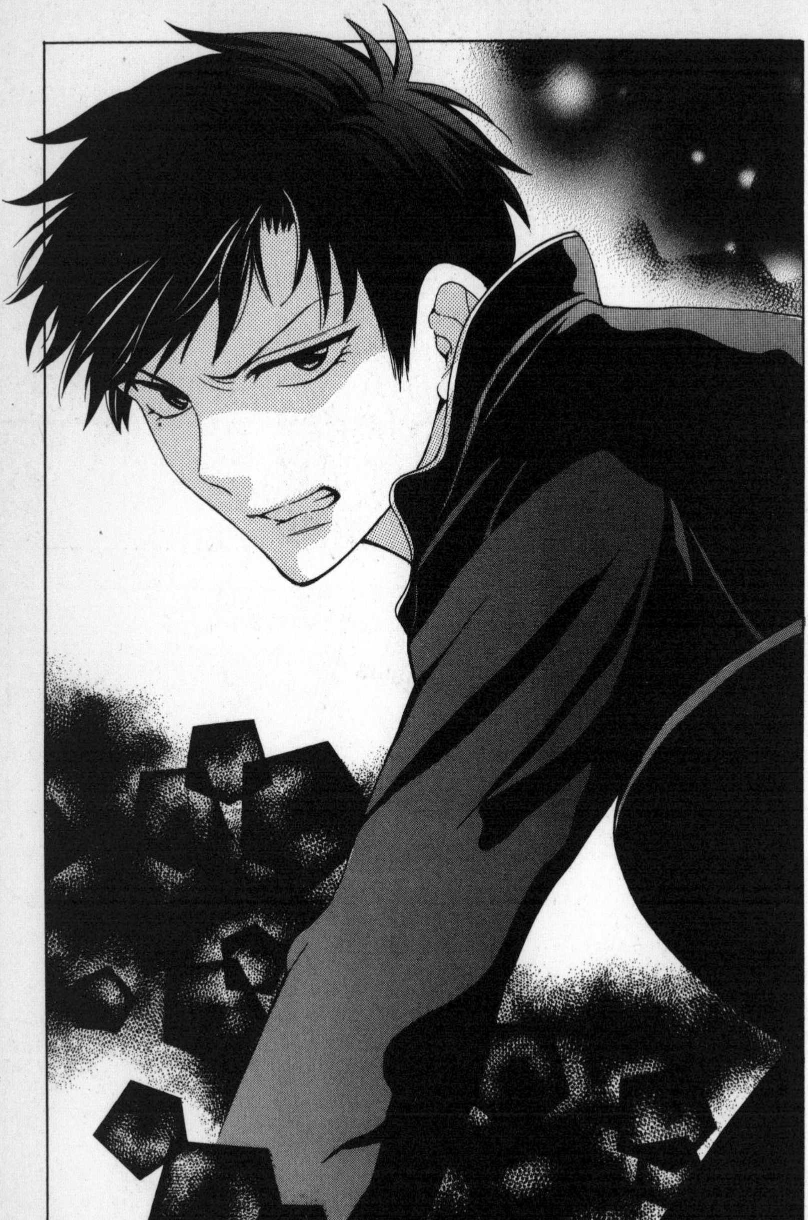

Chapter 60

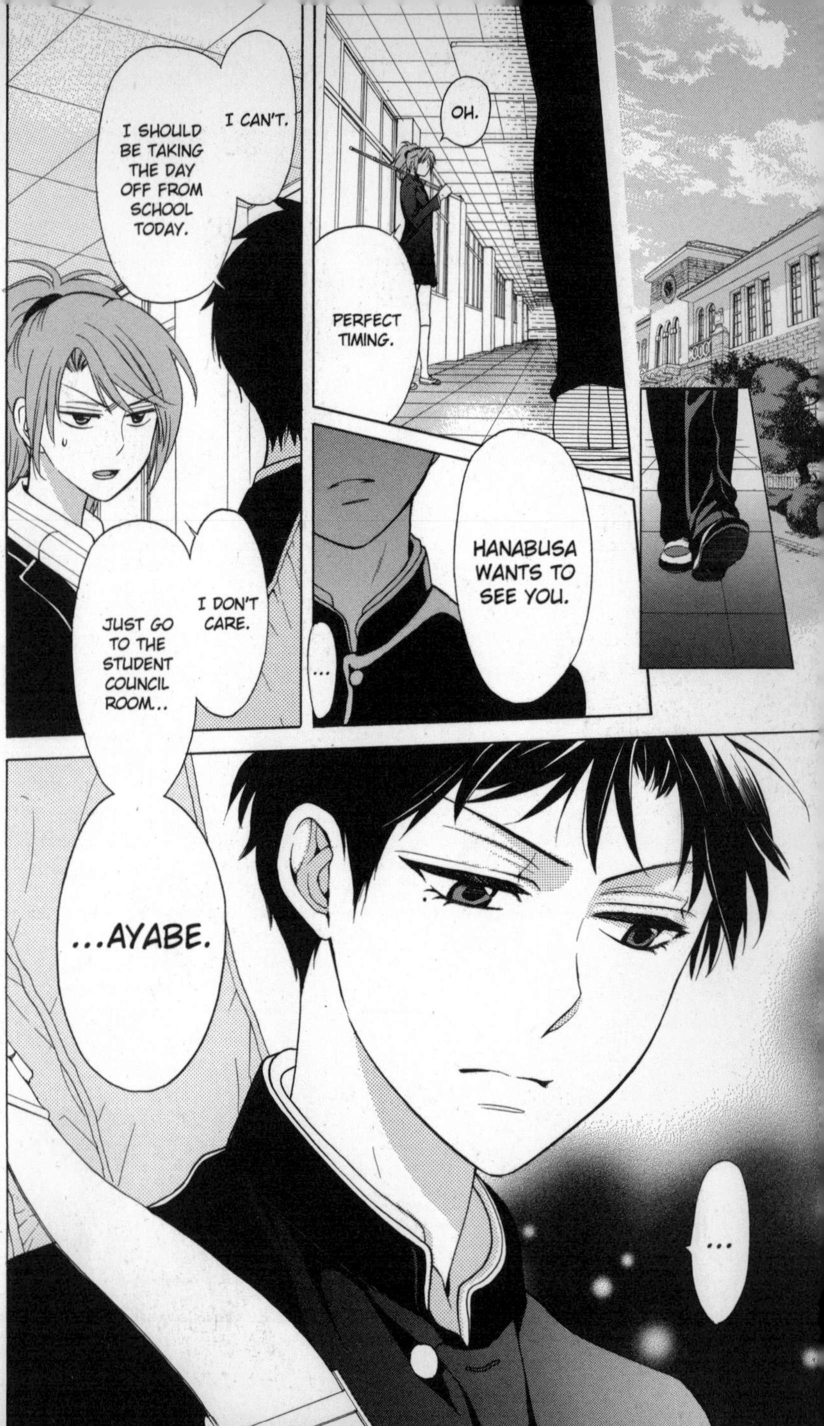
OH.
PERFECT TIMING.
HANABUSA WANTS TO SEE YOU.
...
I CAN'T.
I SHOULD BE TAKING THE DAY OFF FROM SCHOOL TODAY.
I DON'T CARE.
JUST GO TO THE STUDENT COUNCIL ROOM...
...AYABE.
...

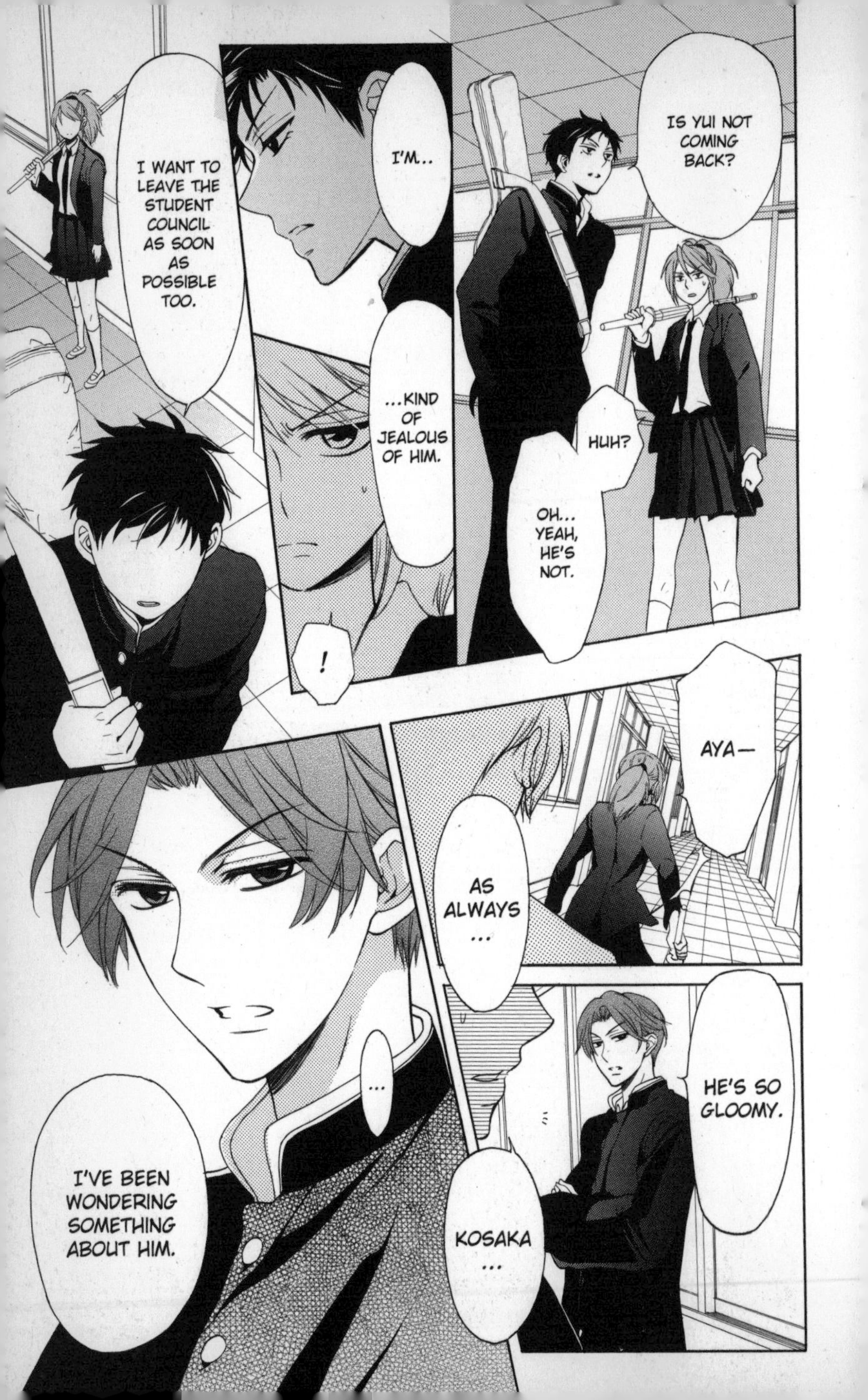
IS YUI NOT COMING BACK?
HUH?
OH... YEAH, HE'S NOT.
I'M...
...KIND OF JEALOUS OF HIM.
!
I WANT TO LEAVE THE STUDENT COUNCIL AS SOON AS POSSIBLE TOO.
AYA—
AS ALWAYS...
HE'S SO GLOOMY.
KOSAKA...
...
I'VE BEEN WONDERING SOMETHING ABOUT HIM.

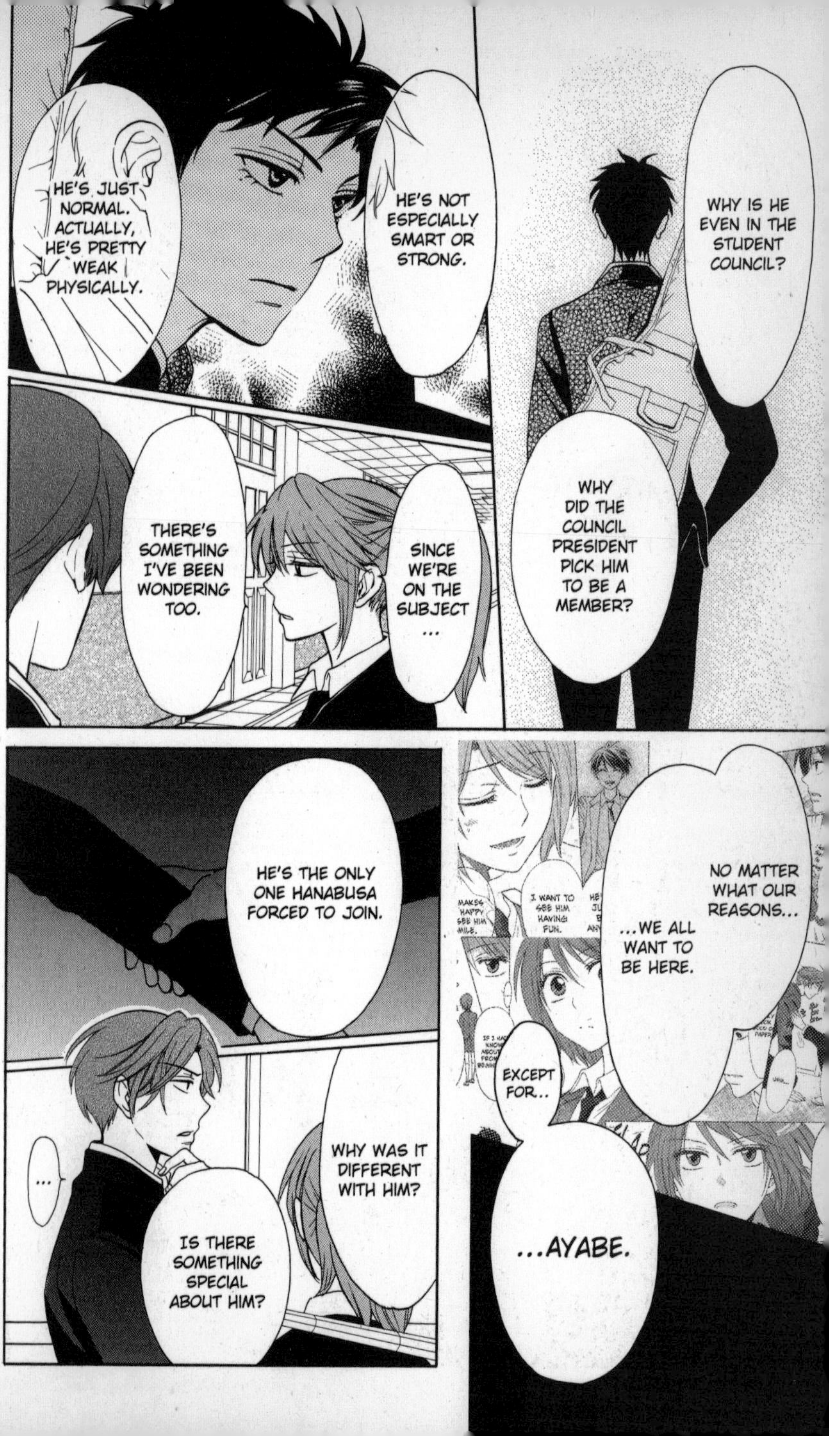
WHY IS HE EVEN IN THE STUDENT COUNCIL?
WHY DID THE COUNCIL PRESIDENT PICK HIM TO BE A MEMBER?
HE'S NOT ESPECIALLY SMART OR STRONG.
HE'S JUST NORMAL. ACTUALLY, HE'S PRETTY WEAK PHYSICALLY.
SINCE WE'RE ON THE SUBJECT...
THERE'S SOMETHING I'VE BEEN WONDERING TOO.
NO MATTER WHAT OUR REASONS...
...WE ALL WANT TO BE HERE.
I WANT TO SEE HIM HAVING FUN.
EXCEPT FOR...
...AYABE.
HE'S THE ONLY ONE HANABUSA FORCED TO JOIN.
WHY WAS IT DIFFERENT WITH HIM?
IS THERE SOMETHING SPECIAL ABOUT HIM?
...

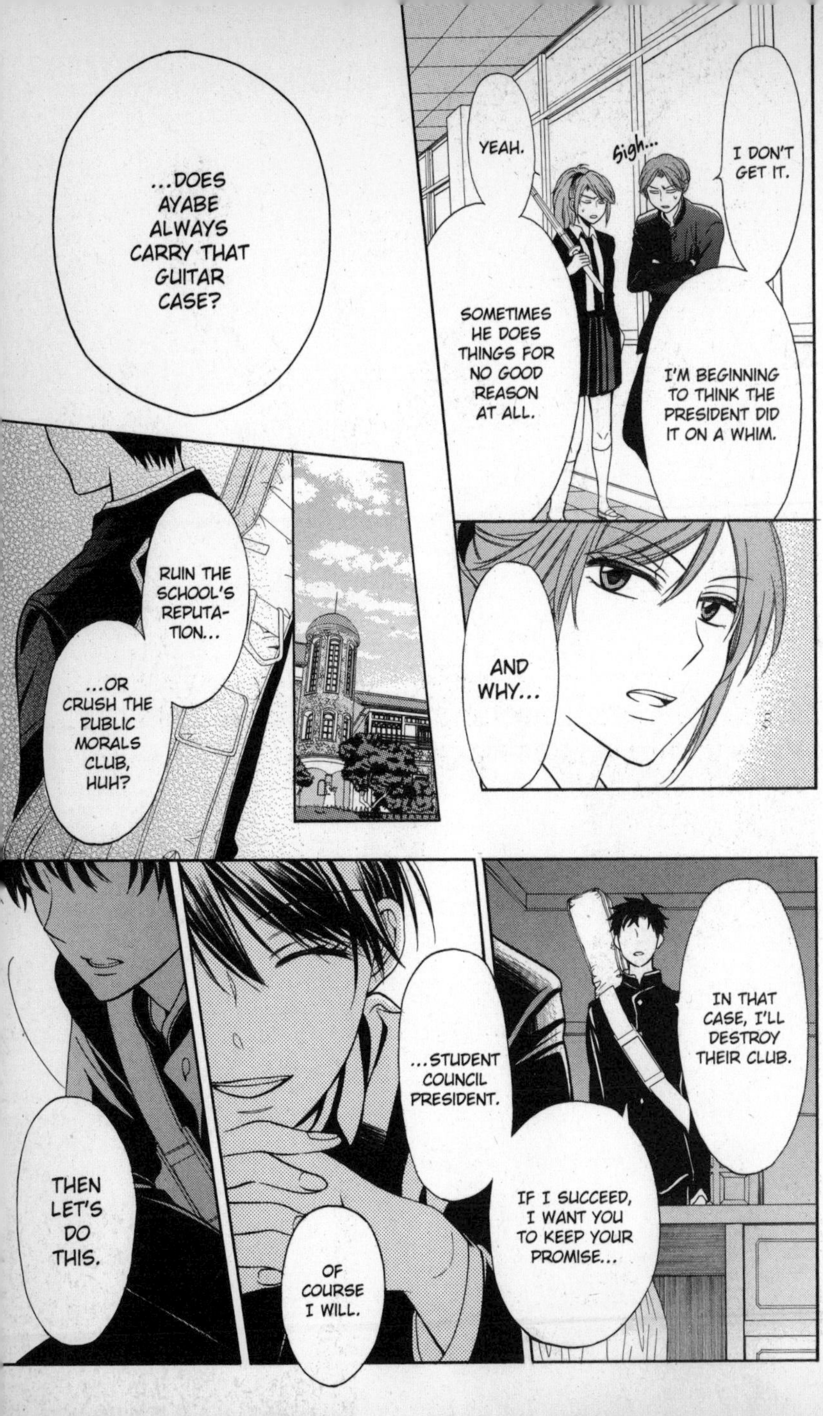
I DON'T GET IT.
Sigh...
YEAH.
I'M BEGINNING TO THINK THE PRESIDENT DID IT ON A WHIM.
SOMETIMES HE DOES THINGS FOR NO GOOD REASON AT ALL.
...DOES AYABE ALWAYS CARRY THAT GUITAR CASE?
AND WHY...
RUIN THE SCHOOL'S REPUTA-TION...
...OR CRUSH THE PUBLIC MORALS CLUB, HUH?
IN THAT CASE, I'LL DESTROY THEIR CLUB.
...STUDENT COUNCIL PRESIDENT.
IF I SUCCEED, I WANT YOU TO KEEP YOUR PROMISE...
OF COURSE I WILL.
THEN LET'S DO THIS.

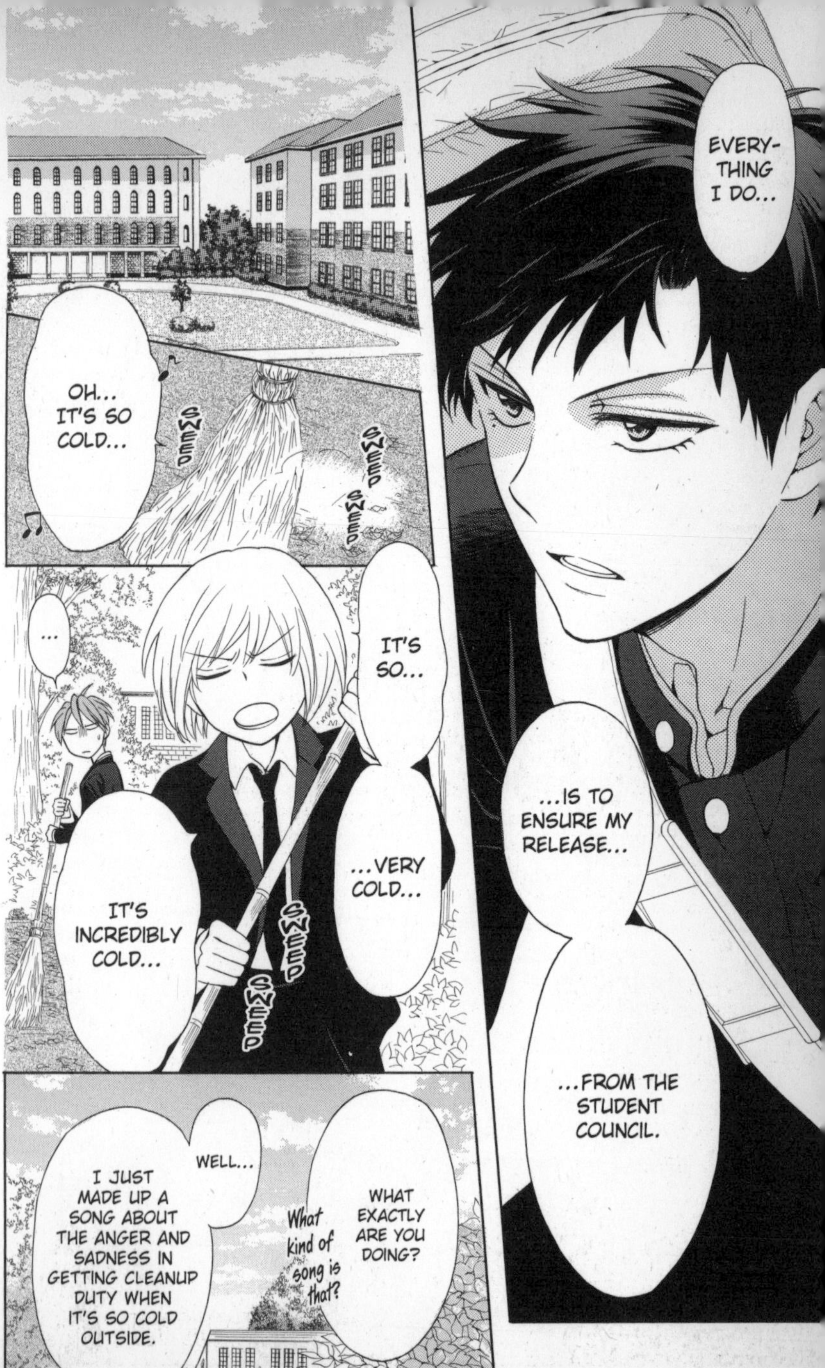
EVERY-THING I DO...
...IS TO ENSURE MY RELEASE...
...FROM THE STUDENT COUNCIL.
OH... IT'S SO COLD...
SWEEP
SWEEP SWEEP
IT'S SO...
...VERY COLD...
...
IT'S JUST INCREDIBLY COLD...
SWEEP SWEEP
WHAT EXACTLY ARE YOU DOING?
What kind of song is that?
WELL...
I JUST MADE UP A SONG ABOUT THE ANGER AND SADNESS IN GETTING CLEANUP DUTY WHEN IT'S SO COLD OUTSIDE.

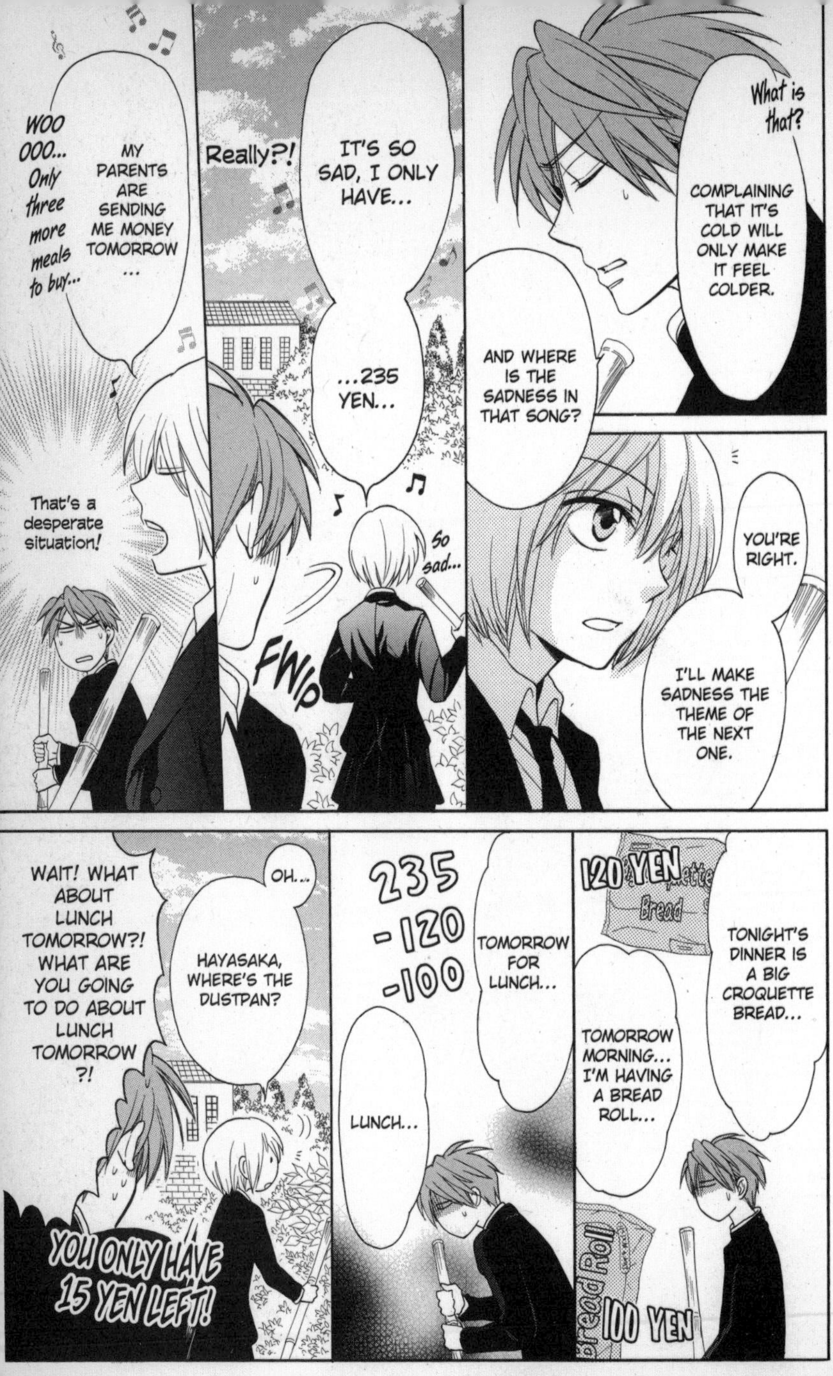

What is that?
COMPLAINING THAT IT'S COLD WILL ONLY MAKE IT FEEL COLDER.
AND WHERE IS THE SADNESS IN THAT SONG?
YOU'RE RIGHT.
I'LL MAKE SADNESS THE THEME OF THE NEXT ONE.
IT'S SO SAD, I ONLY HAVE...
...235 YEN...
Really?!
So sad...
FWIP
MY PARENTS ARE SENDING ME MONEY TOMORROW...
WOO OOO... Only three more meals to buy...
That's a desperate situation!
120 YEN
Bread
TONIGHT'S DINNER IS A BIG CROQUETTE BREAD...
TOMORROW MORNING... I'M HAVING A BREAD ROLL...
Bread Roll
100 YEN
TOMORROW FOR LUNCH...
235 -120 -100
LUNCH...
OH...
HAYASAKA, WHERE'S THE DUSTPAN?
WAIT! WHAT ABOUT LUNCH TOMORROW?! WHAT ARE YOU GOING TO DO ABOUT LUNCH TOMORROW?!
YOU ONLY HAVE 15 YEN LEFT!

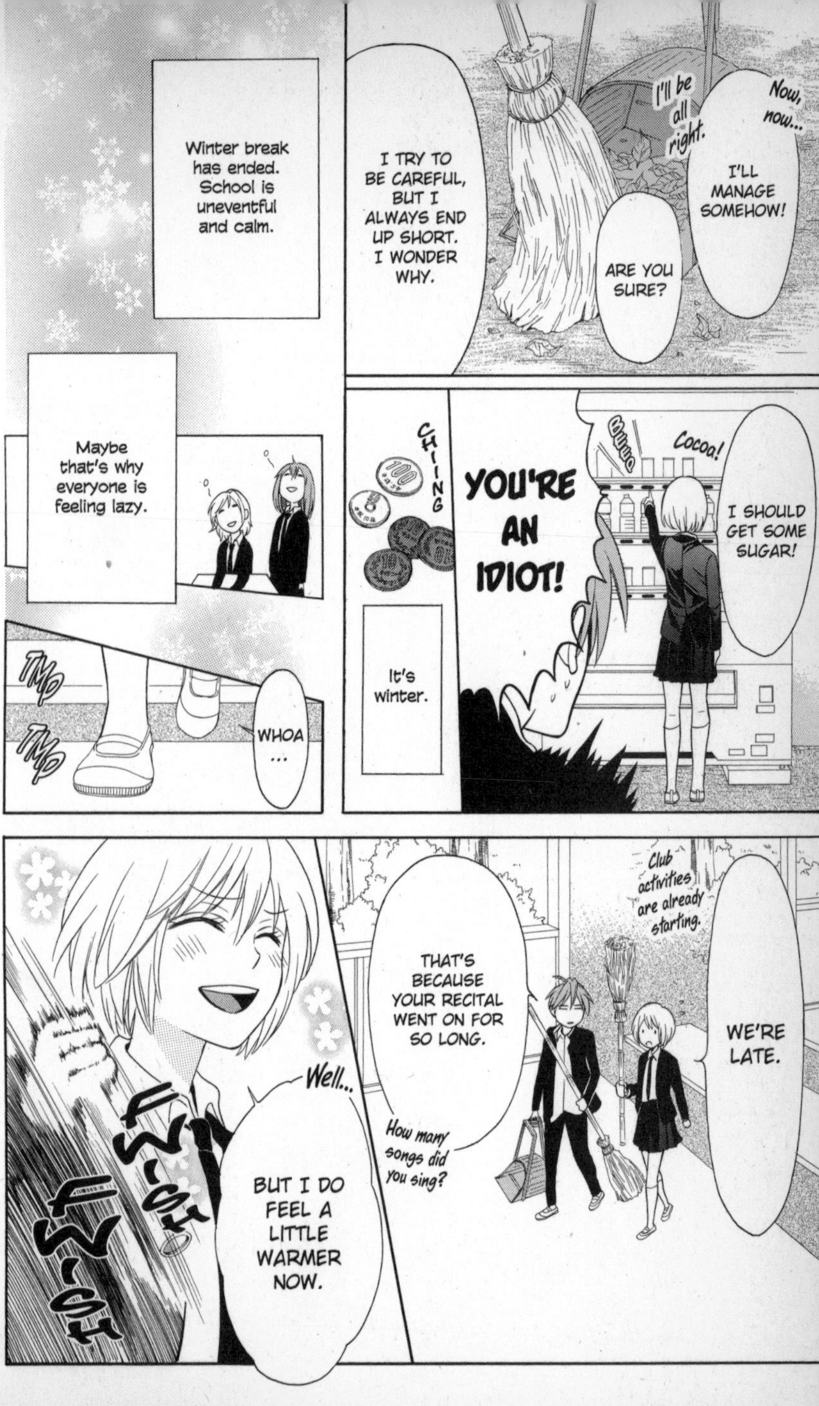

Now, now...
I'll be all right.
I'LL MANAGE SOMEHOW!
ARE YOU SURE?
I TRY TO BE CAREFUL, BUT I ALWAYS END UP SHORT. I WONDER WHY.
Winter break has ended. School is uneventful and calm.
Cocoa!
I SHOULD GET SOME SUGAR!
YOU'RE AN IDIOT!
CHING
It's winter.
Maybe that's why everyone is feeling lazy.
WHOA...
TMP
TMP
Club activities are already starting.
WE'RE LATE.
THAT'S BECAUSE YOUR RECITAL WENT ON FOR SO LONG.
How many songs did you sing?
Well...
BUT I DO FEEL A LITTLE WARMER NOW.
FWISH
FWISH

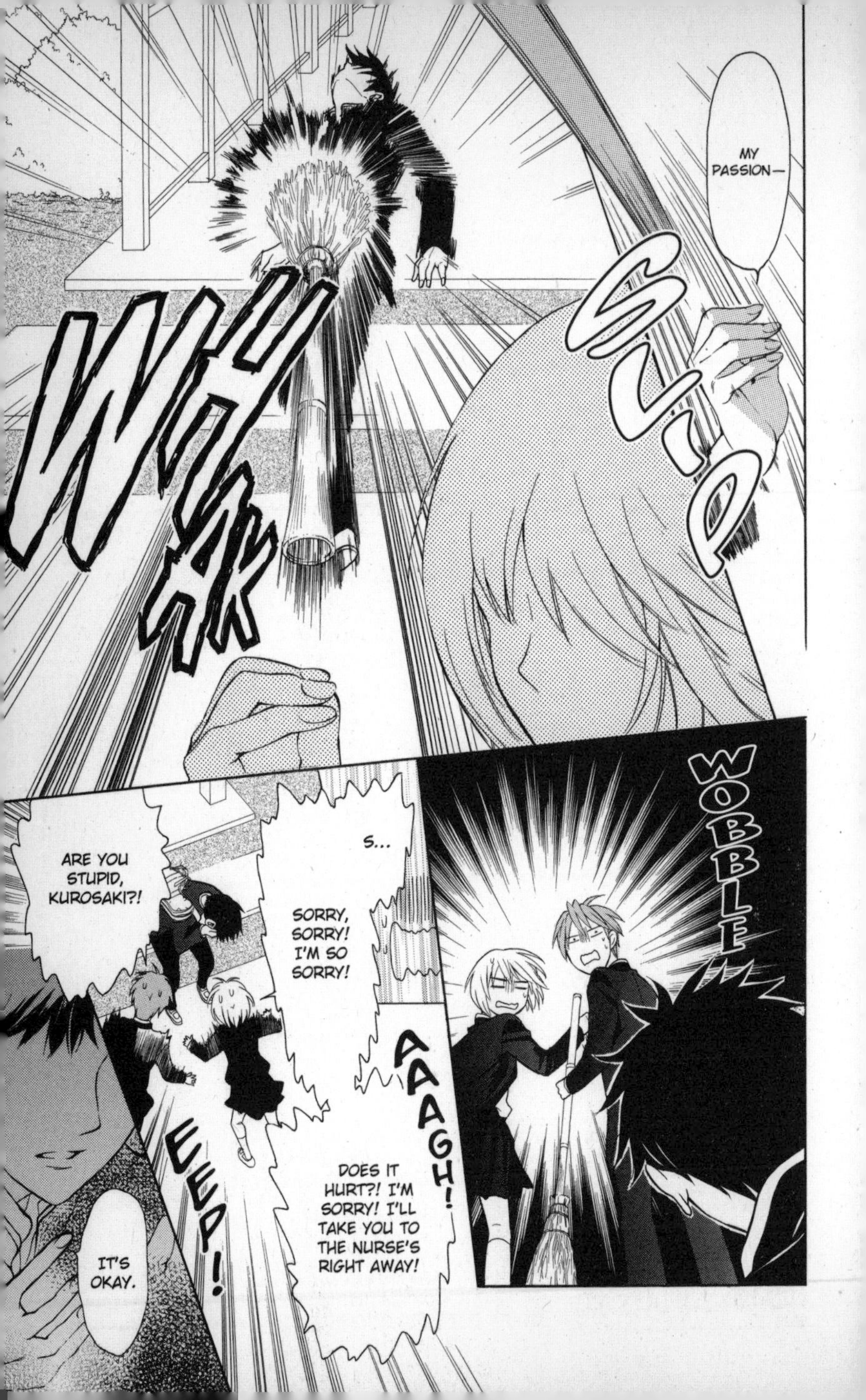
MY PASSION—
WOBBLE
S...
SORRY, SORRY! I'M SO SORRY!
AAAGH!
DOES IT HURT?! I'M SORRY! I'LL TAKE YOU TO THE NURSE'S RIGHT AWAY!
EEP!
ARE YOU STUPID, KUROSAKI?!
IT'S OKAY.

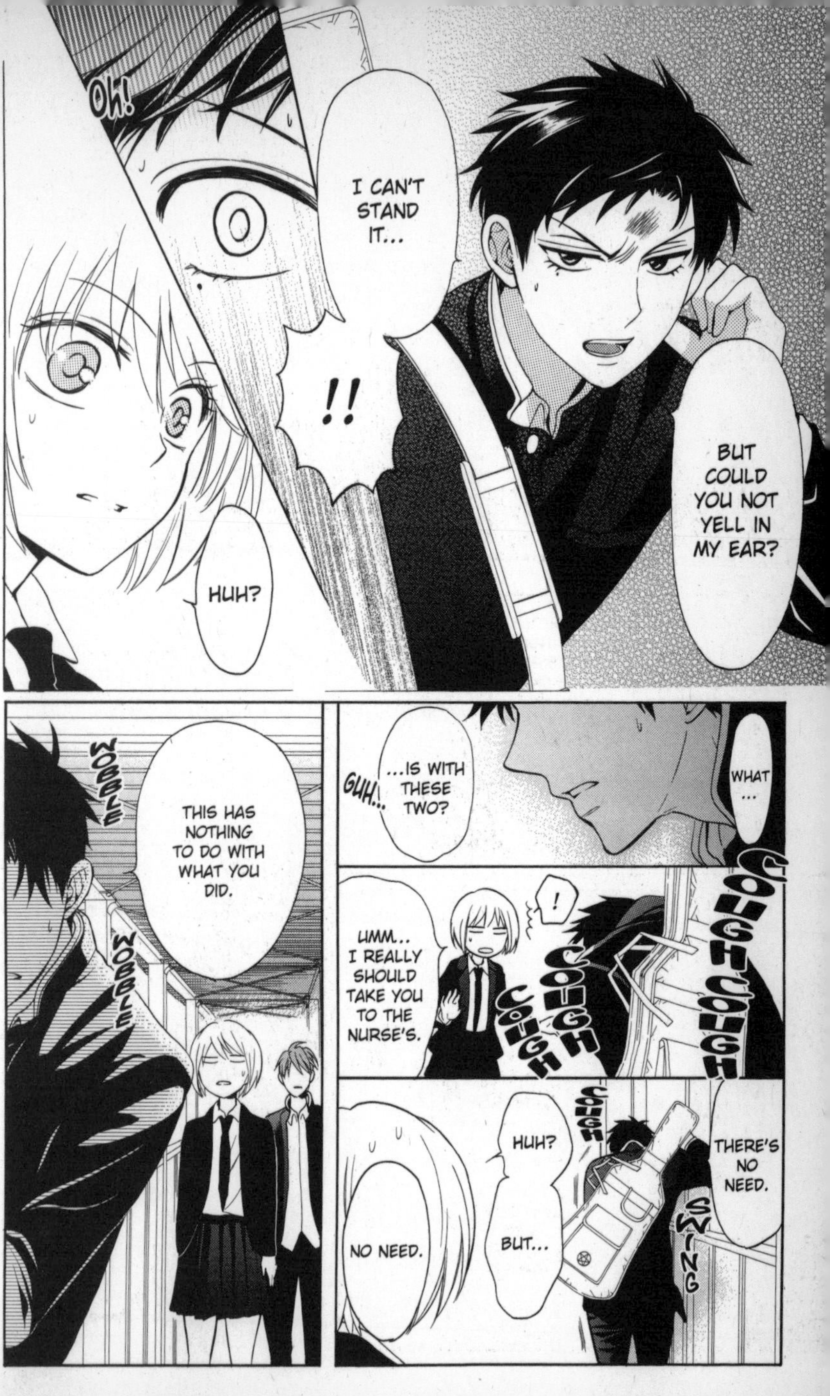
I CAN'T STAND IT...
BUT COULD YOU NOT YELL IN MY EAR?
Oh!
!!
HUH?
WHAT...
...IS WITH THESE TWO?
GUH!..
COUGH COUGH
COUGH
COUGH
!
UMM... I REALLY SHOULD TAKE YOU TO THE NURSE'S.
THERE'S NO NEED.
SWING
COUGH
HUH?
BUT...
NO NEED.
WOBBLE
WOBBLE
THIS HAS NOTHING TO DO WITH WHAT YOU DID.

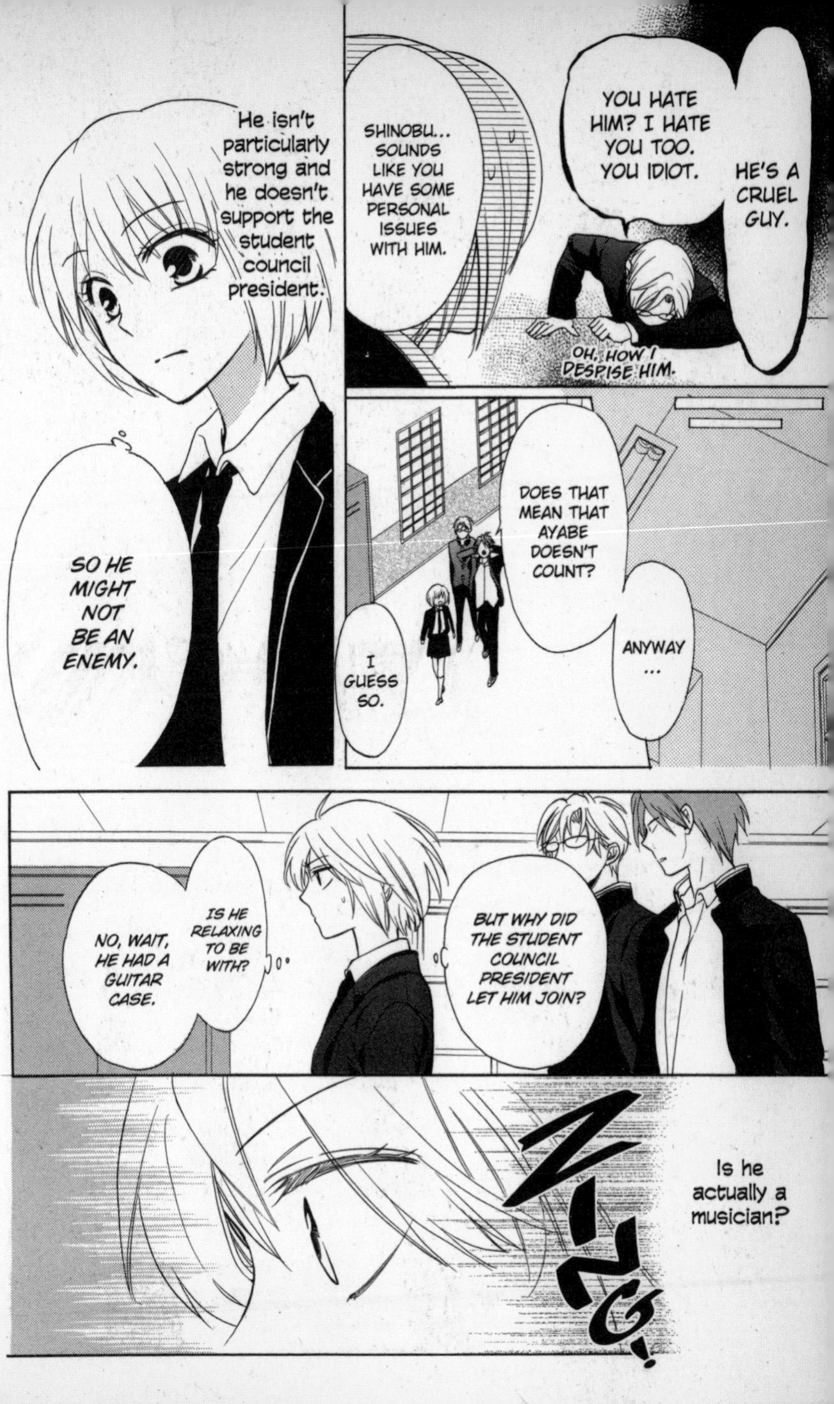
HE'S A CRUEL GUY.
YOU HATE HIM? I HATE YOU TOO. YOU IDIOT.
OH, HOW I DESPISE HIM.
SHINOBU... SOUNDS LIKE YOU HAVE SOME PERSONAL ISSUES WITH HIM.
DOES THAT MEAN THAT AYABE DOESN'T COUNT?
ANYWAY...
I GUESS SO.
He isn't particularly strong and he doesn't support the student council president.
SO HE MIGHT NOT BE AN ENEMY.
BUT WHY DID THE STUDENT COUNCIL PRESIDENT LET HIM JOIN?
IS HE RELAXING TO BE WITH?
NO, WAIT, HE HAD A GUITAR CASE.
Is he actually a musician?
NNG!

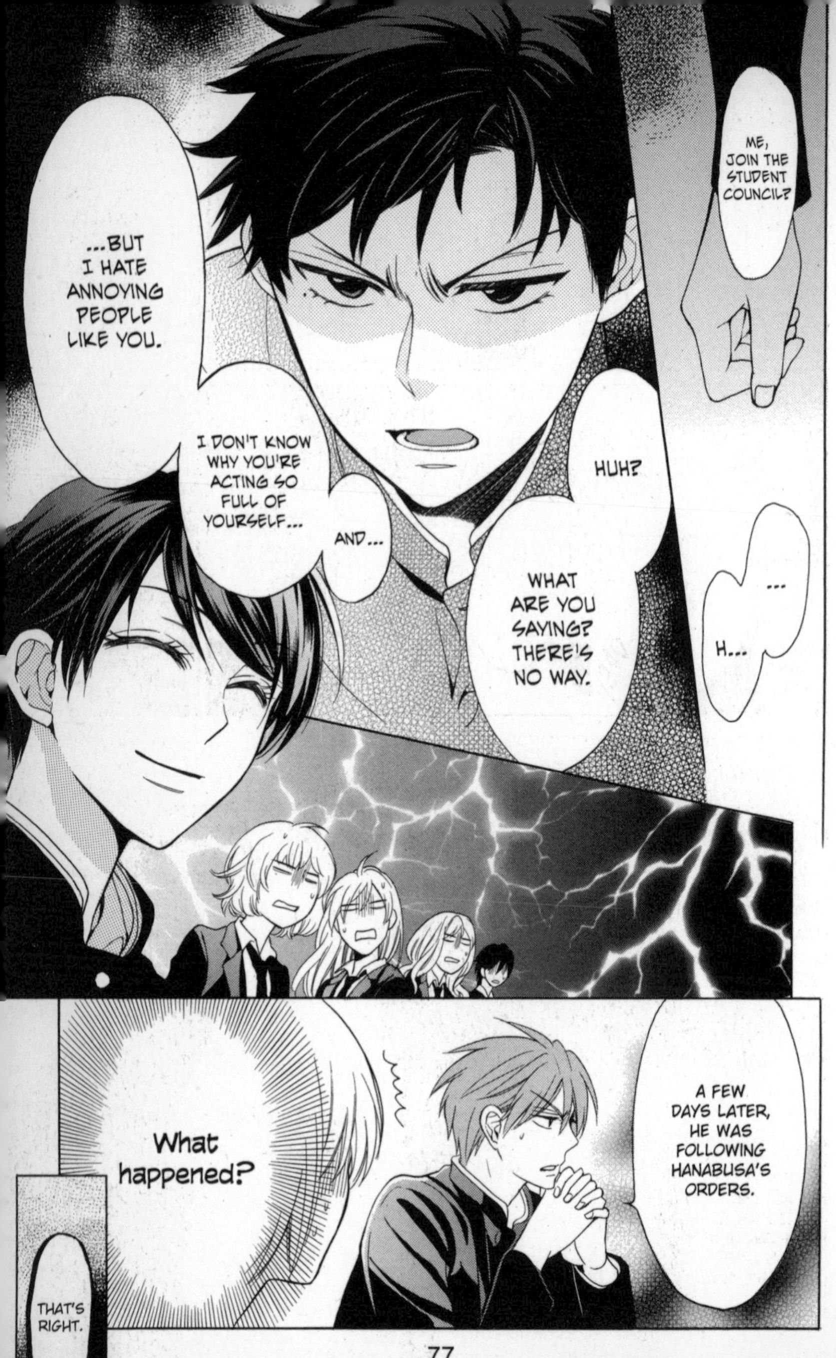
ME, JOIN THE STUDENT COUNCIL?
...
H...
HUH?
WHAT ARE YOU SAYING? THERE'S NO WAY.
AND...
I DON'T KNOW WHY YOU'RE ACTING SO FULL OF YOURSELF...
...BUT I HATE ANNOYING PEOPLE LIKE YOU.
A FEW DAYS LATER, HE WAS FOLLOWING HANABUSA'S ORDERS.
What happened?
THAT'S RIGHT.

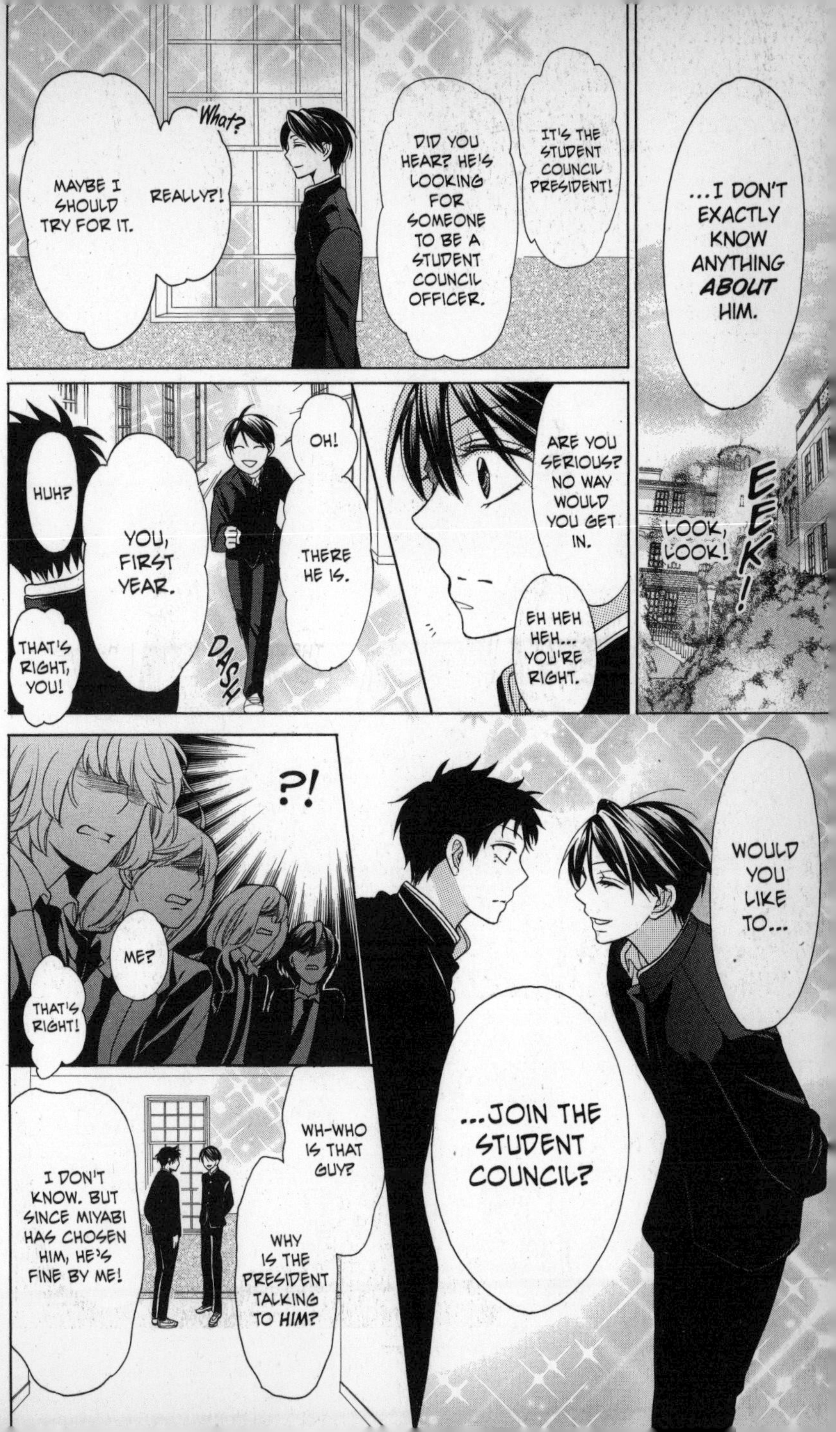
...I DON'T EXACTLY KNOW ANYTHING **ABOUT** HIM.
EEK!
LOOK, LOOK!
IT'S THE STUDENT COUNCIL PRESIDENT!
DID YOU HEAR? HE'S LOOKING FOR SOMEONE TO BE A STUDENT COUNCIL OFFICER.
What?
REALLY?!
MAYBE I SHOULD TRY FOR IT.
ARE YOU SERIOUS? NO WAY WOULD YOU GET IN.
EH HEH HEH... YOU'RE RIGHT.
OH!
THERE HE IS.
DASH
YOU, FIRST YEAR.
HUH?
THAT'S RIGHT, YOU!
WOULD YOU LIKE TO...
...JOIN THE STUDENT COUNCIL?
?!
ME?
THAT'S RIGHT!
WH-WHO IS THAT GUY?
WHY IS THE PRESIDENT TALKING TO **HIM**?
I DON'T KNOW. BUT SINCE MIYABI HAS CHOSEN HIM, HE'S FINE BY ME!

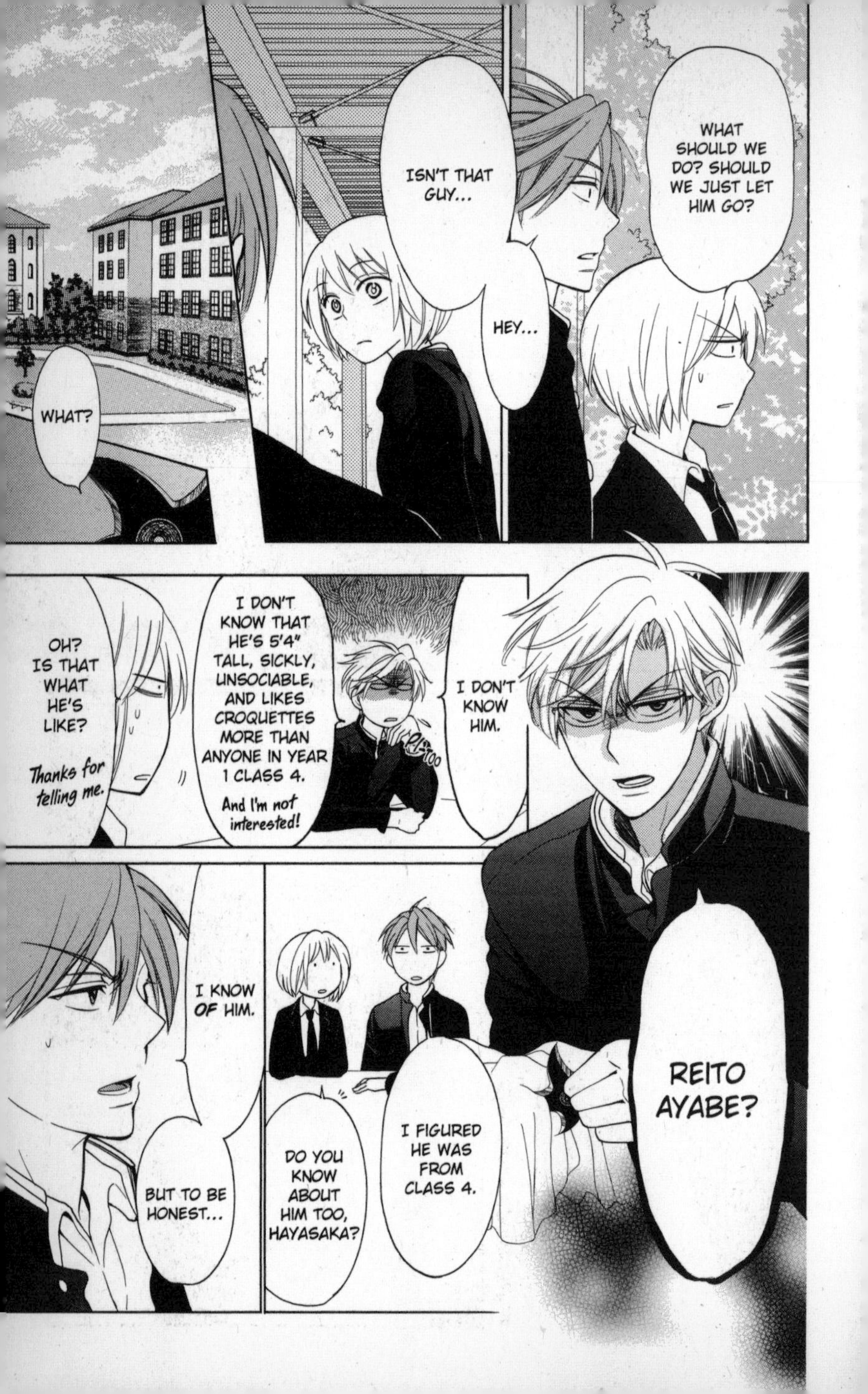
WHAT SHOULD WE DO? SHOULD WE JUST LET HIM GO?
ISN'T THAT GUY...
HEY...
WHAT?
REITO AYABE?
I DON'T KNOW HIM.
I DON'T KNOW THAT HE'S 5'4" TALL, SICKLY, UNSOCIABLE, AND LIKES CROQUETTES MORE THAN ANYONE IN YEAR 1 CLASS 4.
And I'm not interested!
OH? IS THAT WHAT HE'S LIKE?
Thanks for telling me.
I FIGURED HE WAS FROM CLASS 4.
DO YOU KNOW ABOUT HIM TOO, HAYASAKA?
I KNOW OF HIM.
BUT TO BE HONEST...

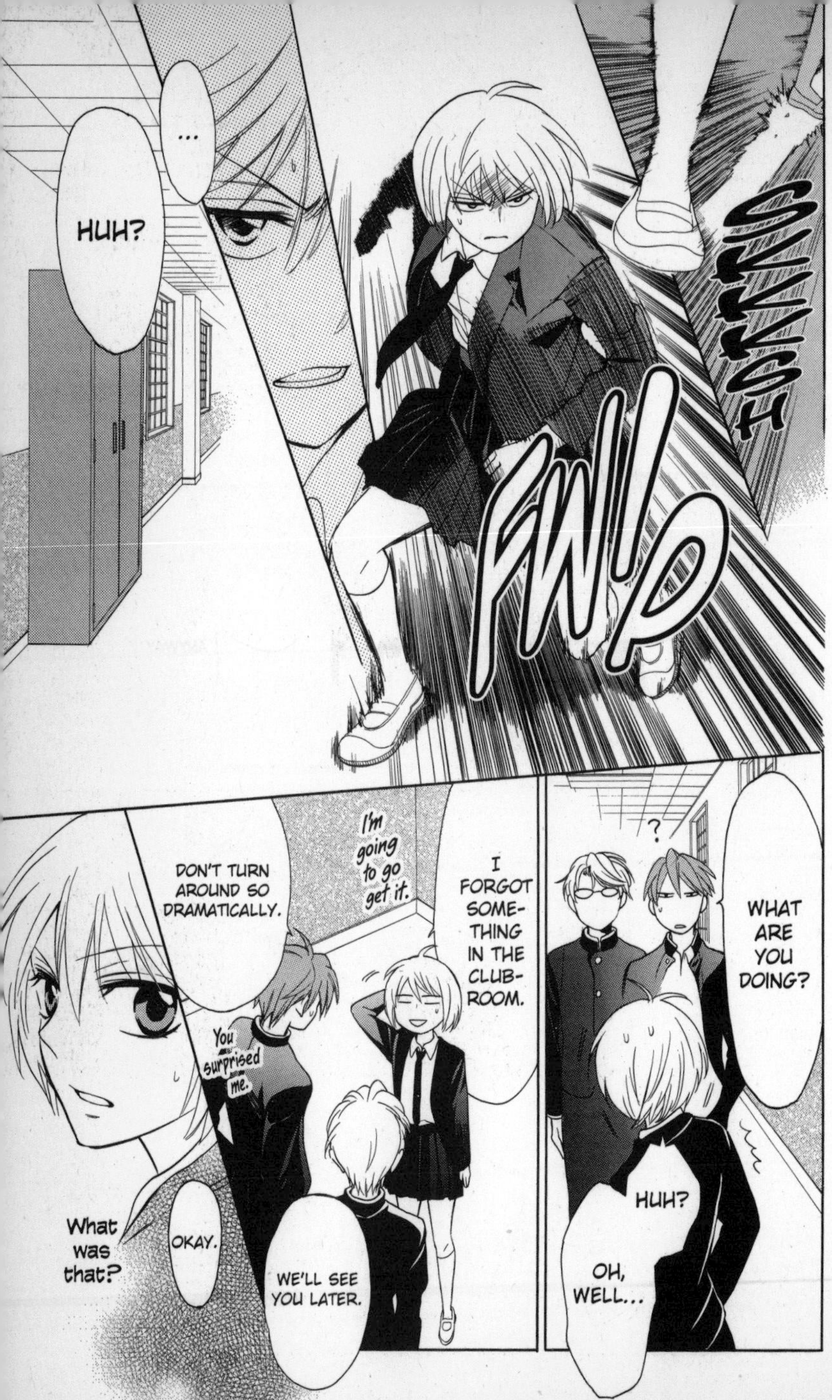
SWWWSH
FWIP
...
HUH?
WHAT ARE YOU DOING?
?
HUH?
OH, WELL...
I FORGOT SOME-THING IN THE CLUB-ROOM.
I'm going to go get it.
OKAY.
WE'LL SEE YOU LATER.
DON'T TURN AROUND SO DRAMATICALLY.
You surprised me.
What was that?

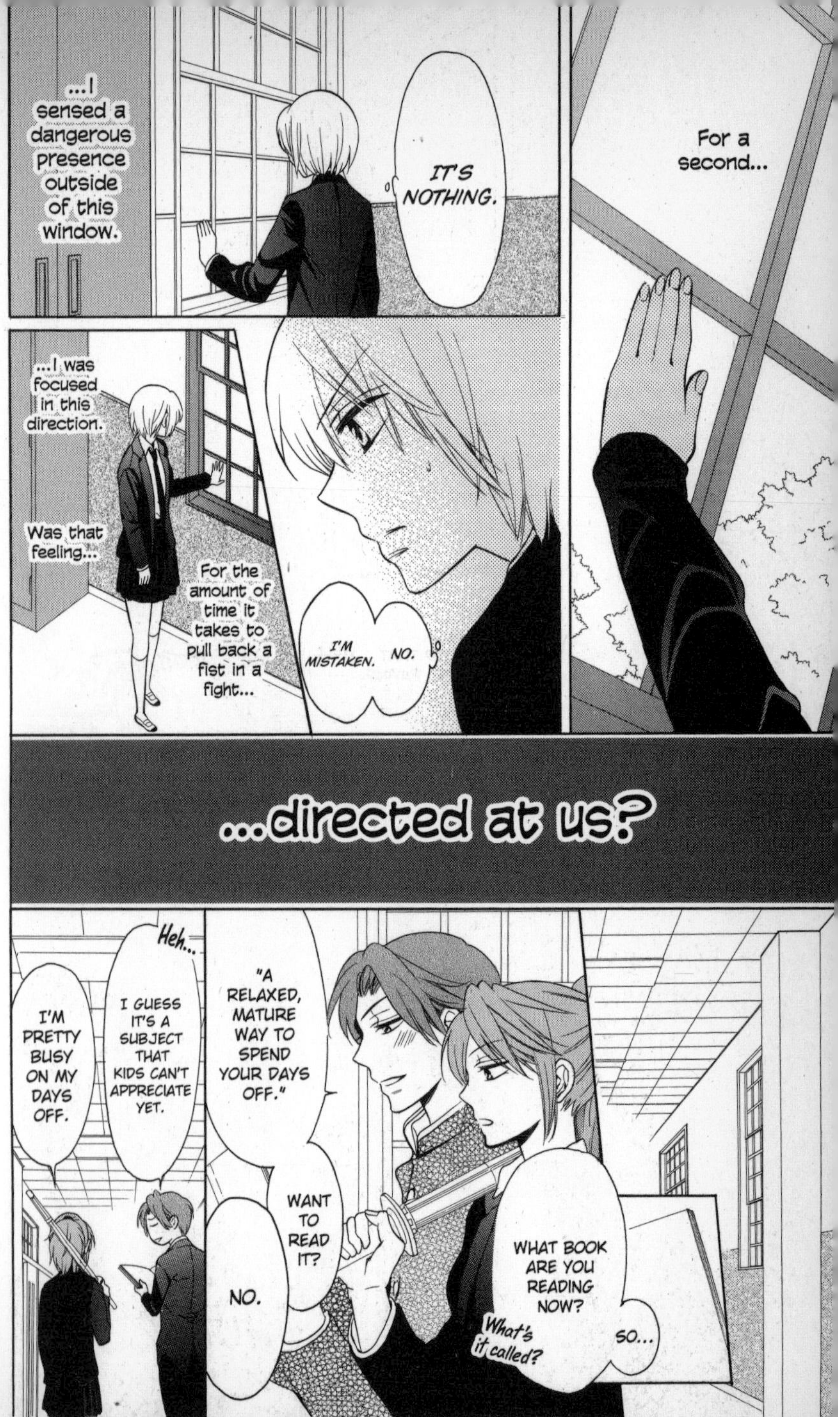
For a second...
IT'S NOTHING.
...I sensed a dangerous presence outside of this window.
NO.
I'M MISTAKEN.
For the amount of time it takes to pull back a fist in a fight...
...I was focused in this direction.
Was that feeling...
...directed at us?
SO...
WHAT BOOK ARE YOU READING NOW?
What's it called?
WANT TO READ IT?
NO.
"A RELAXED, MATURE WAY TO SPEND YOUR DAYS OFF."
Heh...
I GUESS IT'S A SUBJECT THAT KIDS CAN'T APPRECIATE YET.
I'M PRETTY BUSY ON MY DAYS OFF.

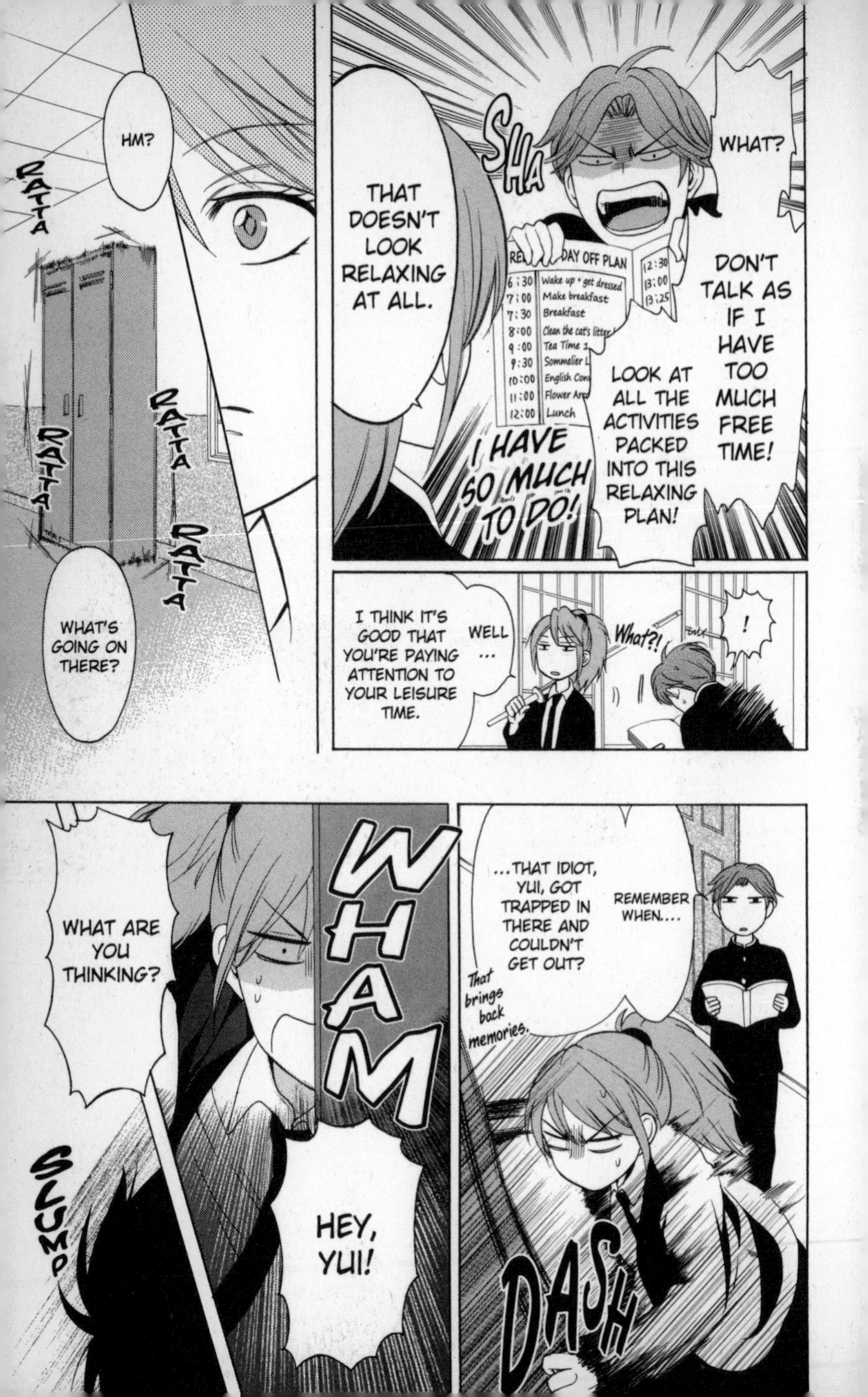

WHAT?
SHA
THAT DOESN'T LOOK RELAXING AT ALL.
DAY OFF PLAN
6:30 Wake up + get dressed
7:00 Make breakfast
7:30 Breakfast
8:00 Clean the cat's litter
9:00 Tea Time
9:30 Sommelier
10:00 English
11:00 Flower
12:00 Lunch
12:30
13:00
13:25
DON'T TALK AS IF I HAVE TOO MUCH FREE TIME!
LOOK AT ALL THE ACTIVITIES PACKED INTO THIS RELAXING PLAN!
I HAVE SO MUCH TO DO!
!
What?!
WELL ...
I THINK IT'S GOOD THAT YOU'RE PAYING ATTENTION TO YOUR LEISURE TIME.
HM?
RATTA
RATTA
RATTA
RATTA
WHAT'S GOING ON THERE?
REMEMBER WHEN....
...THAT IDIOT, YUI, GOT TRAPPED IN THERE AND COULDN'T GET OUT?
That brings back memories.
DASH
WHAM
WHAT ARE YOU THINKING?
HEY, YUI!
SLUMP

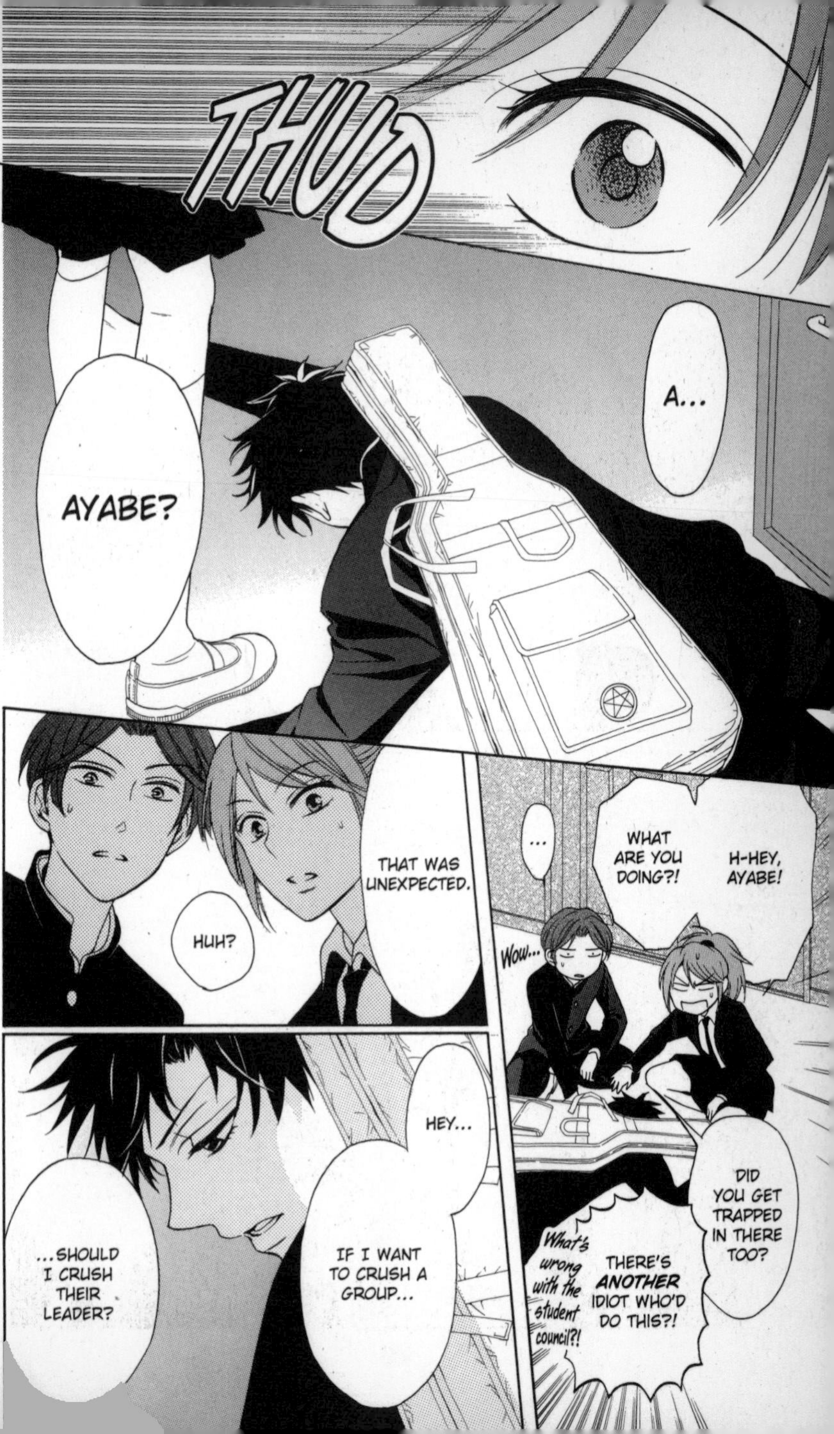
THUD
A...
AYABE?
H-HEY, AYABE!
WHAT ARE YOU DOING?!
...
Wow...
DID YOU GET TRAPPED IN THERE TOO?
THERE'S ANOTHER IDIOT WHO'D DO THIS?!
What's wrong with the student council?!
THAT WAS UNEXPECTED.
HUH?
HEY...
IF I WANT TO CRUSH A GROUP...
...SHOULD I CRUSH THEIR LEADER?

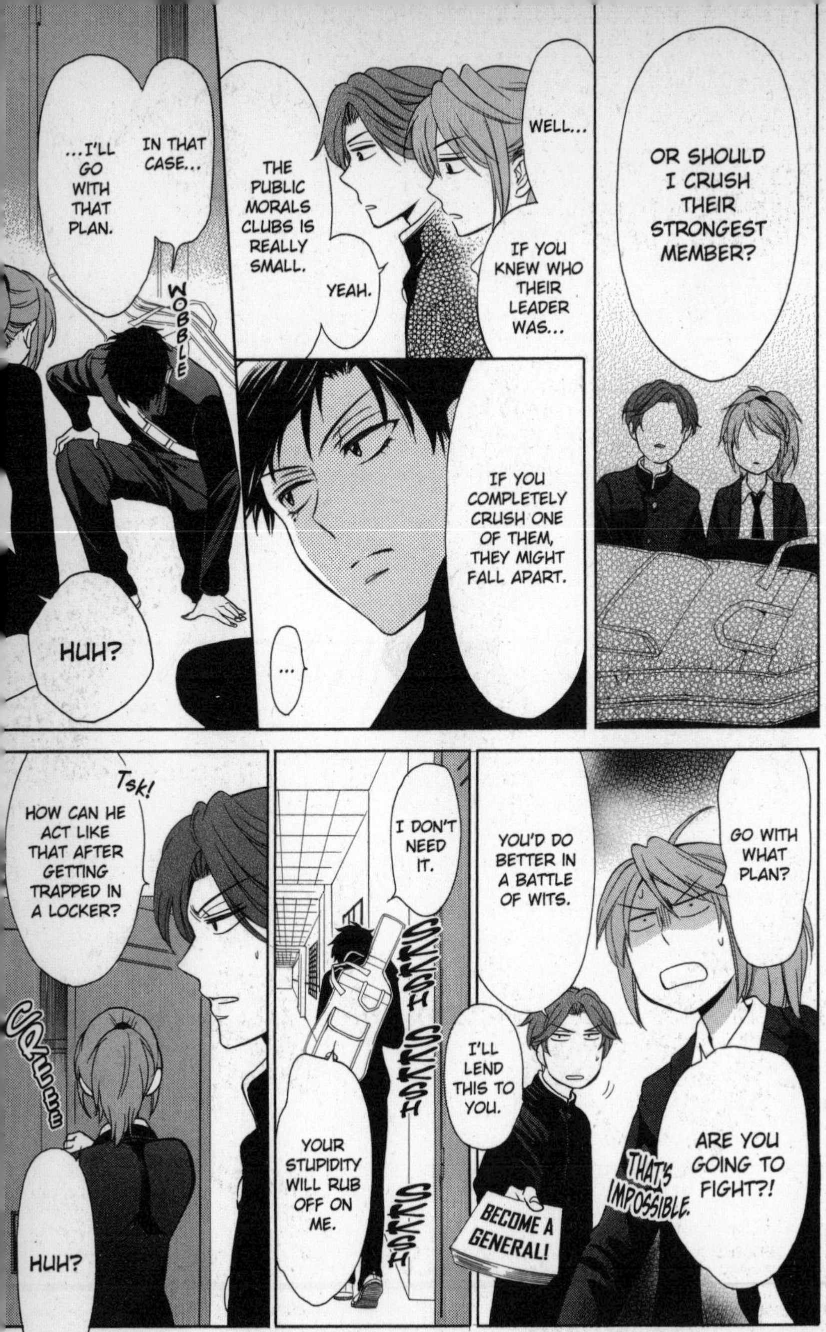
OR SHOULD I CRUSH THEIR STRONGEST MEMBER?
WELL...
IF YOU KNEW WHO THEIR LEADER WAS...
THE PUBLIC MORALS CLUBS IS REALLY SMALL.
YEAH.
IF YOU COMPLETELY CRUSH ONE OF THEM, THEY MIGHT FALL APART.
...
IN THAT CASE...
...I'LL GO WITH THAT PLAN.
WOBBLE
HUH?
GO WITH WHAT PLAN?
YOU'D DO BETTER IN A BATTLE OF WITS.
ARE YOU GOING TO FIGHT?!
THAT'S IMPOSSIBLE.
I'LL LEND THIS TO YOU.
BECOME A GENERAL!
I DON'T NEED IT.
SWISH SWISH
YOUR STUPIDITY WILL RUB OFF ON ME.
SWISH
Tsk!
HOW CAN HE ACT LIKE THAT AFTER GETTING TRAPPED IN A LOCKER?
HUH?

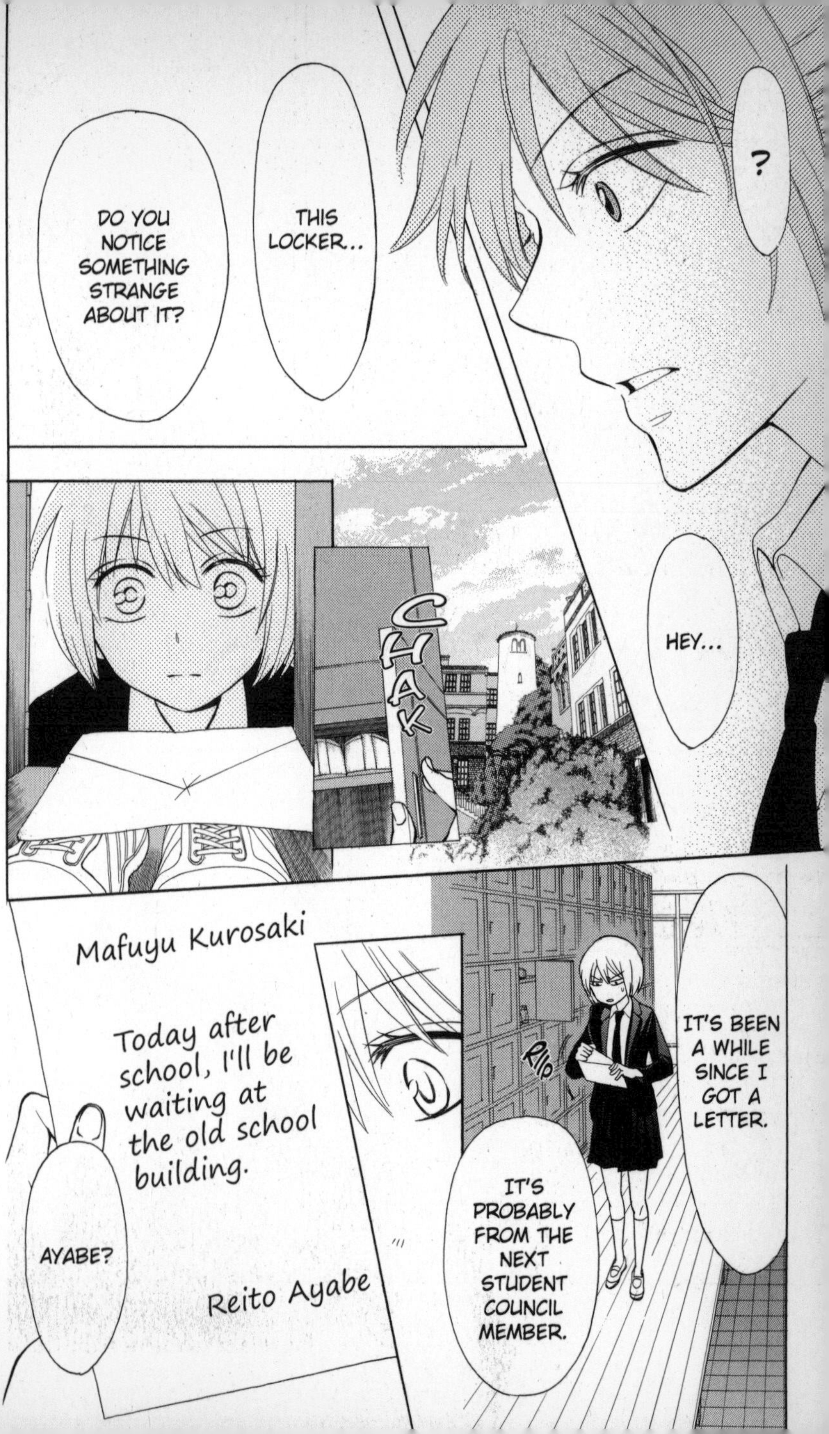
?
THIS LOCKER...
DO YOU NOTICE SOMETHING STRANGE ABOUT IT?
HEY...
CHAK
IT'S BEEN A WHILE SINCE I GOT A LETTER.
RIP
IT'S PROBABLY FROM THE NEXT STUDENT COUNCIL MEMBER.
Mafuyu Kurosaki
Today after school, I'll be waiting at the old school building.
Reito Ayabe
AYABE?

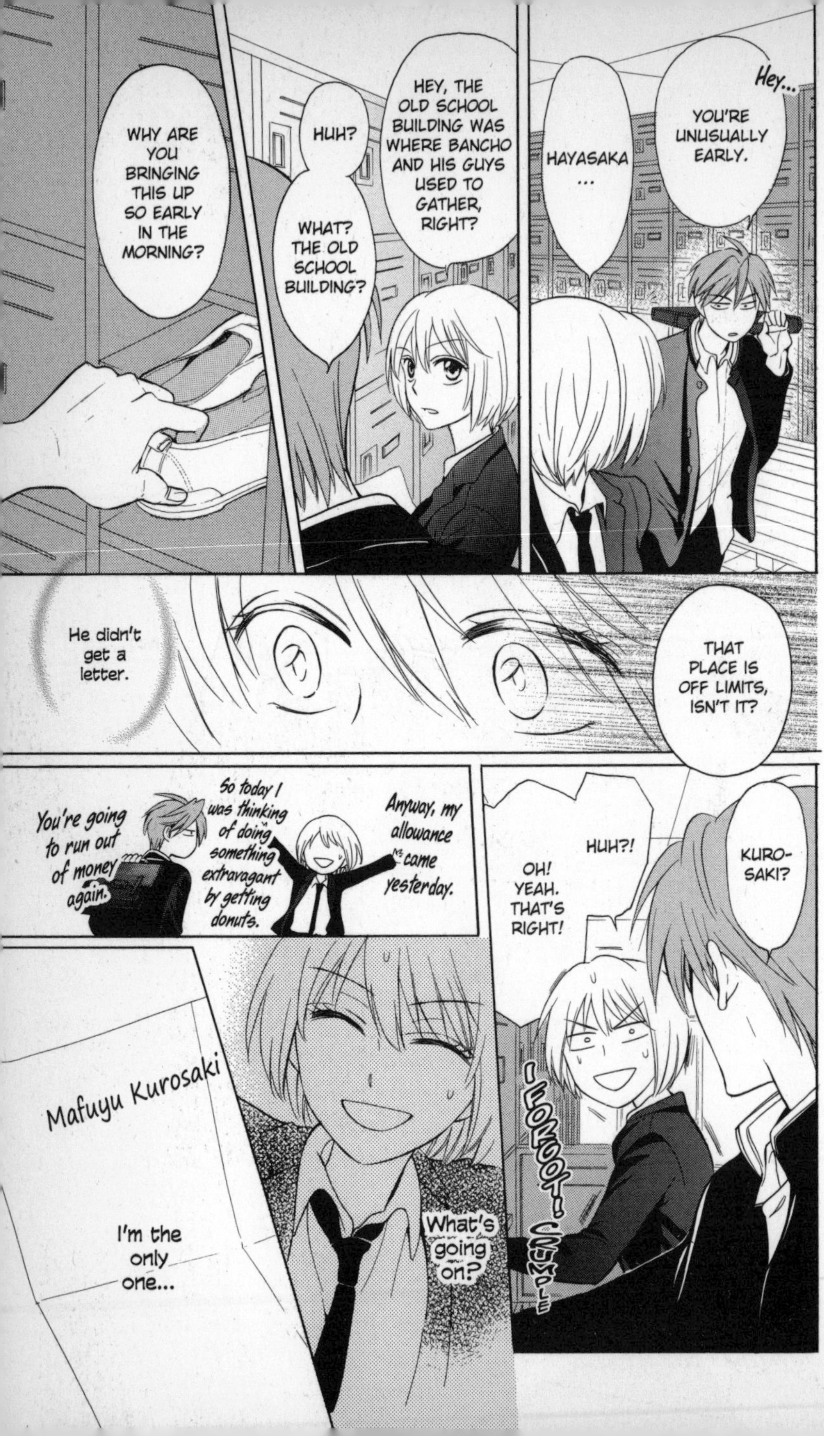
Hey...
YOU'RE UNUSUALLY EARLY.
HAYASAKA...
HEY, THE OLD SCHOOL BUILDING WAS WHERE BANCHO AND HIS GUYS USED TO GATHER, RIGHT?
HUH?
WHAT? THE OLD SCHOOL BUILDING?
WHY ARE YOU BRINGING THIS UP SO EARLY IN THE MORNING?
THAT PLACE IS OFF LIMITS, ISN'T IT?
He didn't get a letter.
KURO-SAKI?
HUH?!
OH! YEAH. THAT'S RIGHT!
Anyway, my allowance came yesterday.
So today I was thinking of doing something extravagant by getting donuts.
You're going to run out of money again.
CRUMPLE
What's going on?
Mafuyu Kurosaki
I'm the only one...

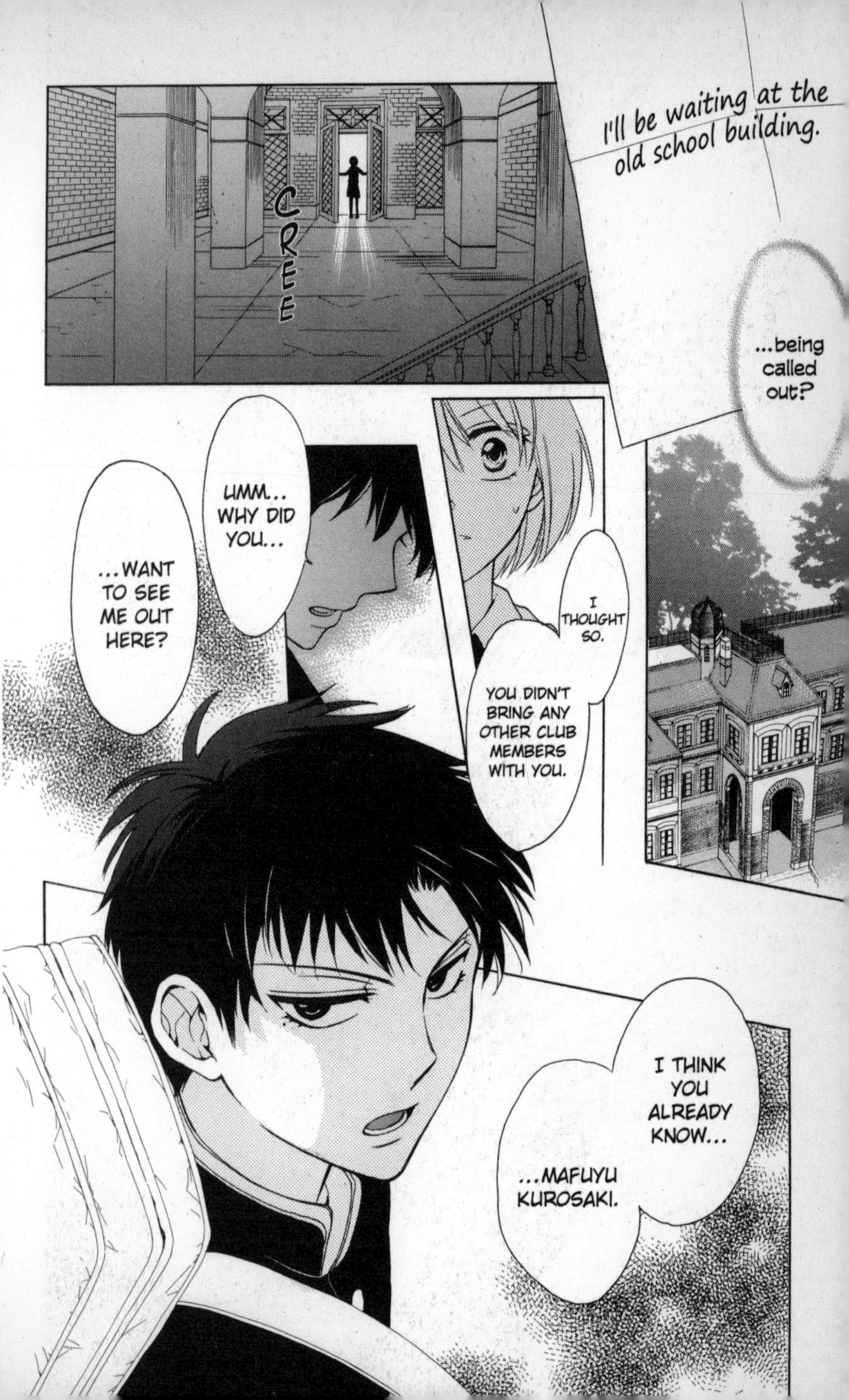
I'll be waiting at the old school building.
CREE
...being called out?
I THOUGHT SO.
YOU DIDN'T BRING ANY OTHER CLUB MEMBERS WITH YOU.
UMM... WHY DID YOU...
...WANT TO SEE ME OUT HERE?
I THINK YOU ALREADY KNOW...
...MAFUYU KUROSAKI.

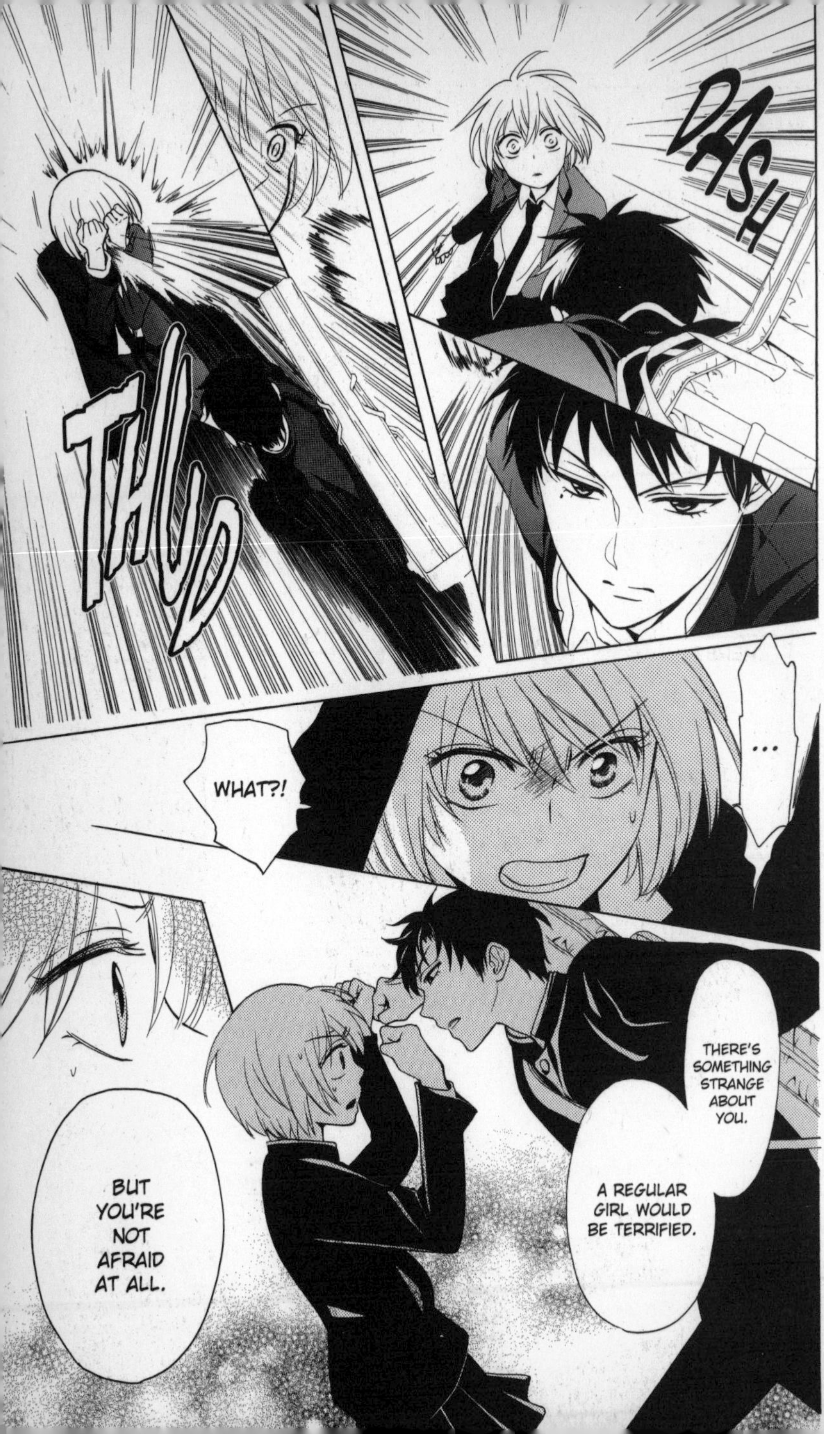
DASH
THUD
...
WHAT?!
THERE'S SOMETHING STRANGE ABOUT YOU.
A REGULAR GIRL WOULD BE TERRIFIED.
BUT YOU'RE NOT AFRAID AT ALL.

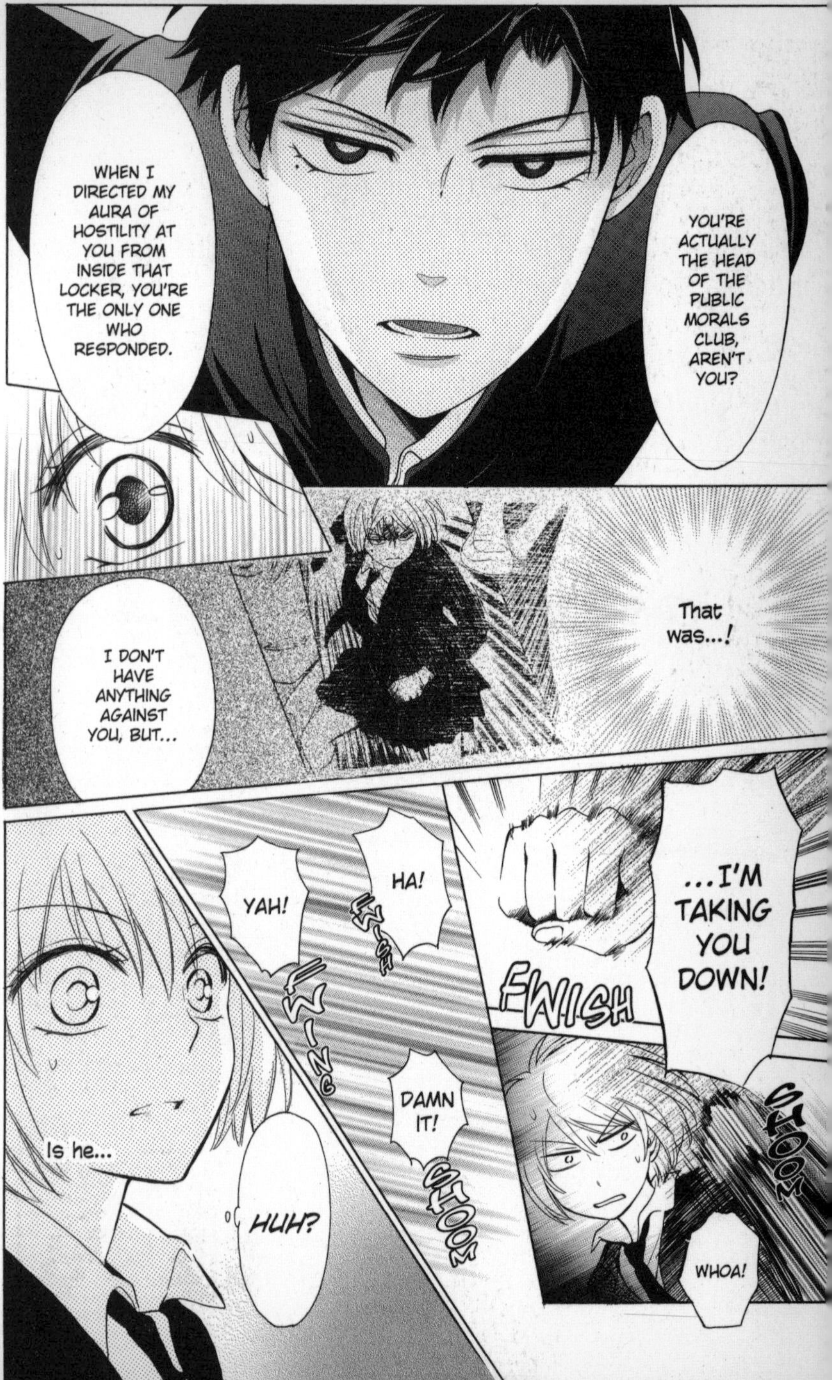
YOU'RE ACTUALLY THE HEAD OF THE PUBLIC MORALS CLUB, AREN'T YOU?
WHEN I DIRECTED MY AURA OF HOSTILITY AT YOU FROM INSIDE THAT LOCKER, YOU'RE THE ONLY ONE WHO RESPONDED.
That was...!
I DON'T HAVE ANYTHING AGAINST YOU, BUT...
...I'M TAKING YOU DOWN!
FWISH
SHOOOM
WHOA!
HA!
FWISH
YAH!
FWING
DAMN IT!
SHOOOM
HUH?
Is he...

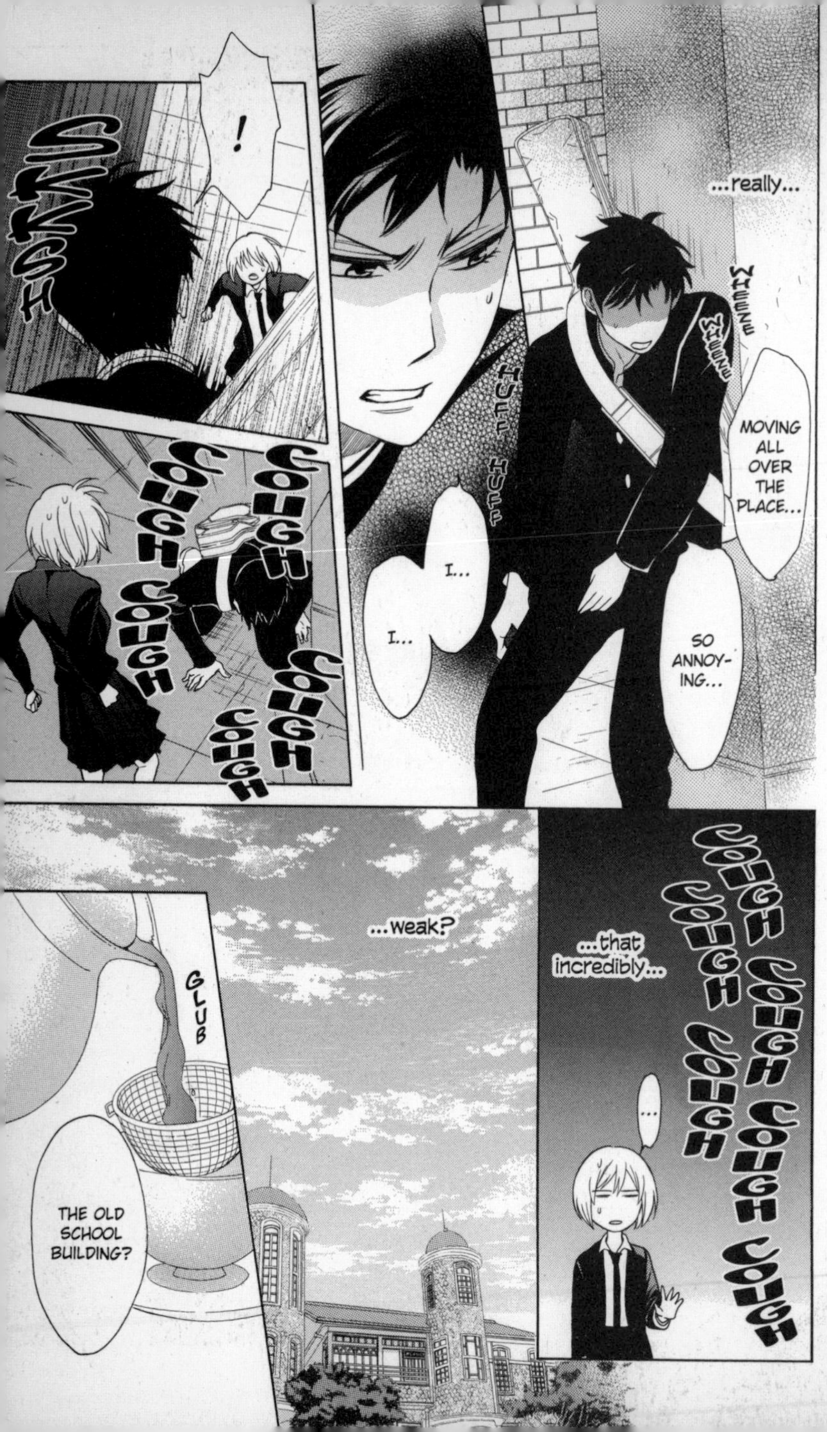

...really...
WHEEZE WHEEZE
MOVING ALL OVER THE PLACE...
SO ANNOY-ING...
HUFF HUFF
I...
I...
!
SKRSH
COUGH COUGH COUGH COUGH
COUGH COUGH
...that incredibly...
COUGH COUGH COUGH COUGH COUGH COUGH
...
...weak?
GLUB
THE OLD SCHOOL BUILDING?

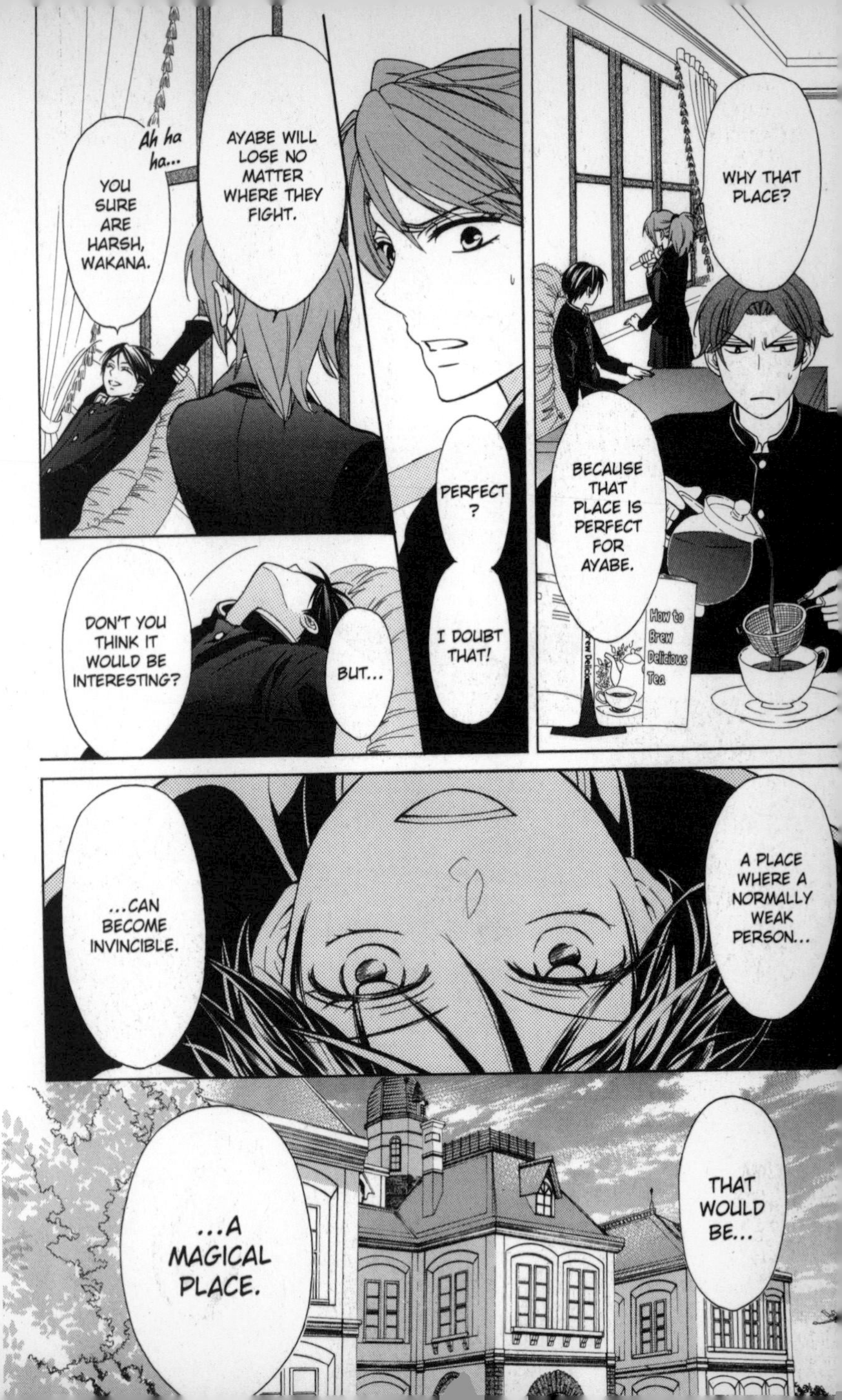
WHY THAT PLACE?
BECAUSE THAT PLACE IS PERFECT FOR AYABE.
How to Brew Delicious Tea
PERFECT?
I DOUBT THAT!
AYABE WILL LOSE NO MATTER WHERE THEY FIGHT.
Ah ha ha...
YOU SURE ARE HARSH, WAKANA.
BUT...
DON'T YOU THINK IT WOULD BE INTERESTING?
A PLACE WHERE A NORMALLY WEAK PERSON...
...CAN BECOME INVINCIBLE.
THAT WOULD BE...
...A MAGICAL PLACE.

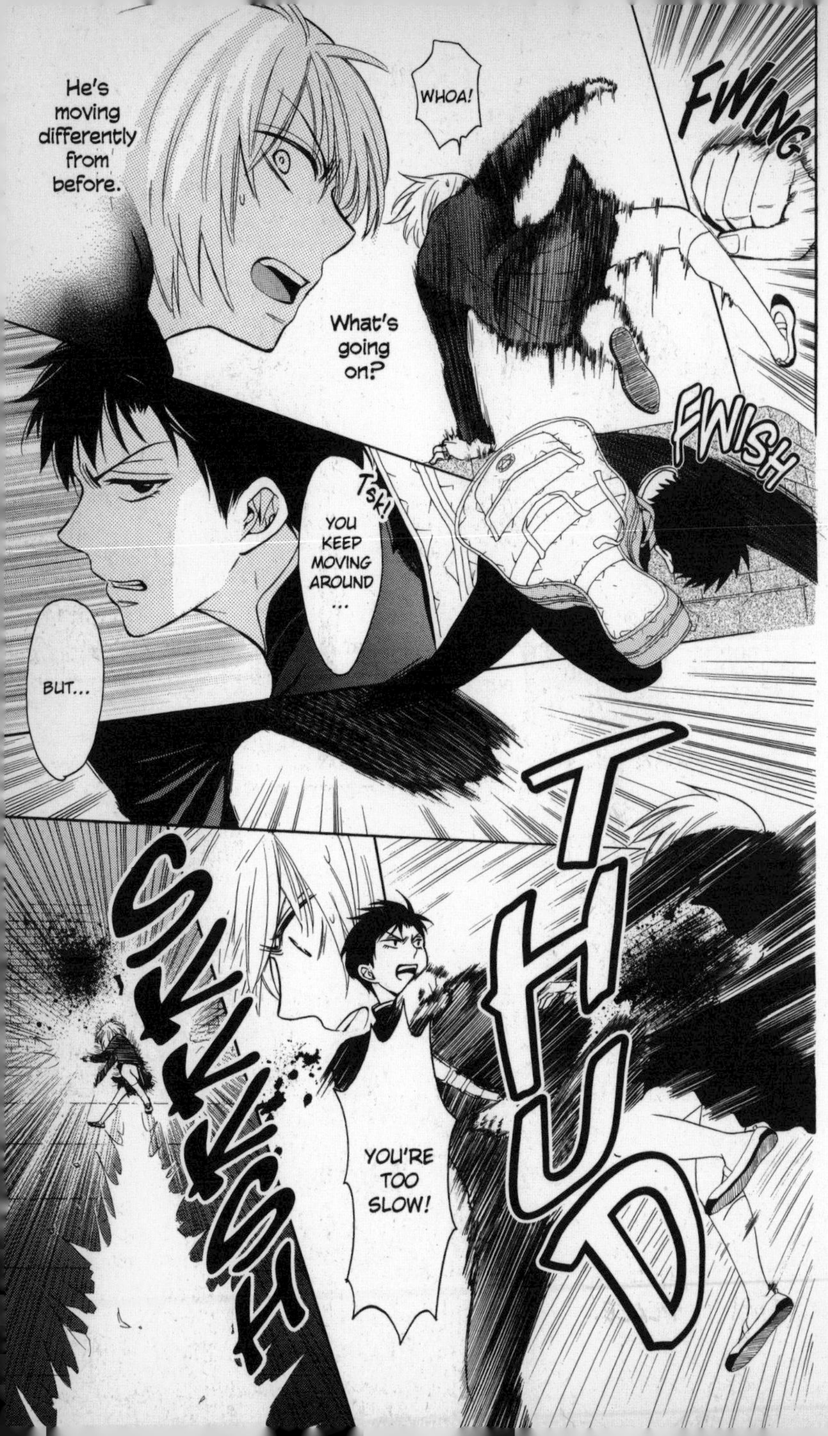
FWING
WHOA!
He's moving differently from before.
What's going on?
FWISH
Tsk!
YOU KEEP MOVING AROUND...
BUT...
THUD
YOU'RE TOO SLOW!

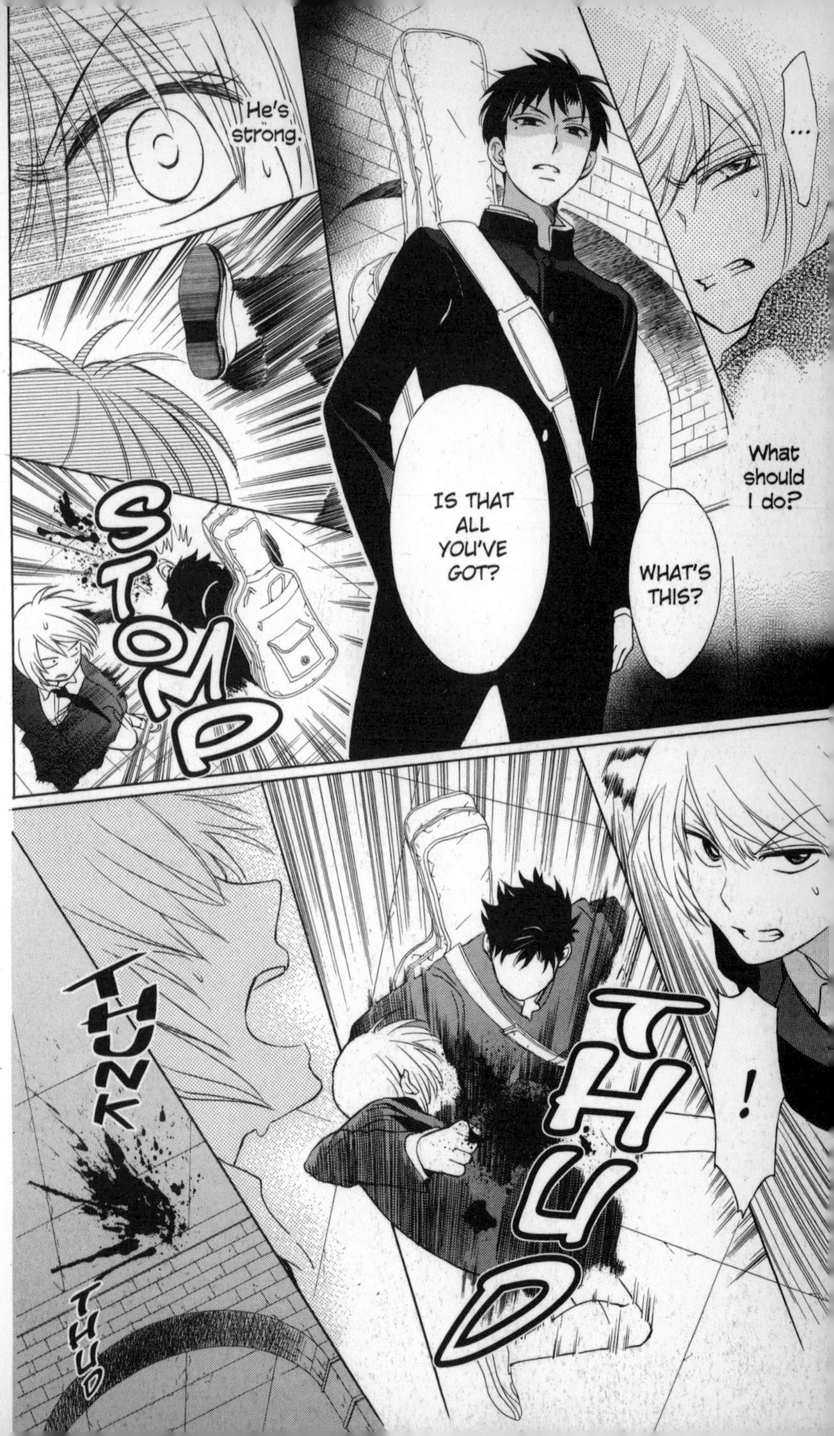
...
What should I do?
WHAT'S THIS?
IS THAT ALL YOU'VE GOT?
He's strong.
STOMP
!
THUD
THUNK
THUD

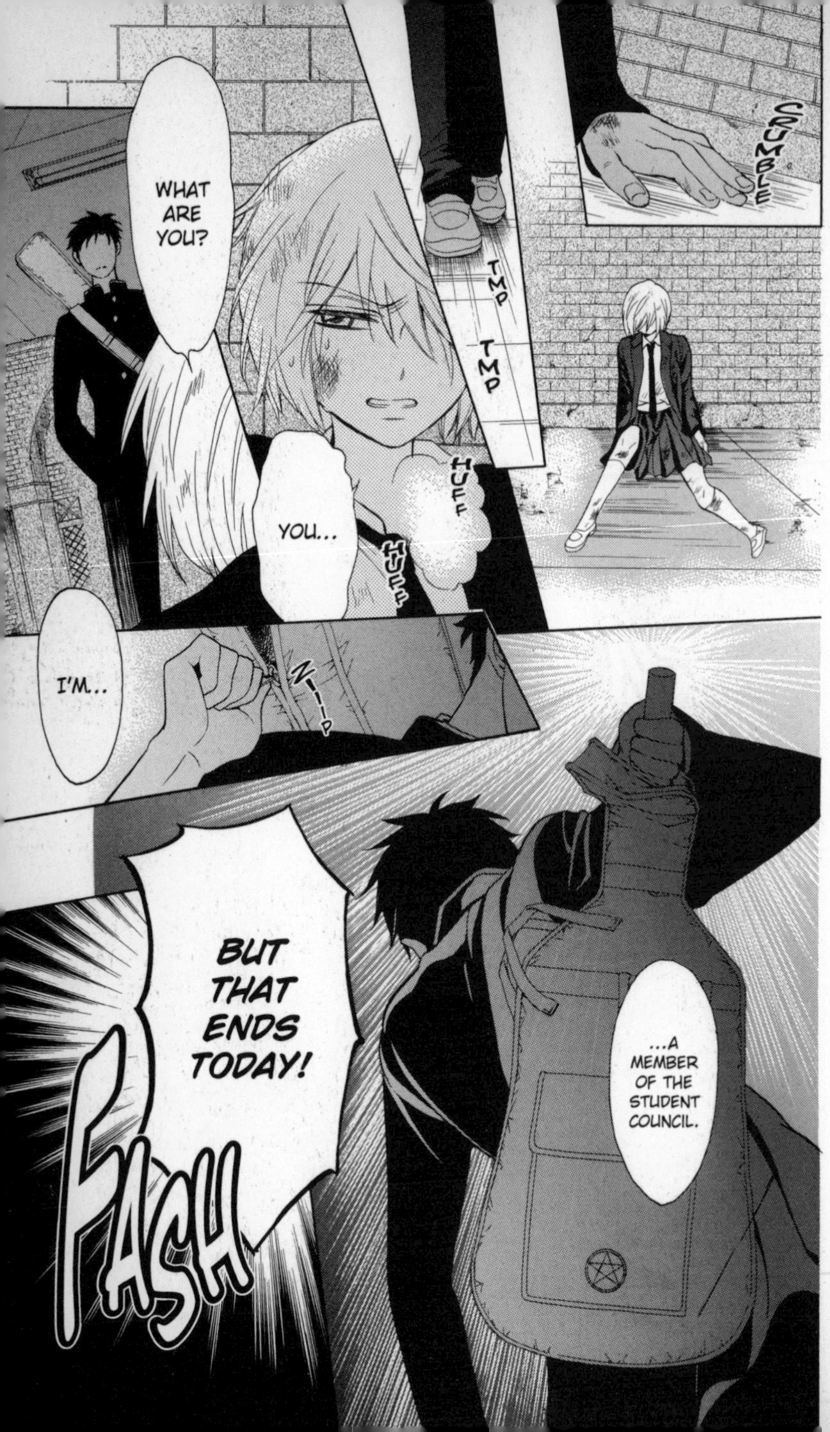
CRUMBLE
TMP
TMP
WHAT ARE YOU?
HUFF
HUFF
YOU...
I'M...
ZIIIP
...A MEMBER OF THE STUDENT COUNCIL.
BUT THAT ENDS TODAY!
FASH

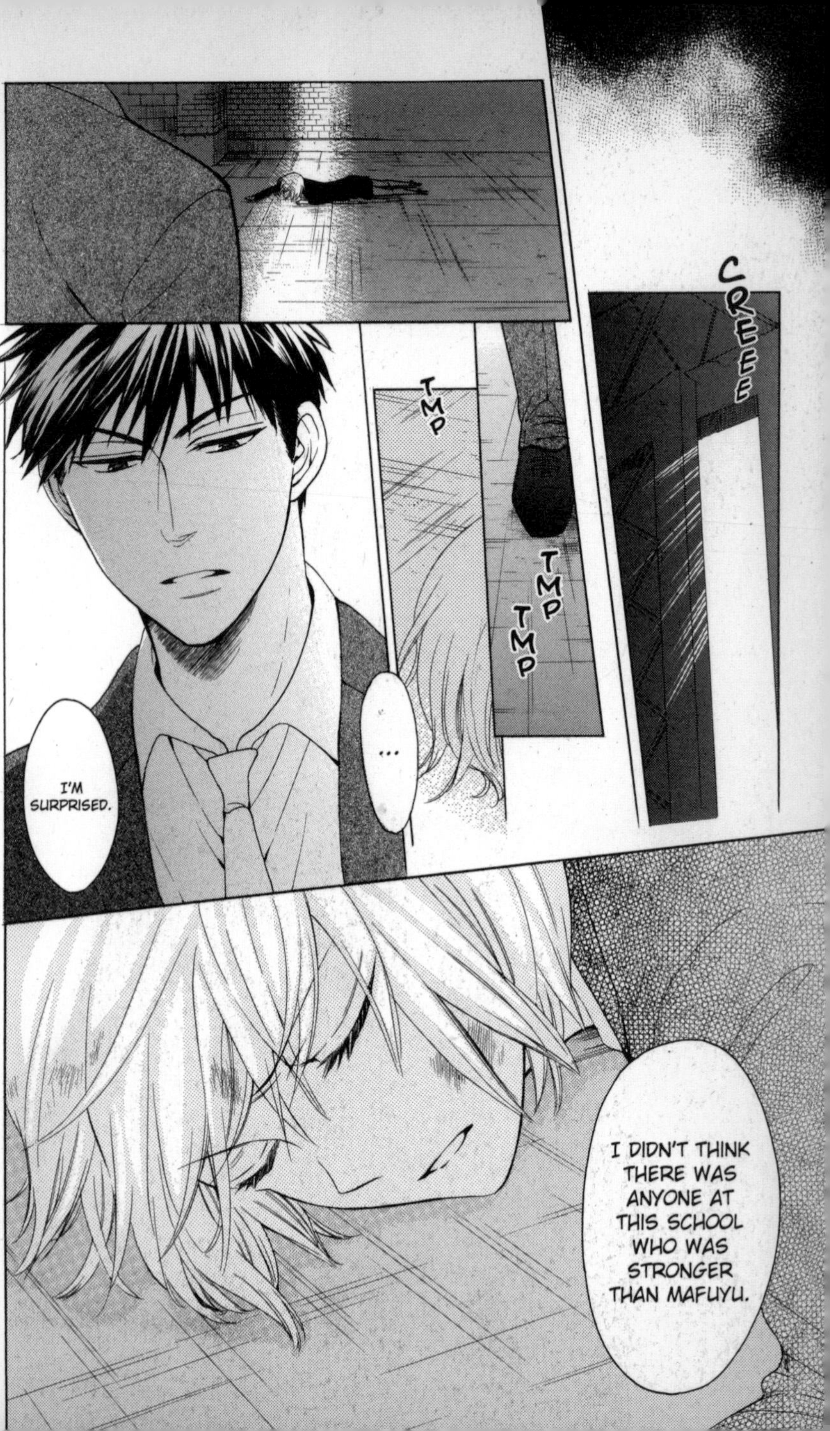
CREEE
TMP
TMP
TMP
...
I'M SURPRISED.
I DIDN'T THINK THERE WAS ANYONE AT THIS SCHOOL WHO WAS STRONGER THAN MAFUYU.

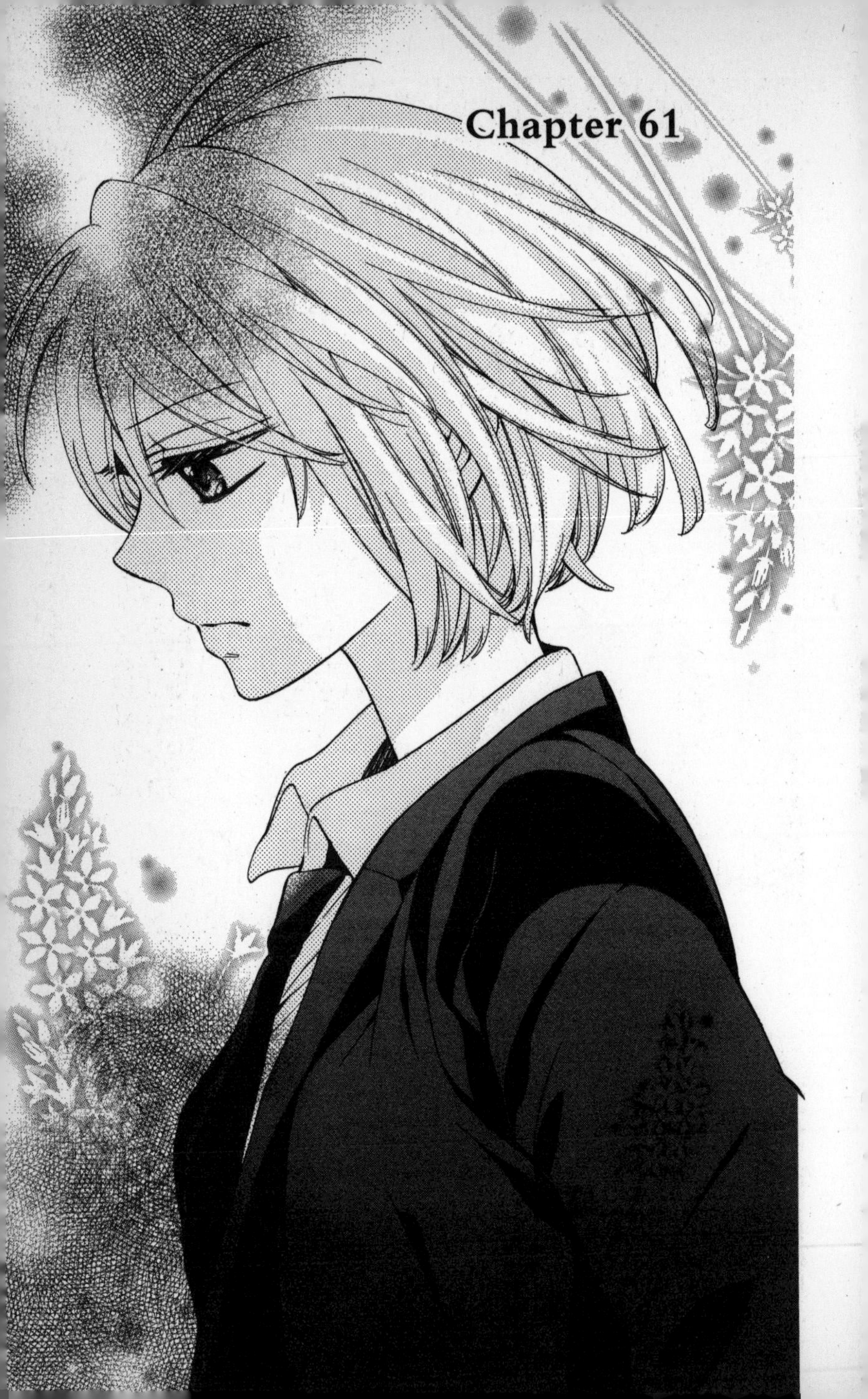
Chapter 61

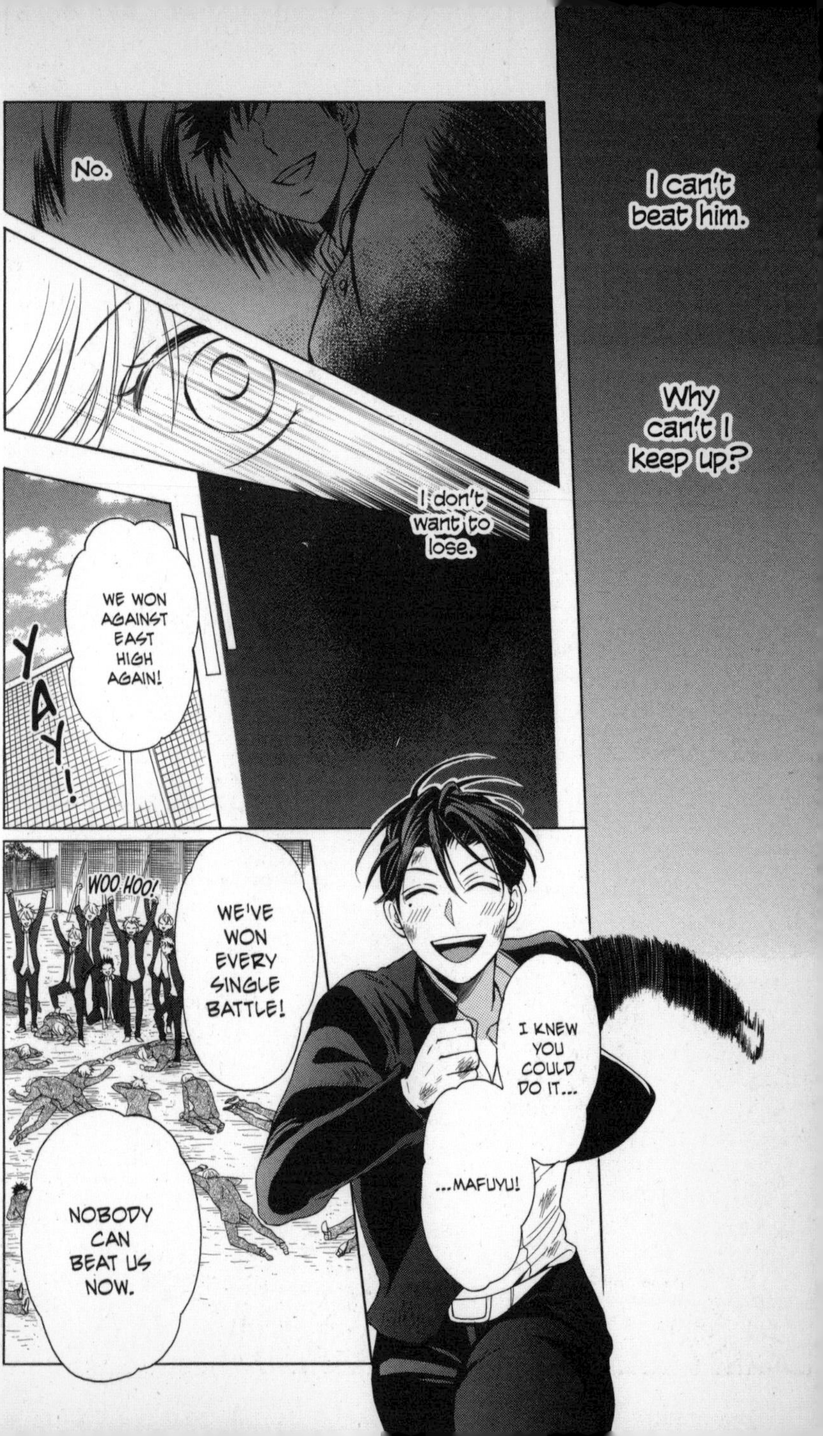
I can't beat him.
Why can't I keep up?
No.
I don't want to lose.
WE WON AGAINST EAST HIGH AGAIN!
YAY!
I KNEW YOU COULD DO IT...
...MAFUYU!
WE'VE WON EVERY SINGLE BATTLE!
WOO HOO!
NOBODY CAN BEAT US NOW.

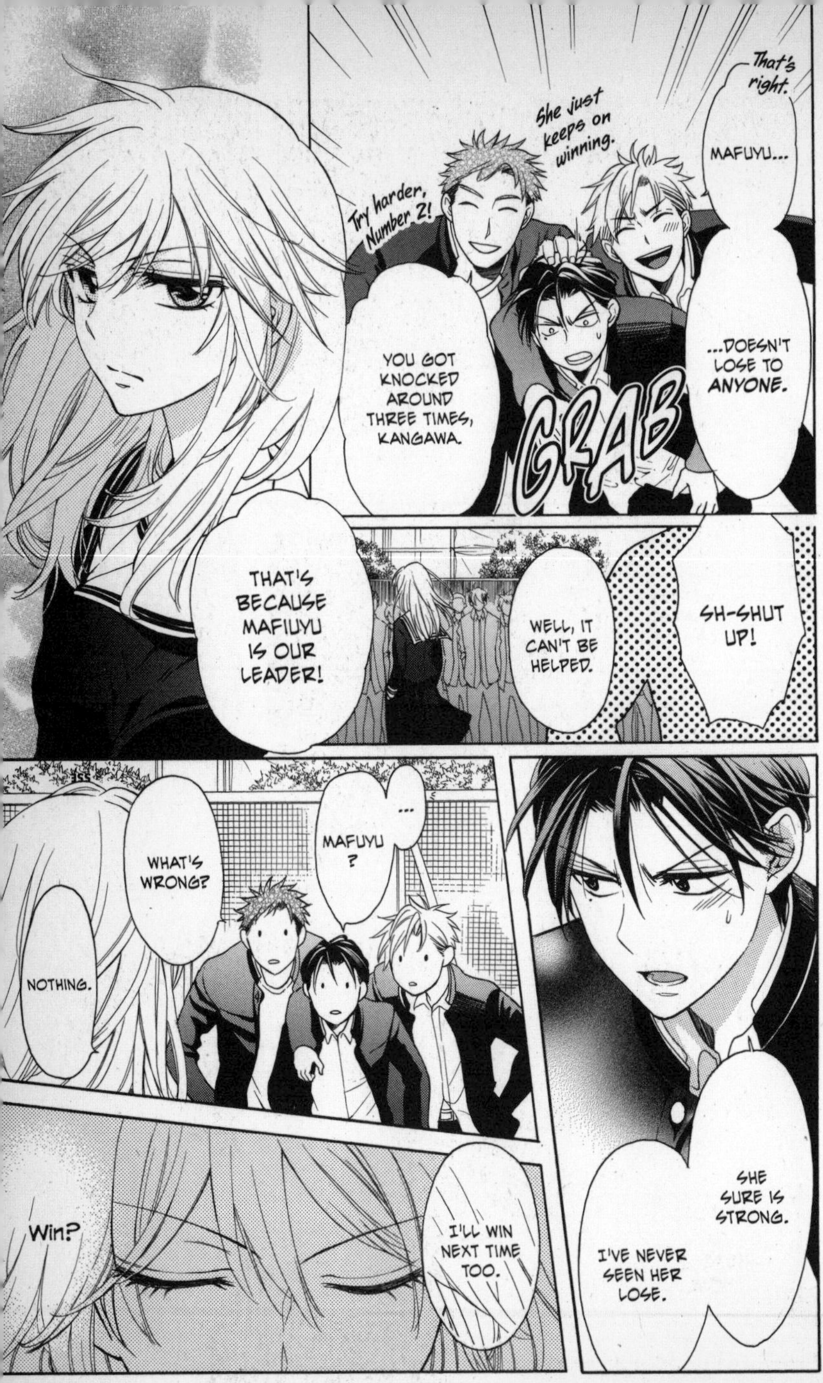
That's right.
MAFUYU...
...DOESN'T LOSE TO ANYONE.
She just keeps on winning.
Try harder, Number 2!
YOU GOT KNOCKED AROUND THREE TIMES, KANGAWA.
GRAB
SH-SHUT UP!
WELL, IT CAN'T BE HELPED.
THAT'S BECAUSE MAFUYU IS OUR LEADER!
SHE SURE IS STRONG.
I'VE NEVER SEEN HER LOSE.
...
MAFUYU?
WHAT'S WRONG?
NOTHING.
I'LL WIN NEXT TIME TOO.
Win?

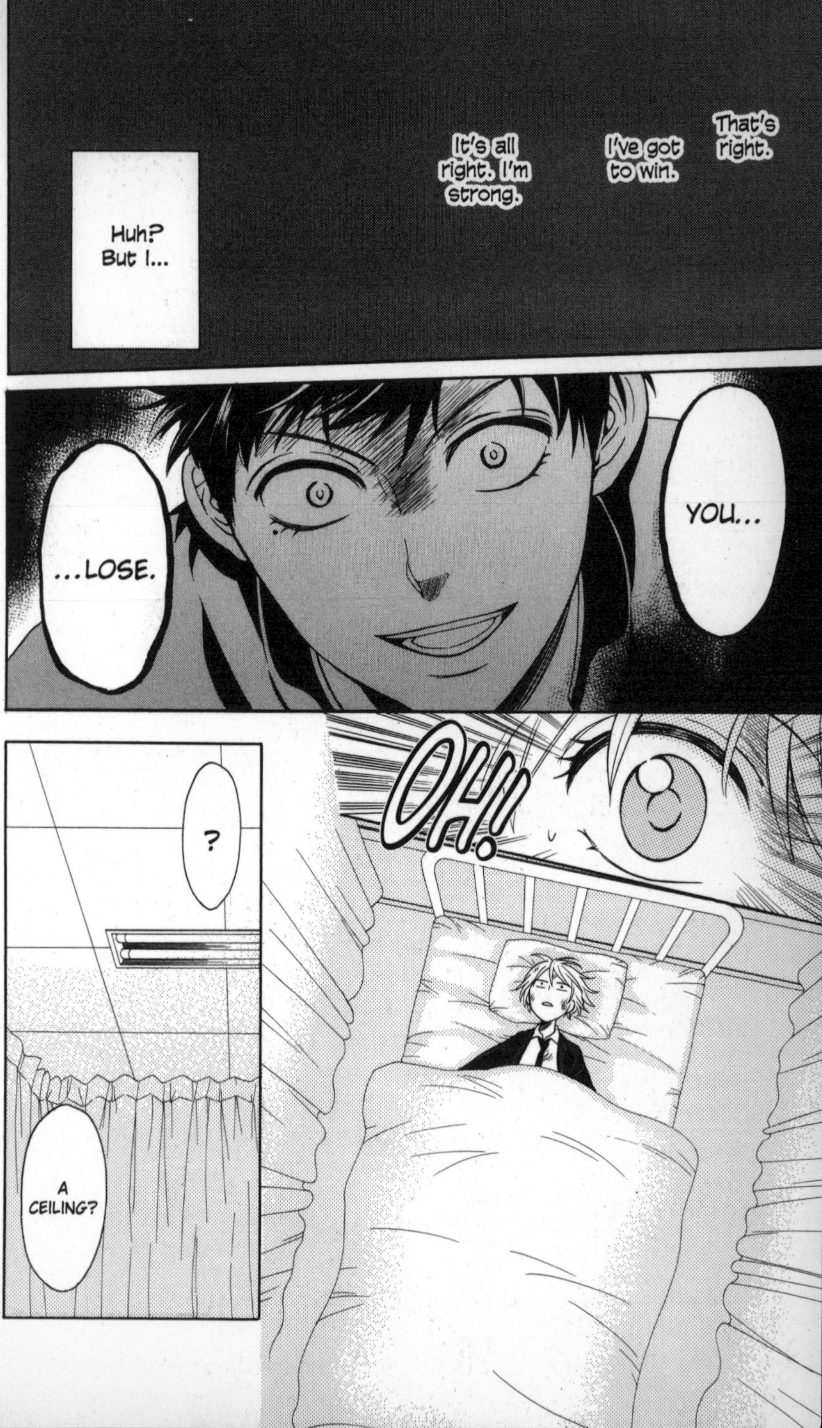
That's right.
I've got to win.
It's all right. I'm strong.
Huh? But I...
YOU...
...LOSE.
OH!
?
A CEILING?

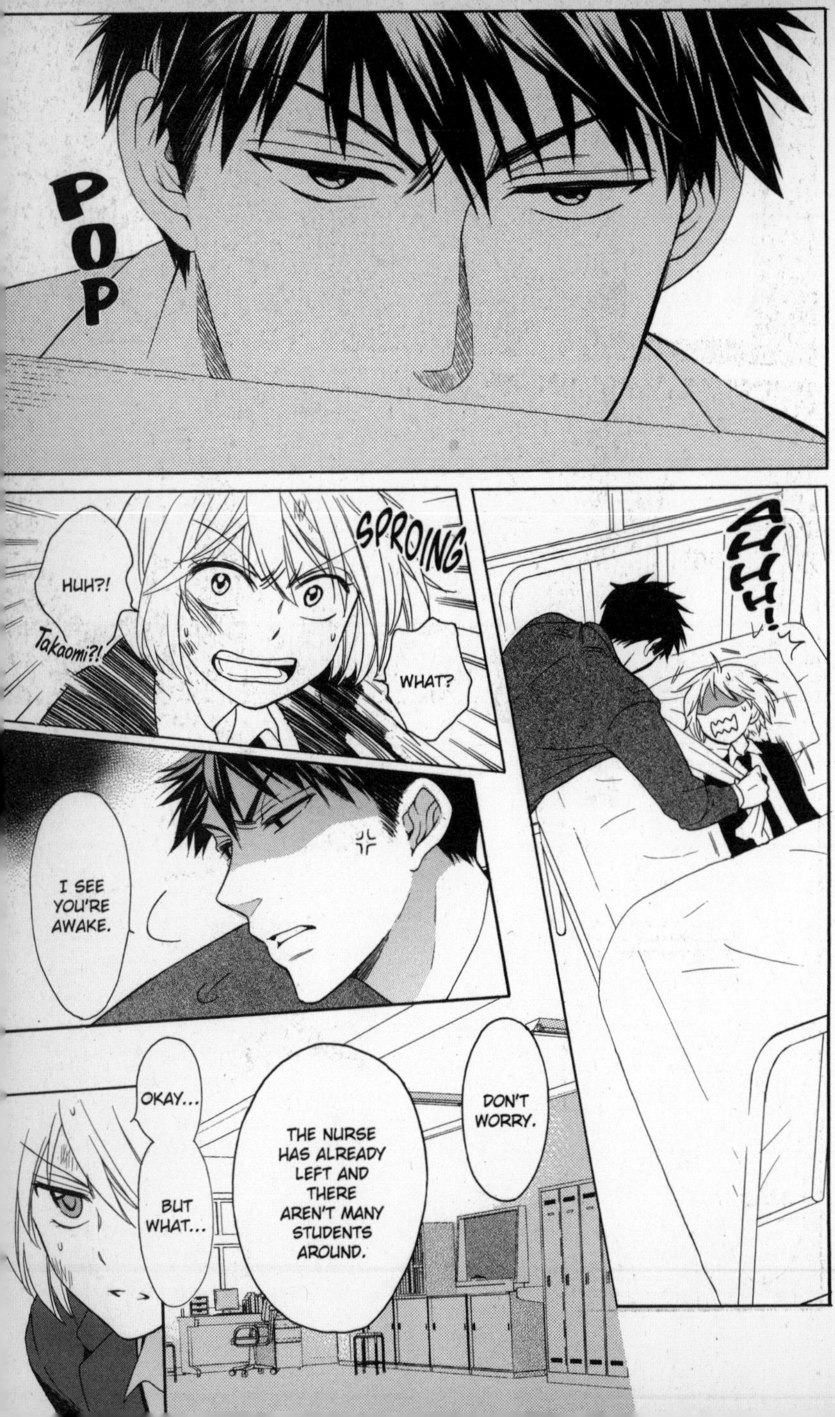
POP
AHHH!!
SPROING
HUH?!
Takaomi?!
WHAT?
I SEE YOU'RE AWAKE.
DON'T WORRY.
THE NURSE HAS ALREADY LEFT AND THERE AREN'T MANY STUDENTS AROUND.
OKAY...
BUT WHAT...

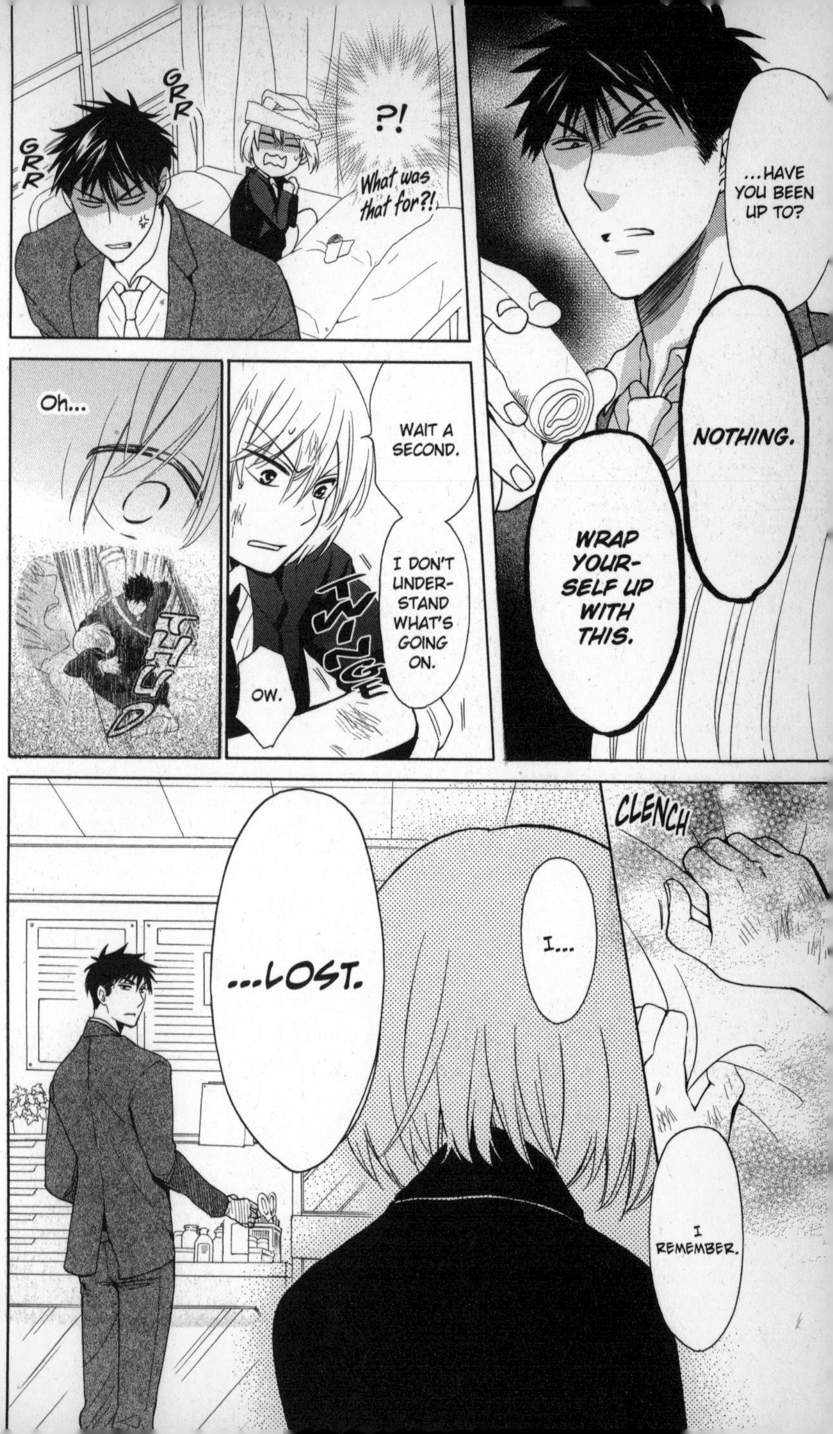
...HAVE YOU BEEN UP TO?
NOTHING.
WRAP YOURSELF UP WITH THIS.
GRR
GRR
?!
What was that for?!
WAIT A SECOND.
I DON'T UNDERSTAND WHAT'S GOING ON.
TWINGE
OW.
Oh...
THUD
CLENCH
I...
...LOST.
I REMEMBER.

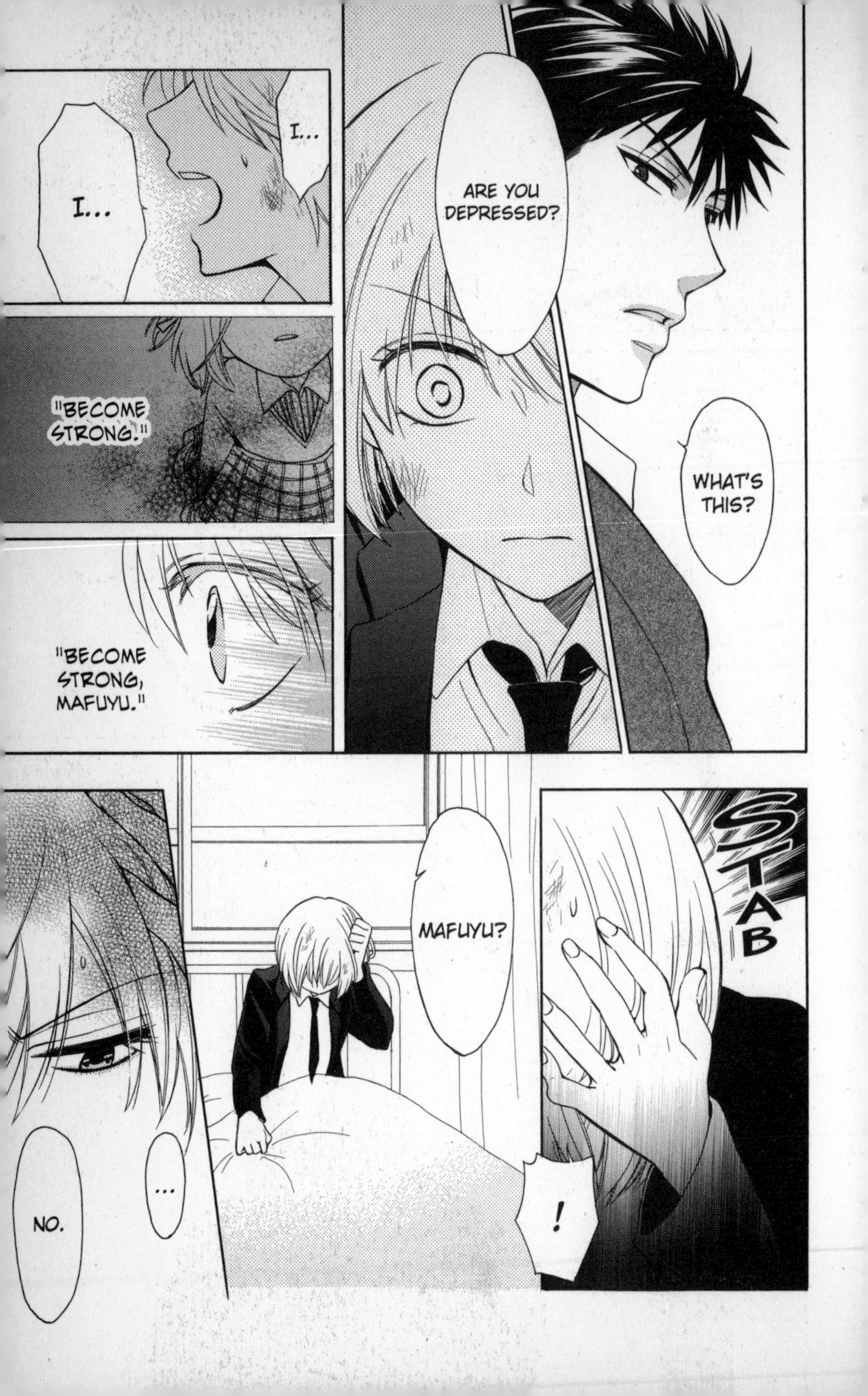
ARE YOU DEPRESSED?
WHAT'S THIS?
I...
I...
"BECOME STRONG."
"BECOME STRONG, MAFUYU."
STAB
!
MAFUYU?
...
NO.

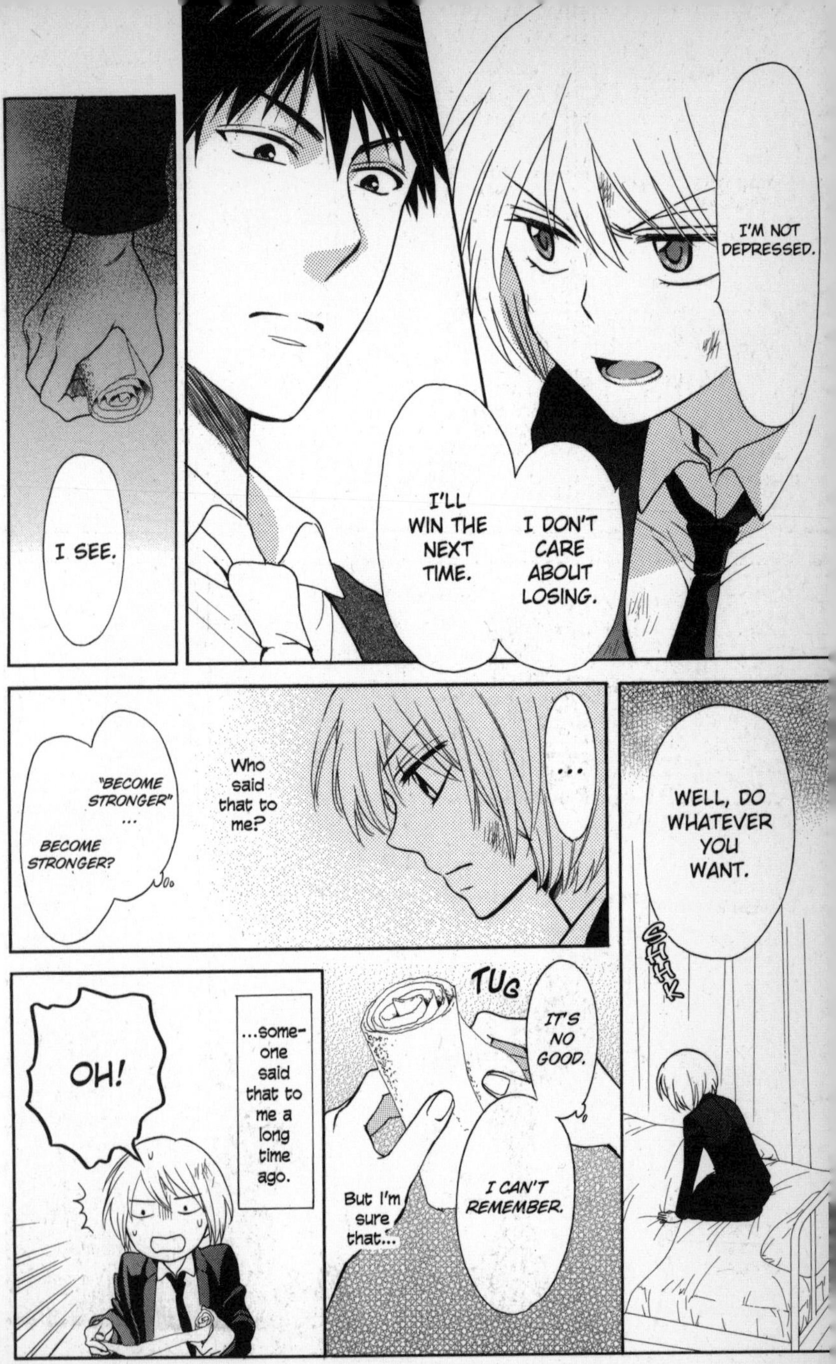
I'M NOT DEPRESSED.
I DON'T CARE ABOUT LOSING.
I'LL WIN THE NEXT TIME.
I SEE.
WELL, DO WHATEVER YOU WANT.
...
Who said that to me?
"BECOME STRONGER" ... BECOME STRONGER?
TUG
IT'S NO GOOD.
I CAN'T REMEMBER.
But I'm sure that...
...some-one said that to me a long time ago.
OH!

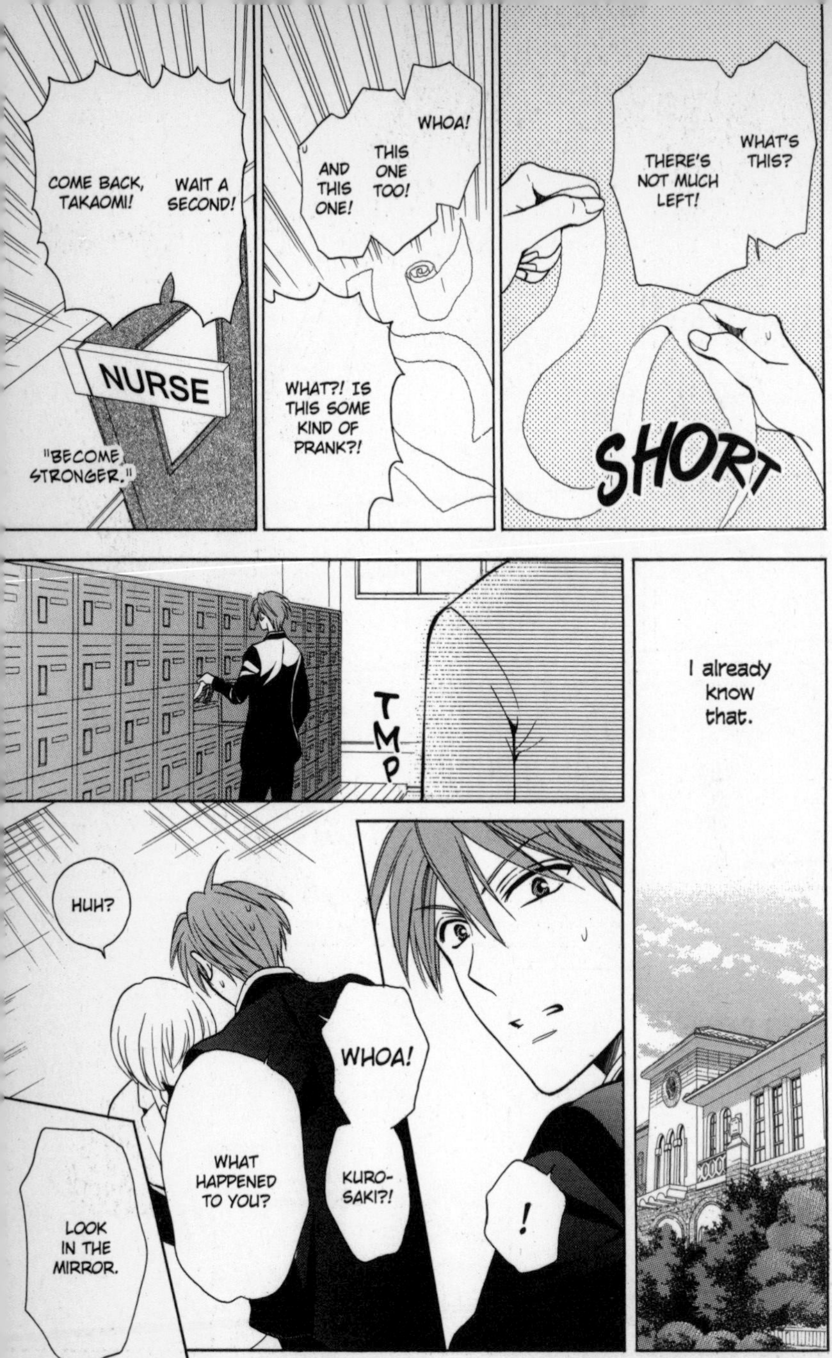
WHAT'S THIS?
THERE'S NOT MUCH LEFT!
SHORT
WHOA!
THIS ONE TOO!
AND THIS ONE!
WHAT?! IS THIS SOME KIND OF PRANK?!
WAIT A SECOND!
COME BACK, TAKAOMI!
NURSE
"BECOME STRONGER."
I already know that.
TMP
!
WHOA!
HUH?
KURO-SAKI?!
WHAT HAPPENED TO YOU?
LOOK IN THE MIRROR.

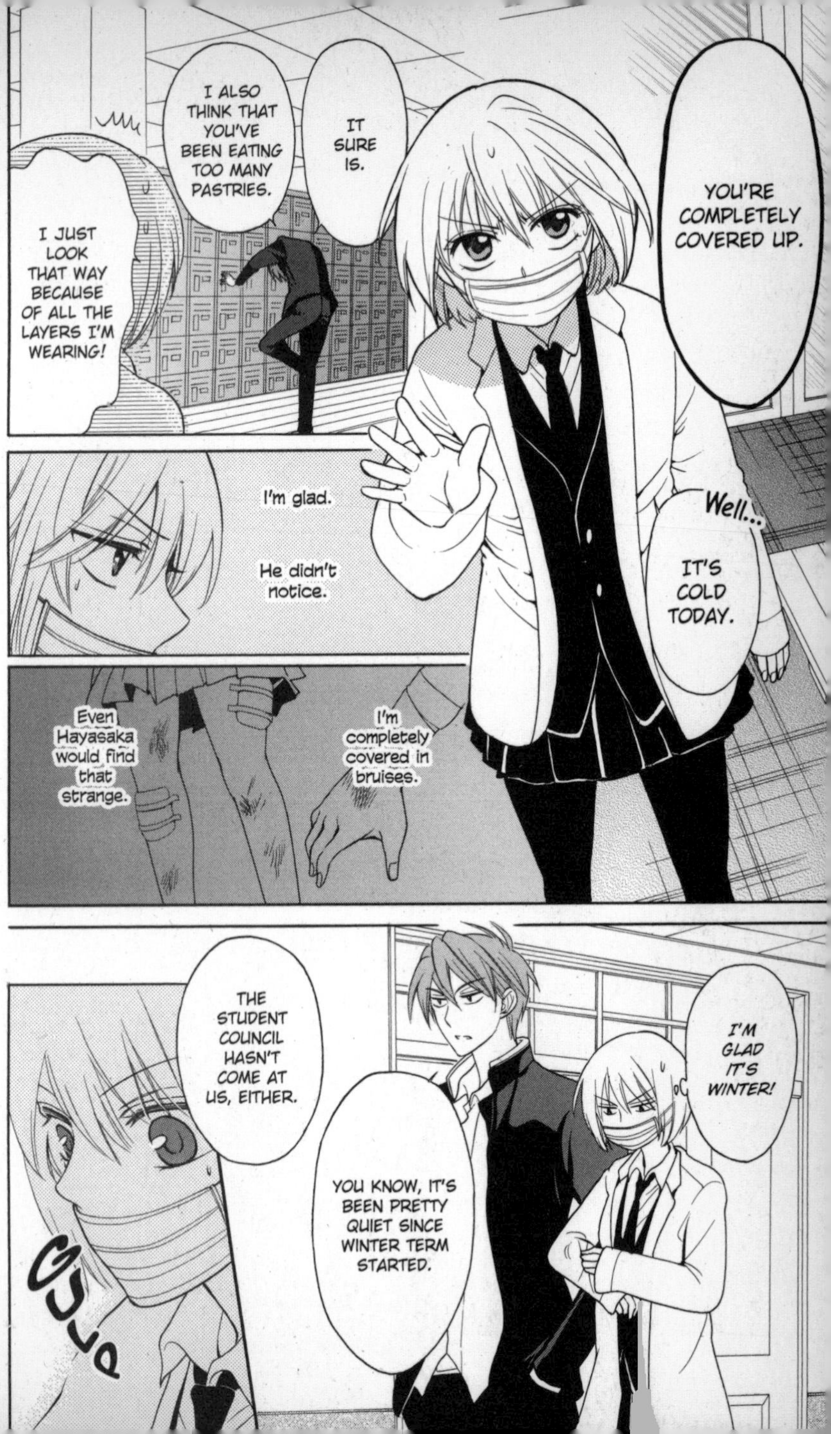
YOU'RE COMPLETELY COVERED UP.
Well...
IT'S COLD TODAY.
IT SURE IS.
I ALSO THINK THAT YOU'VE BEEN EATING TOO MANY PASTRIES.
I JUST LOOK THAT WAY BECAUSE OF ALL THE LAYERS I'M WEARING!
I'm glad.
He didn't notice.
I'm completely covered in bruises.
Even Hayasaka would find that strange.
I'M GLAD IT'S WINTER!
YOU KNOW, IT'S BEEN PRETTY QUIET SINCE WINTER TERM STARTED.
THE STUDENT COUNCIL HASN'T COME AT US, EITHER.

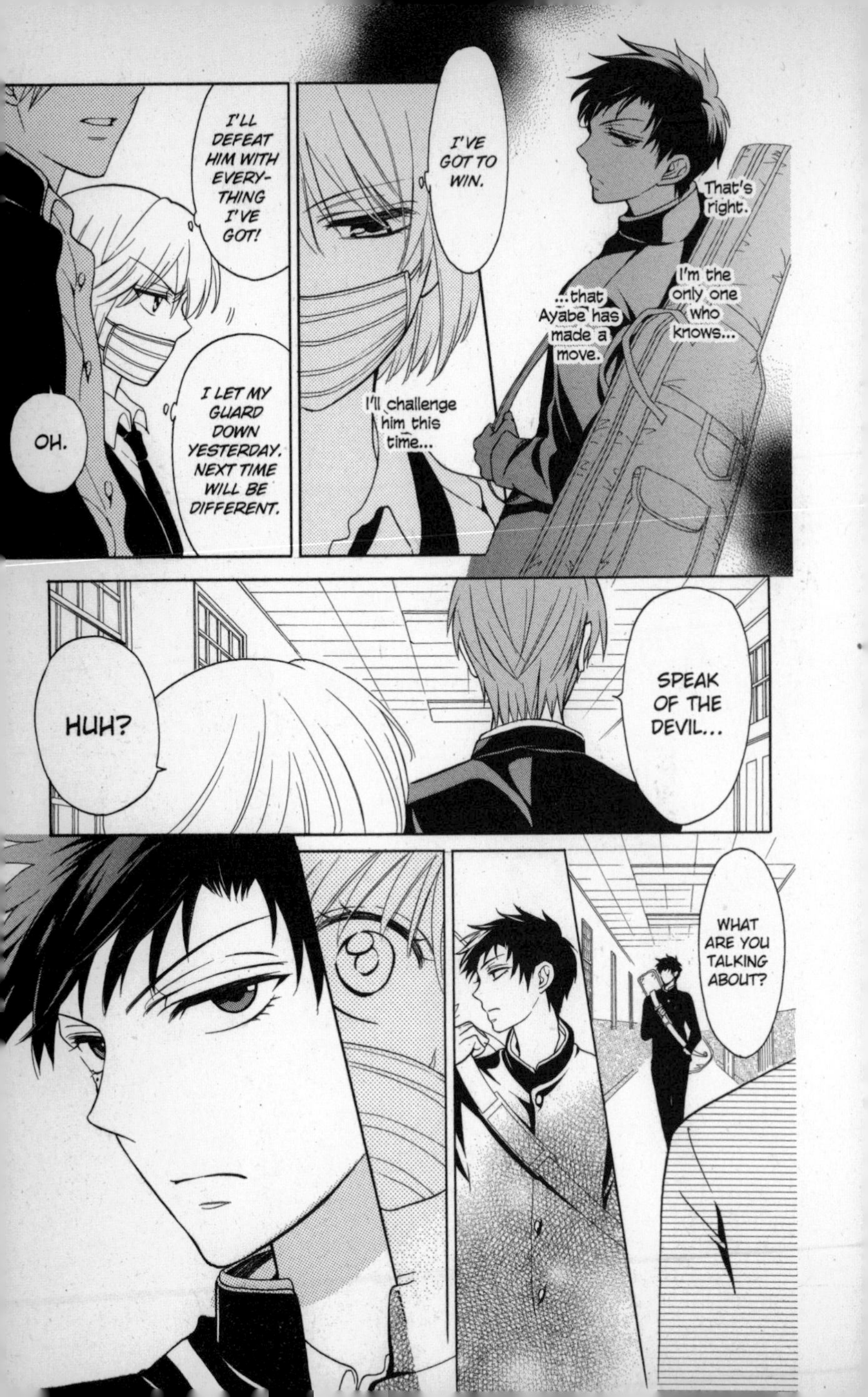
That's right.
I'm the only one who knows...
...that Ayabe has made a move.
I'VE GOT TO WIN.
I'll challenge him this time...
I'LL DEFEAT HIM WITH EVERYTHING I'VE GOT!
I LET MY GUARD DOWN YESTERDAY. NEXT TIME WILL BE DIFFERENT.
OH.
SPEAK OF THE DEVIL...
HUH?
WHAT ARE YOU TALKING ABOUT?

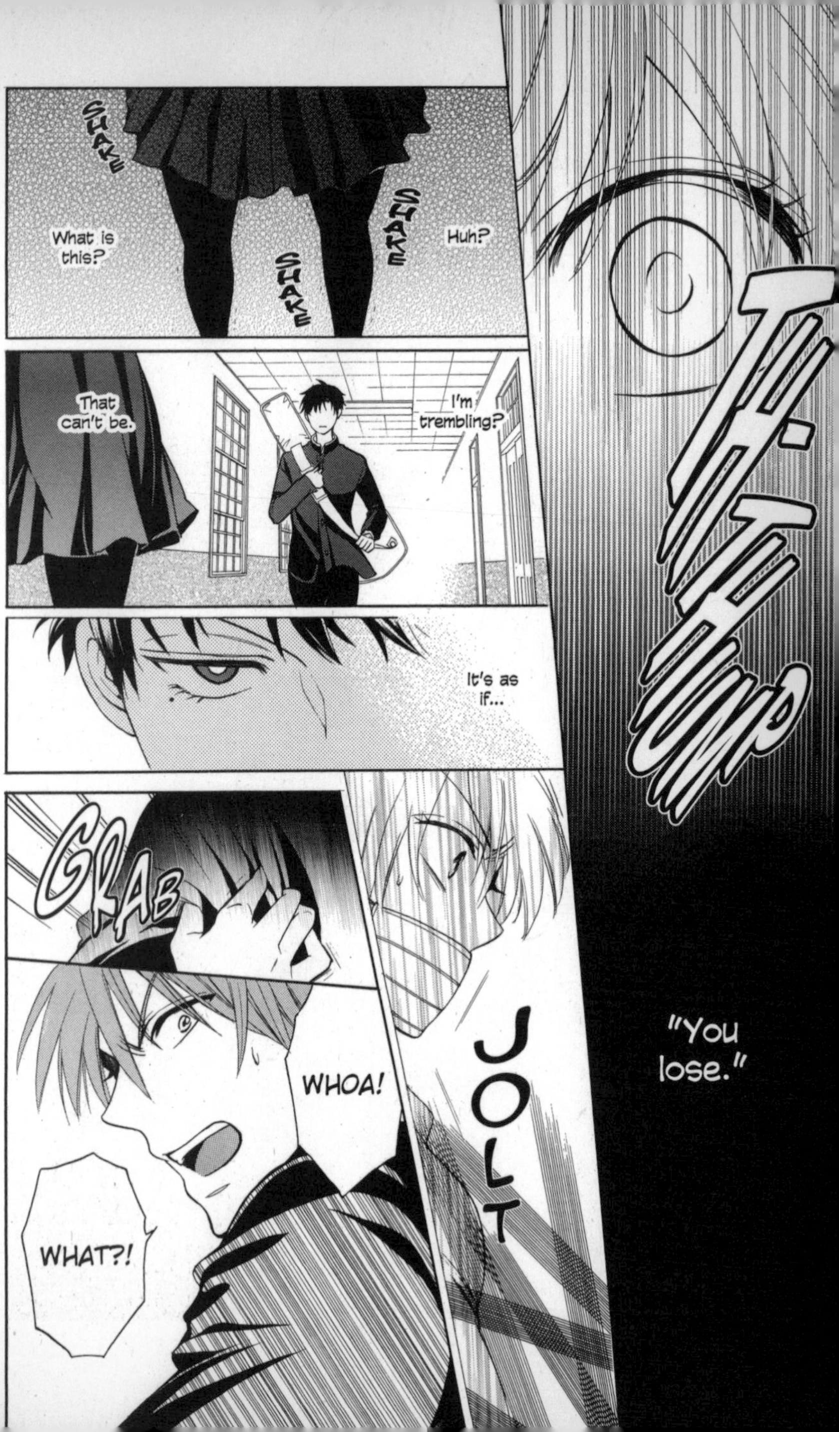
TH-THUMP
"You lose."
Huh?
SHAKE
SHAKE
What is this?
SHAKE
SHAKE
I'm trembling?
That can't be.
It's as if...
GRAB
JOLT
WHOA!
WHAT?!

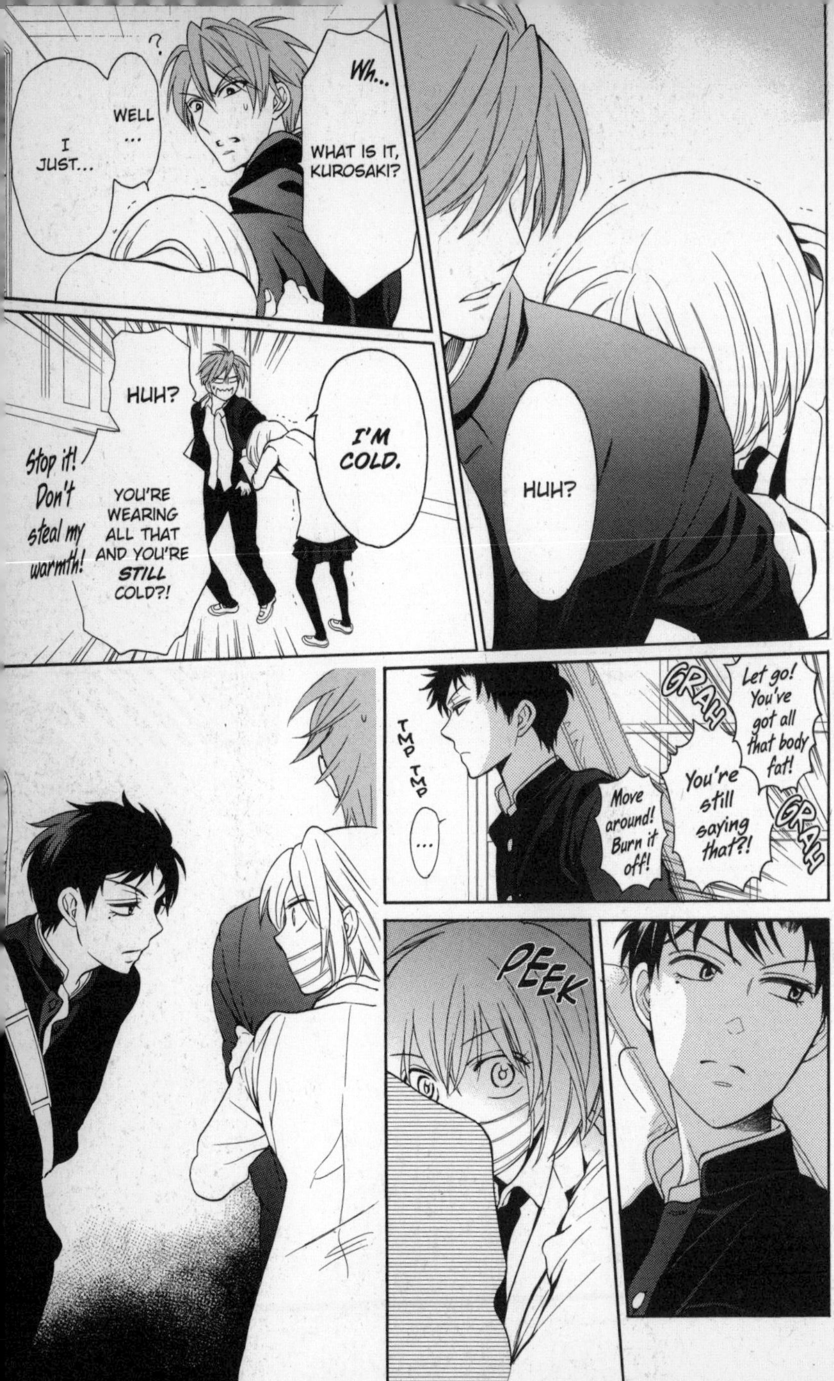

HUH?
Wh... WHAT IS IT, KUROSAKI?
?
WELL...
I JUST...
I'M COLD.
HUH?
YOU'RE WEARING ALL THAT AND YOU'RE STILL COLD?!
Stop it! Don't steal my warmth!
GRAH
Let go! You've got all that body fat!
GRAH
You're still saying that?!
Move around! Burn it off!
TMP TMP
...
PEEK

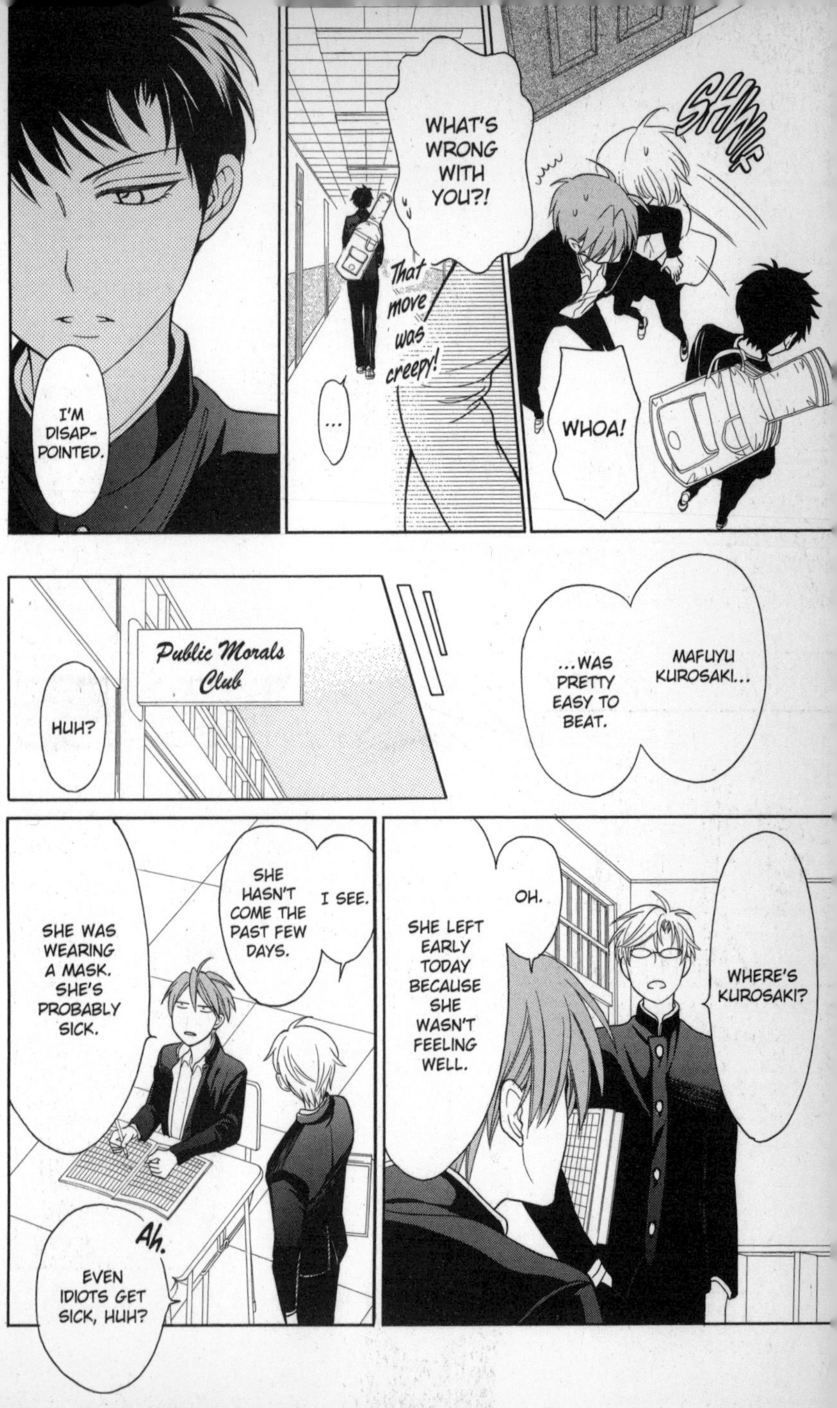
SHWF
WHOA!
WHAT'S WRONG WITH YOU?!
That move was creepy!
...
I'M DISAP-POINTED.
MAFUYU KUROSAKI...
...WAS PRETTY EASY TO BEAT.
Public Morals Club
HUH?
WHERE'S KUROSAKI?
OH.
SHE LEFT EARLY TODAY BECAUSE SHE WASN'T FEELING WELL.
I SEE.
SHE HASN'T COME THE PAST FEW DAYS.
SHE WAS WEARING A MASK. SHE'S PROBABLY SICK.
Ah.
EVEN IDIOTS GET SICK, HUH?

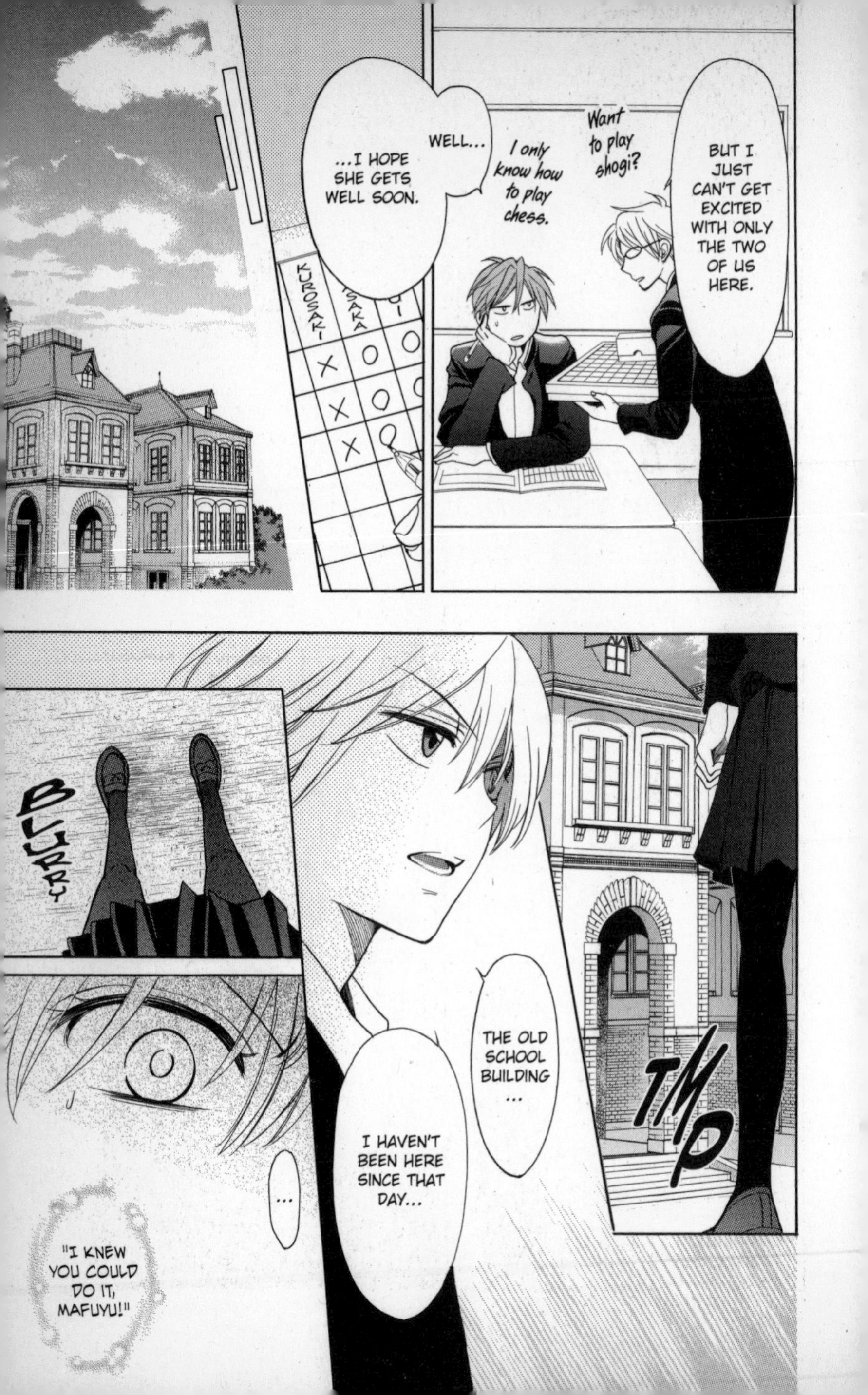
BUT I JUST CAN'T GET EXCITED WITH ONLY THE TWO OF US HERE.
Want to play shogi?
I only know how to play chess.
WELL...
...I HOPE SHE GETS WELL SOON.
KUROSAKI
TMP
THE OLD SCHOOL BUILDING ...
I HAVEN'T BEEN HERE SINCE THAT DAY...
BLURRY
...
"I KNEW YOU COULD DO IT, MAFUYU!"

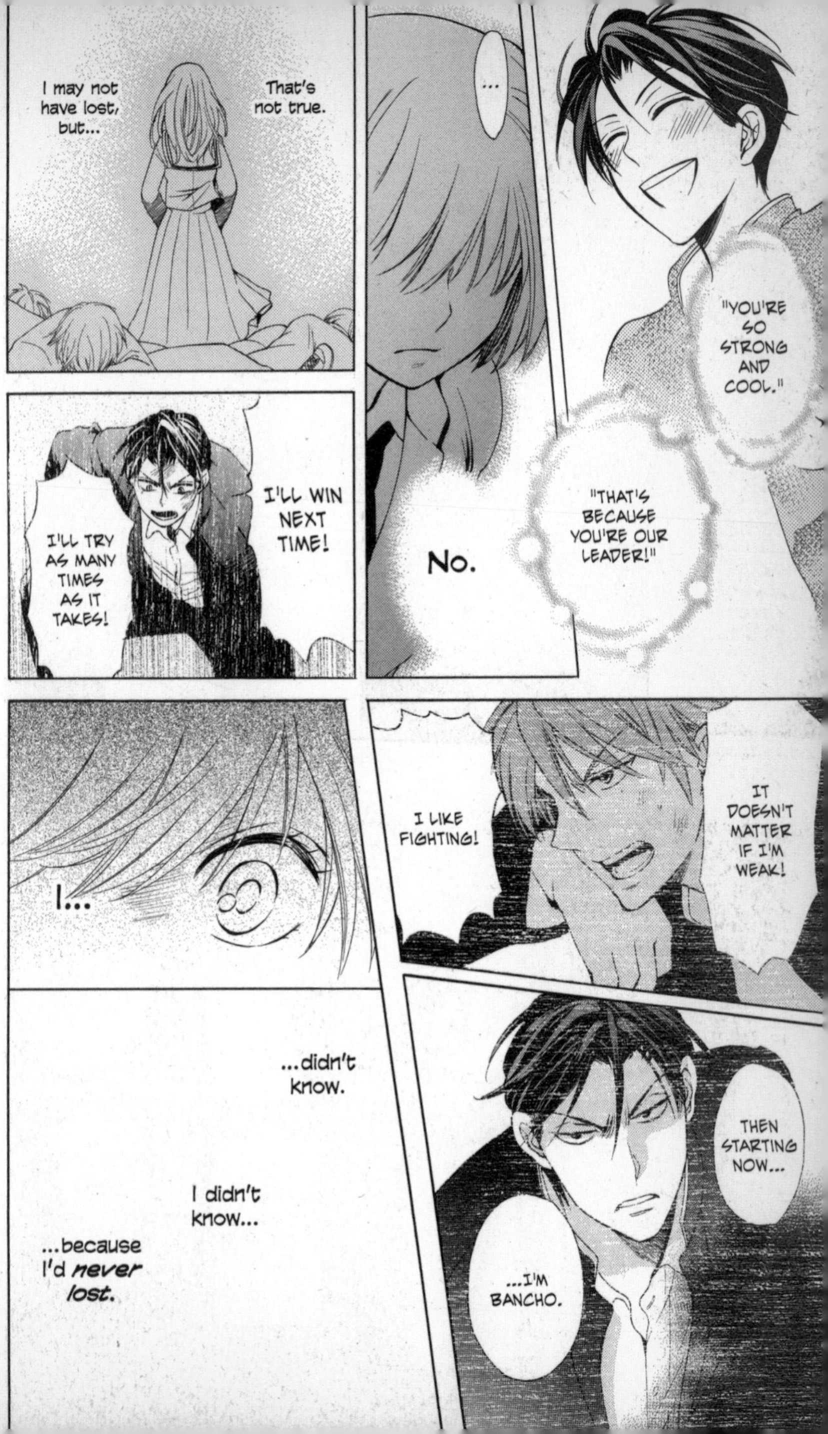
"YOU'RE SO STRONG AND COOL."
"THAT'S BECAUSE YOU'RE OUR LEADER!"
...
No.
That's not true.
I may not have lost, but...
I'LL WIN NEXT TIME!
I'LL TRY AS MANY TIMES AS IT TAKES!
IT DOESN'T MATTER IF I'M WEAK!
I LIKE FIGHTING!
THEN STARTING NOW...
...I'M BANCHO.
I...
...didn't know.
I didn't know...
...because I'd *never lost*.

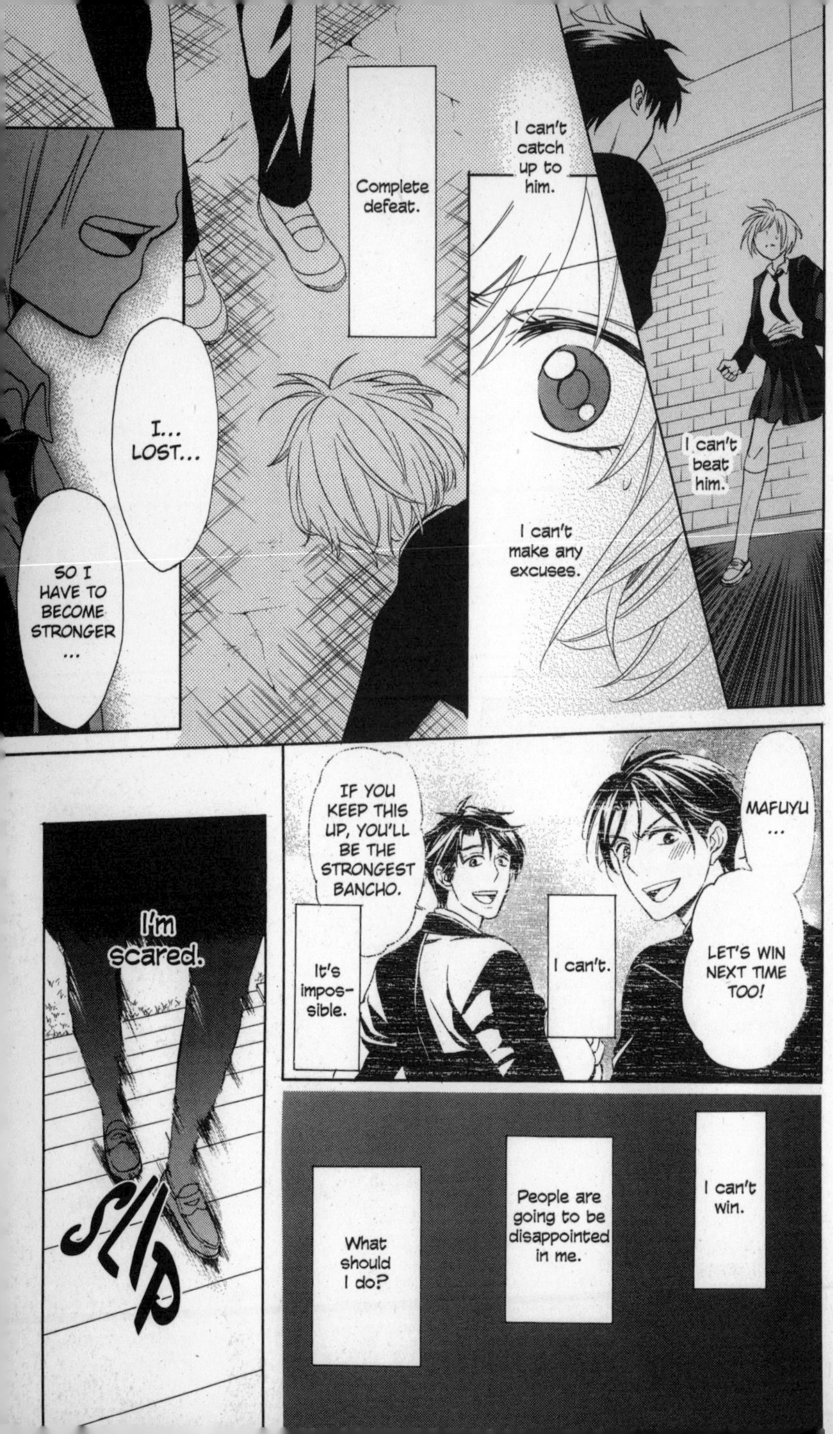

I can't catch up to him.
I can't beat him.
I can't make any excuses.
Complete defeat.
I... LOST...
SO I HAVE TO BECOME STRONGER...
MAFUYU...
LET'S WIN NEXT TIME TOO!
I can't.
IF YOU KEEP THIS UP, YOU'LL BE THE STRONGEST BANCHO.
It's impos-sible.
I can't win.
People are going to be disappointed in me.
What should I do?
I'm scared.
SLIP

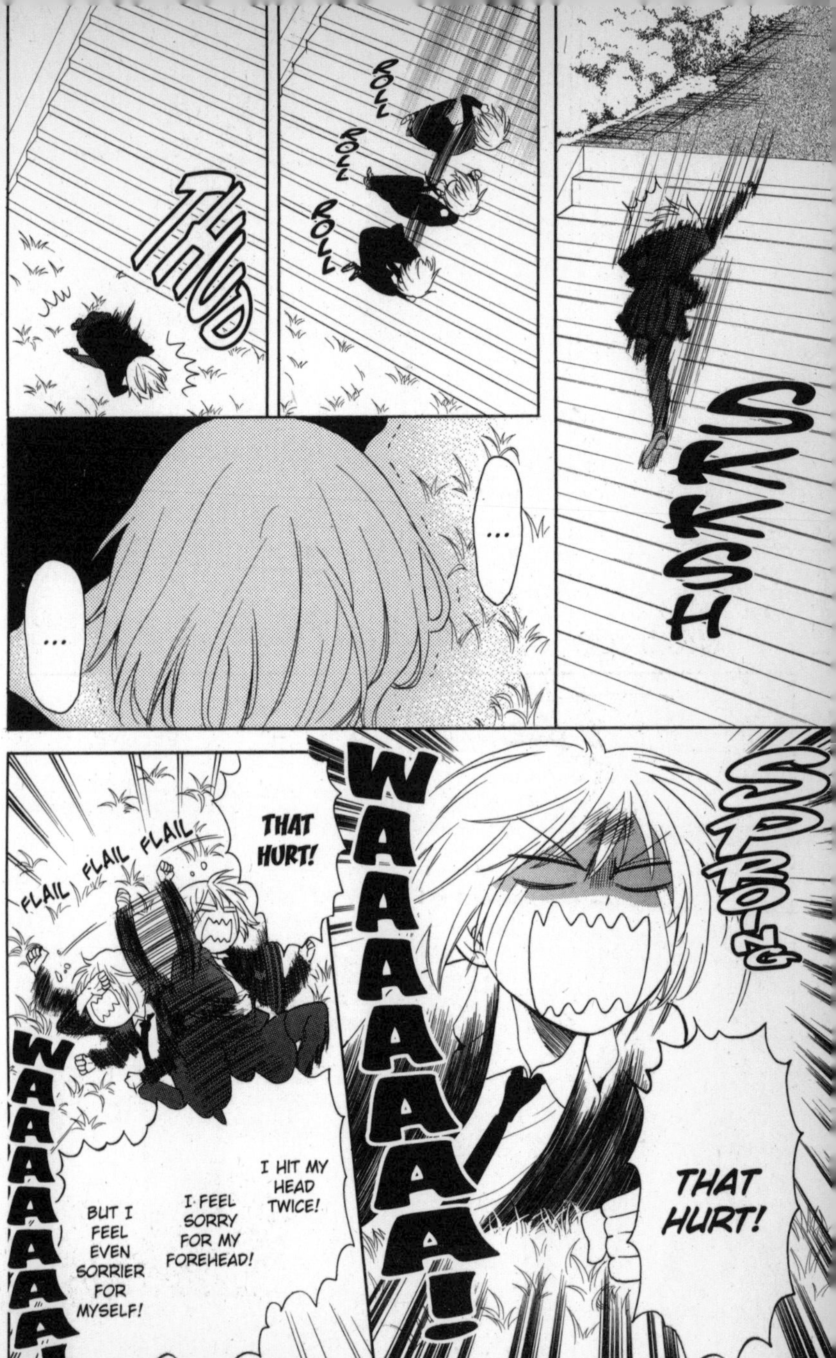
SKKSH
ROLL
ROLL
ROLL
THUD
...
...
SPROING
WAAAAAAA!
THAT HURT!
THAT HURT!
FLAIL FLAIL FLAIL FLAIL
I HIT MY HEAD TWICE!
I FEEL SORRY FOR MY FOREHEAD!
BUT I FEEL EVEN SORRIER FOR MYSELF!
WAAAAAAAAAA!

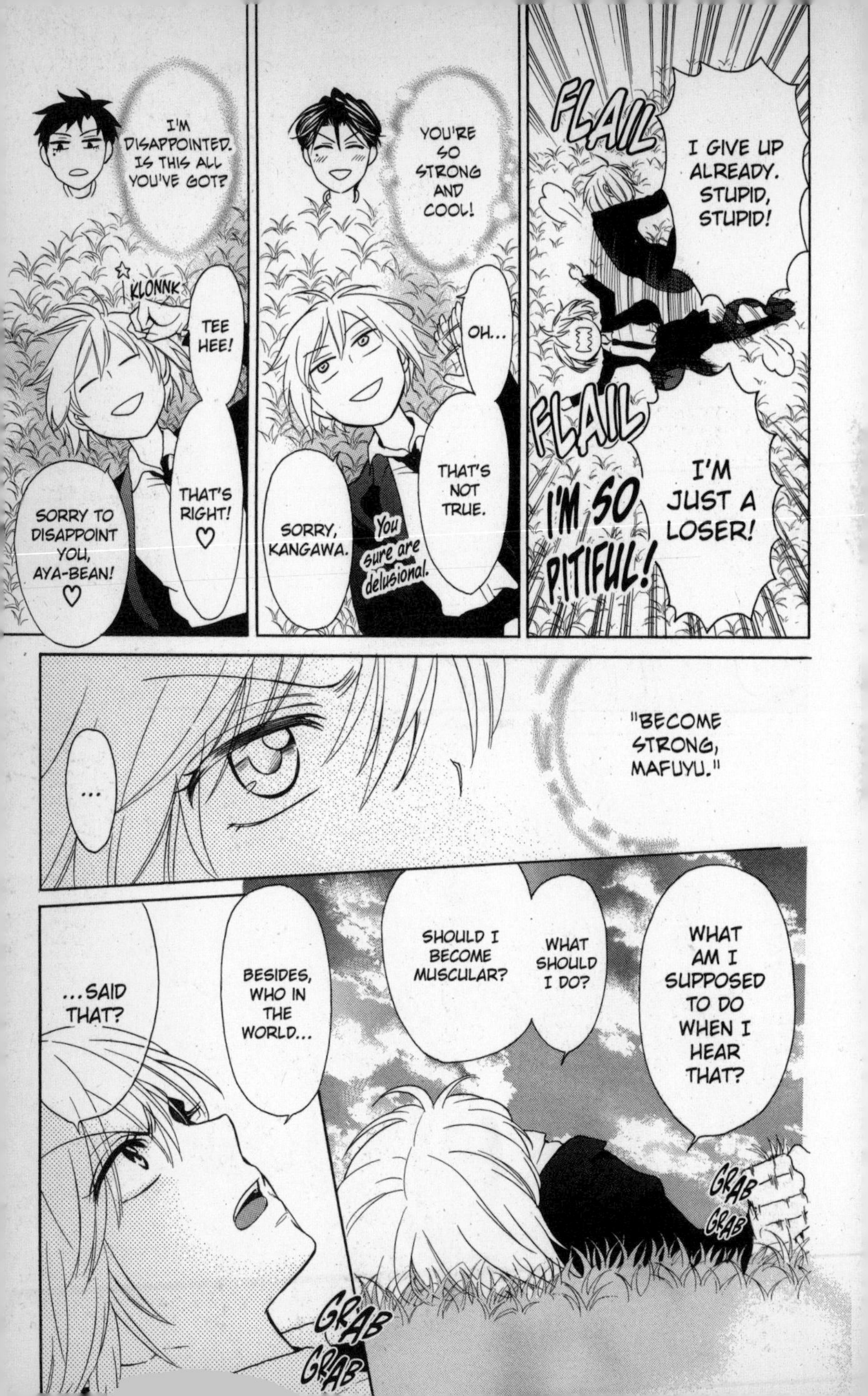
I GIVE UP ALREADY. STUPID, STUPID!
FLAIL
FLAIL
I'M JUST A LOSER!
I'M SO PITIFUL!
YOU'RE SO STRONG AND COOL!
OH...
THAT'S NOT TRUE.
You sure are delusional.
SORRY, KANGAWA.
I'M DISAPPOINTED. IS THIS ALL YOU'VE GOT?
TEE HEE!
KLONNK
THAT'S RIGHT! ♡
SORRY TO DISAPPOINT YOU, AYA-BEAN! ♡
"BECOME STRONG, MAFUYU."
...
WHAT AM I SUPPOSED TO DO WHEN I HEAR THAT?
WHAT SHOULD I DO?
SHOULD I BECOME MUSCULAR?
GRAB GRAB
BESIDES, WHO IN THE WORLD...
...SAID THAT?
GRAB GRAB

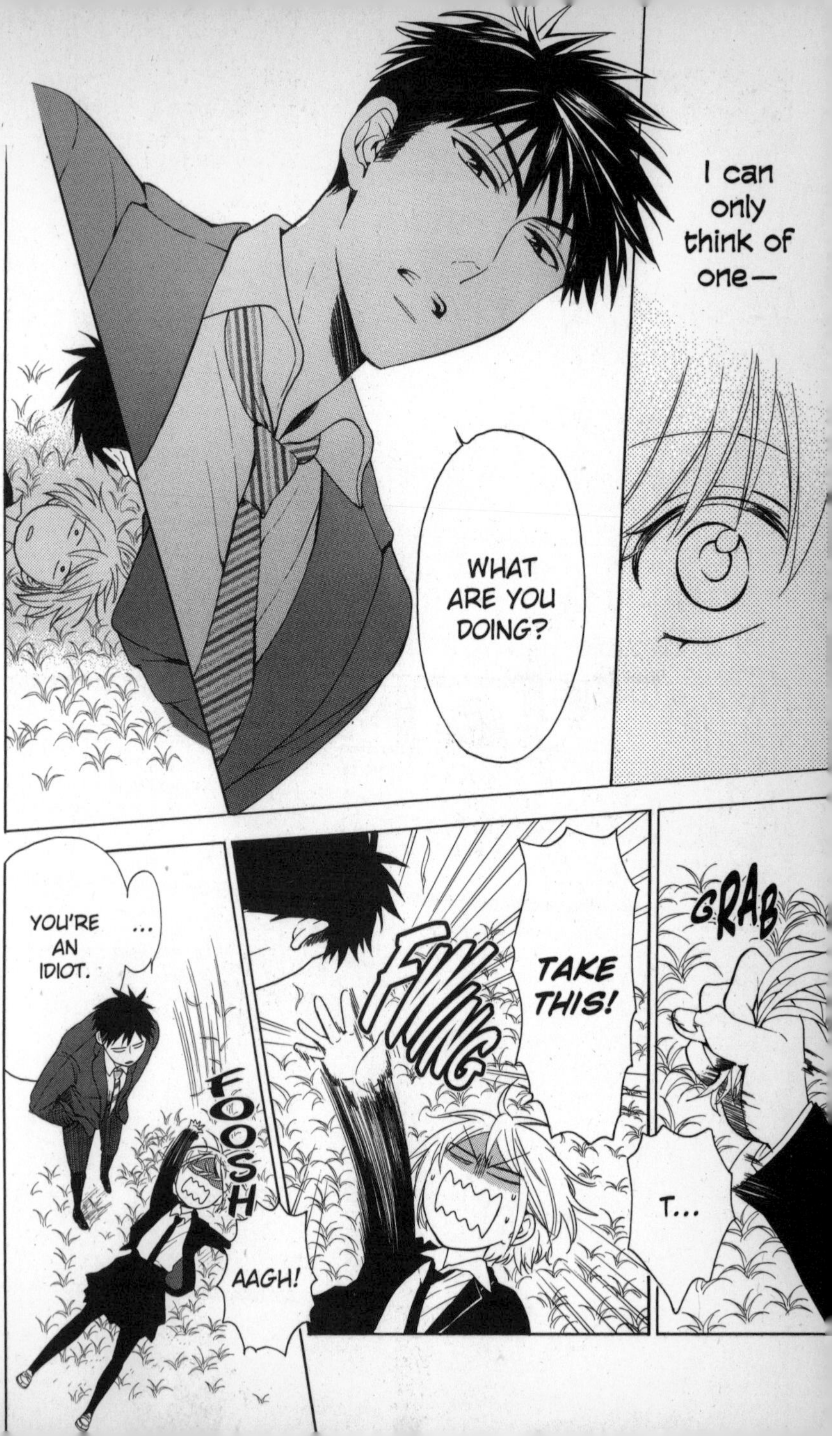
I can only think of one—
WHAT ARE YOU DOING?
GRAB
T...
TAKE THIS!
FWNG
...
YOU'RE AN IDIOT.
FOOSH
AAGH!

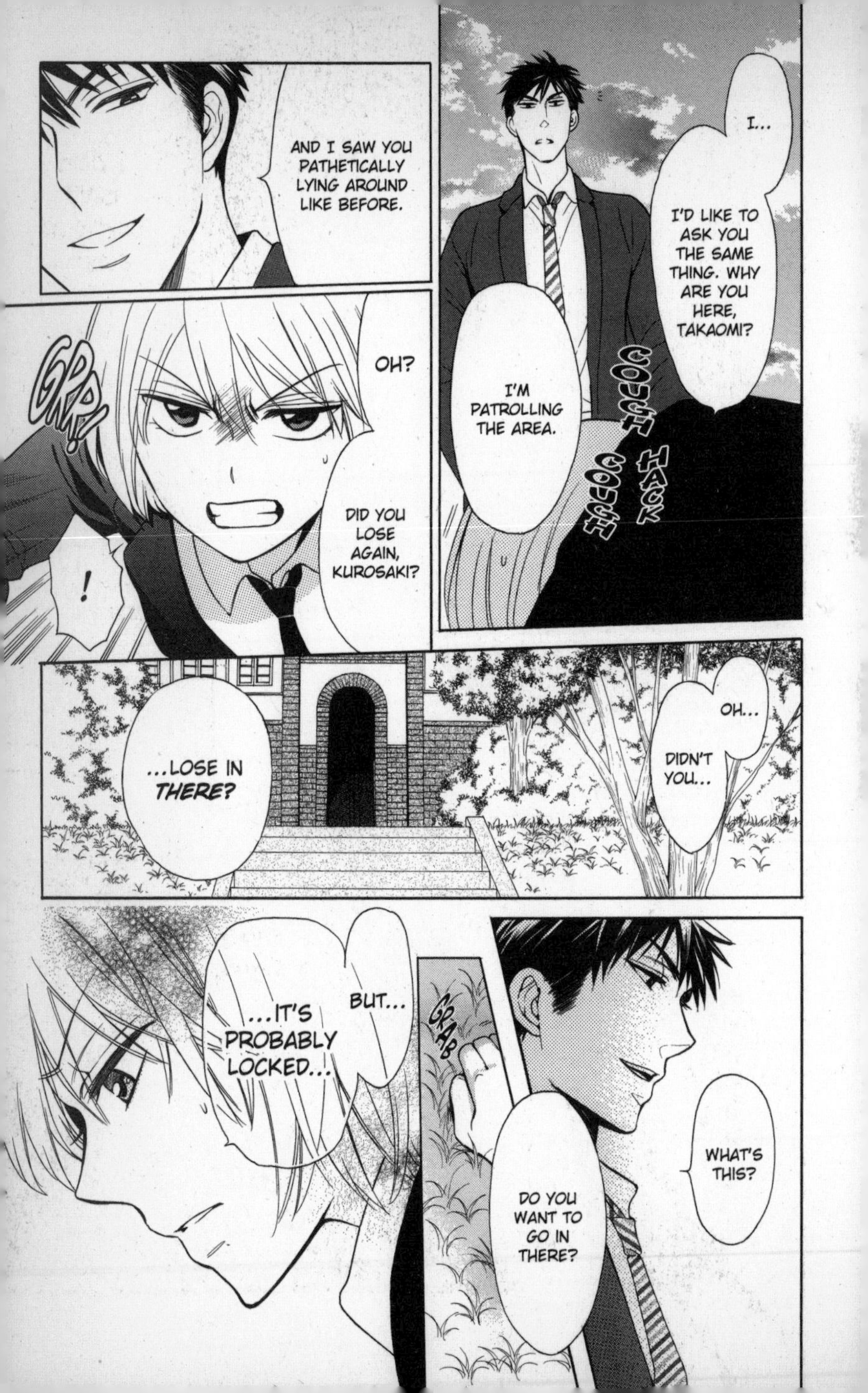
I...
I'D LIKE TO ASK YOU THE SAME THING. WHY ARE YOU HERE, TAKAOMI?
I'M PATROLLING THE AREA.
COUGH HACK
COUGH COUGH
AND I SAW YOU PATHETICALLY LYING AROUND LIKE BEFORE.
OH?
DID YOU LOSE AGAIN, KUROSAKI?
GRR!
!
OH...
DIDN'T YOU...
...LOSE IN THERE?
WHAT'S THIS?
DO YOU WANT TO GO IN THERE?
GRAB
BUT...
...IT'S PROBABLY LOCKED...

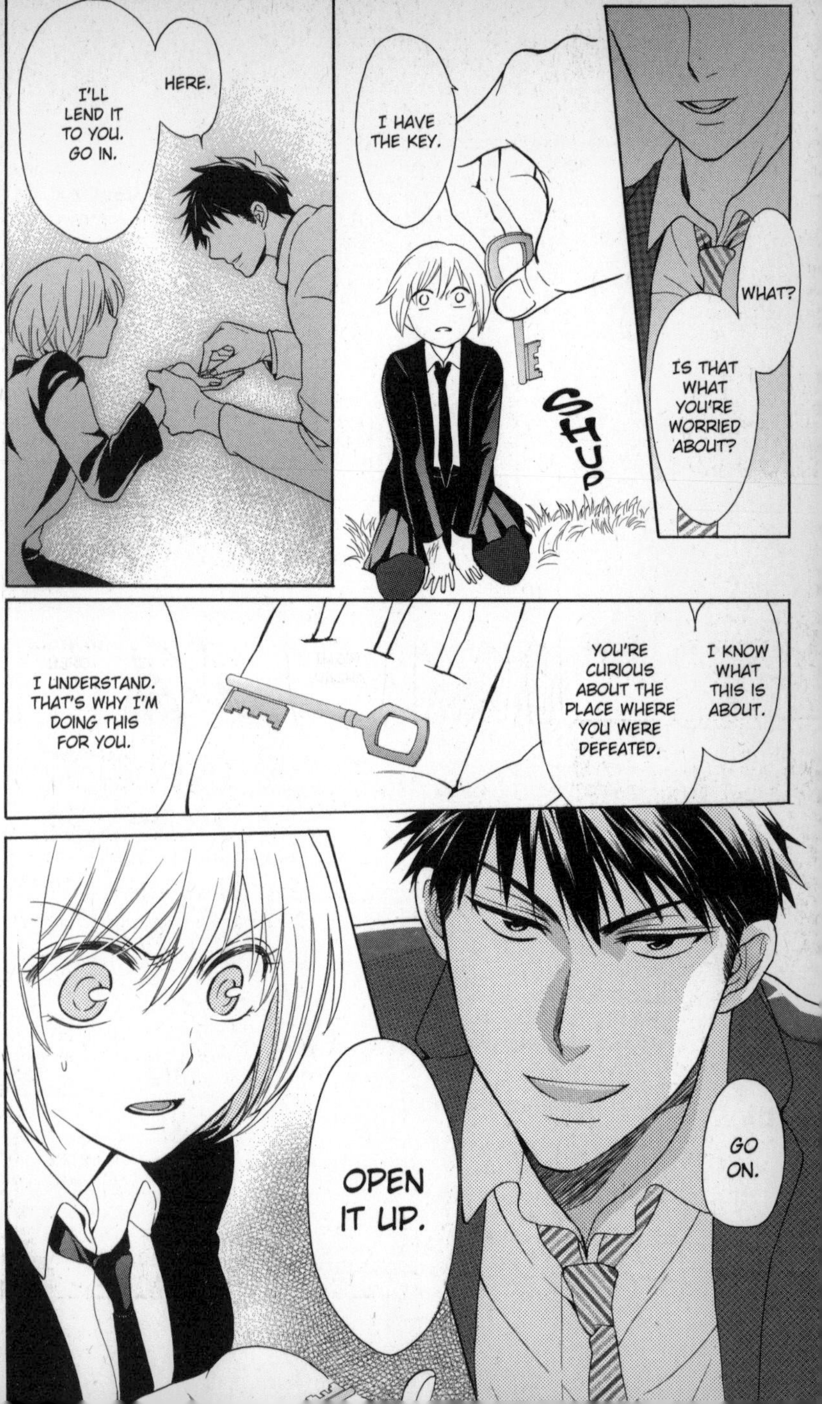
WHAT?
IS THAT WHAT YOU'RE WORRIED ABOUT?
I HAVE THE KEY.
SHUP
HERE.
I'LL LEND IT TO YOU. GO IN.
I KNOW WHAT THIS IS ABOUT.
YOU'RE CURIOUS ABOUT THE PLACE WHERE YOU WERE DEFEATED.
I UNDERSTAND. THAT'S WHY I'M DOING THIS FOR YOU.
GO ON.
OPEN IT UP.

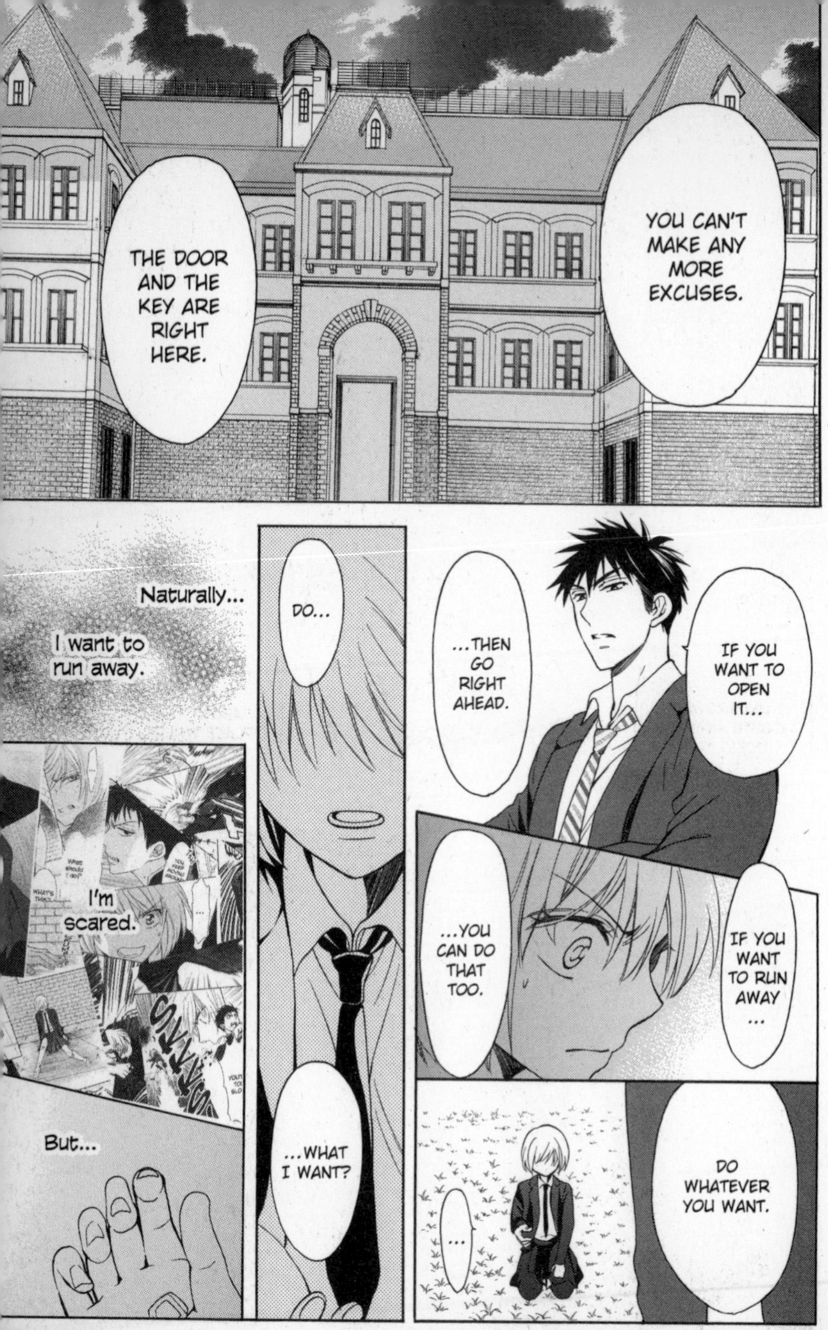
YOU CAN'T MAKE ANY MORE EXCUSES.
THE DOOR AND THE KEY ARE RIGHT HERE.
IF YOU WANT TO OPEN IT...
...THEN GO RIGHT AHEAD.
IF YOU WANT TO RUN AWAY ...
...YOU CAN DO THAT TOO.
DO WHATEVER YOU WANT.
...
DO...
...WHAT I WANT?
Naturally...
I want to run away.
I'm scared.
But...

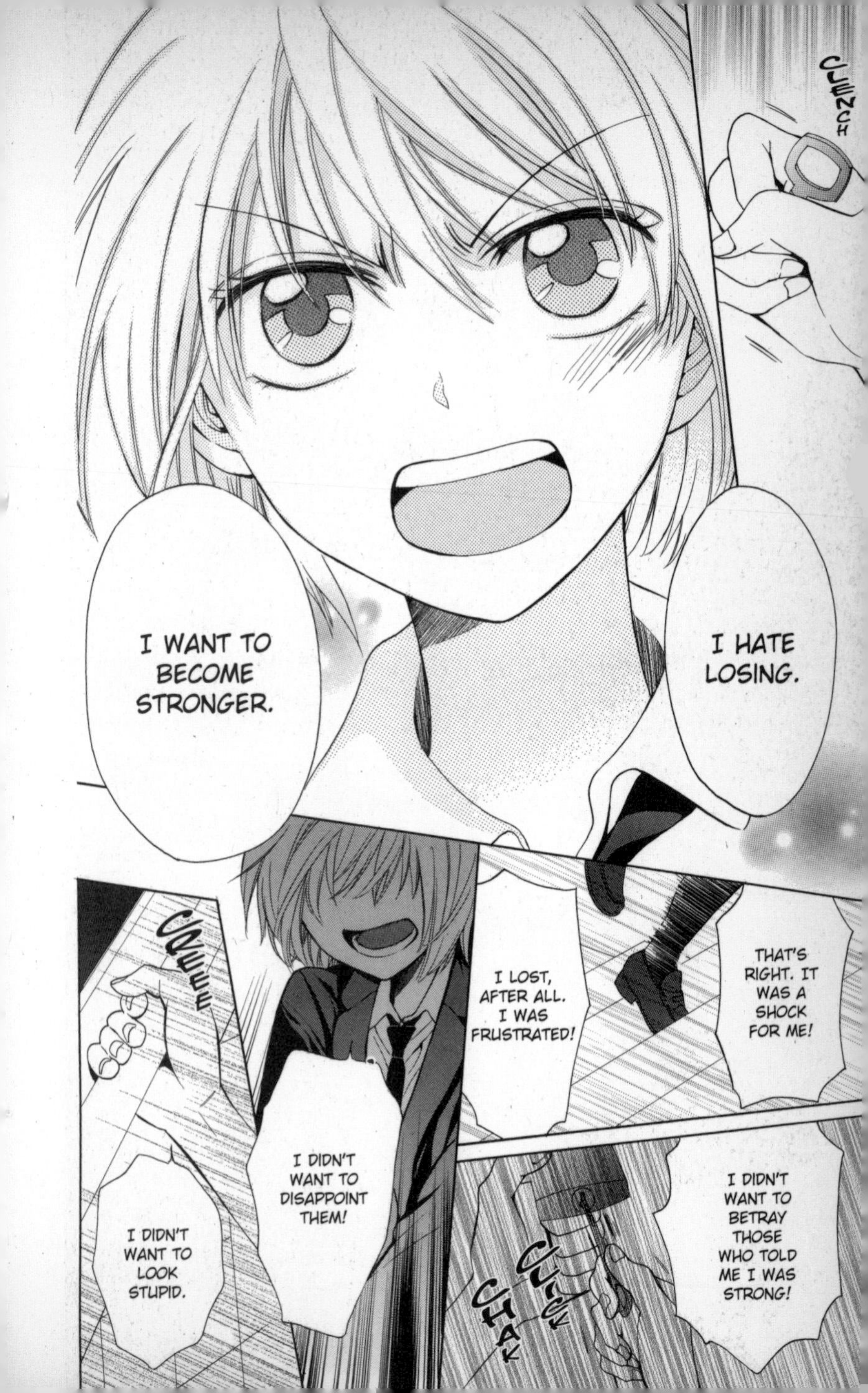
CLENCH
I HATE LOSING.
I WANT TO BECOME STRONGER.
THAT'S RIGHT. IT WAS A SHOCK FOR ME!
I LOST, AFTER ALL. I WAS FRUSTRATED!
CREEE
I DIDN'T WANT TO BETRAY THOSE WHO TOLD ME I WAS STRONG!
CLICK
CHAK
I DIDN'T WANT TO DISAPPOINT THEM!
I DIDN'T WANT TO LOOK STUPID.

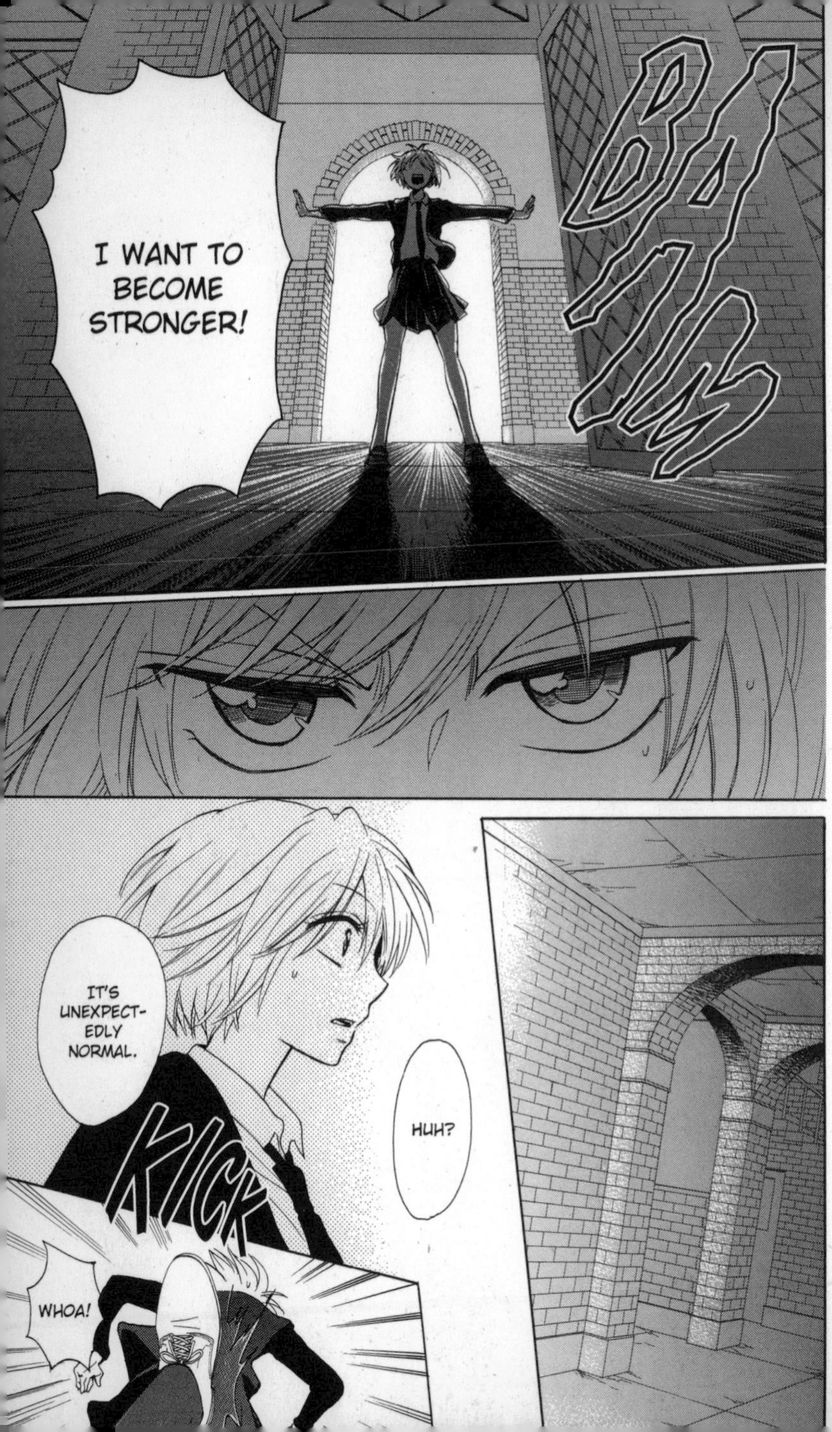
BAM
I WANT TO BECOME STRONGER!
HUH?
IT'S UNEXPECT-EDLY NORMAL.
KICK
WHOA!

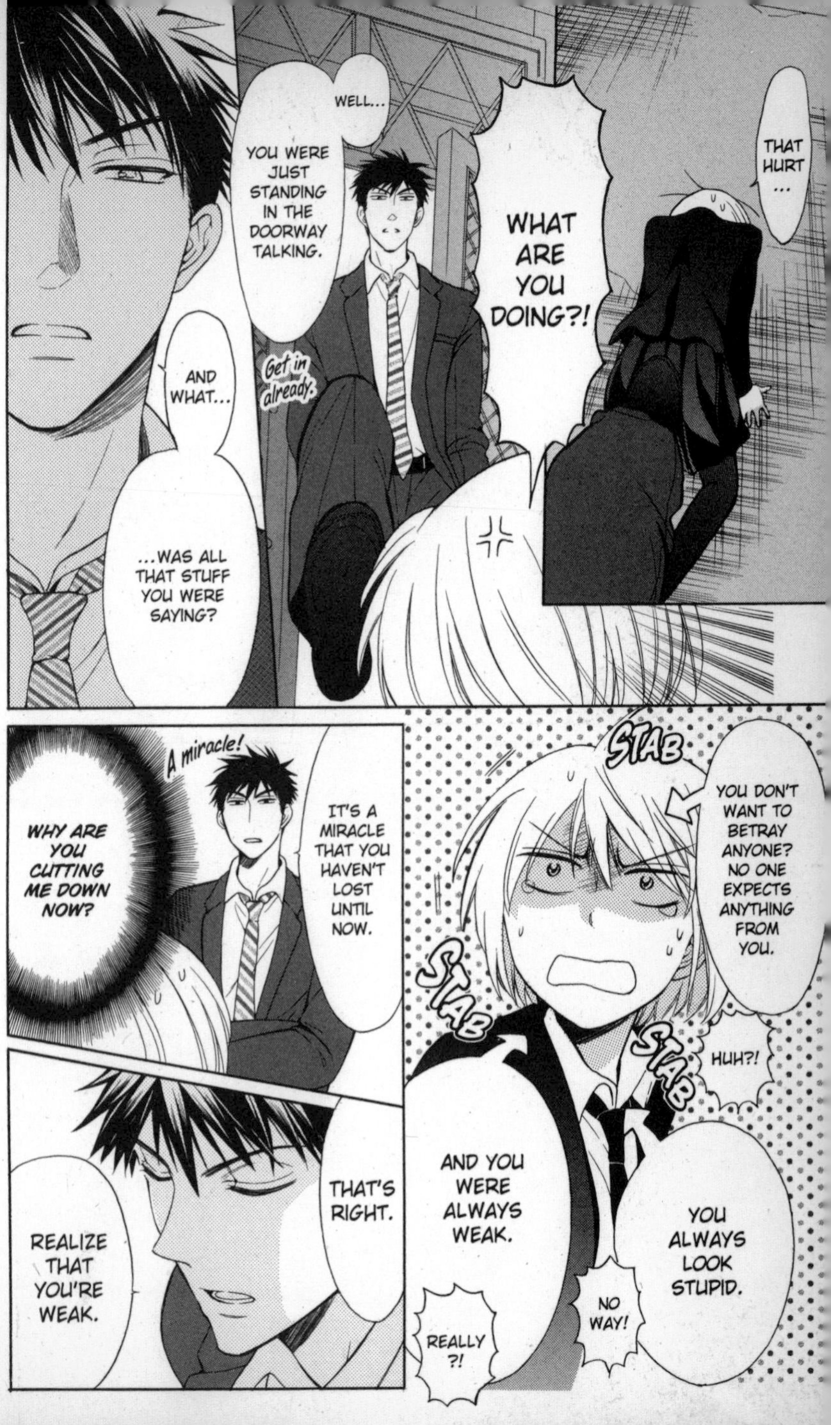
THAT HURT...
WHAT ARE YOU DOING?!
WELL...
YOU WERE JUST STANDING IN THE DOORWAY TALKING.
Get in already.
AND WHAT...
...WAS ALL THAT STUFF YOU WERE SAYING?
STAB
YOU DON'T WANT TO BETRAY ANYONE? NO ONE EXPECTS ANYTHING FROM YOU.
STAB
STAB
HUH?!
YOU ALWAYS LOOK STUPID.
NO WAY!
AND YOU WERE ALWAYS WEAK.
REALLY?!
IT'S A MIRACLE THAT YOU HAVEN'T LOST UNTIL NOW.
A miracle!
WHY ARE YOU CUTTING ME DOWN NOW?
THAT'S RIGHT.
REALIZE THAT YOU'RE WEAK.

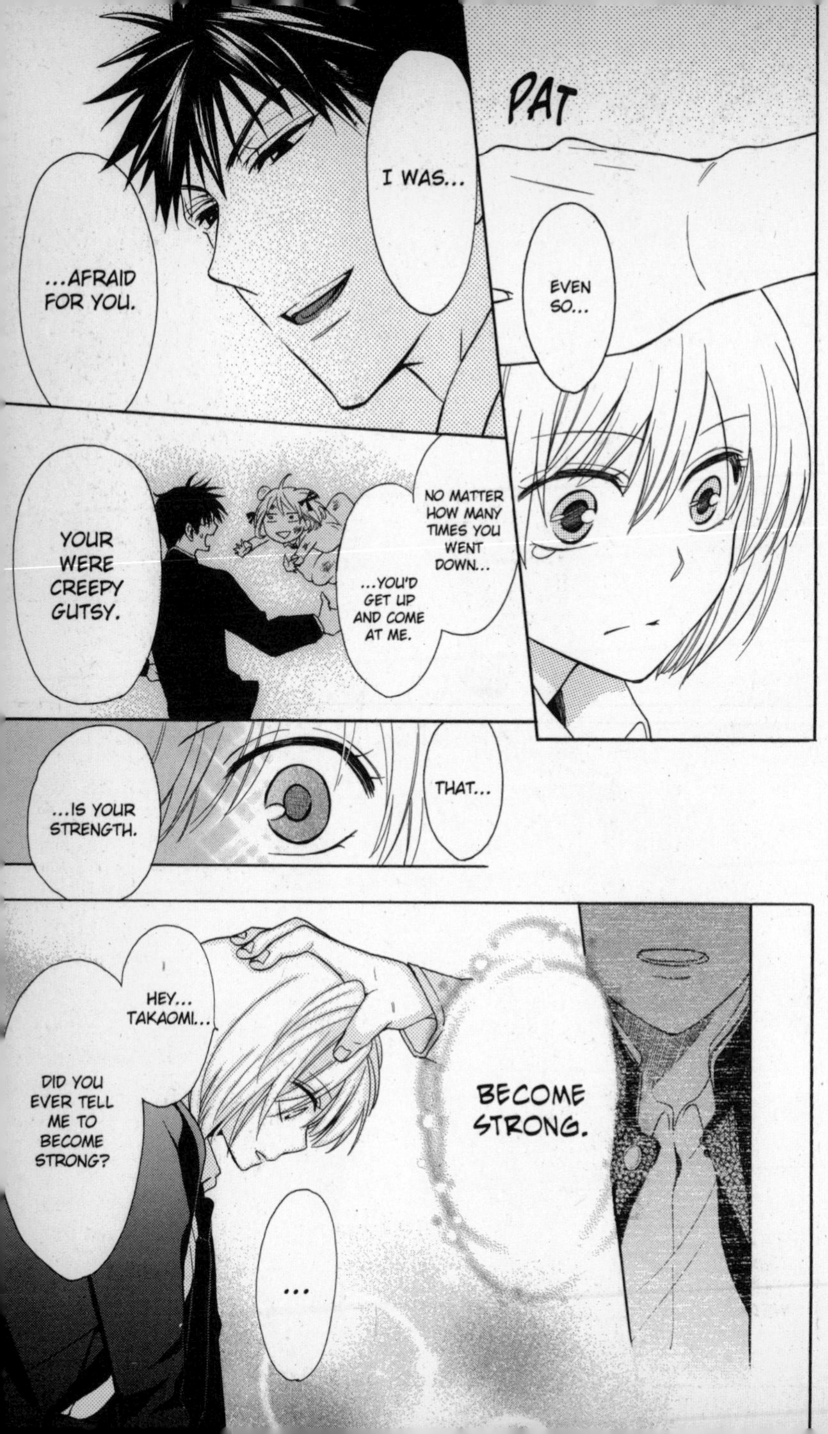
PAT
I WAS...
...AFRAID FOR YOU.
EVEN SO...
NO MATTER HOW MANY TIMES YOU WENT DOWN...
...YOU'D GET UP AND COME AT ME.
YOUR WERE CREEPY GUTSY.
THAT...
...IS YOUR STRENGTH.
BECOME STRONG.
HEY... TAKAOMI...
DID YOU EVER TELL ME TO BECOME STRONG?
...

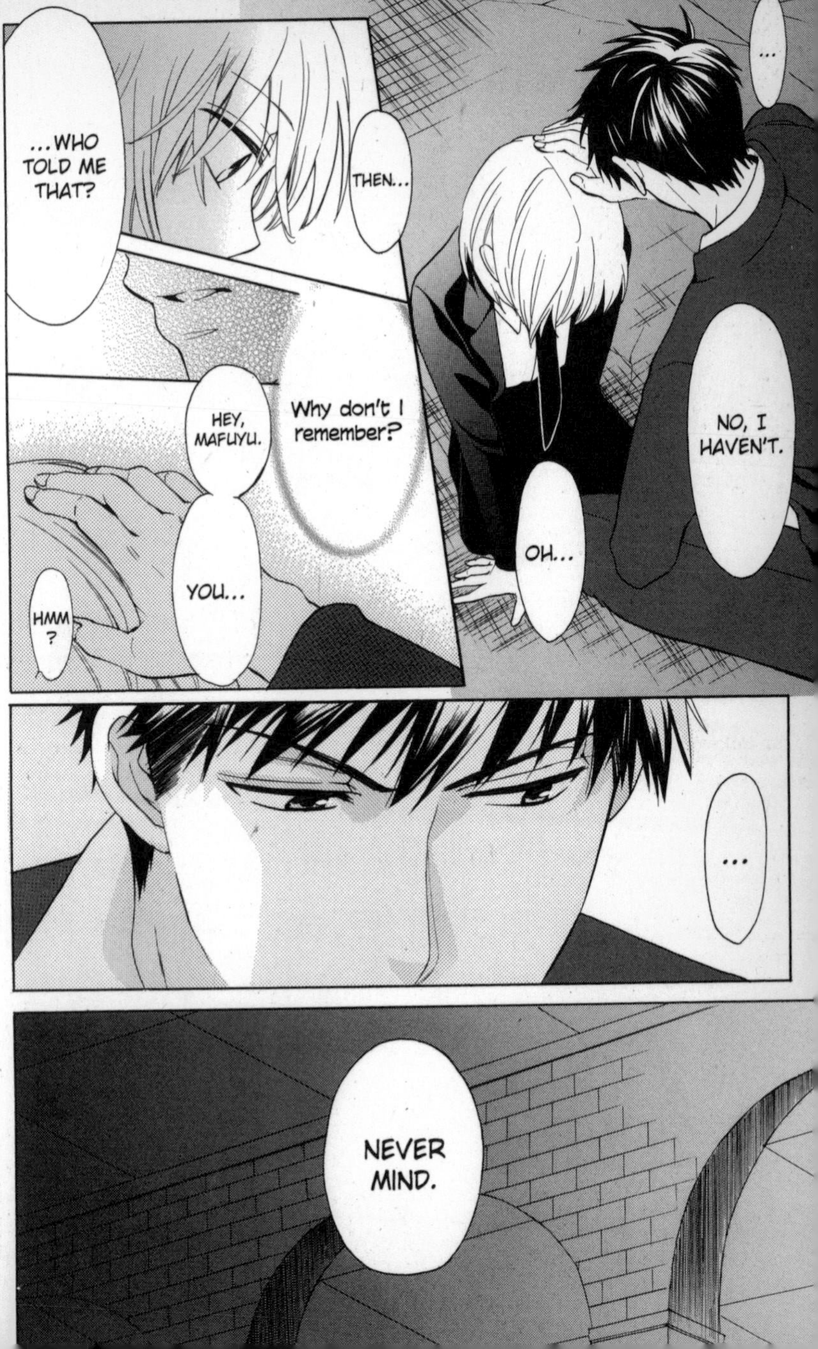
...
NO, I HAVEN'T.
OH...
THEN...
...WHO TOLD ME THAT?
Why don't I remember?
HEY, MAFUYU.
YOU...
HMM?
...
NEVER MIND.

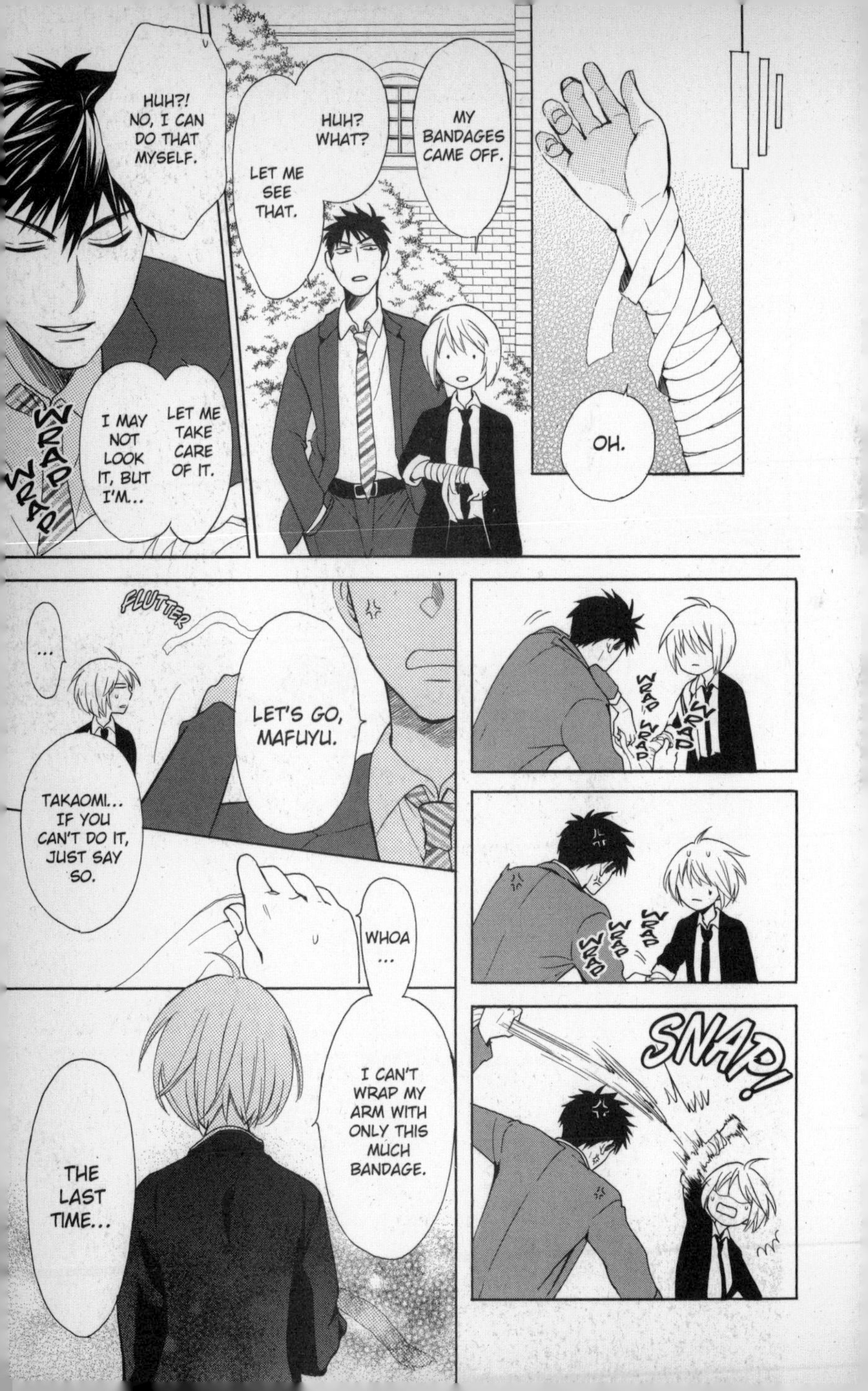
OH.
MY BANDAGES CAME OFF.
HUH? WHAT?
LET ME SEE THAT.
HUH?! NO, I CAN DO THAT MYSELF.
LET ME TAKE CARE OF IT.
I MAY NOT LOOK IT, BUT I'M...
WRAP
WRAP
WRAP WRAP WRAP
WRAP WRAP WRAP
SNAP!
LET'S GO, MAFUYU.
FLUTTER
...
TAKAOMI... IF YOU CAN'T DO IT, JUST SAY SO.
WHOA...
I CAN'T WRAP MY ARM WITH ONLY THIS MUCH BANDAGE.
THE LAST TIME...

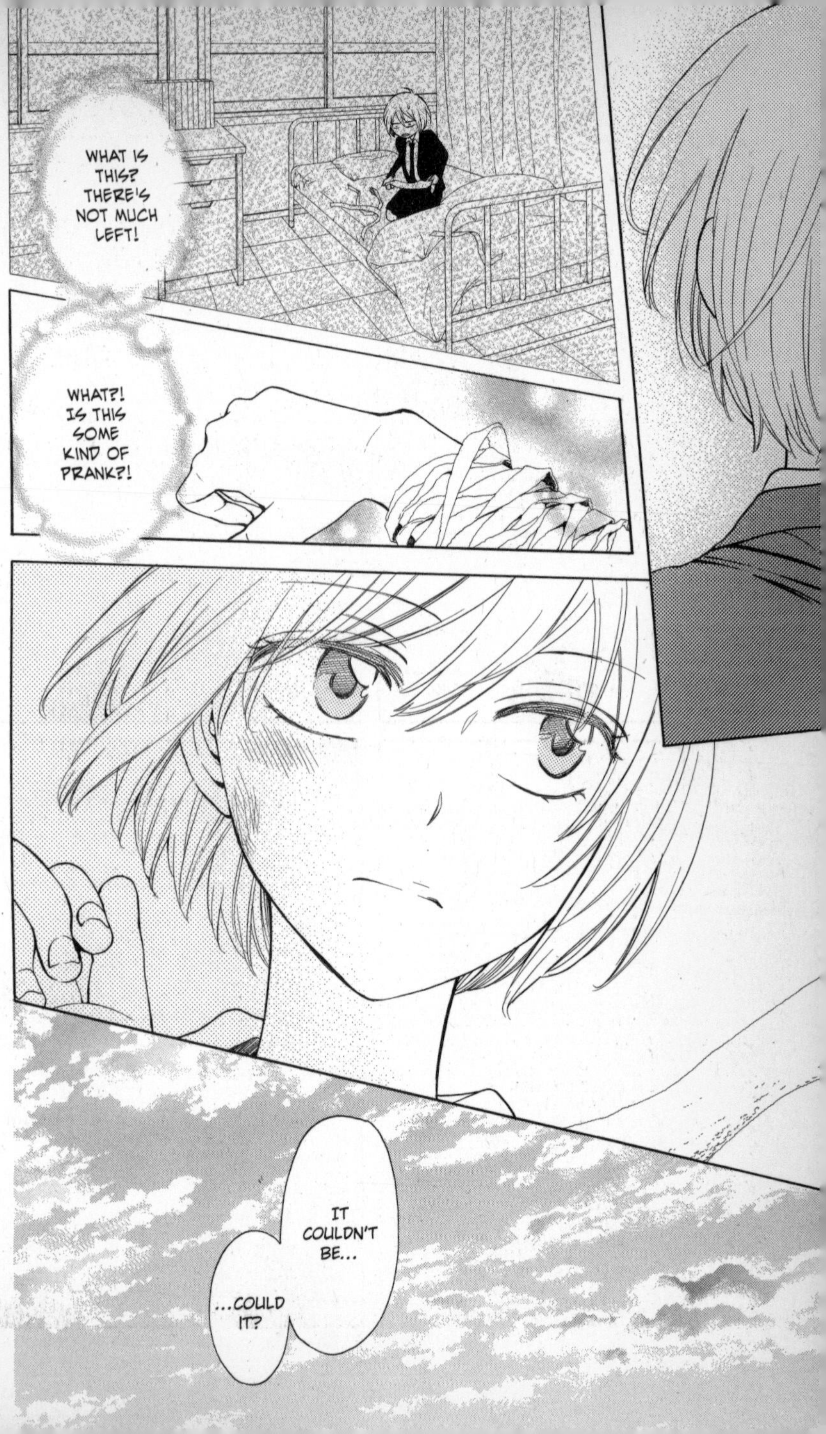
WHAT IS THIS? THERE'S NOT MUCH LEFT!
WHAT?! IS THIS SOME KIND OF PRANK?!
IT COULDN'T BE...
...COULD IT?

GOING ALONE

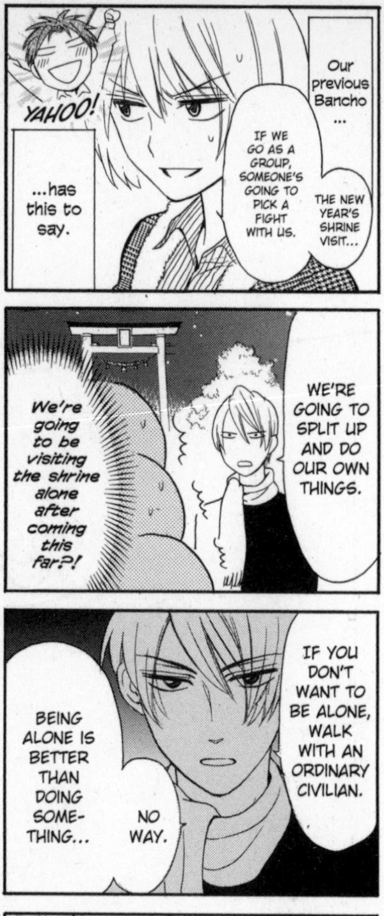
Our previous Bancho ...
THE NEW YEAR'S SHRINE VISIT...
IF WE GO AS A GROUP, SOMEONE'S GOING TO PICK A FIGHT WITH US.
YAHOO!
...has this to say.
WE'RE GOING TO SPLIT UP AND DO OUR OWN THINGS.
We're going to be visiting the shrine alone after coming this far?!
IF YOU DON'T WANT TO BE ALONE, WALK WITH AN ORDINARY CIVILIAN.
NO WAY.
BEING ALONE IS BETTER THAN DOING SOME-THING...
...THAT PATHETIC.
HELLO?
OH, MOM? IS SIS THERE?
GRAND-MA?
AWW, JUST HANG OUT WITH YOUR BIG BROTHER!

NEXT YEAR'S LUCK

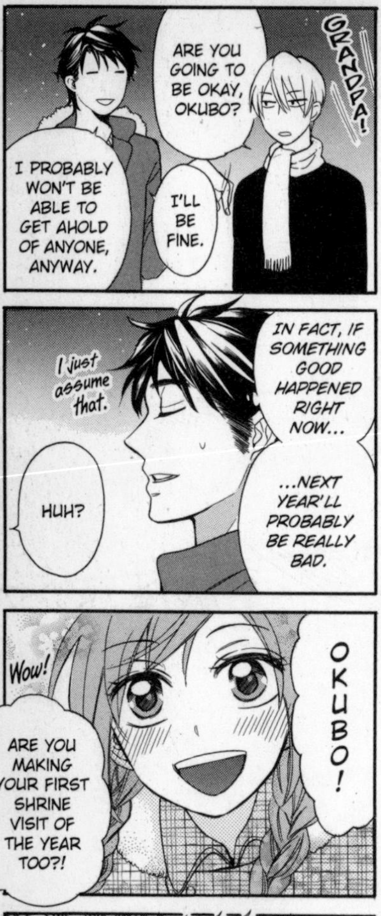
GRANDPA!
ARE YOU GOING TO BE OKAY, OKUBO?
I'LL BE FINE.
I PROBABLY WON'T BE ABLE TO GET AHOLD OF ANYONE, ANYWAY.
IN FACT, IF SOMETHING GOOD HAPPENED RIGHT NOW...
...NEXT YEAR'LL PROBABLY BE REALLY BAD.
I just assume that.
HUH?
OKUBO!
Wow!
ARE YOU MAKING YOUR FIRST SHRINE VISIT OF THE YEAR TOO?!
NEXT YEAR MIGHT BE NO GOOD!
WHAT?!
ALREADY!

Chapter 62

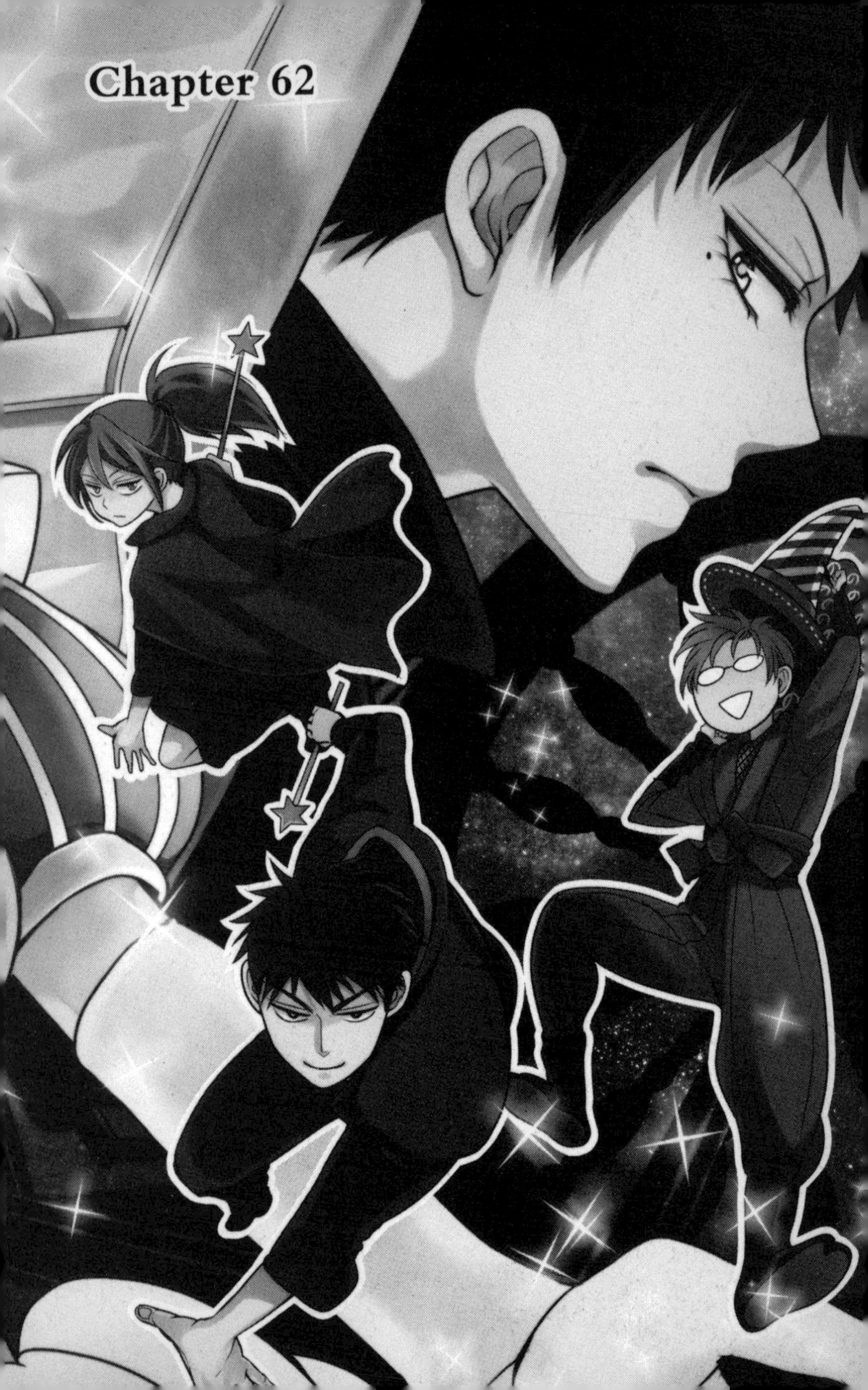

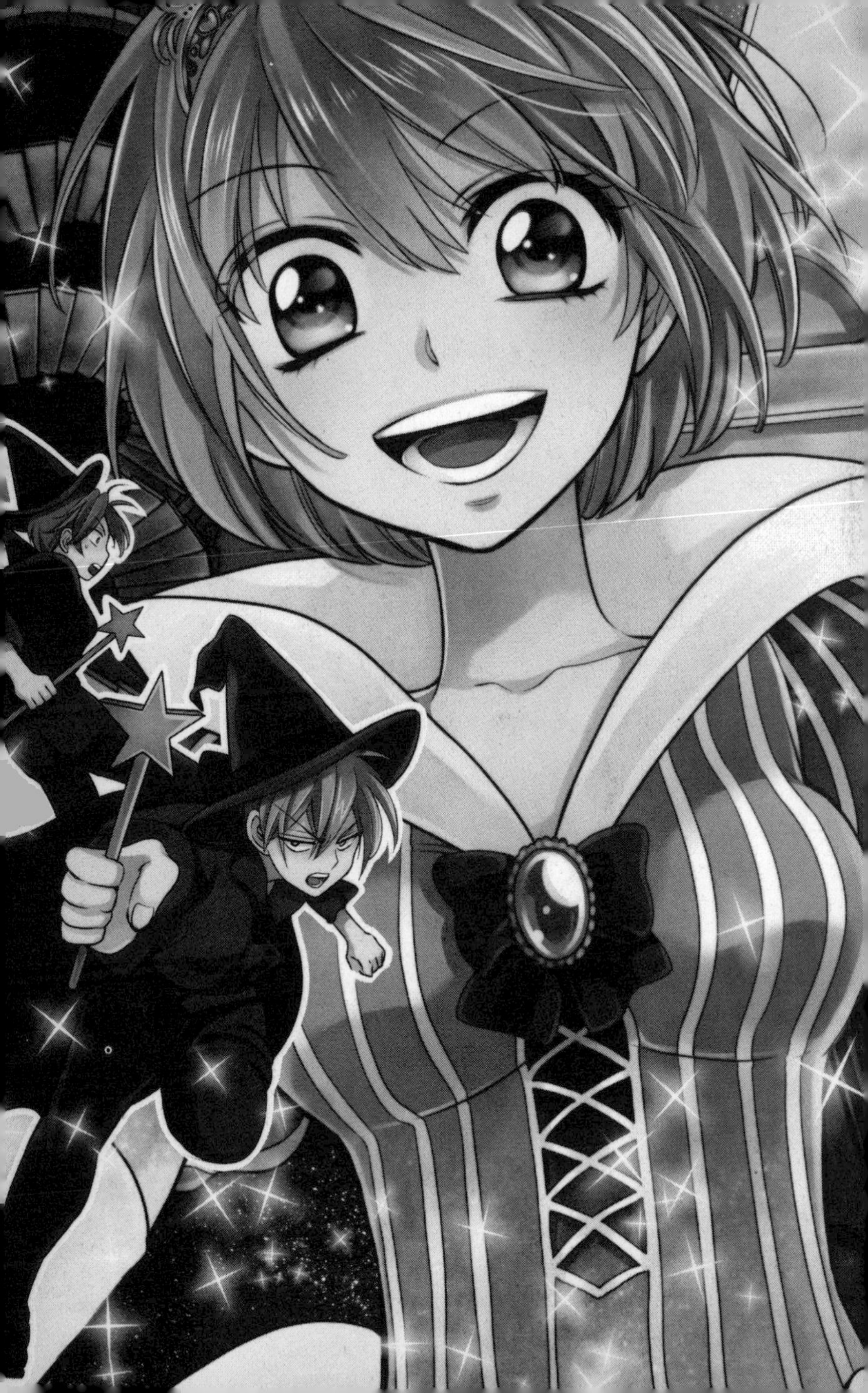

GOOD LUCK TIME

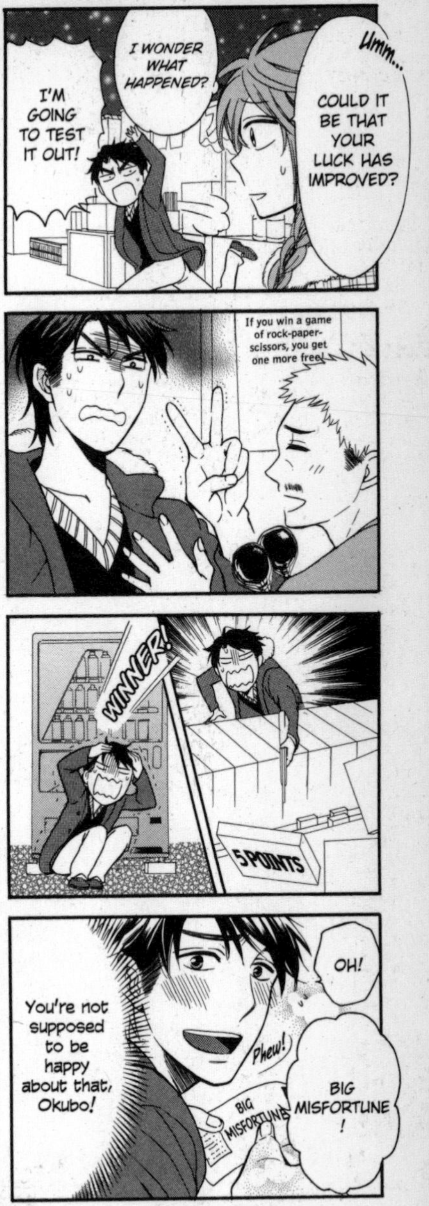
Umm...
COULD IT BE THAT YOUR LUCK HAS IMPROVED?
I WONDER WHAT HAPPENED?
I'M GOING TO TEST IT OUT!
If you win a game of rock-paper-scissors, you get one more free!
WINNER!
5 POINTS
OH!
BIG MISFORTUNE!
Phew!
BIG MISFORTUNE
You're not supposed to be happy about that, Okubo!

FIRST WISH OF THE YEAR

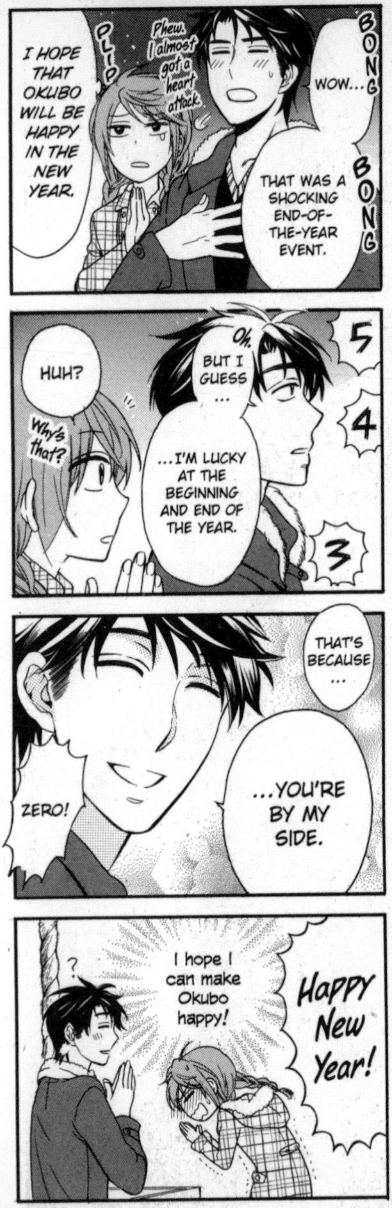
BONG BONG
WOW...
THAT WAS A SHOCKING END-OF-THE-YEAR EVENT.
Phew. I almost got a heart attack.
PLIP
I HOPE THAT OKUBO WILL BE HAPPY IN THE NEW YEAR.
5
Oh.
BUT I GUESS...
4
...I'M LUCKY AT THE BEGINNING AND END OF THE YEAR.
3
HUH?
Why's that?
THAT'S BECAUSE...
...YOU'RE BY MY SIDE.
ZERO!
Happy New Year!
I hope I can make Okubo happy!
?

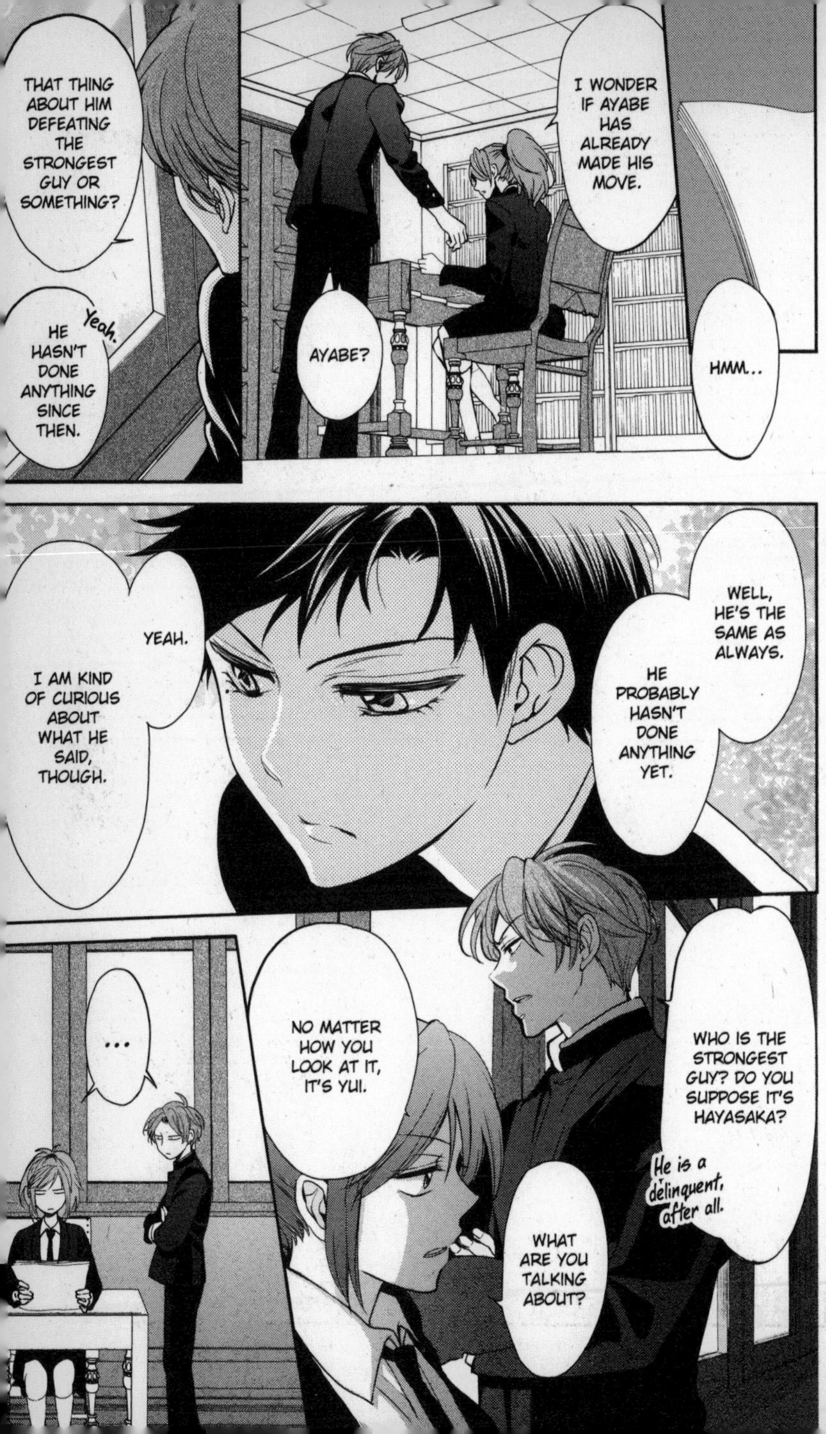
I WONDER IF AYABE HAS ALREADY MADE HIS MOVE.
HMM...
AYABE?
THAT THING ABOUT HIM DEFEATING THE STRONGEST GUY OR SOMETHING?
Yeah.
HE HASN'T DONE ANYTHING SINCE THEN.
WELL, HE'S THE SAME AS ALWAYS.
HE PROBABLY HASN'T DONE ANYTHING YET.
YEAH.
I AM KIND OF CURIOUS ABOUT WHAT HE SAID, THOUGH.
WHO IS THE STRONGEST GUY? DO YOU SUPPOSE IT'S HAYASAKA?
He is a delinquent, after all.
WHAT ARE YOU TALKING ABOUT?
NO MATTER HOW YOU LOOK AT IT, IT'S YUI.
...

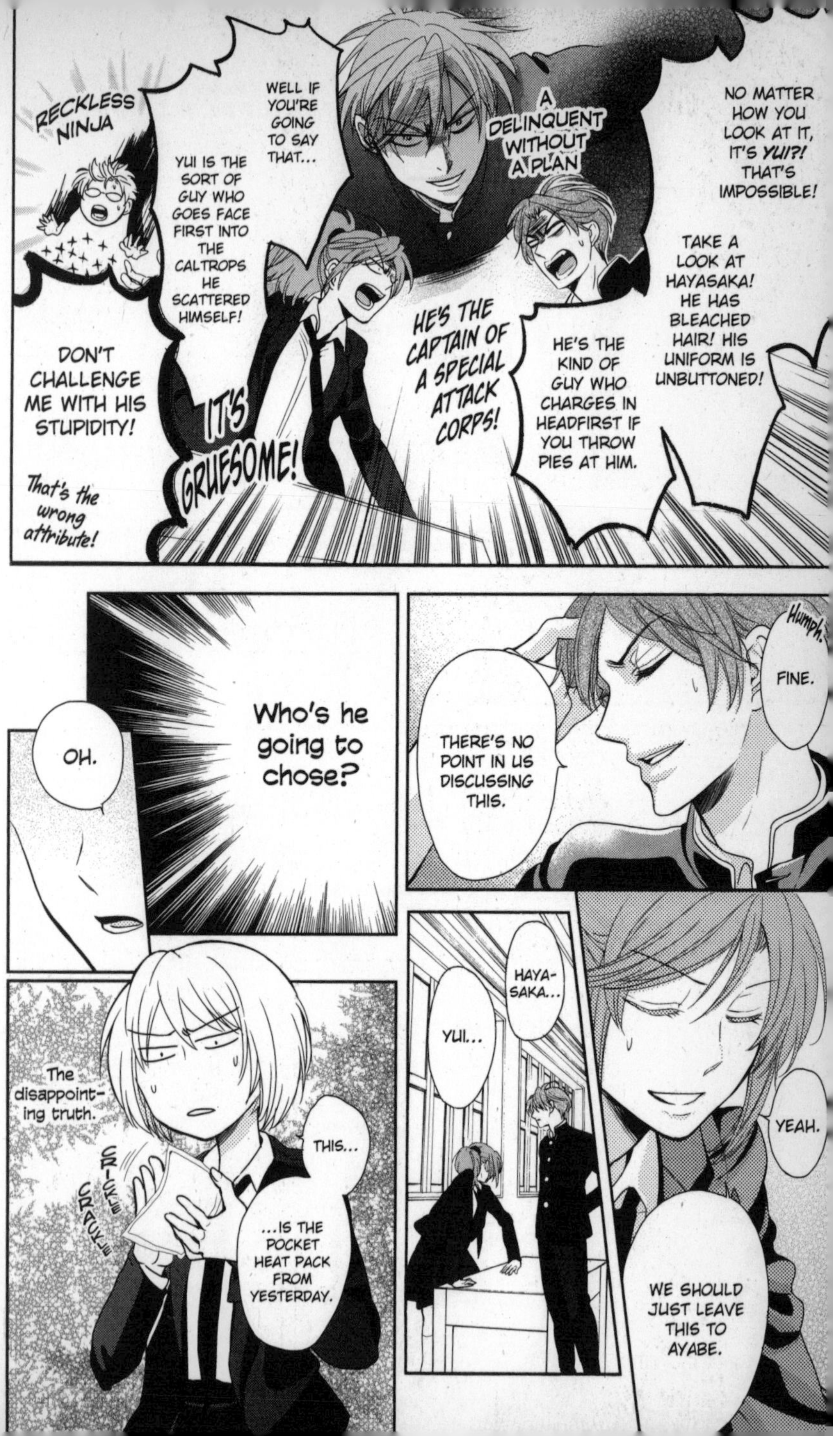
NO MATTER HOW YOU LOOK AT IT, IT'S YUI?! THAT'S IMPOSSIBLE!
TAKE A LOOK AT HAYASAKA! HE HAS BLEACHED HAIR! HIS UNIFORM IS UNBUTTONED!
A DELINQUENT WITHOUT A PLAN
HE'S THE KIND OF GUY WHO CHARGES IN HEADFIRST IF YOU THROW PIES AT HIM.
HE'S THE CAPTAIN OF A SPECIAL ATTACK CORPS!
WELL IF YOU'RE GOING TO SAY THAT...
YUI IS THE SORT OF GUY WHO GOES FACE FIRST INTO THE CALTROPS HE SCATTERED HIMSELF!
IT'S GRUESOME!
RECKLESS NINJA
DON'T CHALLENGE ME WITH HIS STUPIDITY!
That's the wrong attribute!
Humph.
FINE.
THERE'S NO POINT IN US DISCUSSING THIS.
Who's he going to chose?
OH.
YEAH.
WE SHOULD JUST LEAVE THIS TO AYABE.
HAYA-SAKA...
YUI...
THIS...
...IS THE POCKET HEAT PACK FROM YESTERDAY.
CRICKLE CRACKLE
The disappointing truth.

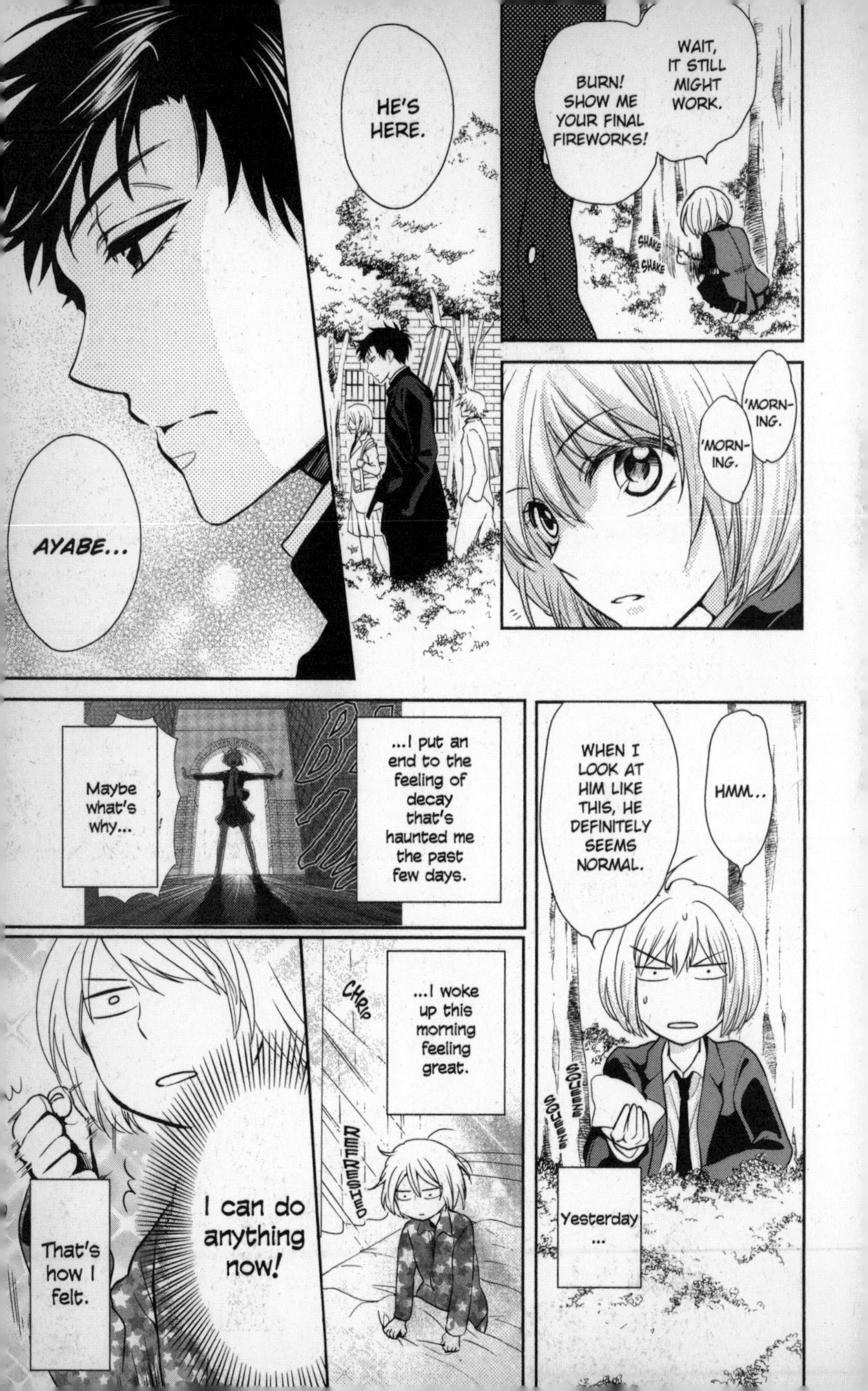
WAIT, IT STILL MIGHT WORK.
BURN! SHOW ME YOUR FINAL FIREWORKS!
SHAKE
SHAKE
'MORN-ING.
'MORN-ING.
HE'S HERE.
AYABE...
HMM..
WHEN I LOOK AT HIM LIKE THIS, HE DEFINITELY SEEMS NORMAL.
Yesterday ...
...I put an end to the feeling of decay that's haunted me the past few days.
Maybe what's why...
...I woke up this morning feeling great.
CHRIP
REFRESHED
I can do anything now!
That's how I felt.

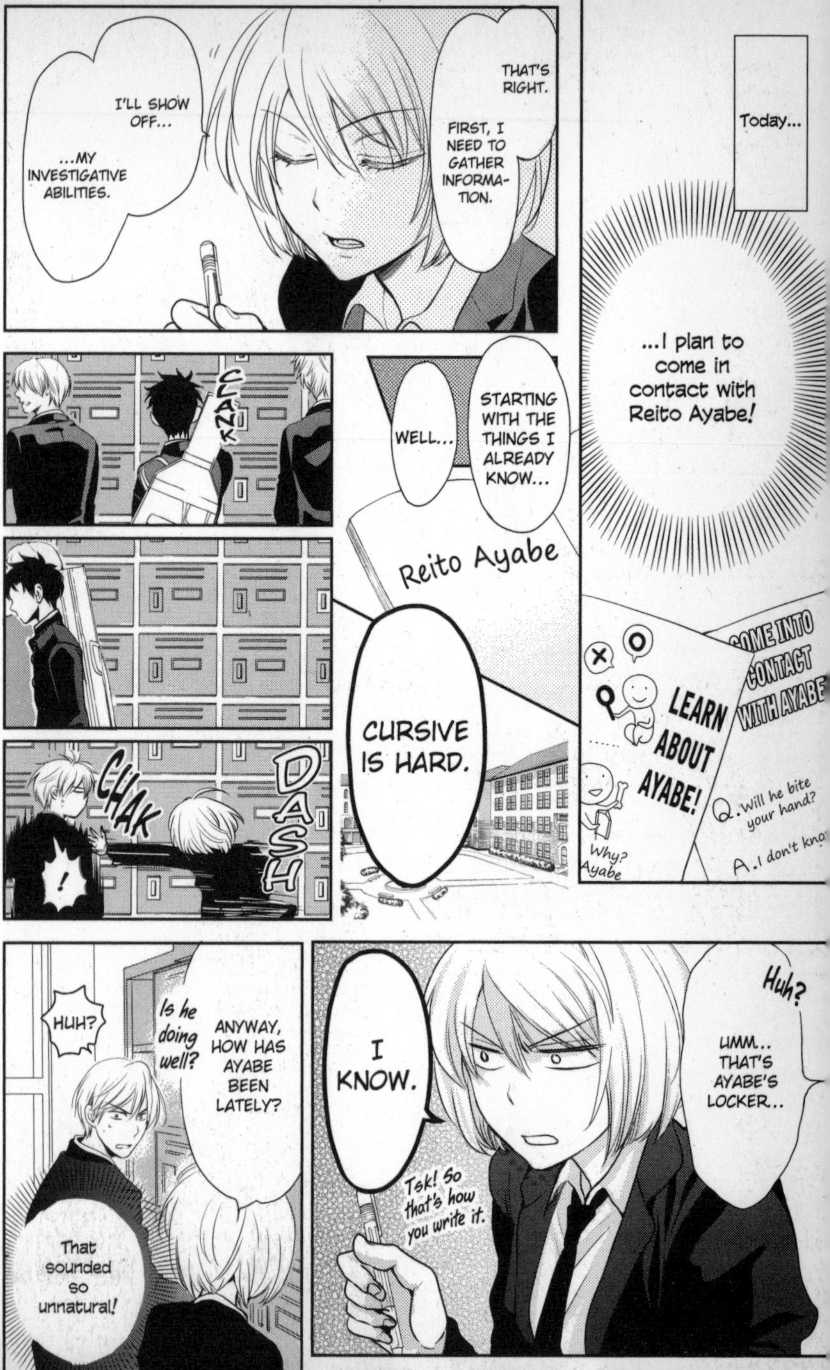
Today...
...I plan to come in contact with Reito Ayabe!
COME INTO CONTACT WITH AYABE
LEARN ABOUT AYABE!
Q. Will he bite your hand?
A. I don't kno
Why? Ayabe
THAT'S RIGHT.
FIRST, I NEED TO GATHER INFORMATION.
I'LL SHOW OFF...
...MY INVESTIGATIVE ABILITIES.
STARTING WITH THE THINGS I ALREADY KNOW...
WELL...
Reito Ayabe
CURSIVE IS HARD.
CLANK
CHAK
DASH
!
Huh?
UMM... THAT'S AYABE'S LOCKER...
I KNOW.
Tsk! So that's how you write it.
ANYWAY, HOW HAS AYABE BEEN LATELY?
Is he doing well?
HUH?
That sounded so unnatural!

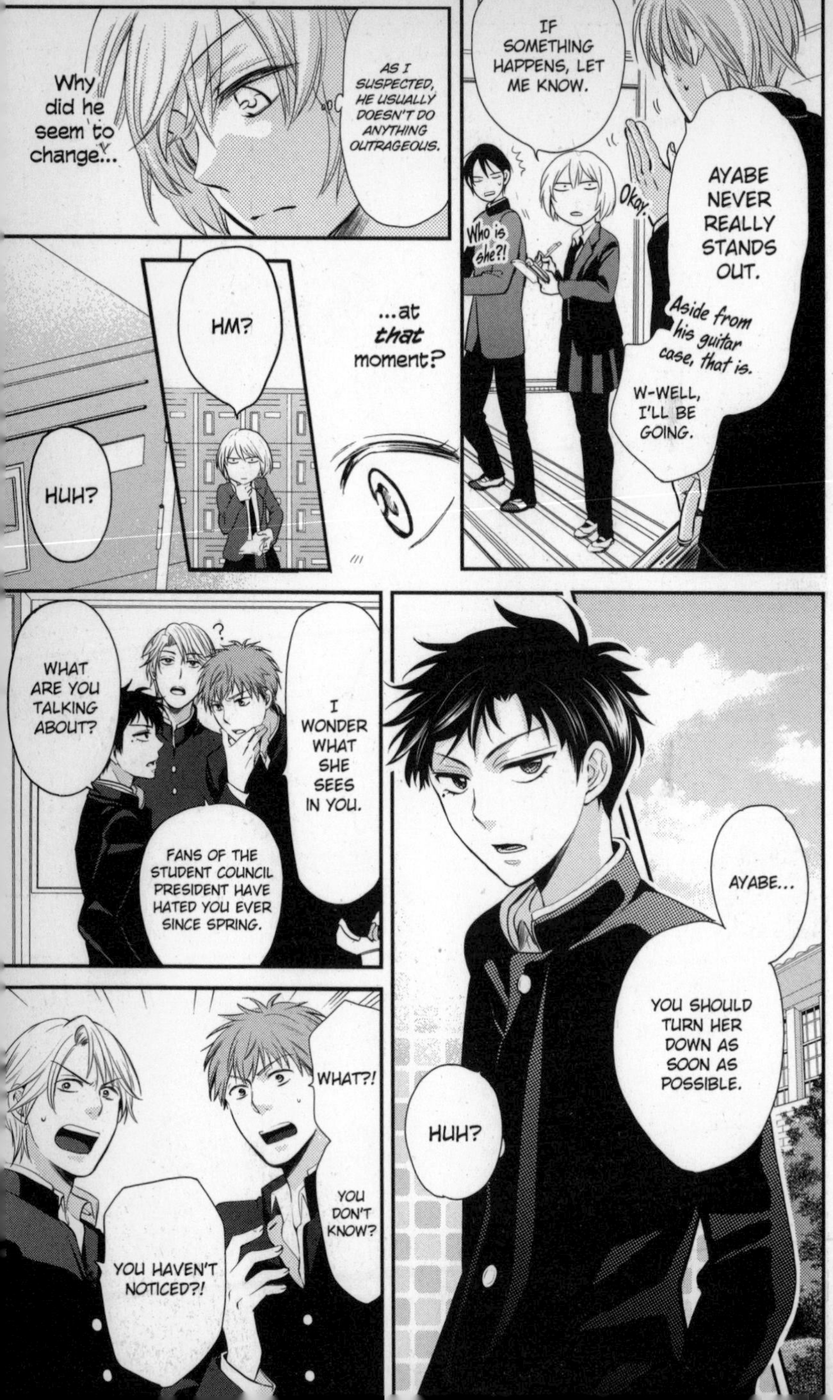
IF SOMETHING HAPPENS, LET ME KNOW.
Okay.
Who is she?!
AYABE NEVER REALLY STANDS OUT.
Aside from his guitar case, that is.
W-WELL, I'LL BE GOING.
AS I SUSPECTED, HE USUALLY DOESN'T DO ANYTHING OUTRAGEOUS.
Why did he seem to change...
HM?
...at *that* moment?
HUH?
AYABE...
YOU SHOULD TURN HER DOWN AS SOON AS POSSIBLE.
HUH?
I WONDER WHAT SHE SEES IN YOU.
WHAT ARE YOU TALKING ABOUT?
FANS OF THE STUDENT COUNCIL PRESIDENT HAVE HATED YOU EVER SINCE SPRING.
WHAT?!
YOU DON'T KNOW?
YOU HAVEN'T NOTICED?!

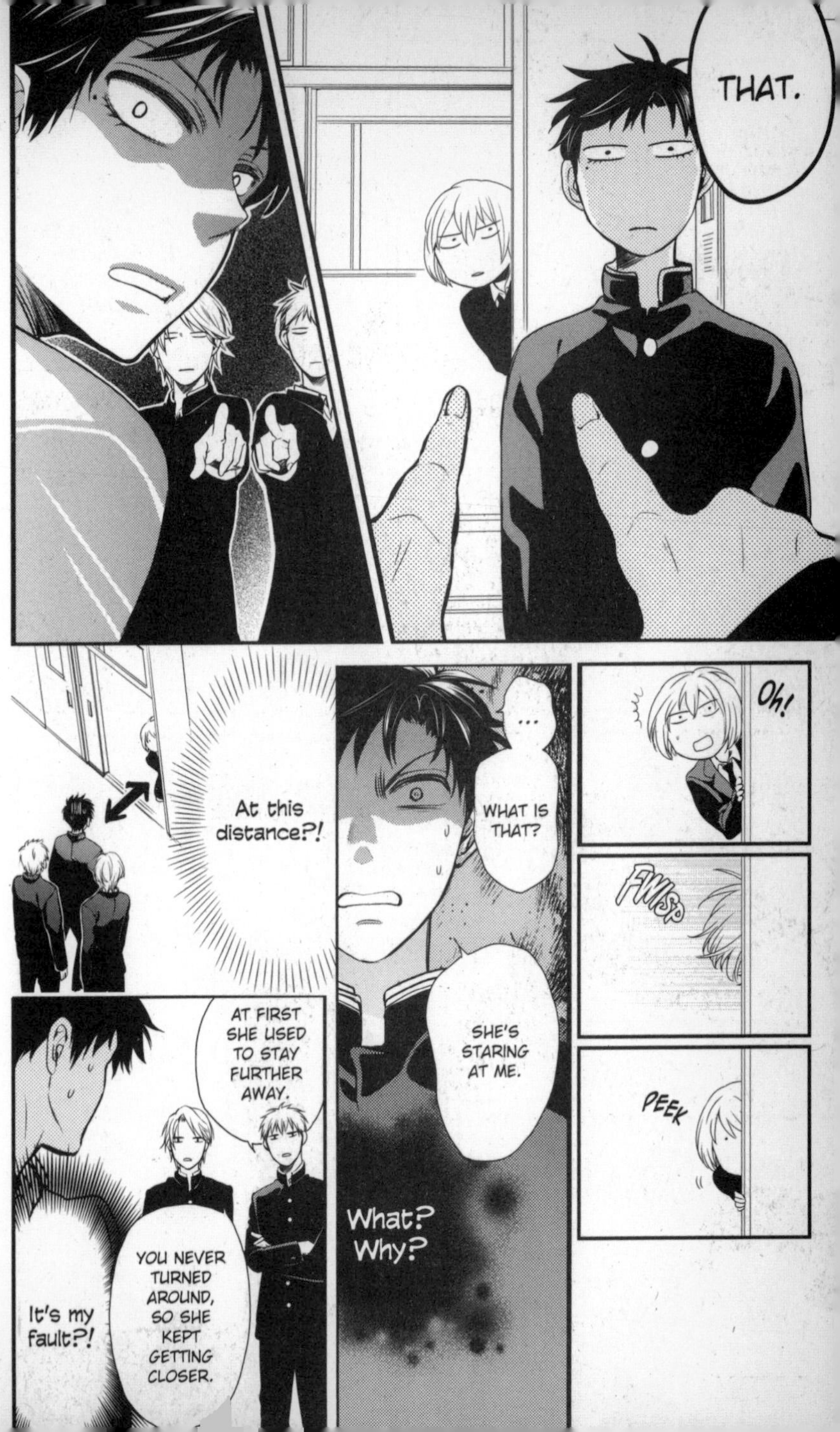
THAT.
Oh!
FWISP
PEEK
...
WHAT IS THAT?
SHE'S STARING AT ME.
What? Why?
At this distance?!
AT FIRST SHE USED TO STAY FURTHER AWAY.
YOU NEVER TURNED AROUND, SO SHE KEPT GETTING CLOSER.
It's my fault?!

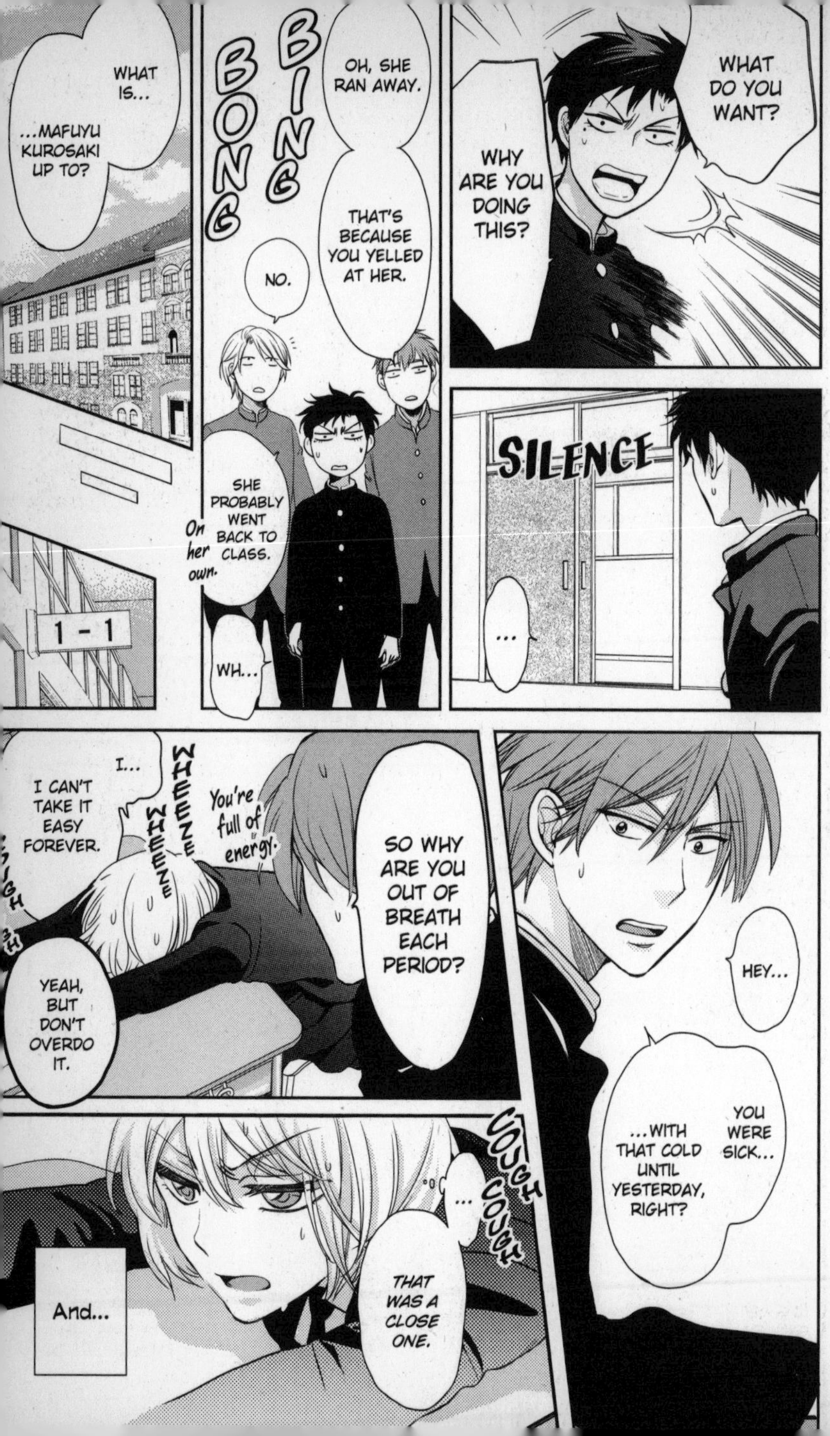
WHAT DO YOU WANT?
WHY ARE YOU DOING THIS?
SILENCE
...
BING BONG
OH, SHE RAN AWAY.
THAT'S BECAUSE YOU YELLED AT HER.
NO.
SHE PROBABLY WENT BACK TO CLASS.
On her own.
WH...
WHAT IS...
...MAFUYU KUROSAKI UP TO?
1 - 1
HEY...
YOU WERE SICK...
...WITH THAT COLD UNTIL YESTERDAY, RIGHT?
SO WHY ARE YOU OUT OF BREATH EACH PERIOD?
You're full of energy.
WHEEZE WHEEZE
I...
I CAN'T TAKE IT EASY FOREVER.
YEAH, BUT DON'T OVERDO IT.
COUGH COUGH
...
THAT WAS A CLOSE ONE.
And...

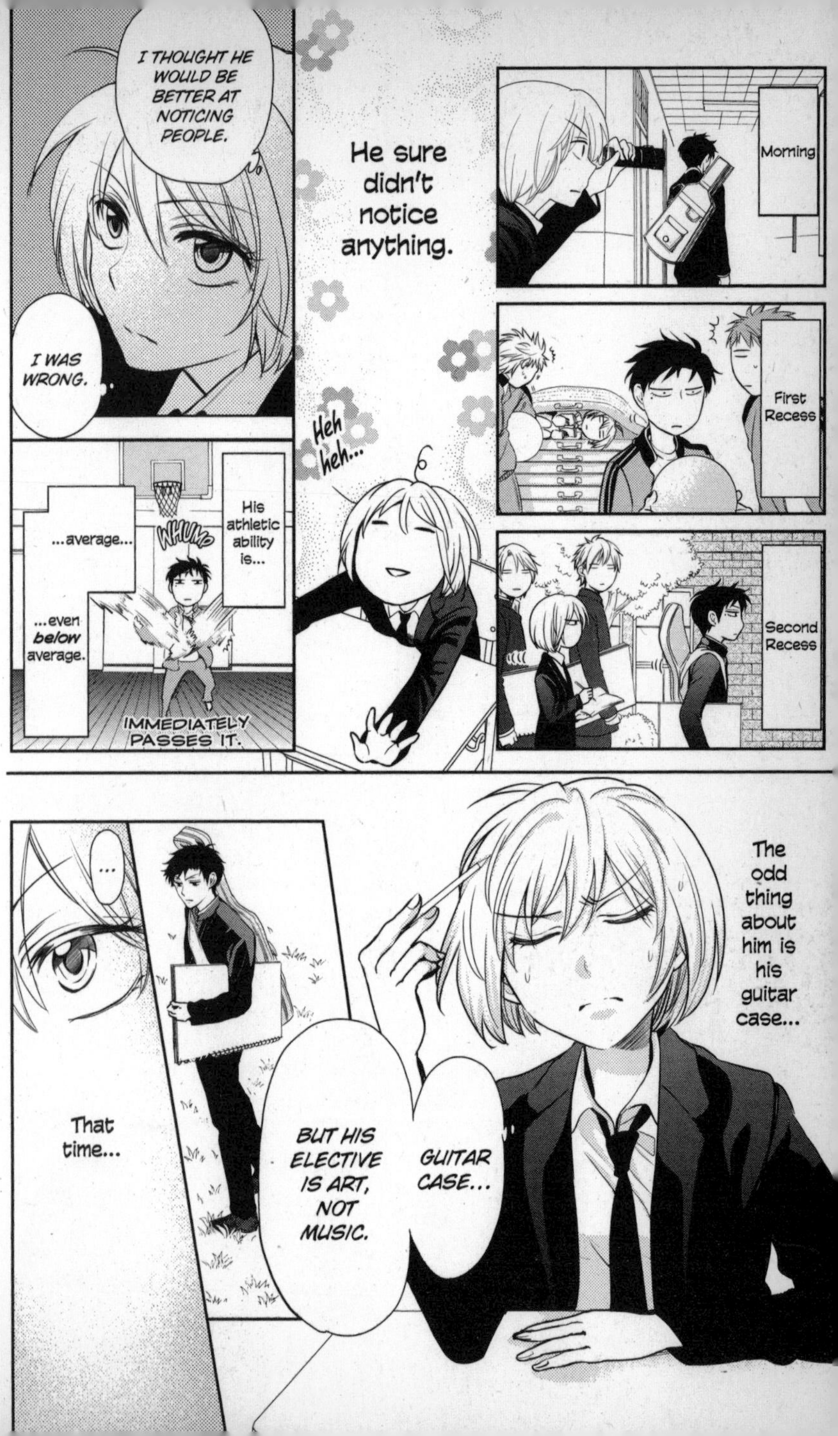
Morning
First Recess
Second Recess
He sure didn't notice anything.
Heh heh...
I THOUGHT HE WOULD BE BETTER AT NOTICING PEOPLE.
I WAS WRONG.
His athletic ability is...
WHUMP
...average...
...even below average.
IMMEDIATELY PASSES IT.
The odd thing about him is his guitar case...
GUITAR CASE...
BUT HIS ELECTIVE IS ART, NOT MUSIC.
...
That time...

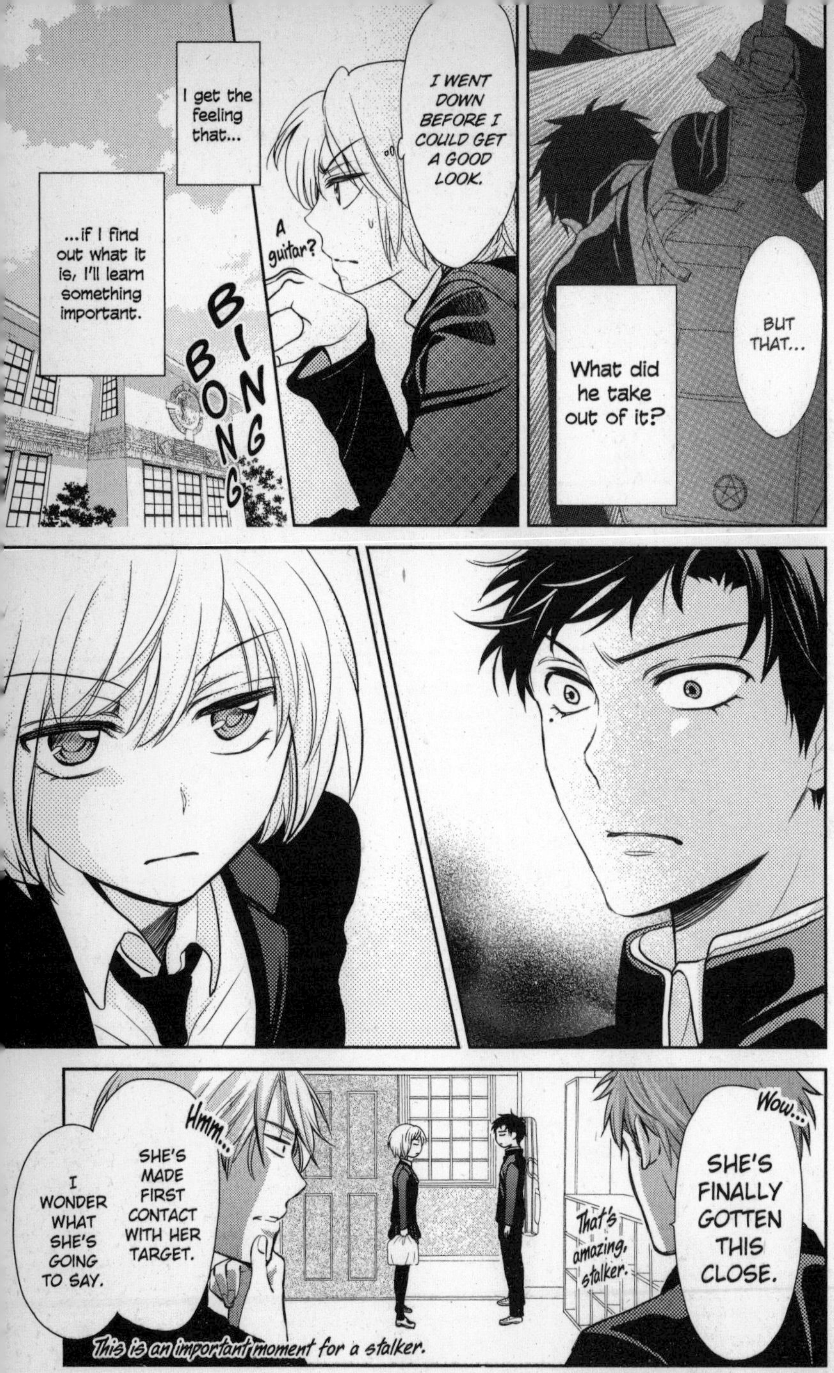
BUT THAT...
What did he take out of it?
I WENT DOWN BEFORE I COULD GET A GOOD LOOK.
A guitar?
I get the feeling that...
...if I find out what it is, I'll learn something important.
BING BONG
Wow...
SHE'S FINALLY GOTTEN THIS CLOSE.
That's amazing, stalker.
SHE'S MADE FIRST CONTACT WITH HER TARGET.
Hmm...
I WONDER WHAT SHE'S GOING TO SAY.
This is an important moment for a stalker.

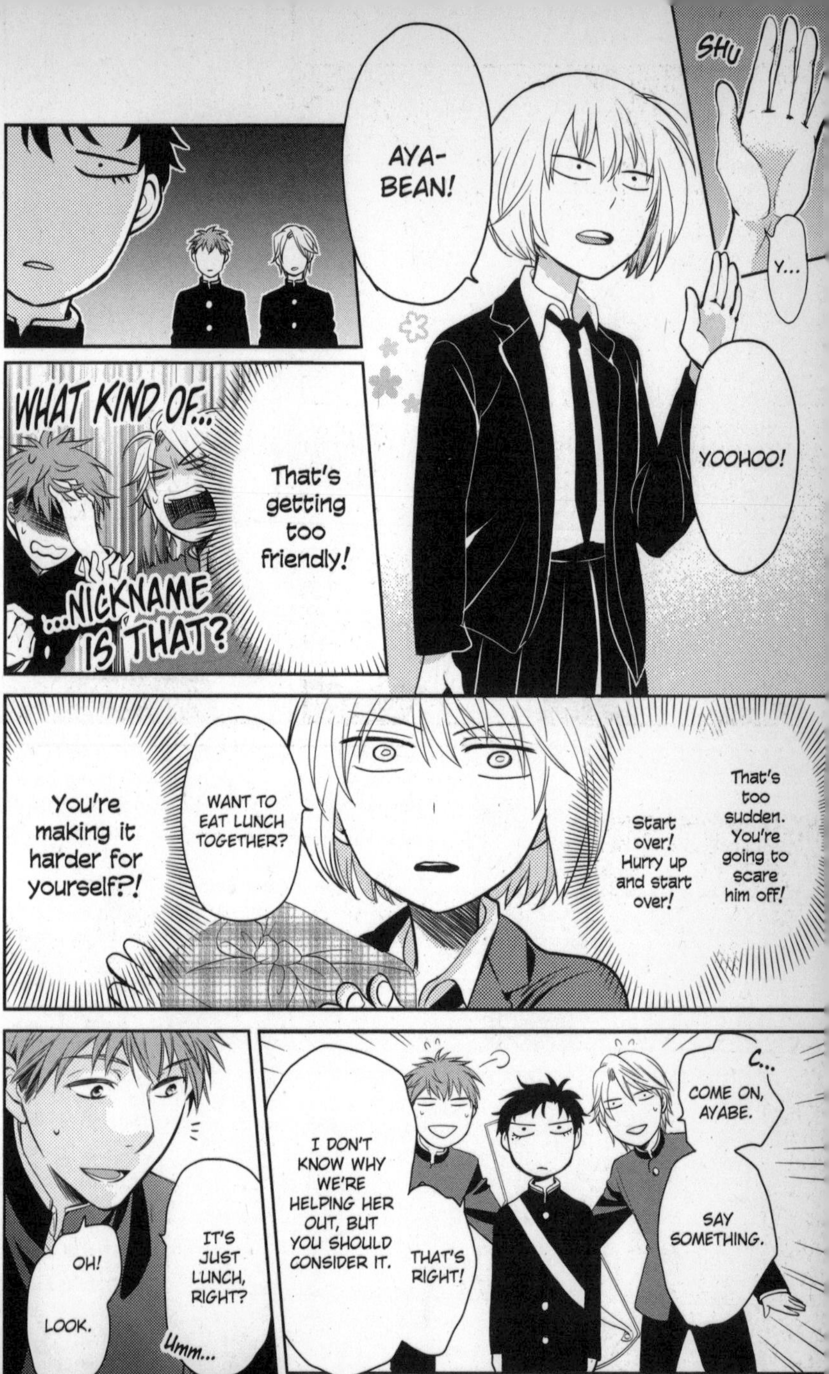
SHU
Y...
YOOHOO!
AYA-BEAN!
WHAT KIND OF... ...NICKNAME IS THAT?
That's getting too friendly!
That's too sudden. You're going to scare him off!
Start over! Hurry up and start over!
WANT TO EAT LUNCH TOGETHER?
You're making it harder for yourself?!
C... COME ON, AYABE.
SAY SOMETHING.
THAT'S RIGHT!
I DON'T KNOW WHY WE'RE HELPING HER OUT, BUT YOU SHOULD CONSIDER IT.
IT'S JUST LUNCH, RIGHT?
Umm...
OH! LOOK.

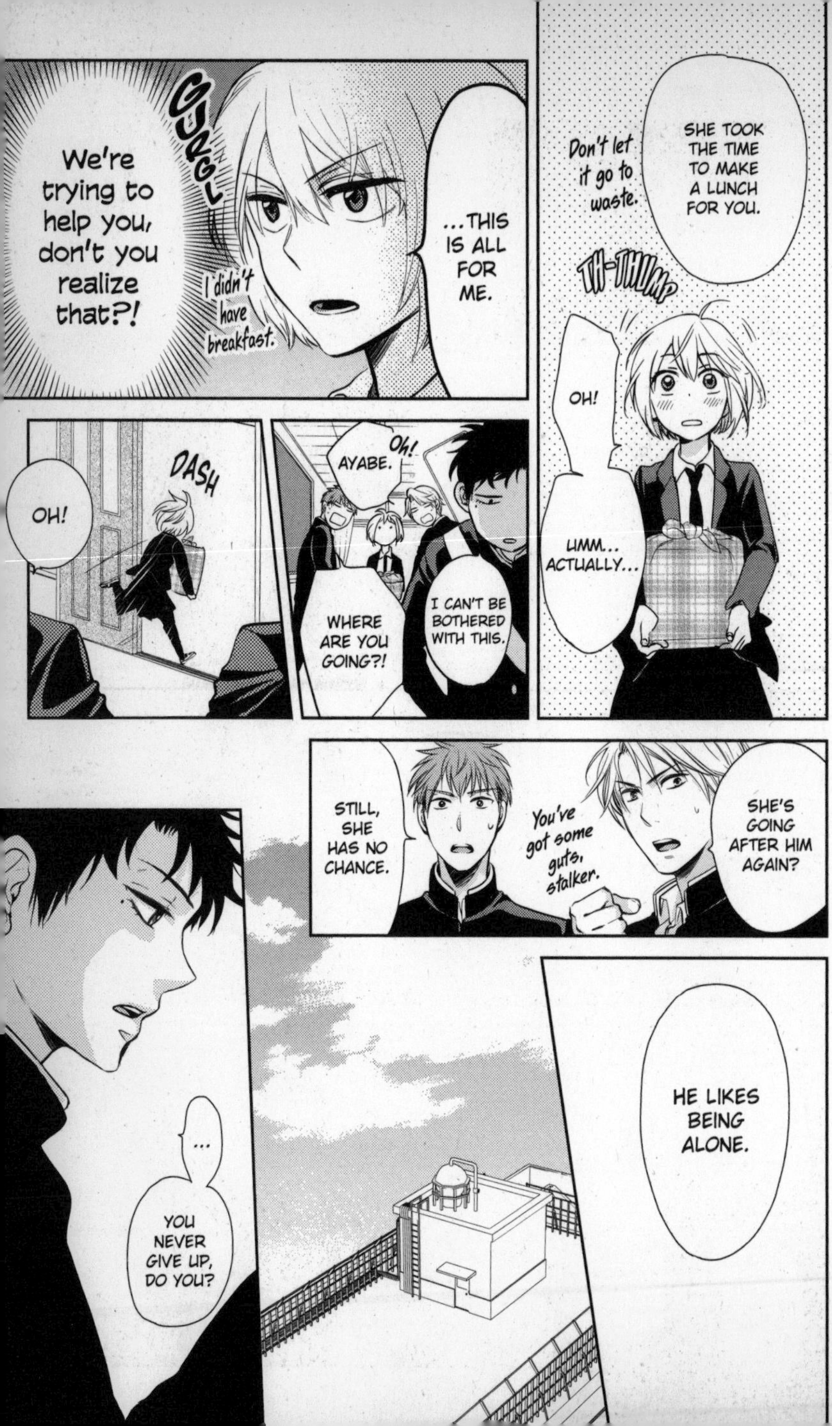
SHE TOOK THE TIME TO MAKE A LUNCH FOR YOU.
Don't let it go to waste.
TH-THUMP
OH!
UMM... ACTUALLY...
...THIS IS ALL FOR ME.
GURGL
I didn't have breakfast.
We're trying to help you, don't you realize that?!
Oh!
AYABE.
I CAN'T BE BOTHERED WITH THIS.
WHERE ARE YOU GOING?!
DASH
OH!
SHE'S GOING AFTER HIM AGAIN?
You've got some guts, stalker.
STILL, SHE HAS NO CHANCE.
HE LIKES BEING ALONE.
...
YOU NEVER GIVE UP, DO YOU?

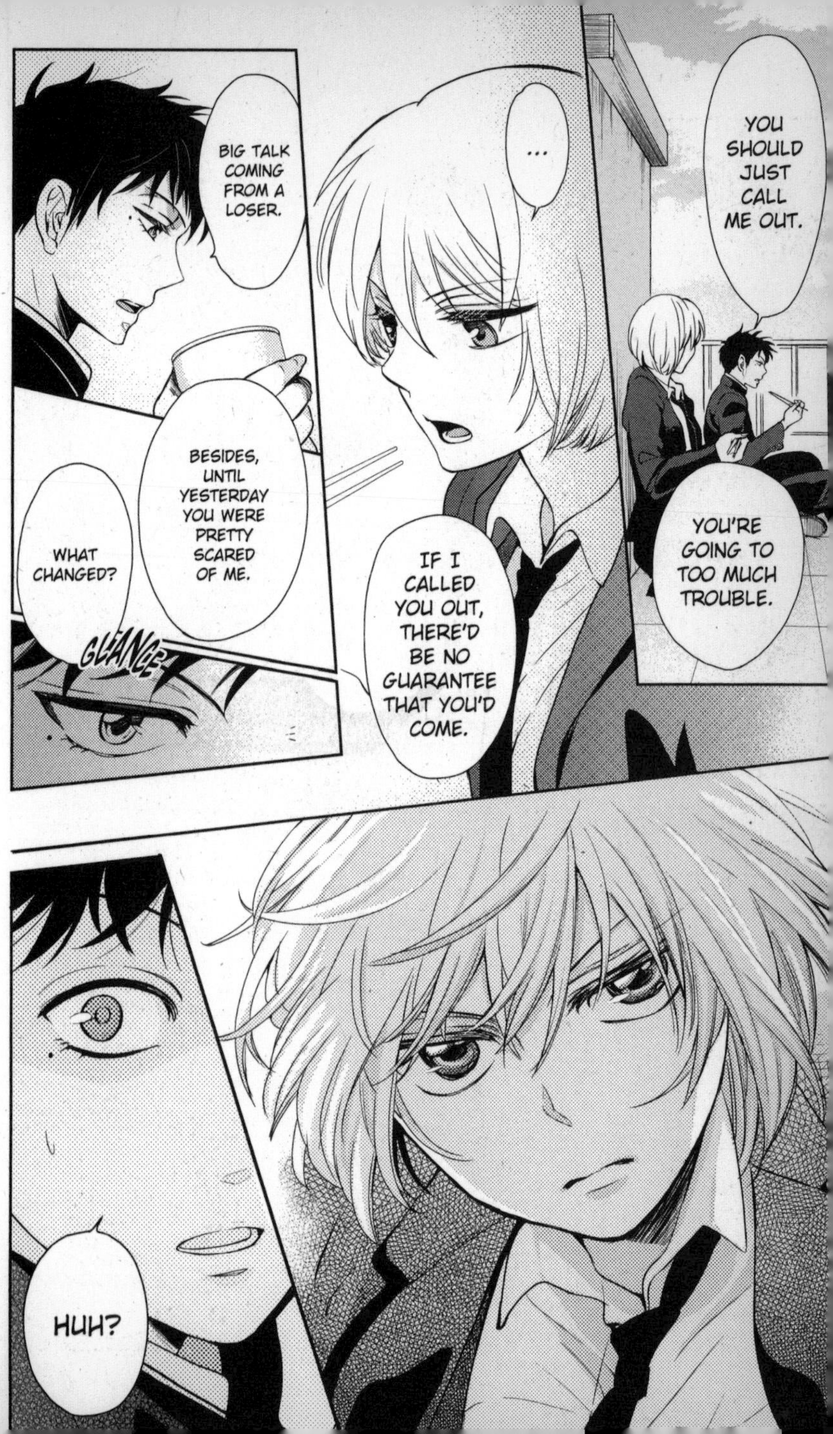
YOU SHOULD JUST CALL ME OUT.
YOU'RE GOING TO TOO MUCH TROUBLE.
...
IF I CALLED YOU OUT, THERE'D BE NO GUARANTEE THAT YOU'D COME.
BIG TALK COMING FROM A LOSER.
BESIDES, UNTIL YESTERDAY YOU WERE PRETTY SCARED OF ME.
WHAT CHANGED?
GLANCE
HUH?

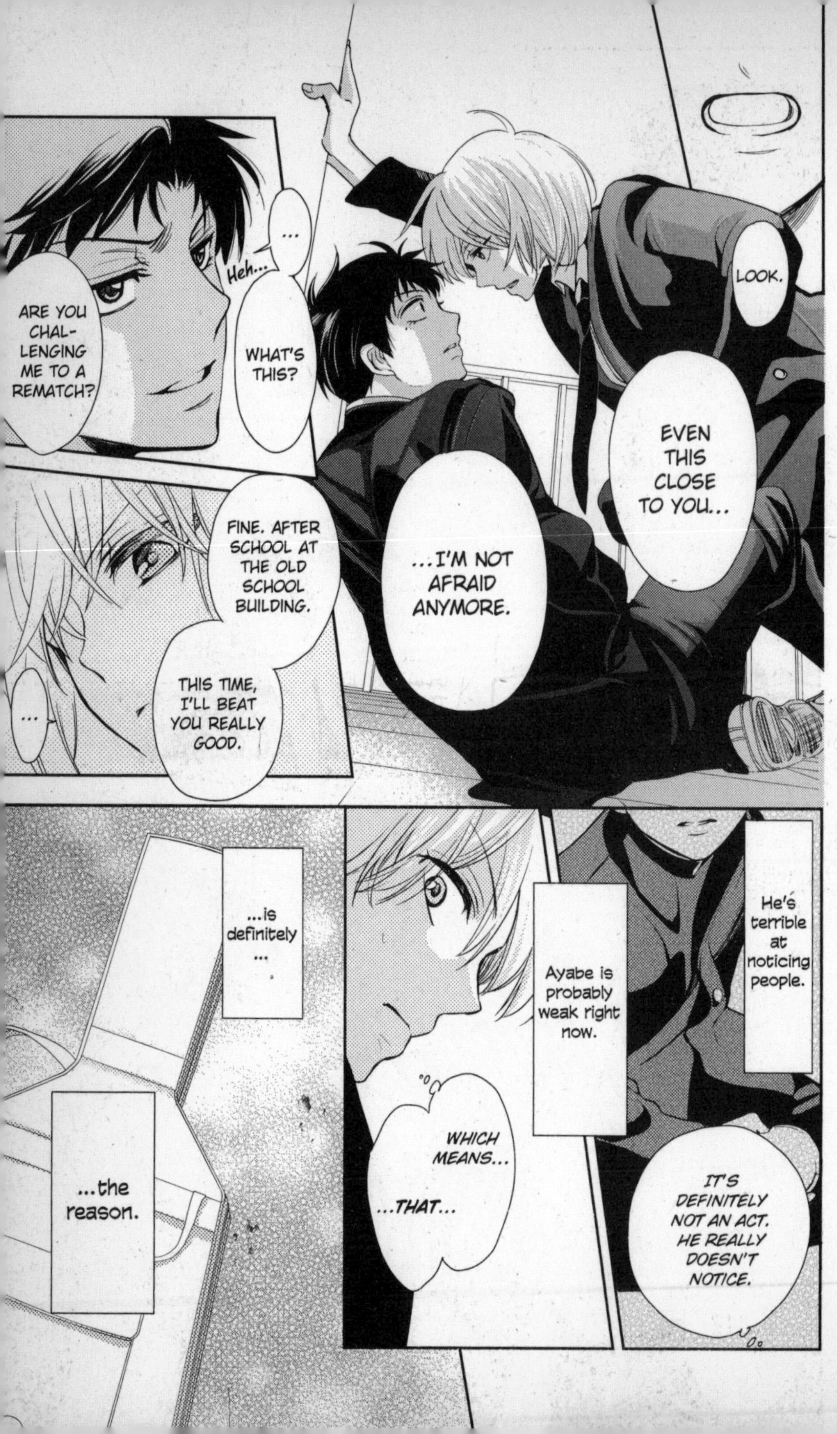
LOOK.
EVEN THIS CLOSE TO YOU...
...I'M NOT AFRAID ANYMORE.
...
Heh... WHAT'S THIS?
ARE YOU CHALLENGING ME TO A REMATCH?
FINE. AFTER SCHOOL AT THE OLD SCHOOL BUILDING.
THIS TIME, I'LL BEAT YOU REALLY GOOD.
...
He's terrible at noticing people.
Ayabe is probably weak right now.
IT'S DEFINITELY NOT AN ACT. HE REALLY DOESN'T NOTICE.
WHICH MEANS...
...THAT...
...is definitely...
...the reason.

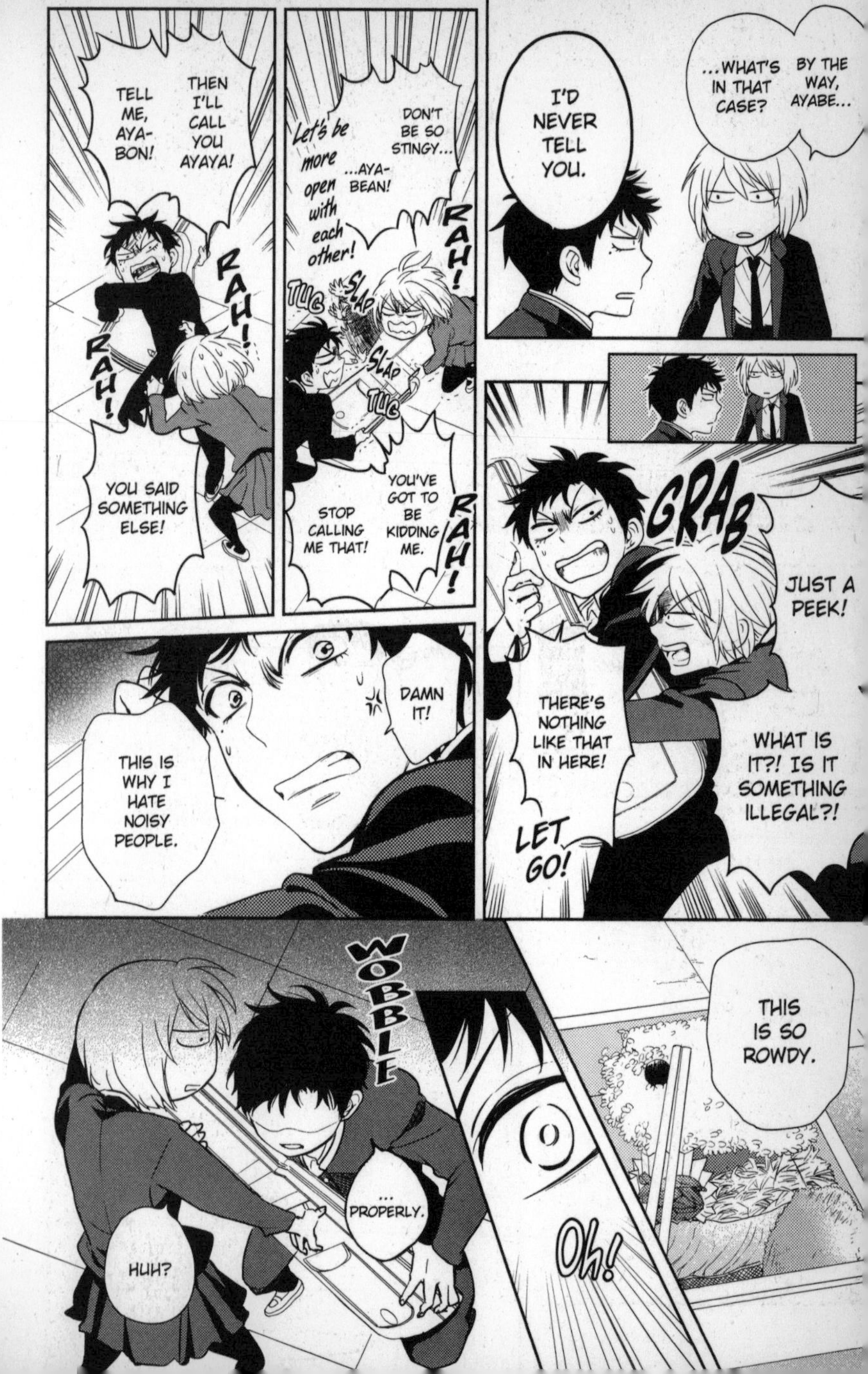
BY THE WAY, AYABE...
...WHAT'S IN THAT CASE?
I'D NEVER TELL YOU.
GRAB
JUST A PEEK!
WHAT IS IT?! IS IT SOMETHING ILLEGAL?!
THERE'S NOTHING LIKE THAT IN HERE!
LET GO!
DON'T BE SO STINGY...
...AYA-BEAN!
Let's be more open with each other!
RAH!
SLAP
TUG
SLAP
TUG
YOU'VE GOT TO BE KIDDING ME.
STOP CALLING ME THAT!
RAH!
THEN I'LL CALL YOU AYAYA!
TELL ME, AYA-BON!
RAH!
RAH!
YOU SAID SOMETHING ELSE!
DAMN IT!
THIS IS WHY I HATE NOISY PEOPLE.
THIS IS SO ROWDY.
Oh!
WOBBLE
...PROPERLY.
HUH?

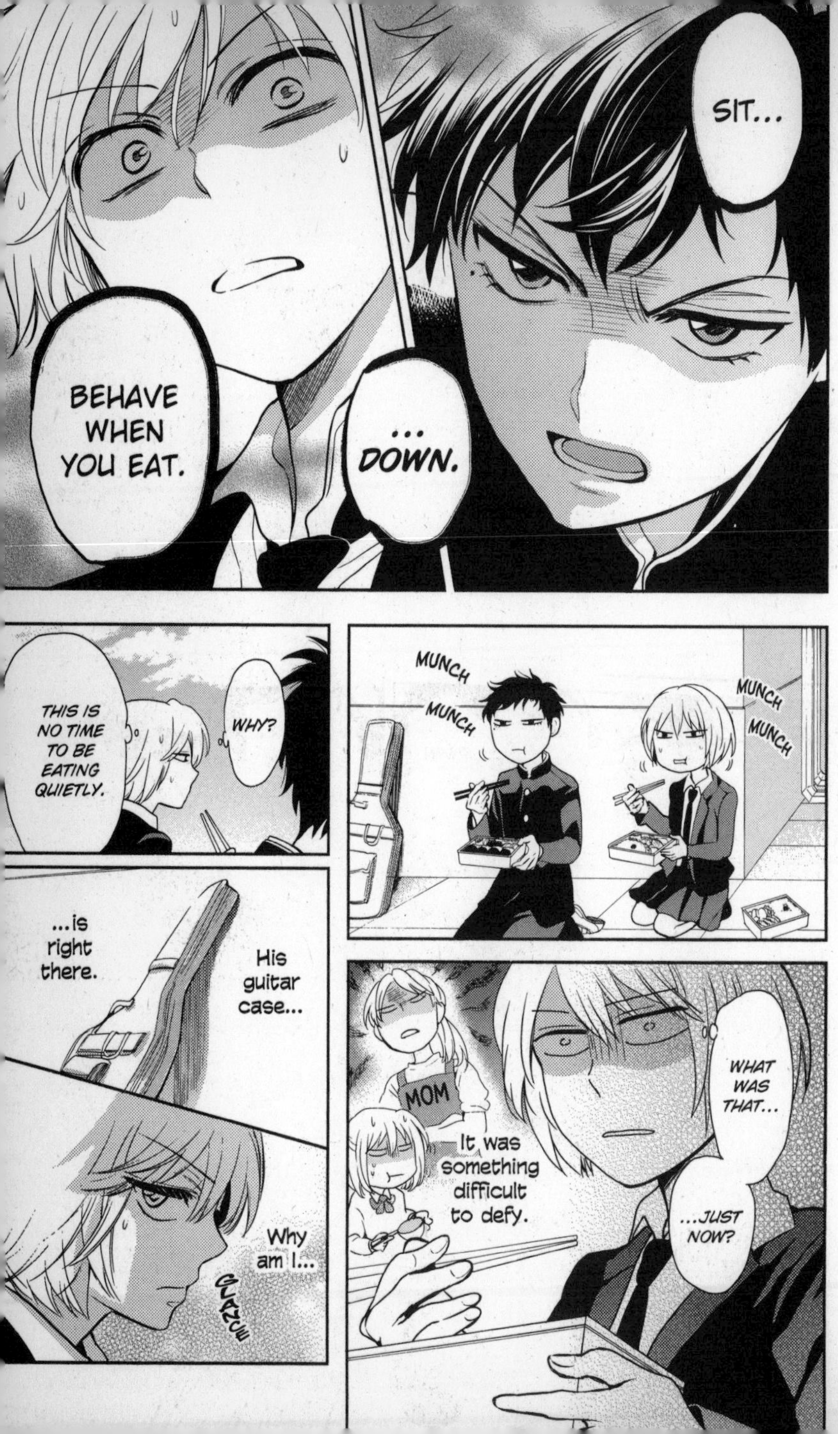
SIT...
...DOWN.
BEHAVE WHEN YOU EAT.
MUNCH MUNCH
MUNCH MUNCH
WHY?
THIS IS NO TIME TO BE EATING QUIETLY.
WHAT WAS THAT...
...JUST NOW?
MOM
It was something difficult to defy.
His guitar case...
...is right there.
Why am I...
GLANCE

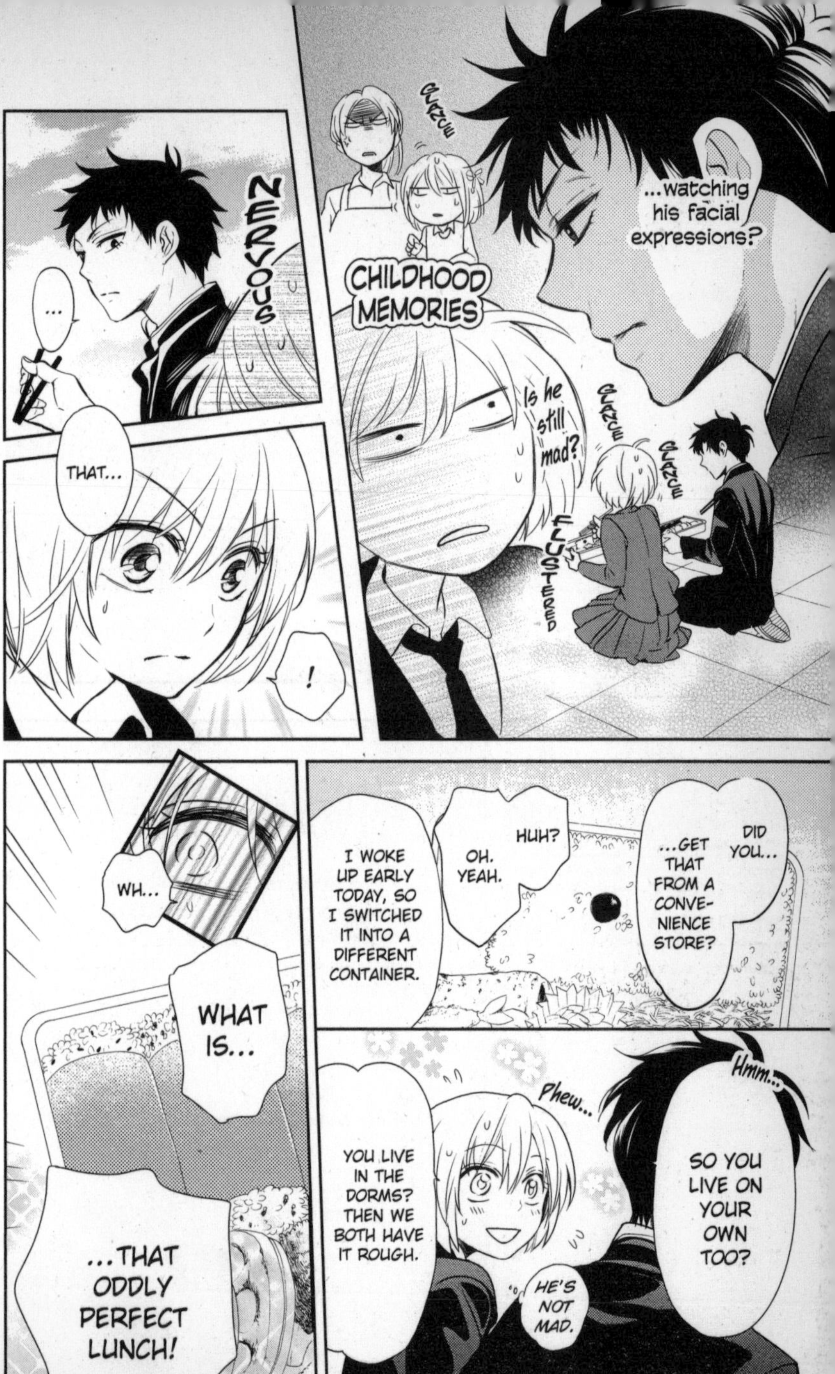
...watching his facial expressions?
GLANCE
CHILDHOOD MEMORIES
Is he still mad?
GLANCE
GLANCE
FLUSTERED
NERVOUS
...
THAT...
!
DID YOU...
...GET THAT FROM A CONVE-NIENCE STORE?
HUH?
OH. YEAH.
I WOKE UP EARLY TODAY, SO I SWITCHED IT INTO A DIFFERENT CONTAINER.
Hmm...
SO YOU LIVE ON YOUR OWN TOO?
Phew...
YOU LIVE IN THE DORMS? THEN WE BOTH HAVE IT ROUGH.
HE'S NOT MAD.
WH...
WHAT IS...
...THAT ODDLY PERFECT LUNCH!

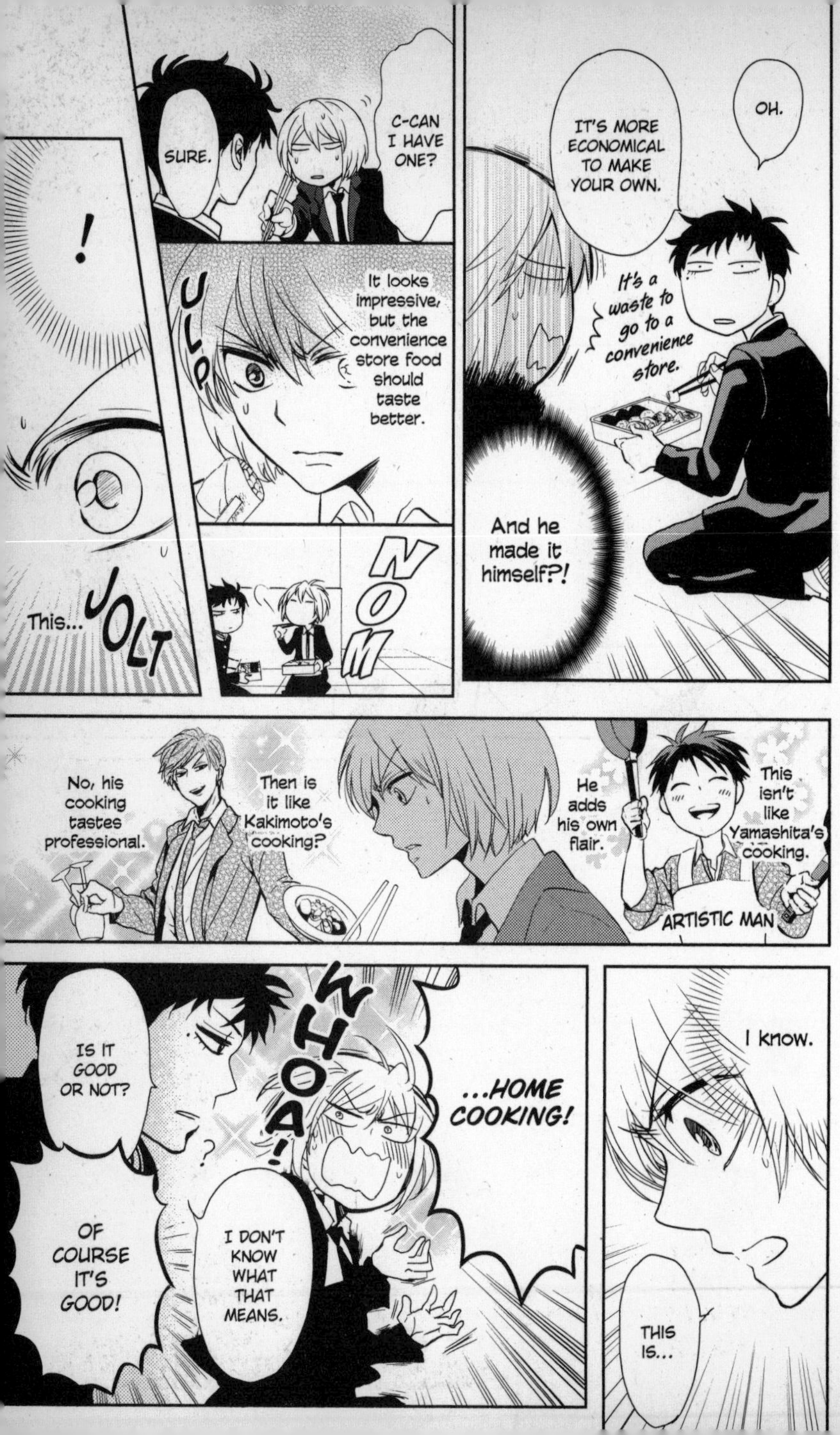
OH.
IT'S MORE ECONOMICAL TO MAKE YOUR OWN.
It's a waste to go to a convenience store.
And he made it himself?!
C-CAN I HAVE ONE?
SURE.
ULP
It looks impressive, but the convenience store food should taste better.
NOM
!
This...
JOLT
This isn't like Yamashita's cooking.
He adds his own flair.
ARTISTIC MAN
Then is it like Kakimoto's cooking?
No, his cooking tastes professional.
I know.
THIS IS...
...HOME COOKING!
WHOA!
IS IT GOOD OR NOT?
I DON'T KNOW WHAT THAT MEANS.
OF COURSE IT'S GOOD!

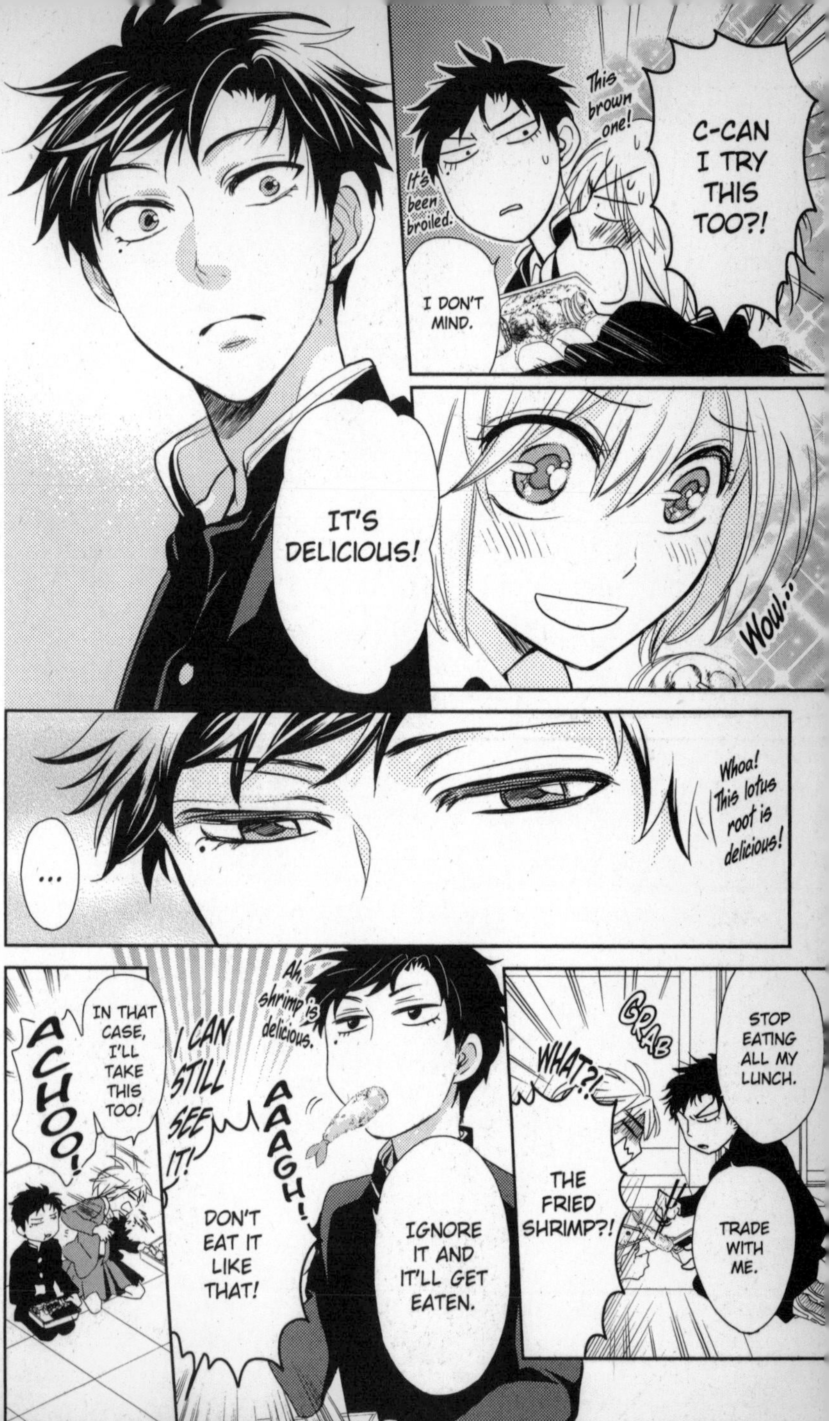
C-CAN I TRY THIS TOO?!
This brown one!
It's been broiled.
I DON'T MIND.
Wow...
IT'S DELICIOUS!
Whoa! This lotus root is delicious!
...
STOP EATING ALL MY LUNCH.
GRAB
WHAT?!
TRADE WITH ME.
THE FRIED SHRIMP?!
Ah, shrimp is delicious.
AAAGH!
IGNORE IT AND IT'LL GET EATEN.
I CAN STILL SEE IT!
DON'T EAT IT LIKE THAT!
IN THAT CASE, I'LL TAKE THIS TOO!
ACHOO!

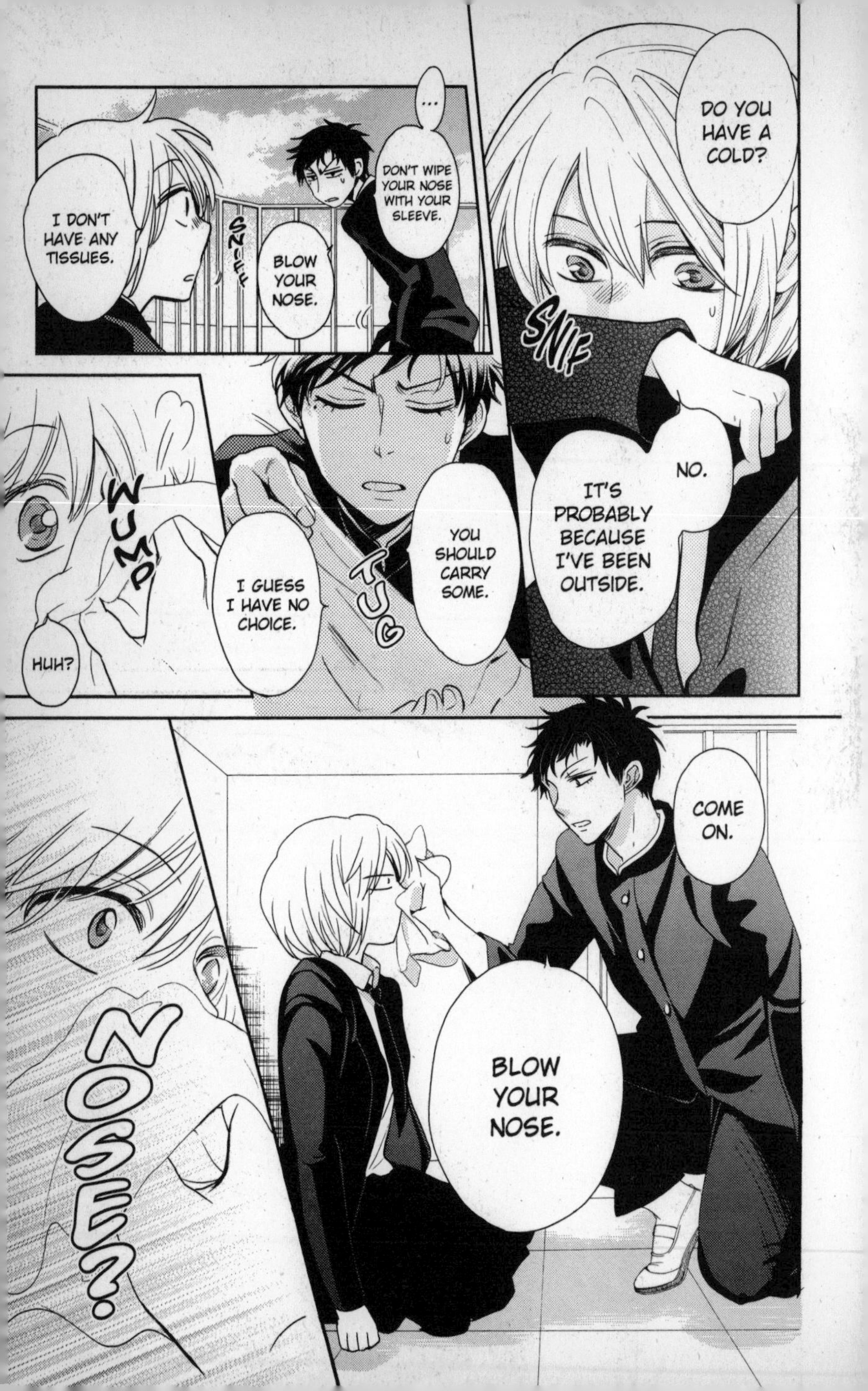
DO YOU HAVE A COLD?
SNIF
NO.
IT'S PROBABLY BECAUSE I'VE BEEN OUTSIDE.
...
DON'T WIPE YOUR NOSE WITH YOUR SLEEVE.
BLOW YOUR NOSE.
SNIFF
I DON'T HAVE ANY TISSUES.
YOU SHOULD CARRY SOME.
TUG
I GUESS I HAVE NO CHOICE.
WUMP
HUH?
COME ON.
BLOW YOUR NOSE.
NOSE?

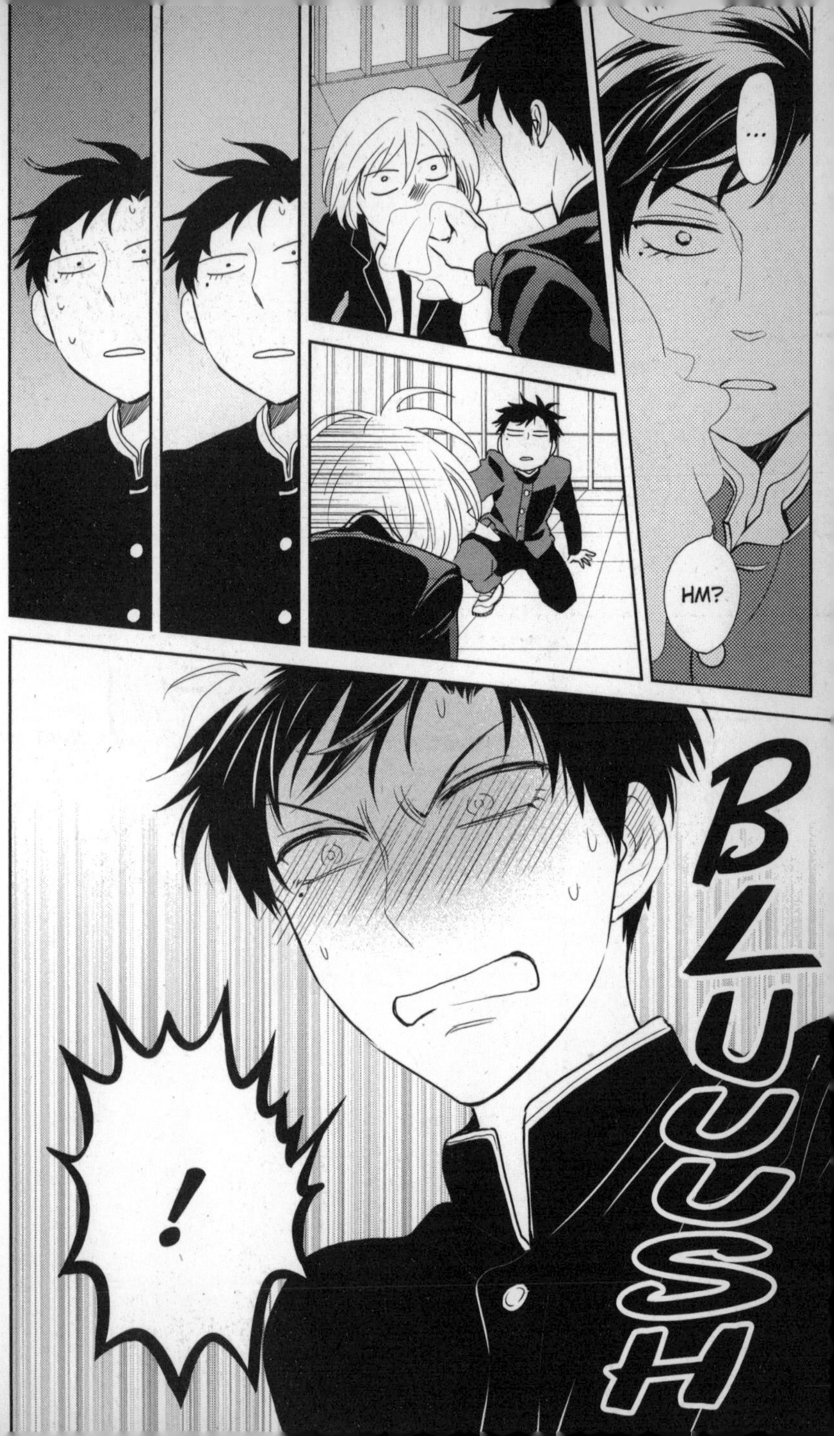
...
HM?
BLUUUSH
!

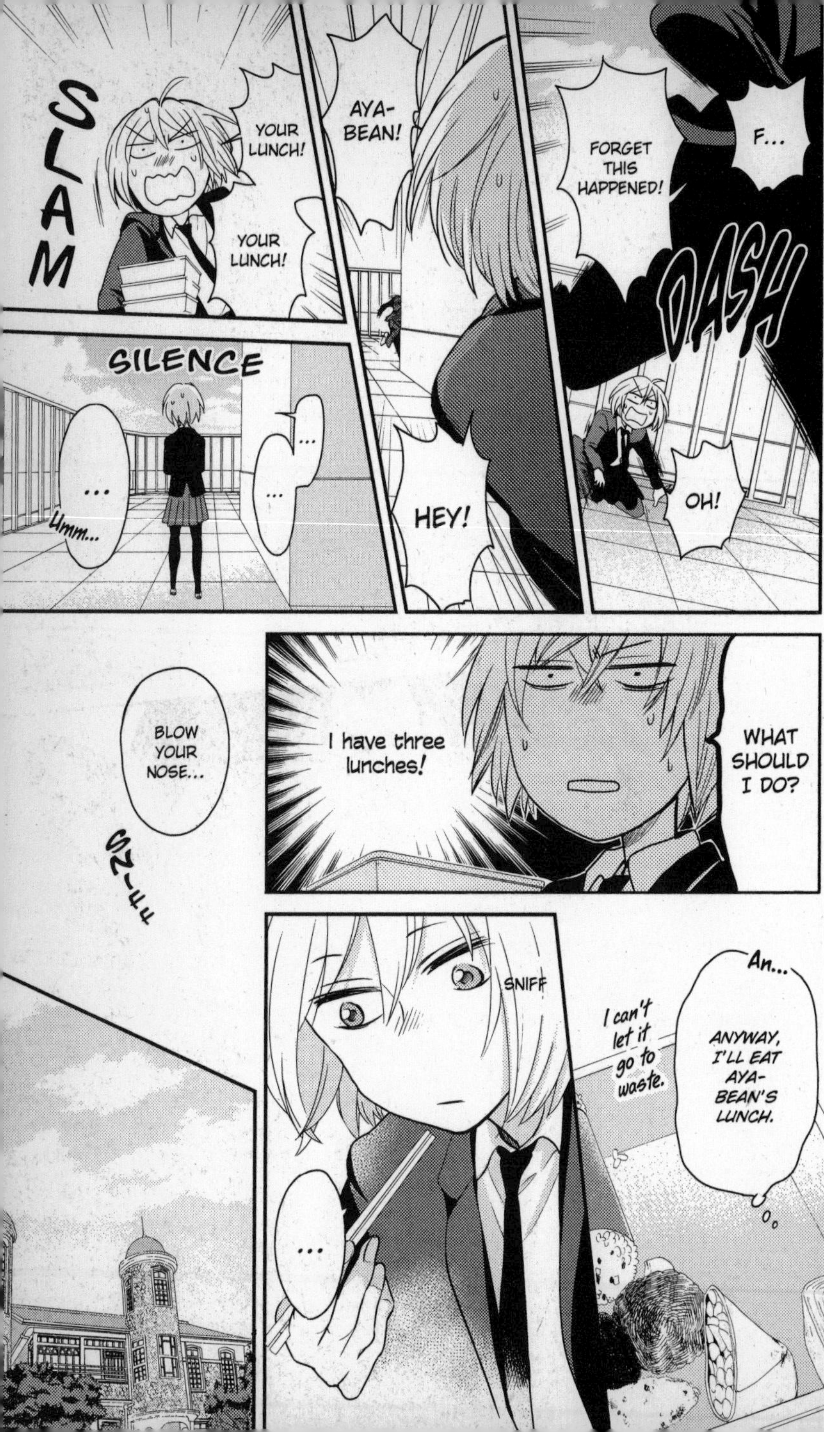
F...
FORGET THIS HAPPENED!
DASH
OH!
AYA-BEAN!
HEY!
YOUR LUNCH!
YOUR LUNCH!
SLAM
SILENCE
...
...
...
Umm...
WHAT SHOULD I DO?
I have three lunches!
BLOW YOUR NOSE...
An...
ANYWAY, I'LL EAT AYA-BEAN'S LUNCH.
I can't let it go to waste.
SNIFF
...

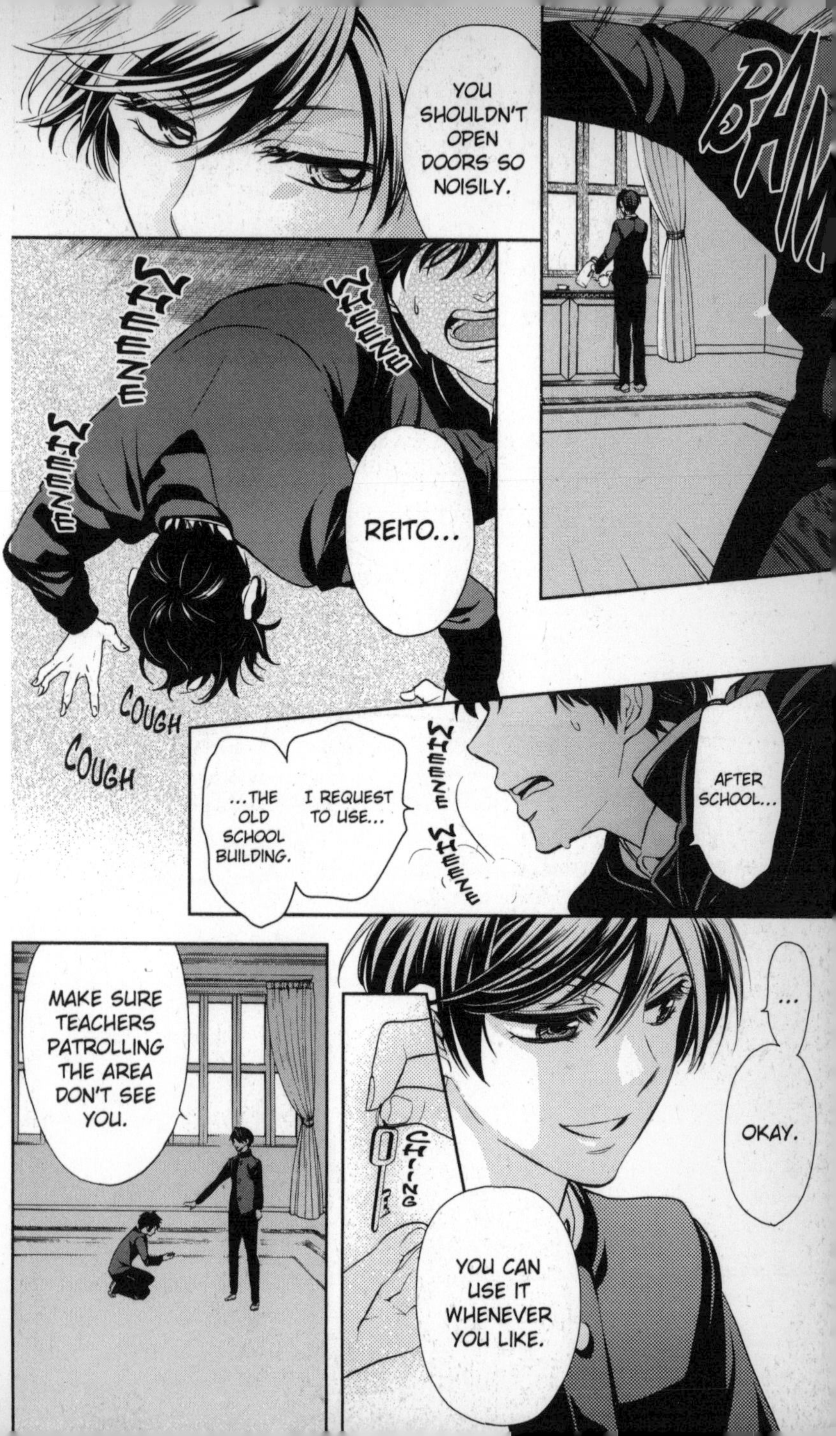
BAM
YOU SHOULDN'T OPEN DOORS SO NOISILY.
WHEEZE
WHEEZE
WHEEZE
REITO...
COUGH
COUGH
AFTER SCHOOL...
WHEEZE WHEEZE
WHEEZE
I REQUEST TO USE...
...THE OLD SCHOOL BUILDING.
... OKAY.
CHING
YOU CAN USE IT WHENEVER YOU LIKE.
MAKE SURE TEACHERS PATROLLING THE AREA DON'T SEE YOU.

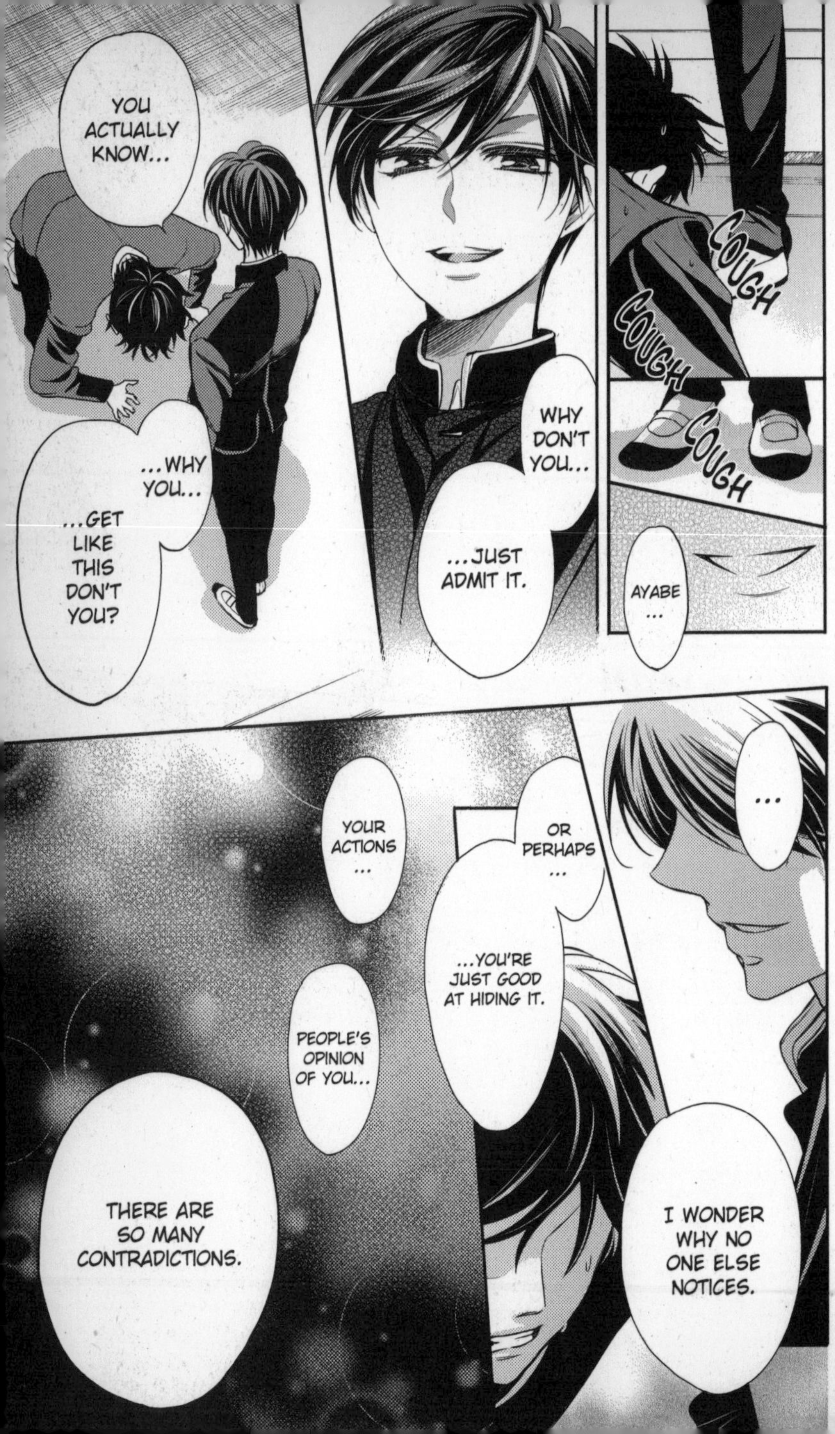
COUGH
COUGH
COUGH
AYABE ...
WHY DON'T YOU...
...JUST ADMIT IT.
YOU ACTUALLY KNOW...
...WHY YOU...
...GET LIKE THIS DON'T YOU?
...
I WONDER WHY NO ONE ELSE NOTICES.
YOUR ACTIONS ...
PEOPLE'S OPINION OF YOU...
THERE ARE SO MANY CONTRADICTIONS.
OR PERHAPS ...
...YOU'RE JUST GOOD AT HIDING IT.

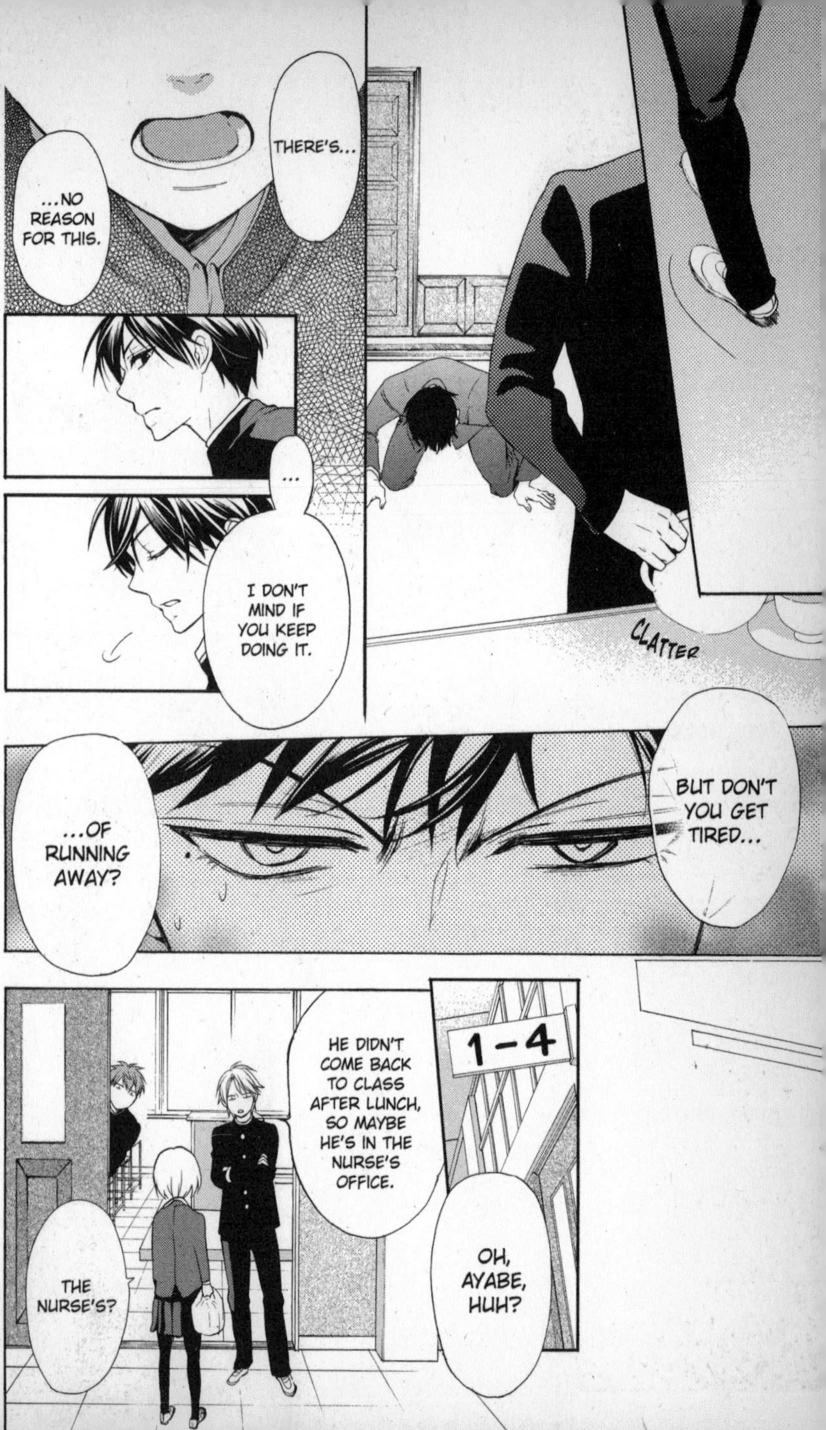
CLATTER
THERE'S...
...NO REASON FOR THIS.
...
I DON'T MIND IF YOU KEEP DOING IT.
BUT DON'T YOU GET TIRED...
...OF RUNNING AWAY?
1-4
OH, AYABE, HUH?
HE DIDN'T COME BACK TO CLASS AFTER LUNCH, SO MAYBE HE'S IN THE NURSE'S OFFICE.
THE NURSE'S?

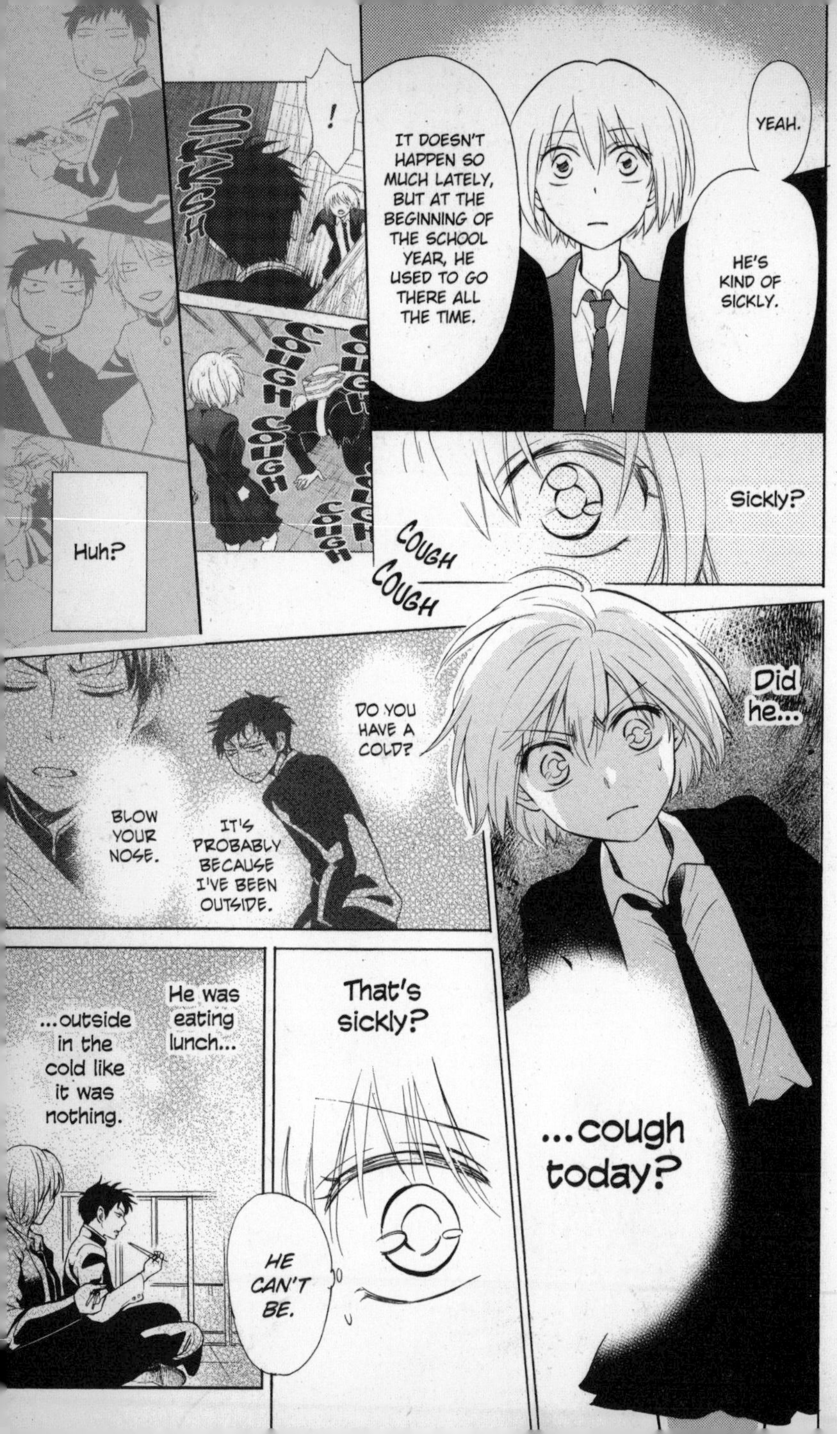

YEAH.
HE'S KIND OF SICKLY.
IT DOESN'T HAPPEN SO MUCH LATELY, BUT AT THE BEGINNING OF THE SCHOOL YEAR, HE USED TO GO THERE ALL THE TIME.
Sickly?
COUGH COUGH
!
SWISH
COUGH COUGH COUGH
COUGH COUGH
COUGH
Huh?
Did he...
...cough today?
DO YOU HAVE A COLD?
IT'S PROBABLY BECAUSE I'VE BEEN OUTSIDE.
BLOW YOUR NOSE.
That's sickly?
HE CAN'T BE.
He was eating lunch...
...outside in the cold like it was nothing.

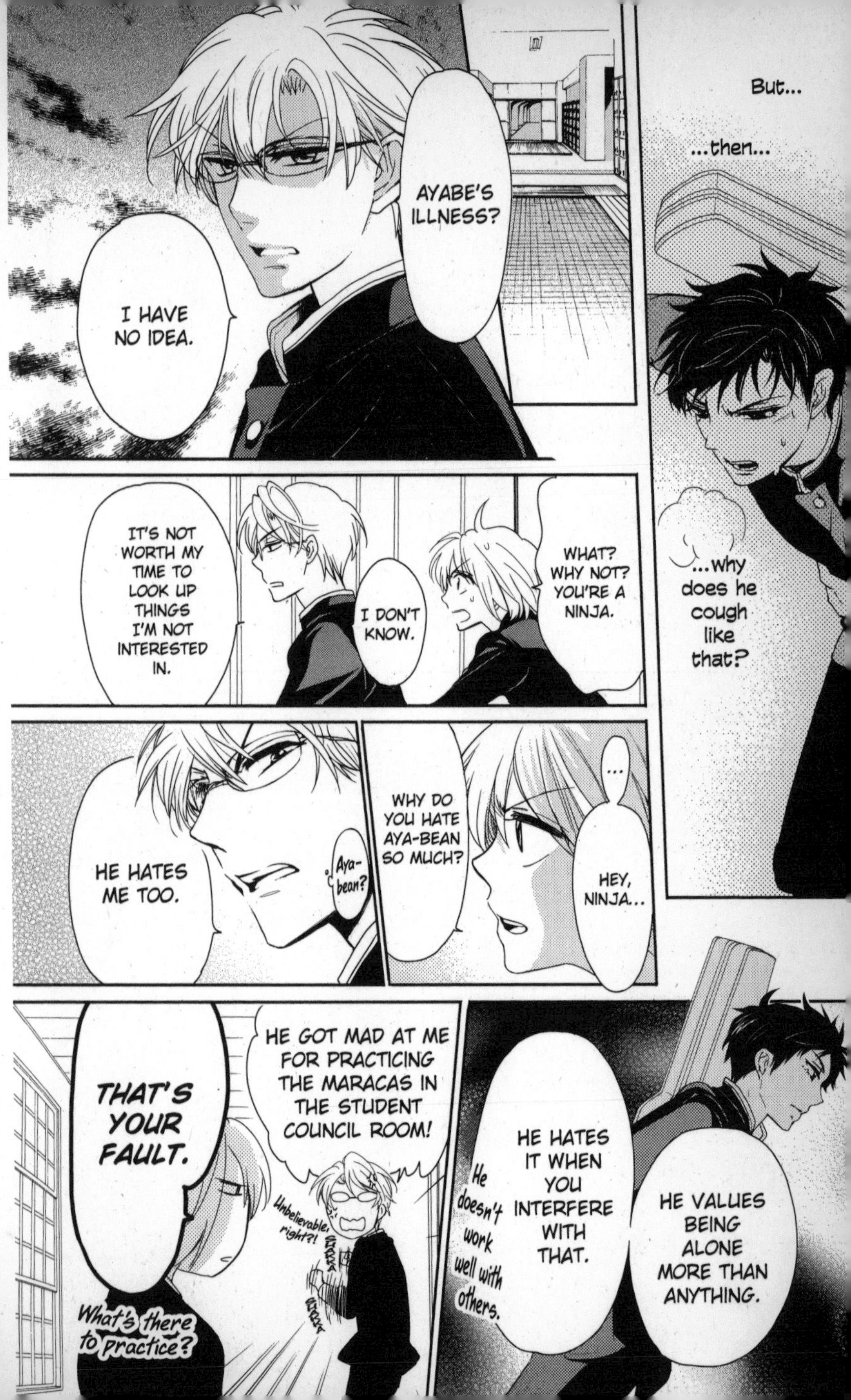
But...
...then...
...why does he cough like that?
AYABE'S ILLNESS?
I HAVE NO IDEA.
WHAT? WHY NOT? YOU'RE A NINJA.
I DON'T KNOW.
IT'S NOT WORTH MY TIME TO LOOK UP THINGS I'M NOT INTERESTED IN.
...
HEY, NINJA...
WHY DO YOU HATE AYA-BEAN SO MUCH?
Aya-bean?
HE HATES ME TOO.
HE VALUES BEING ALONE MORE THAN ANYTHING.
HE HATES IT WHEN YOU INTERFERE WITH THAT.
He doesn't work well with others.
HE GOT MAD AT ME FOR PRACTICING THE MARACAS IN THE STUDENT COUNCIL ROOM!
Unbelievable, right?!
THAT'S YOUR FAULT.
What's there to practice?

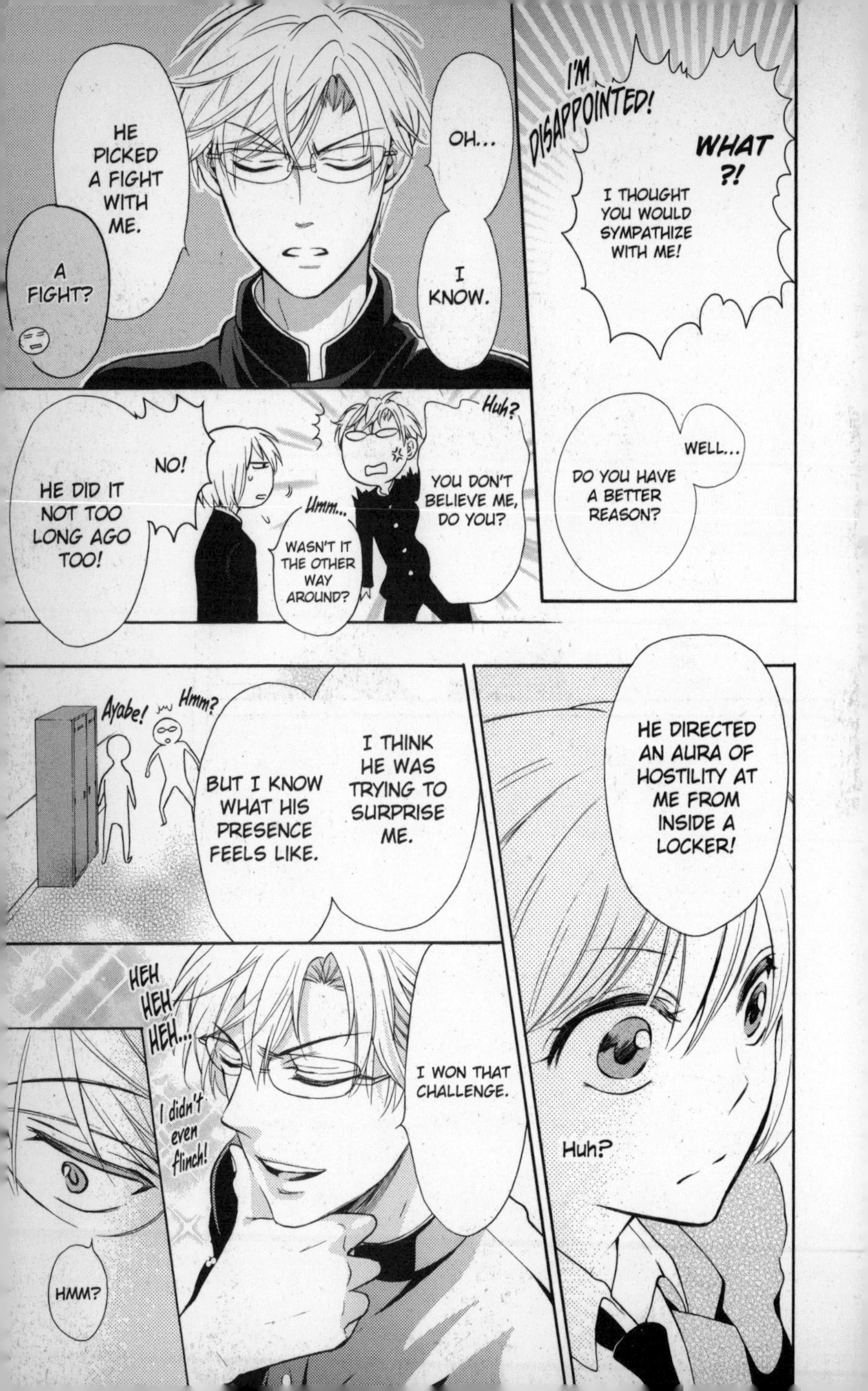
I'M DISAPPOINTED!
WHAT?!
I THOUGHT YOU WOULD SYMPATHIZE WITH ME!
WELL...
DO YOU HAVE A BETTER REASON?
OH...
I KNOW.
HE PICKED A FIGHT WITH ME.
A FIGHT?
Huh?
YOU DON'T BELIEVE ME, DO YOU?
Umm...
WASN'T IT THE OTHER WAY AROUND?
NO!
HE DID IT NOT TOO LONG AGO TOO!
HE DIRECTED AN AURA OF HOSTILITY AT ME FROM INSIDE A LOCKER!
Huh?
I THINK HE WAS TRYING TO SURPRISE ME.
BUT I KNOW WHAT HIS PRESENCE FEELS LIKE.
Hmm?
Ayabe!
I WON THAT CHALLENGE.
HEH HEH HEH...
I didn't even flinch!
HMM?

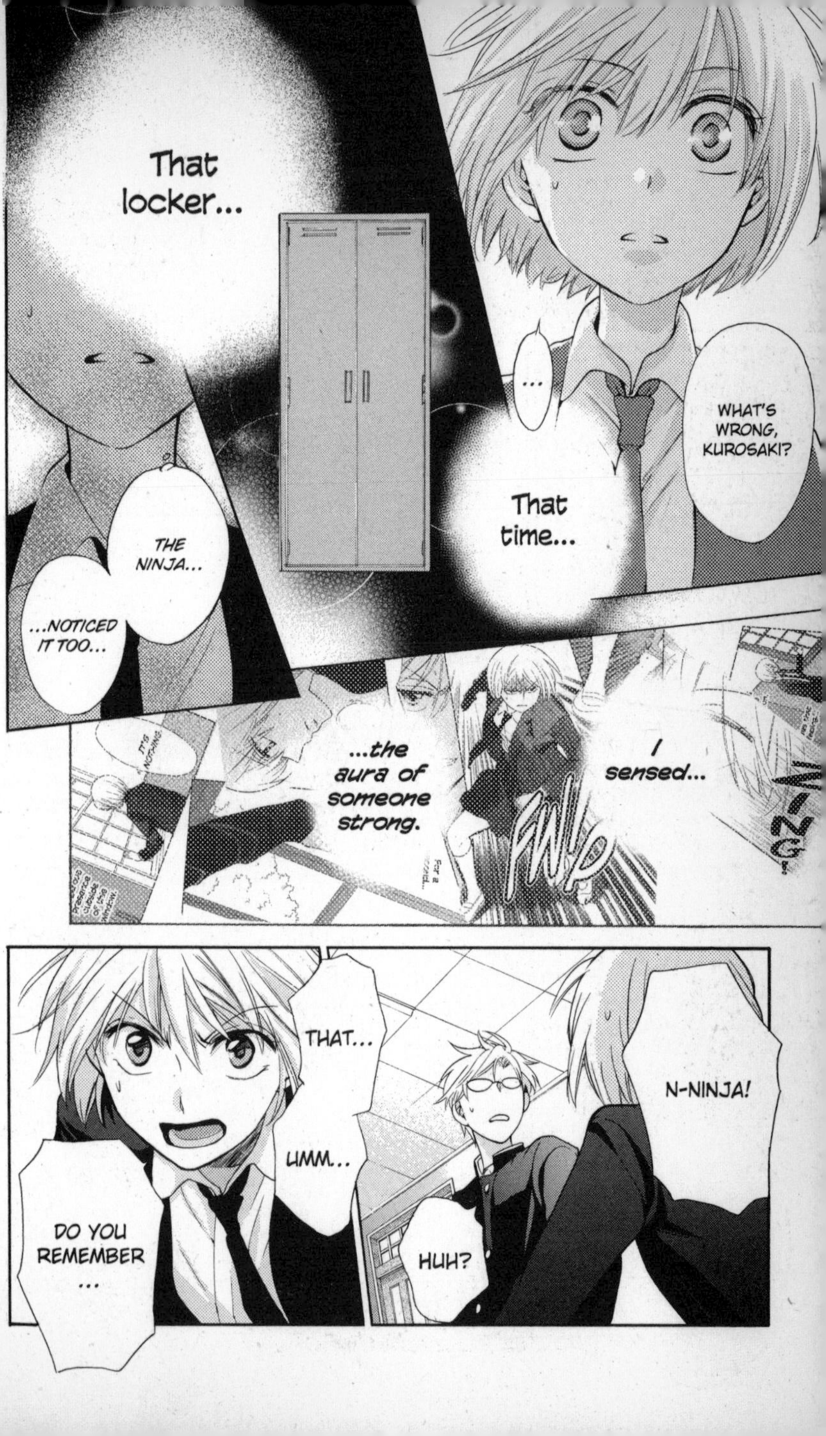
WHAT'S WRONG, KUROSAKI?
...
That time...
That locker...
THE NINJA...
...NOTICED IT TOO...
I sensed...
FWIP
...the aura of someone strong.
IT'S NOTHING.
your presence outside of the window.
N-NINJA!
HUH?
THAT...
UMM...
DO YOU REMEMBER ...

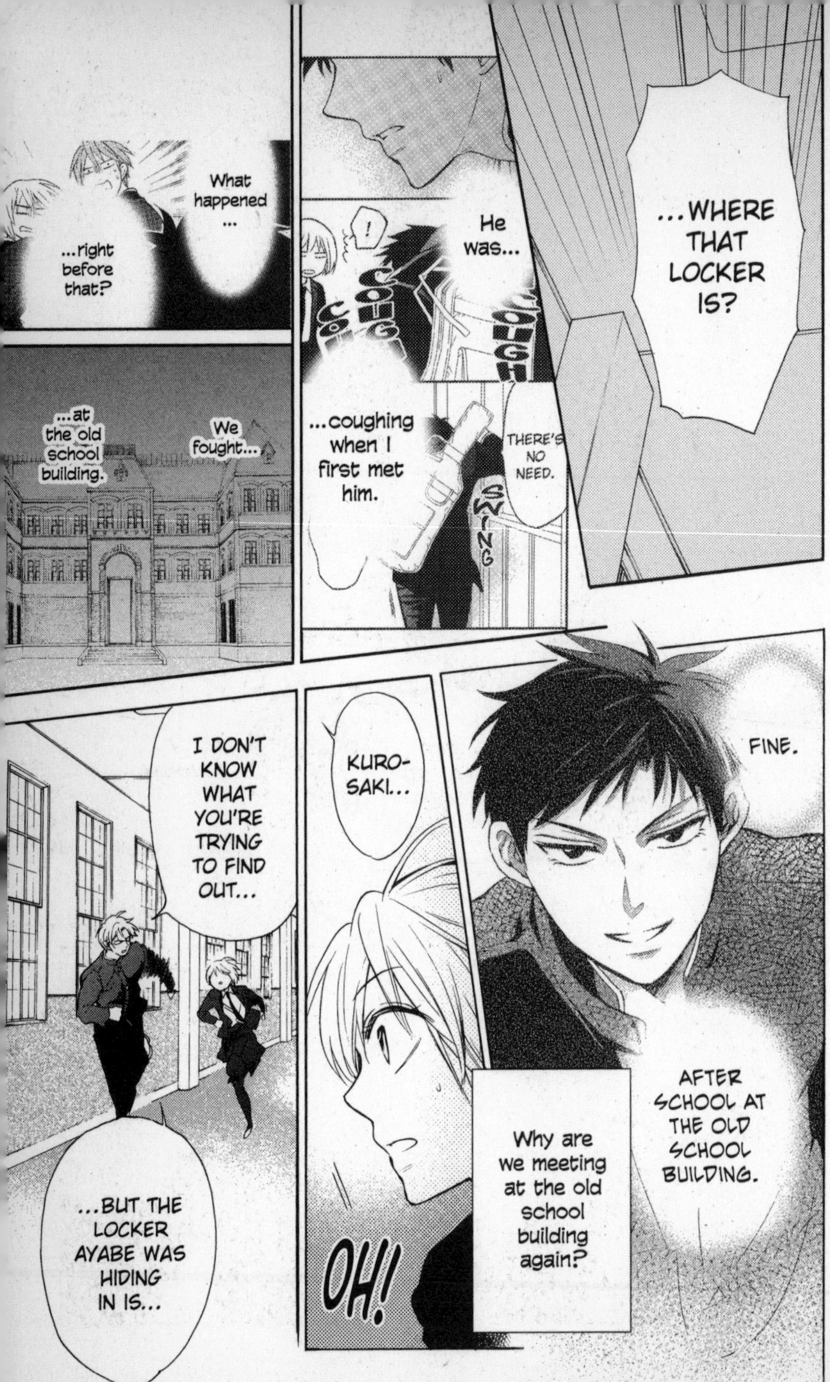
...WHERE THAT LOCKER IS?
He was...
COUGH
COUGH
COUGH
...coughing when I first met him.
THERE'S NO NEED.
SWING
What happened ...
...right before that?
We fought...
...at the old school building.
FINE.
AFTER SCHOOL AT THE OLD SCHOOL BUILDING.
KURO-SAKI...
Why are we meeting at the old school building again?
OH!
I DON'T KNOW WHAT YOU'RE TRYING TO FIND OUT...
...BUT THE LOCKER AYABE WAS HIDING IN IS...

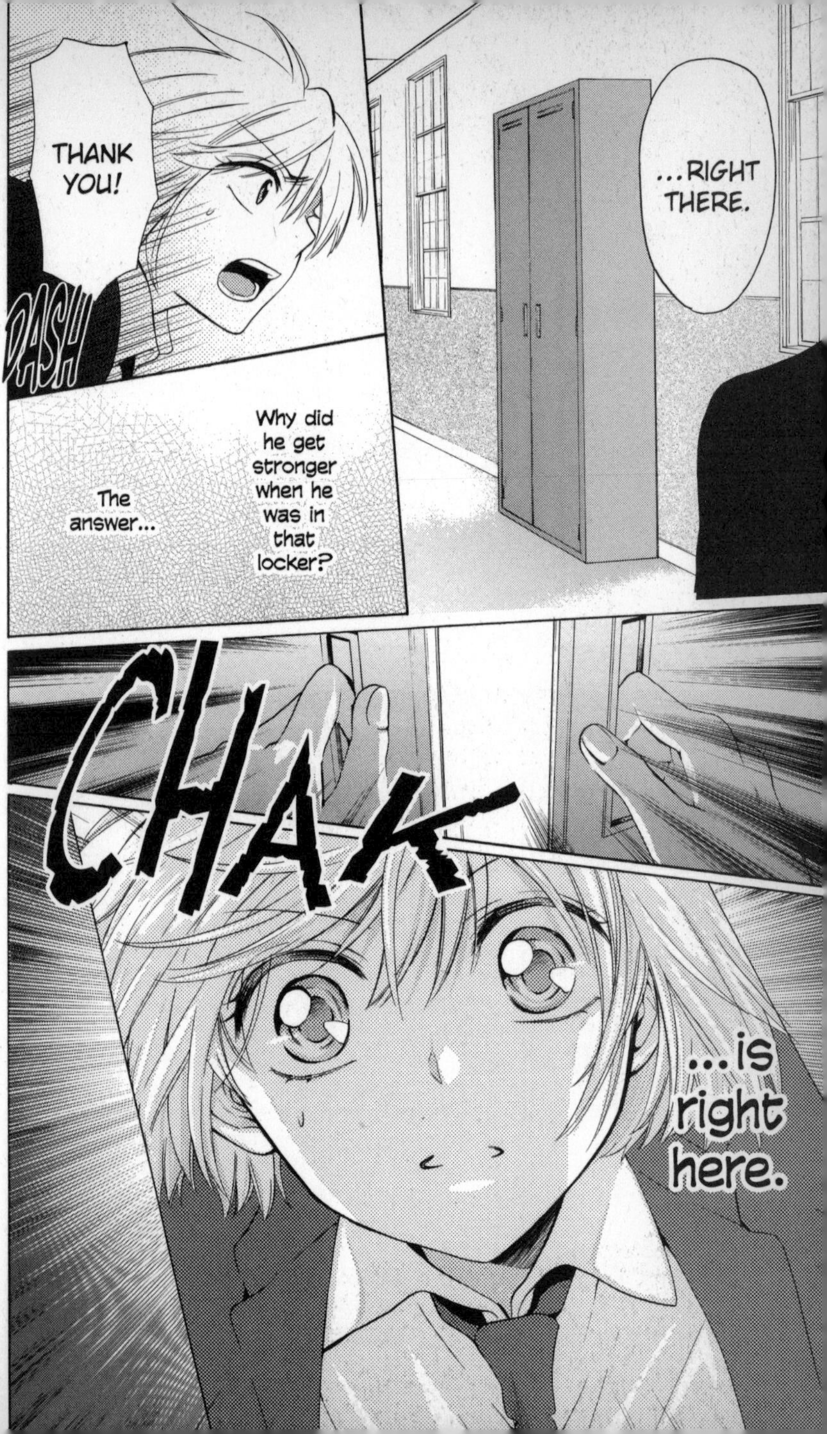
...RIGHT THERE.
THANK YOU!
DASH
Why did he get stronger when he was in that locker?
The answer...
CHAK
...is right here.

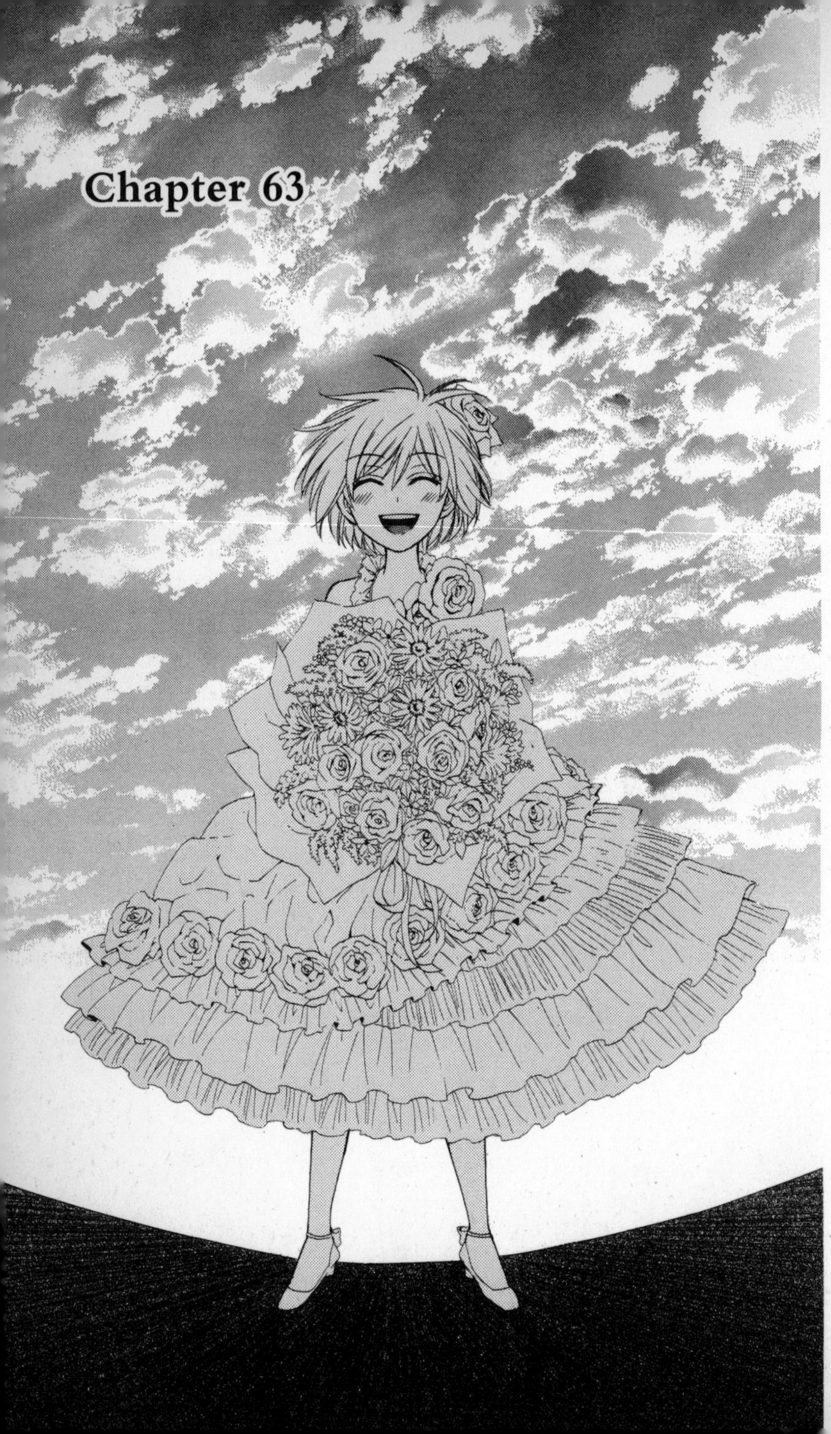
Chapter 63

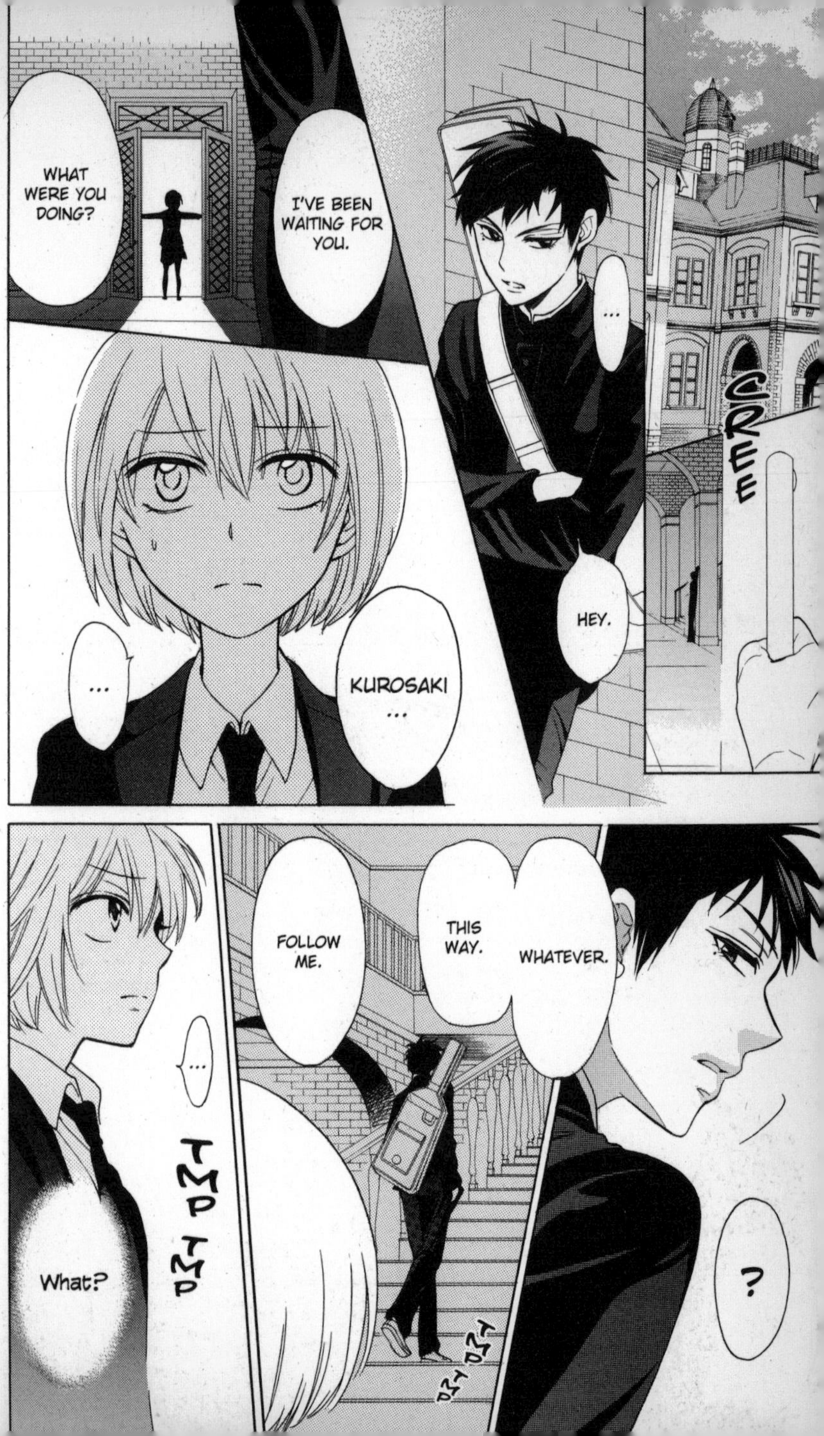
CREE
...
HEY.
I'VE BEEN WAITING FOR YOU.
WHAT WERE YOU DOING?
KUROSAKI...
...
WHATEVER.
THIS WAY.
?
FOLLOW ME.
TMP TMP
...
TMP TMP
What?

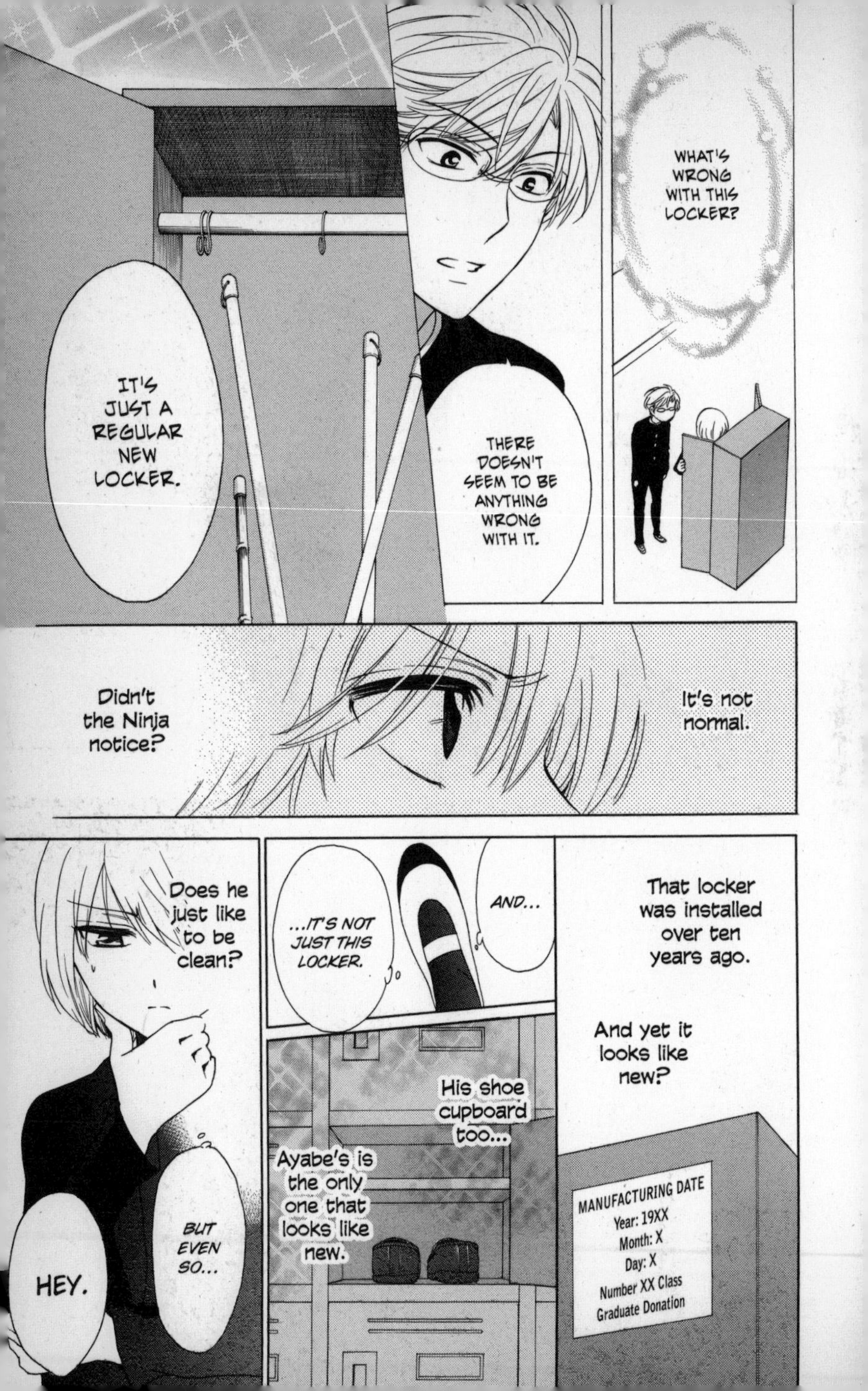
WHAT'S WRONG WITH THIS LOCKER?
THERE DOESN'T SEEM TO BE ANYTHING WRONG WITH IT.
IT'S JUST A REGULAR NEW LOCKER.
It's not normal.
Didn't the Ninja notice?
That locker was installed over ten years ago.
And yet it looks like new?
MANUFACTURING DATE
Year: 19XX
Month: X
Day: X
Number XX Class
Graduate Donation
AND...
...IT'S NOT JUST THIS LOCKER.
His shoe cupboard too...
Ayabe's is the only one that looks like new.
Does he just like to be clean?
BUT EVEN SO...
HEY.

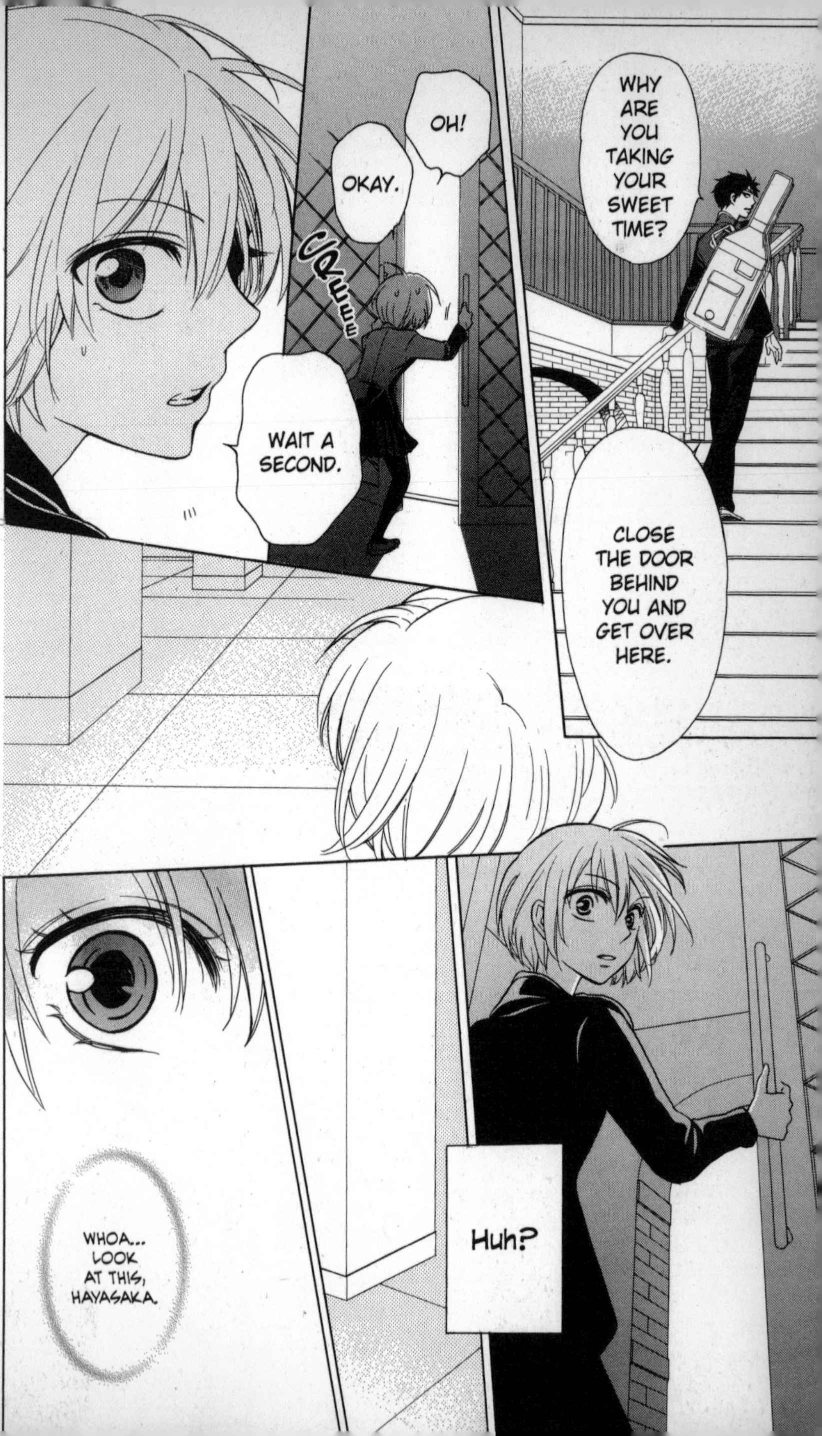
WHY ARE YOU TAKING YOUR SWEET TIME?
CLOSE THE DOOR BEHIND YOU AND GET OVER HERE.
OH!
OKAY.
CREEEE
WAIT A SECOND.
Huh?
WHOA... LOOK AT THIS, HAYASAKA.

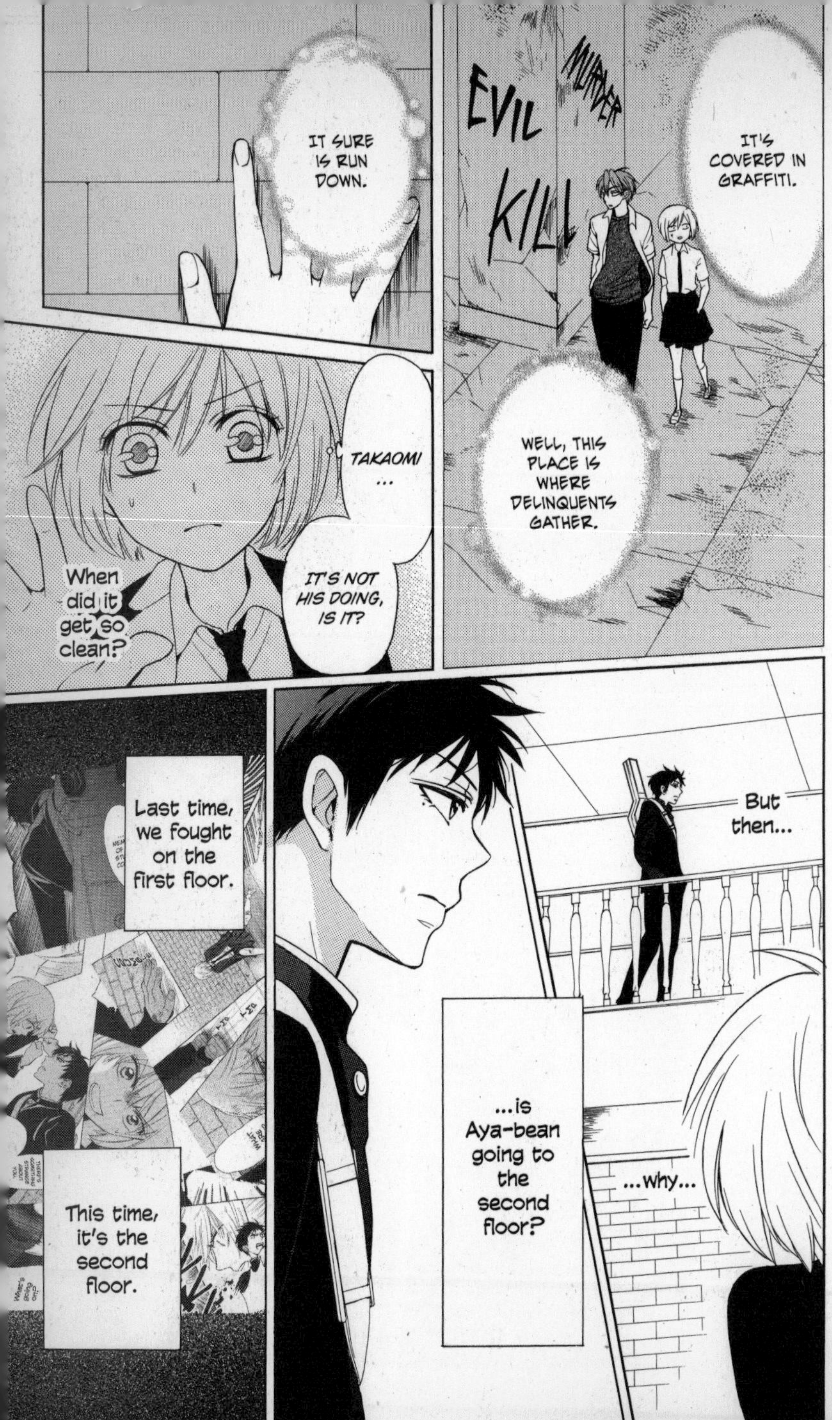
MURDER
EVIL
KILL
IT'S COVERED IN GRAFFITI.
WELL, THIS PLACE IS WHERE DELINQUENTS GATHER.
IT SURE IS RUN DOWN.
TAKAOMI ...
IT'S NOT HIS DOING, IS IT?
When did it get so clean?
But then...
...why...
...is Aya-bean going to the second floor?
Last time, we fought on the first floor.
This time, it's the second floor.

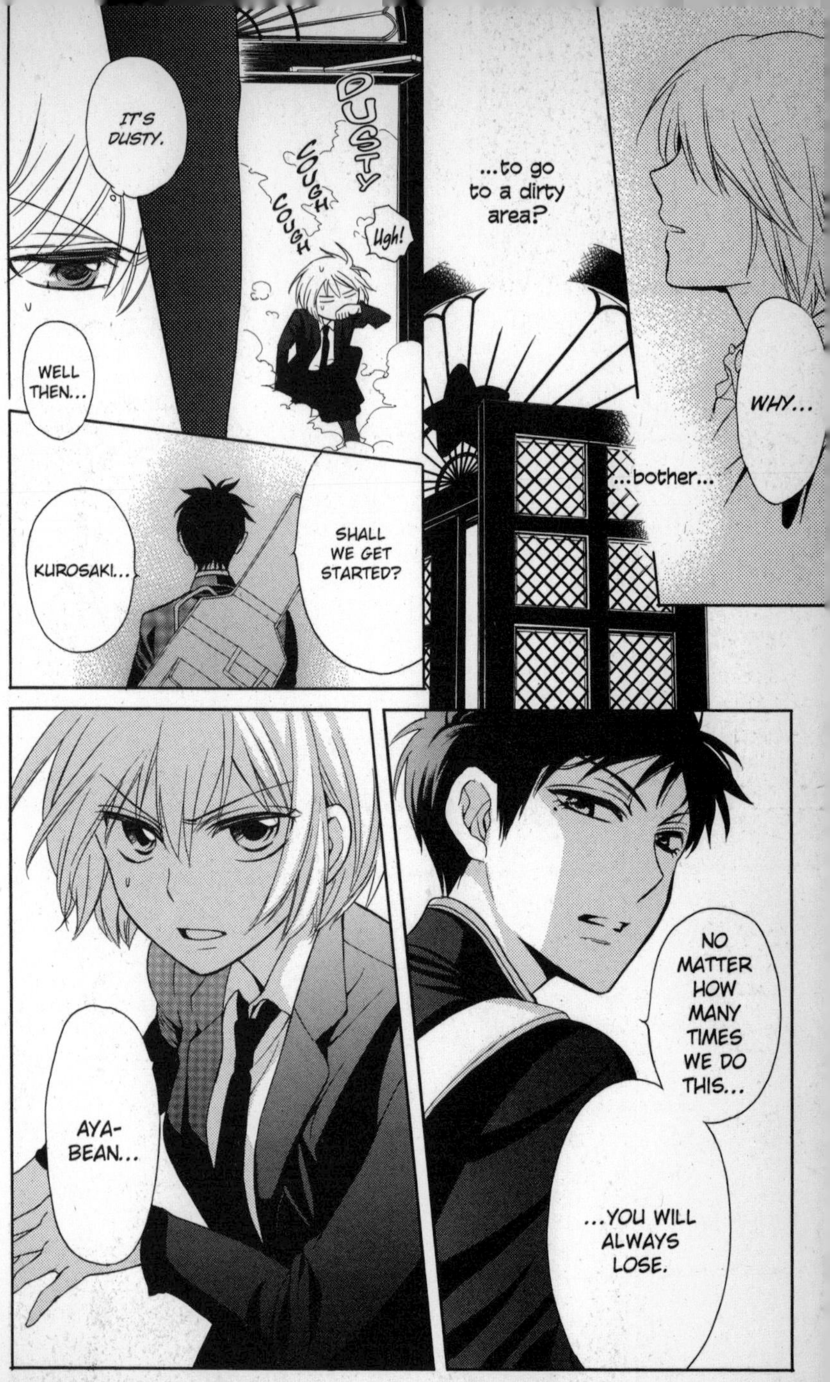
WHY...
...bother...
...to go to a dirty area?
DUSTY
COUGH COUGH
Ugh!
IT'S DUSTY.
WELL THEN...
SHALL WE GET STARTED?
KUROSAKI...
NO MATTER HOW MANY TIMES WE DO THIS...
...YOU WILL ALWAYS LOSE.
AYA-BEAN...

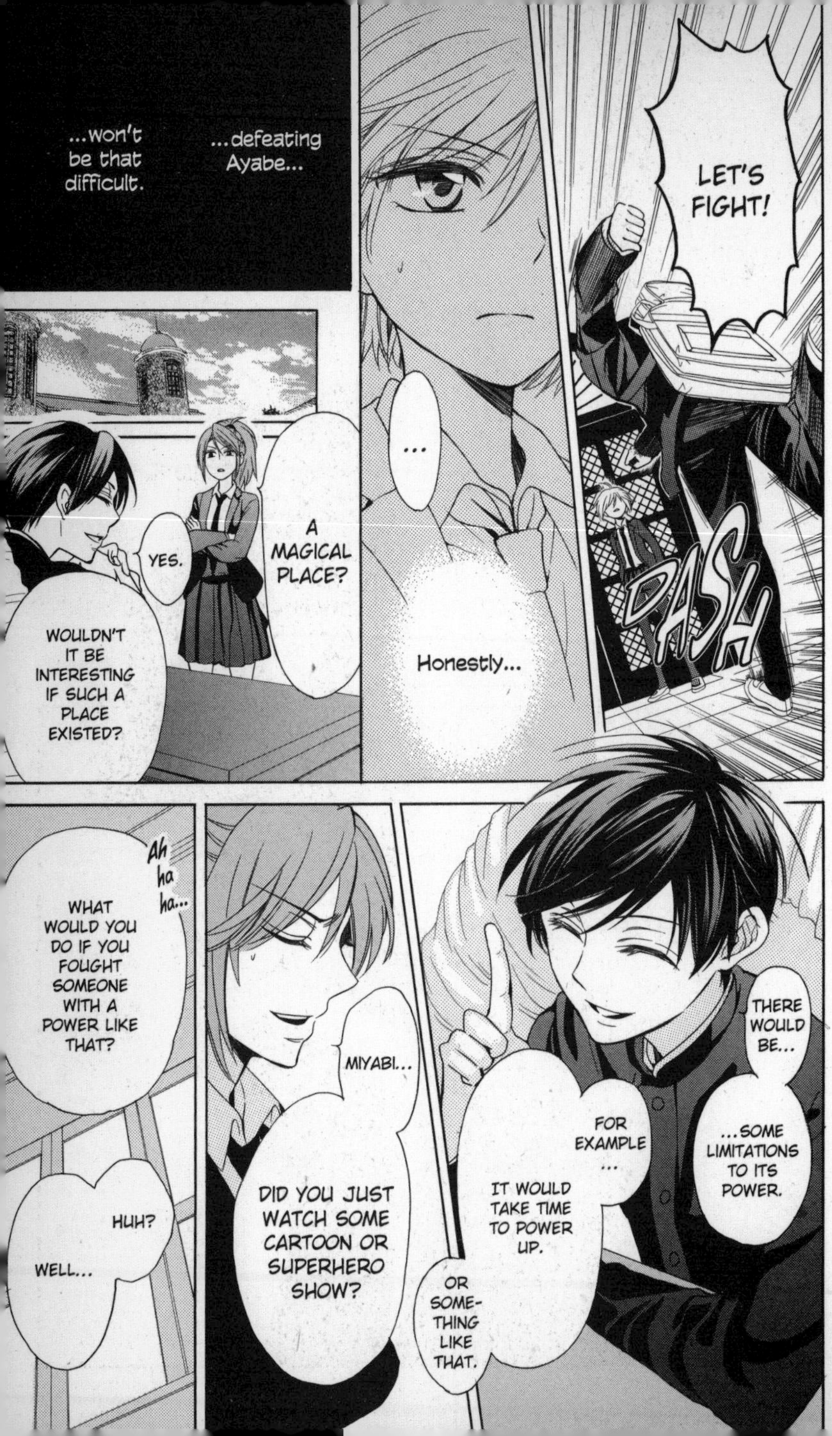
LET'S FIGHT!
DASH
...
Honestly...
...defeating Ayabe...
...won't be that difficult.
A MAGICAL PLACE?
YES.
WOULDN'T IT BE INTERESTING IF SUCH A PLACE EXISTED?
THERE WOULD BE...
...SOME LIMITATIONS TO ITS POWER.
FOR EXAMPLE...
IT WOULD TAKE TIME TO POWER UP.
OR SOME-THING LIKE THAT.
MIYABI...
DID YOU JUST WATCH SOME CARTOON OR SUPERHERO SHOW?
Ah ha ha...
WHAT WOULD YOU DO IF YOU FOUGHT SOMEONE WITH A POWER LIKE THAT?
HUH?
WELL...

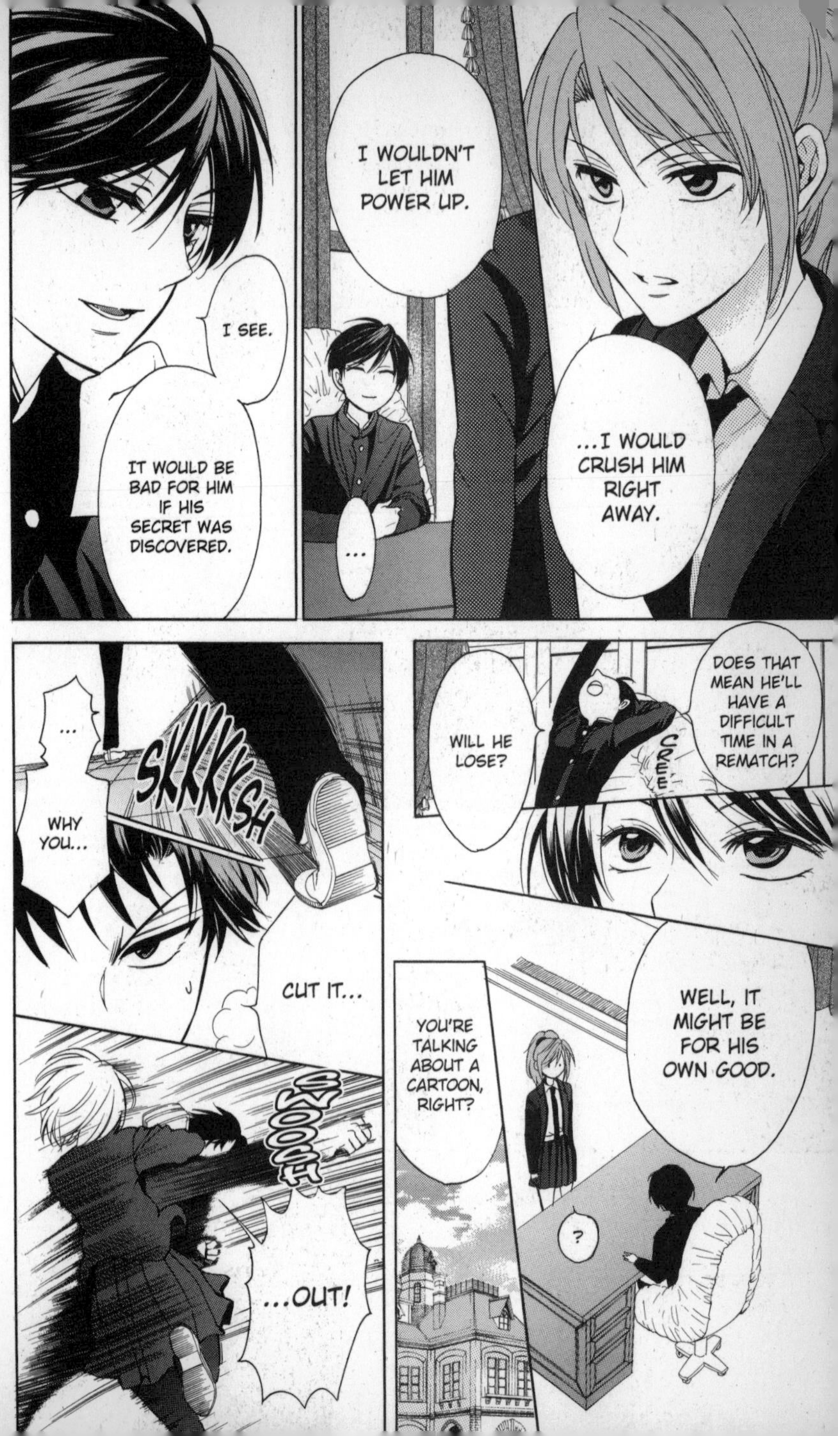

I WOULDN'T LET HIM POWER UP.
...I WOULD CRUSH HIM RIGHT AWAY.
...
I SEE.
IT WOULD BE BAD FOR HIM IF HIS SECRET WAS DISCOVERED.
DOES THAT MEAN HE'LL HAVE A DIFFICULT TIME IN A REMATCH?
CREE
WILL HE LOSE?
WELL, IT MIGHT BE FOR HIS OWN GOOD.
YOU'RE TALKING ABOUT A CARTOON, RIGHT?
?
...
SKKKKSH
WHY YOU...
CUT IT...
SWOOSH
...OUT!

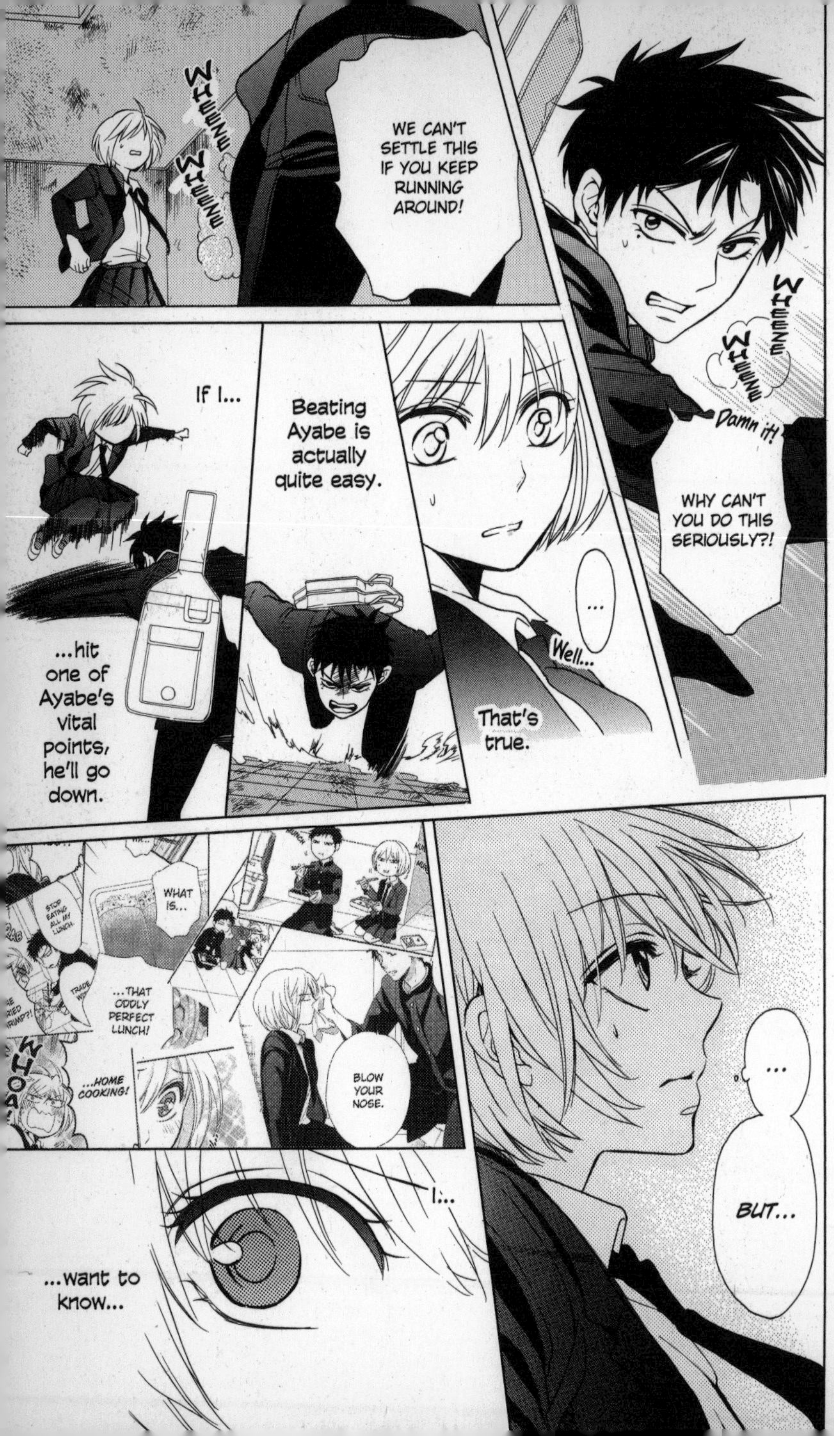
WHEEZE
WHEEZE
Damn it!
WHY CAN'T YOU DO THIS SERIOUSLY?!
WE CAN'T SETTLE THIS IF YOU KEEP RUNNING AROUND!
WHEEZE
WHEEZE
...
Well...
That's true.
Beating Ayabe is actually quite easy.
If I...
...hit one of Ayabe's vital points, he'll go down.
...
BUT...
BLOW YOUR NOSE.
WHAT IS...
...THAT ODDLY PERFECT LUNCH!
STOP EATING ALL MY LUNCH.
...HOME COOKING!
WHOA!
I...
...want to know...

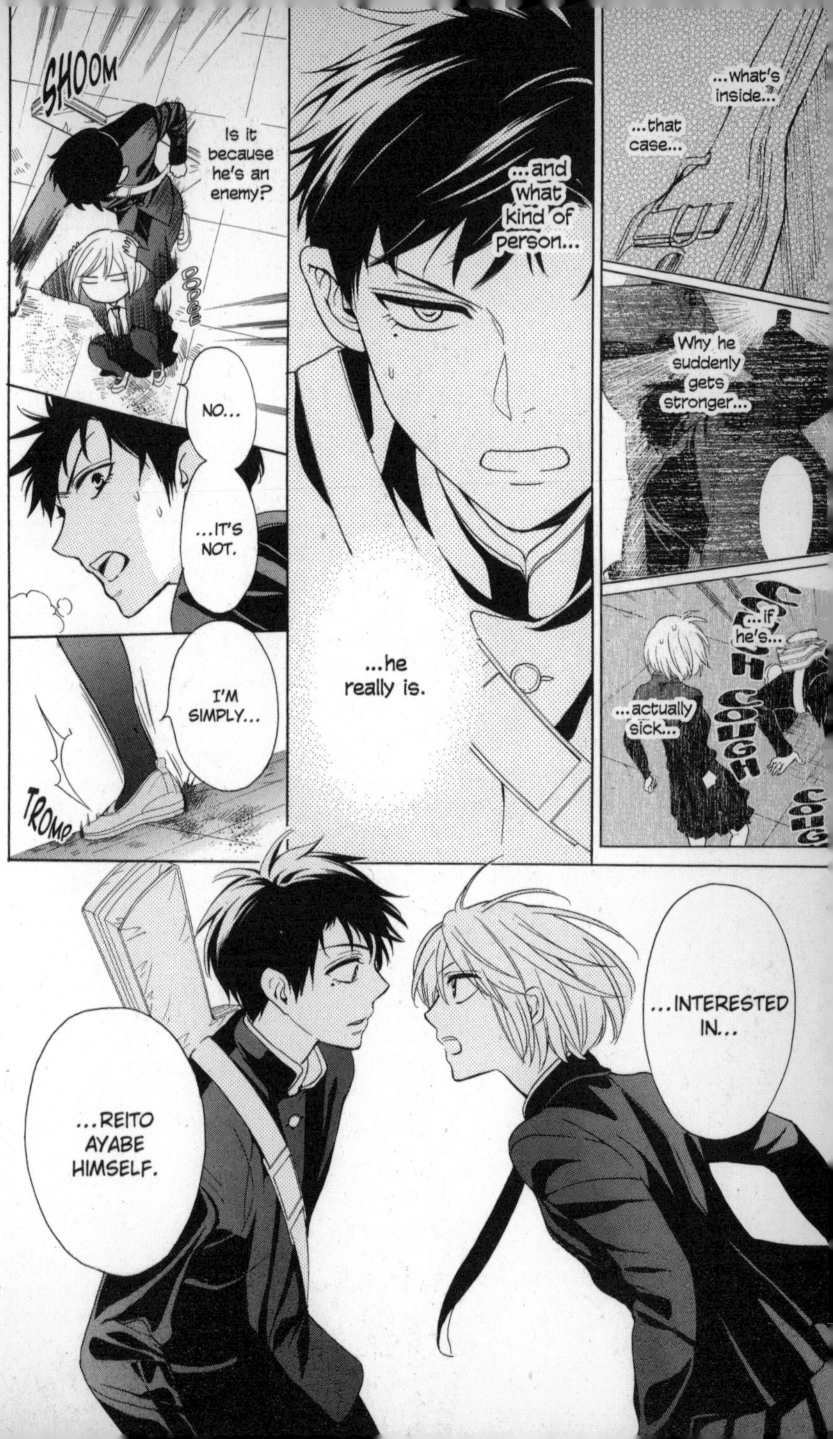
...what's inside...
...that case...
Why he suddenly gets stronger...
...if he's...
...actually sick...
COUGH
COUGH
...and what kind of person...
...he really is.
SHOOM
Is it because he's an enemy?
DODGE
NO...
...IT'S NOT.
I'M SIMPLY...
TROMP
...INTERESTED IN...
...REITO AYABE HIMSELF.

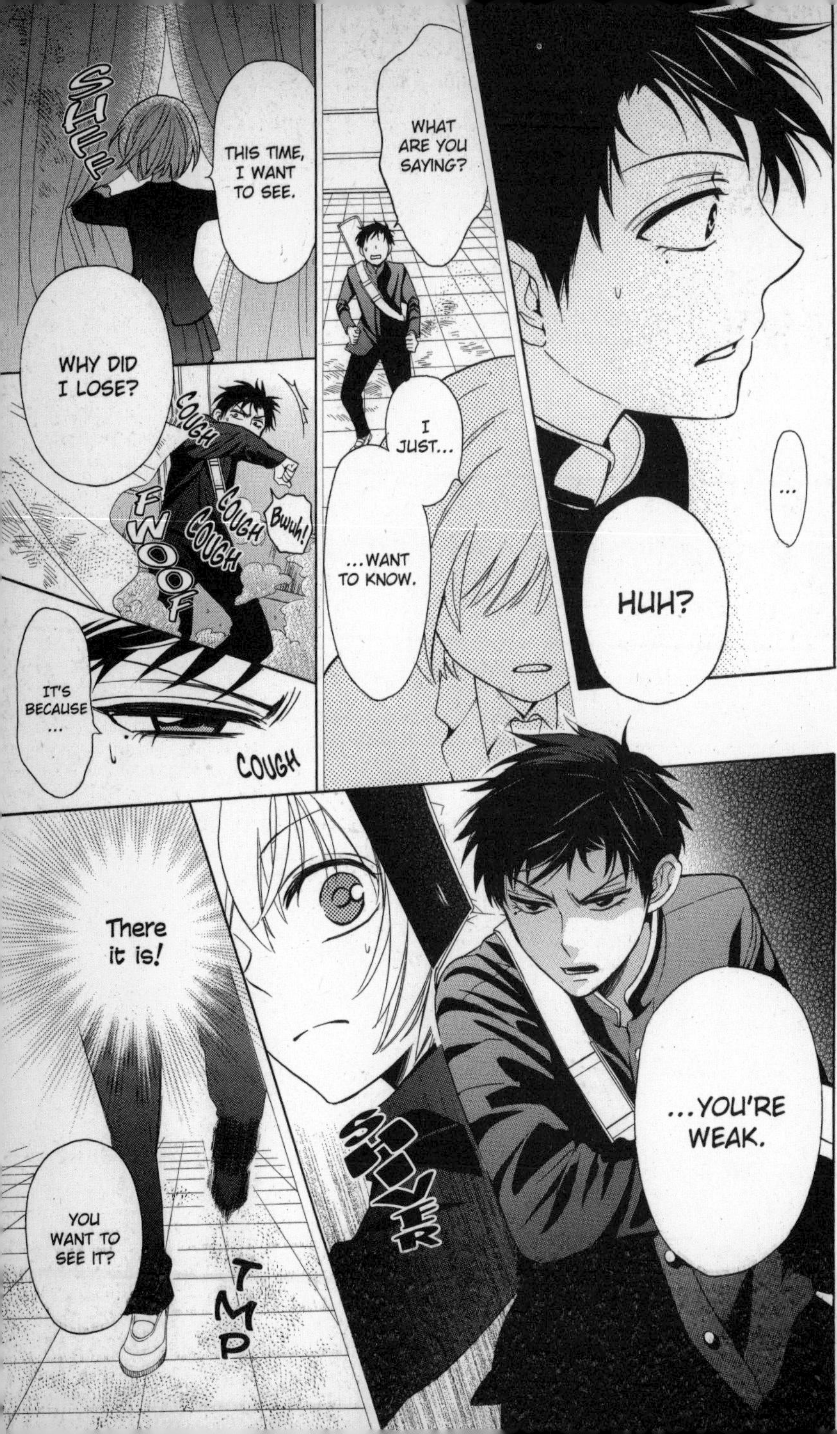
...
HUH?
WHAT ARE YOU SAYING?
I JUST...
...WANT TO KNOW.
SHFF
THIS TIME, I WANT TO SEE.
WHY DID I LOSE?
COUGH
Bwuh!
COUGH
COUGH
FWOOF
IT'S BECAUSE ...
COUGH
...YOU'RE WEAK.
SHIVER
There it is!
YOU WANT TO SEE IT?
TMP

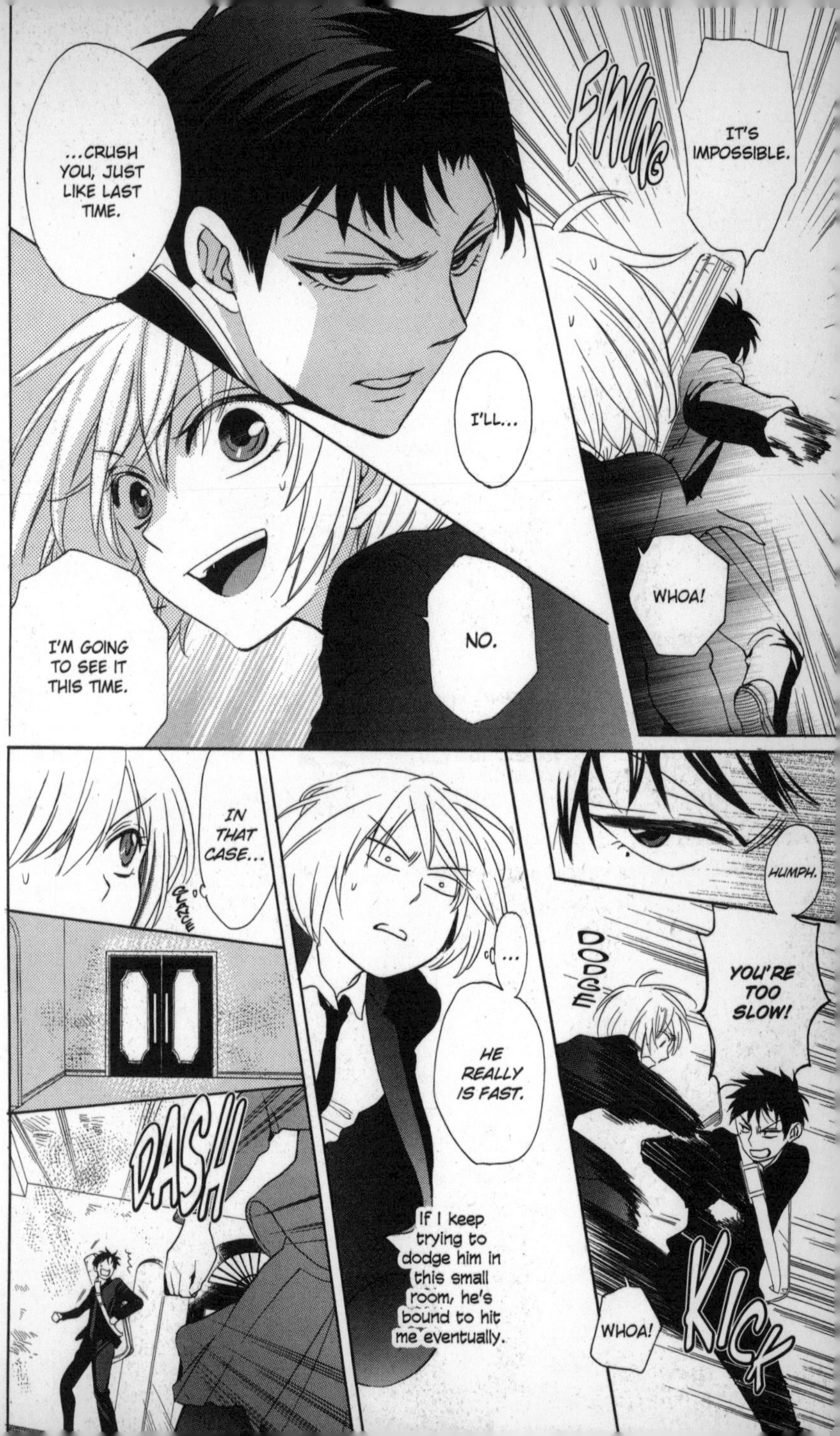
FWING
IT'S IMPOSSIBLE.
WHOA!
I'LL...
...CRUSH YOU, JUST LIKE LAST TIME.
NO.
I'M GOING TO SEE IT THIS TIME.
HUMPH.
DODGE
YOU'RE TOO SLOW!
KICK
WHOA!
...
HE REALLY IS FAST.
If I keep trying to dodge him in this small room, he's bound to hit me eventually.
IN THAT CASE...
DASH

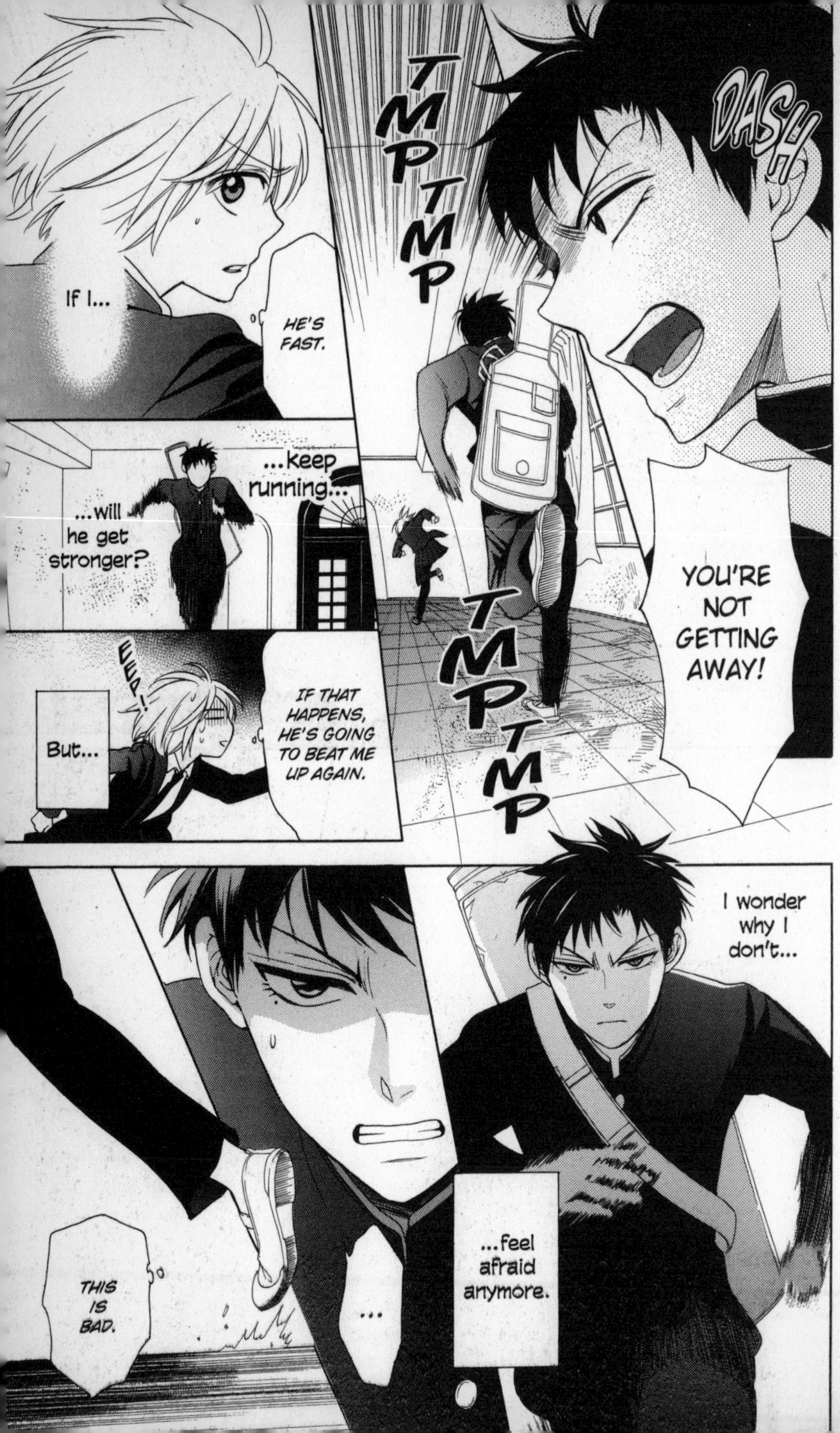
DASH
TMP TMP
TMP
YOU'RE NOT GETTING AWAY!
TMP TMP
TMP
HE'S FAST.
If I...
...keep running...
...will he get stronger?
IF THAT HAPPENS, HE'S GOING TO BEAT ME UP AGAIN.
EEP!
But...
I wonder why I don't...
...feel afraid anymore.
...
THIS IS BAD.

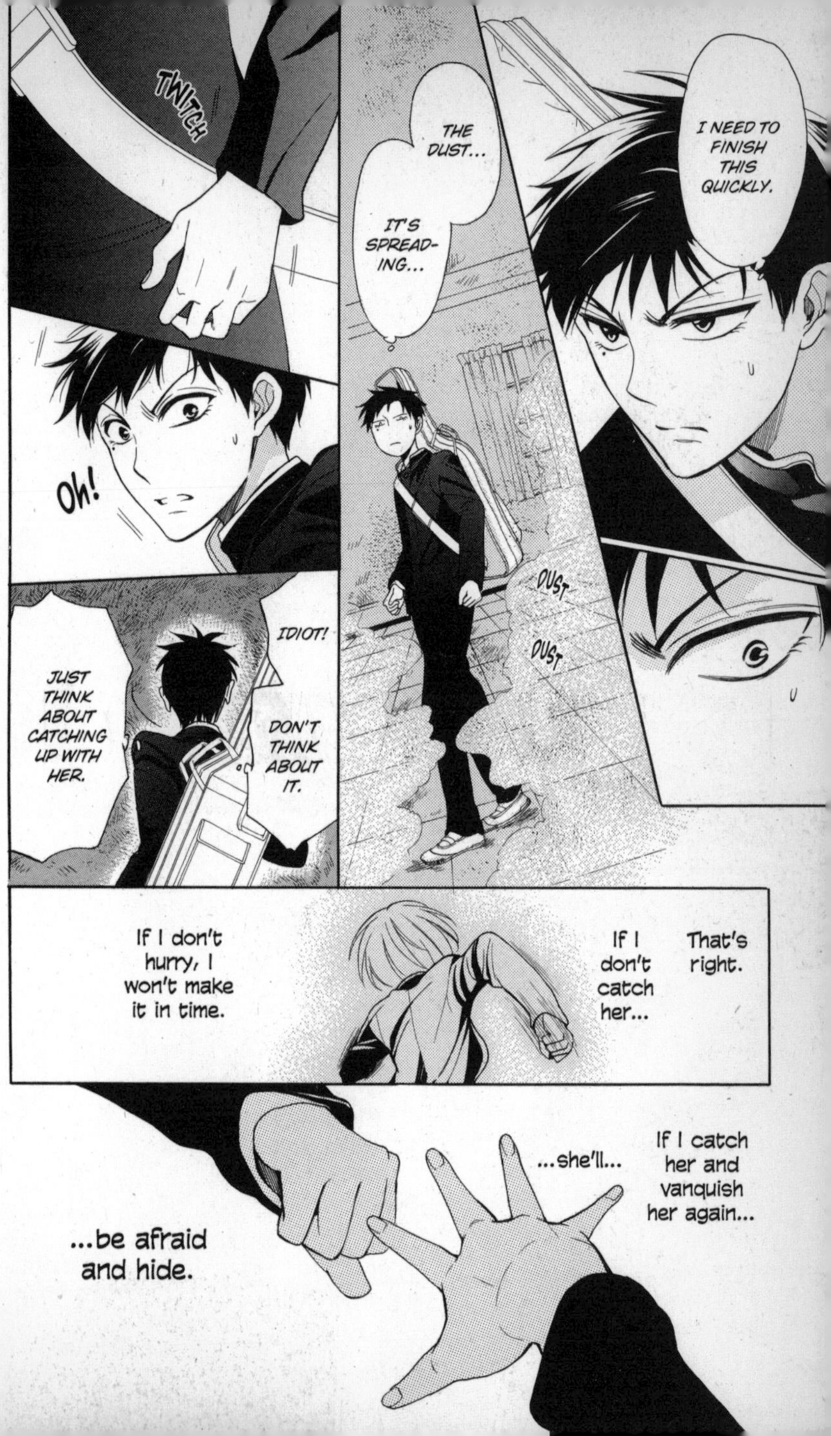
I NEED TO FINISH THIS QUICKLY.
THE DUST...
IT'S SPREADING...
DUST
DUST
TWITCH
Oh!
IDIOT!
DON'T THINK ABOUT IT.
JUST THINK ABOUT CATCHING UP WITH HER.
That's right.
If I don't catch her...
If I don't hurry, I won't make it in time.
If I catch her and vanquish her again...
...she'll...
...be afraid and hide.

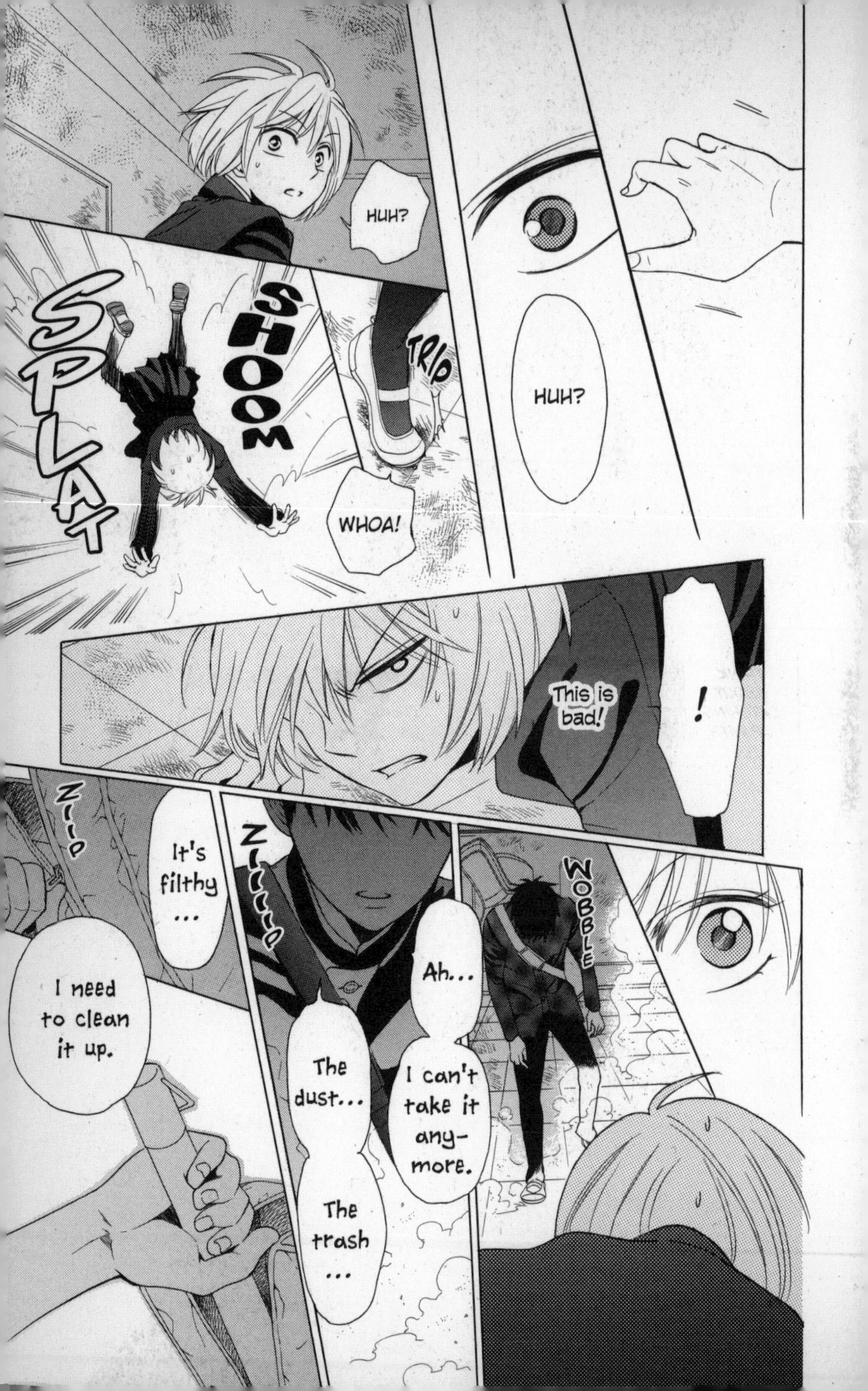

HUH?
HUH?
TRIP
WHOA!
SHOOM
SPLAT
!
This is bad!
WOBBLE
Zirrrrip
Ah...
I can't take it anymore.
The dust...
The trash...
Zrip
It's filthy...
I need to clean it up.

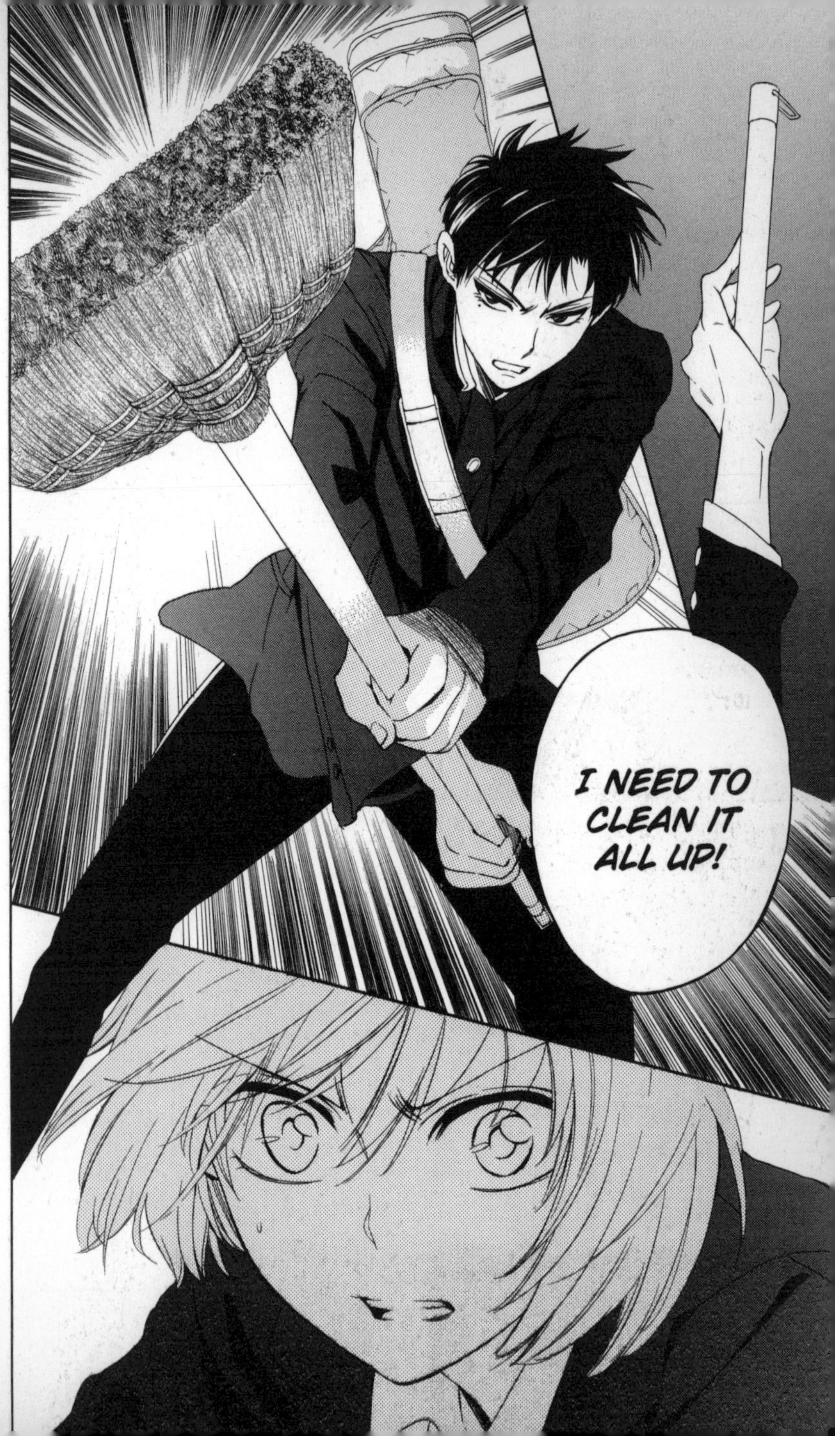
I NEED TO CLEAN IT ALL UP!

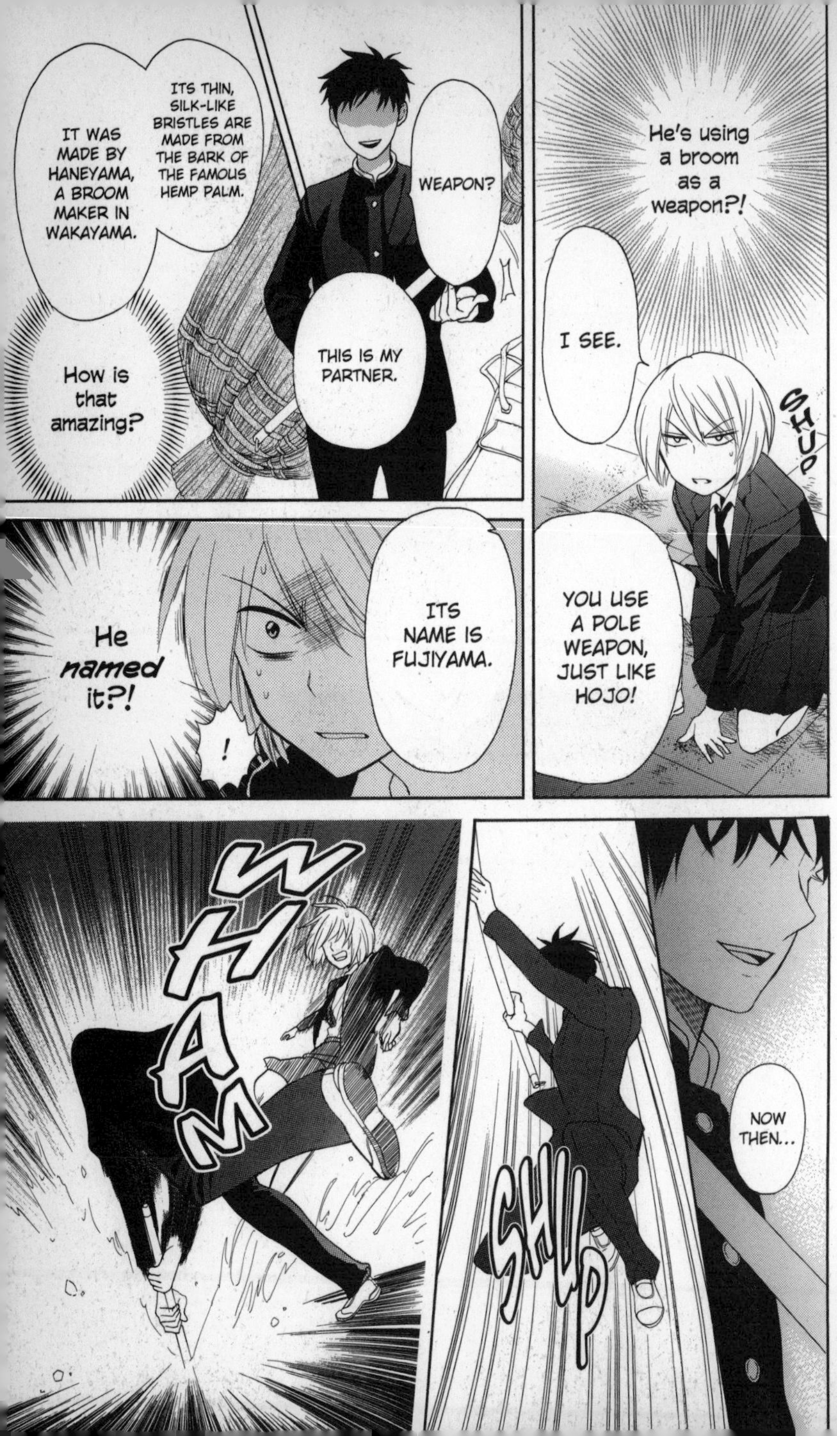
He's using a broom as a weapon?!
I SEE.
SHUP
YOU USE A POLE WEAPON, JUST LIKE HOJO!
WEAPON?
THIS IS MY PARTNER.
ITS THIN, SILK-LIKE BRISTLES ARE MADE FROM THE BARK OF THE FAMOUS HEMP PALM.
IT WAS MADE BY HANEYAMA, A BROOM MAKER IN WAKAYAMA.
How is that amazing?
ITS NAME IS FUJIYAMA.
!
He *named* it?!
NOW THEN...
SHUP
WHAM

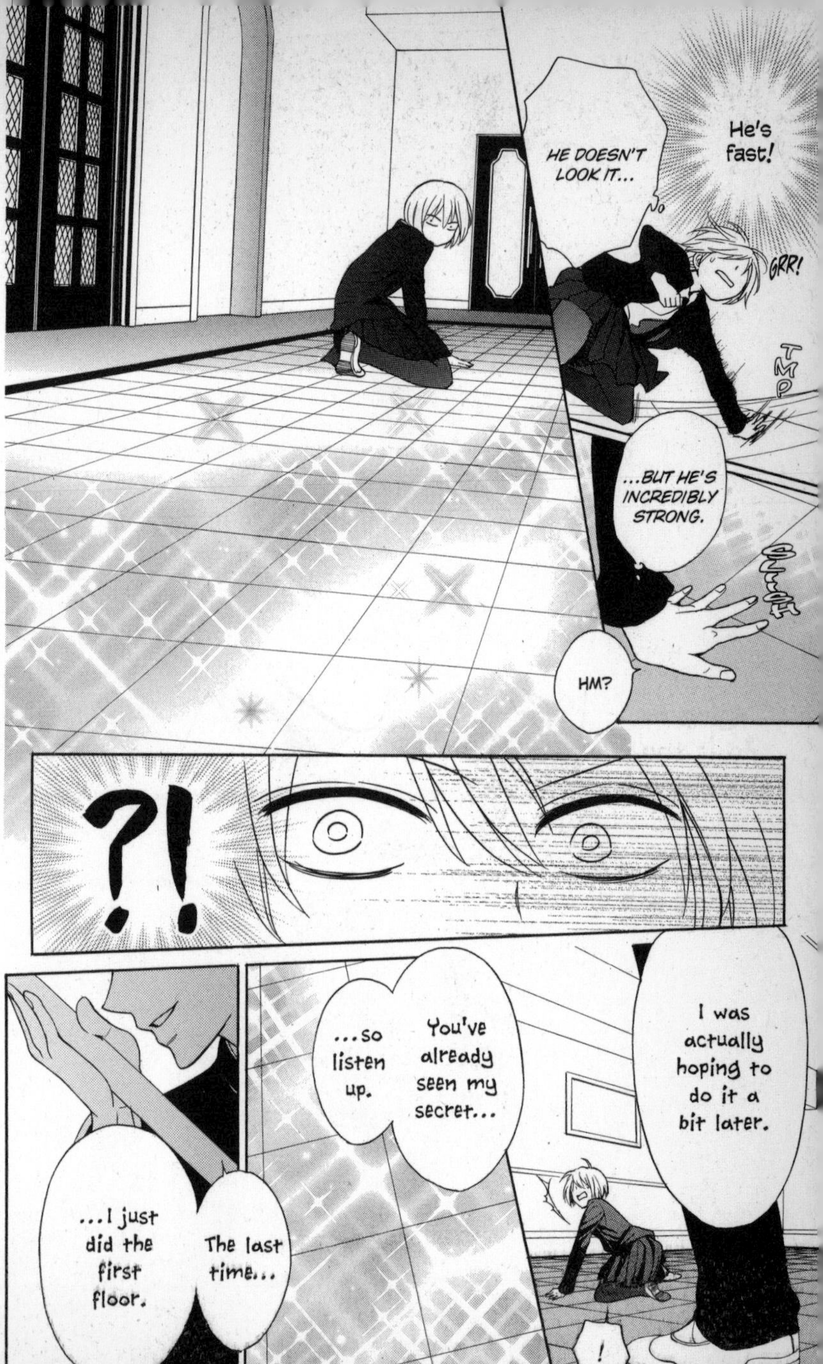
He's fast!
HE DOESN'T LOOK IT...
GRR!
TMP
...BUT HE'S INCREDIBLY STRONG.
HM?
?!
I was actually hoping to do it a bit later.
You've already seen my secret...
...so listen up.
!
The last time...
...I just did the first floor.

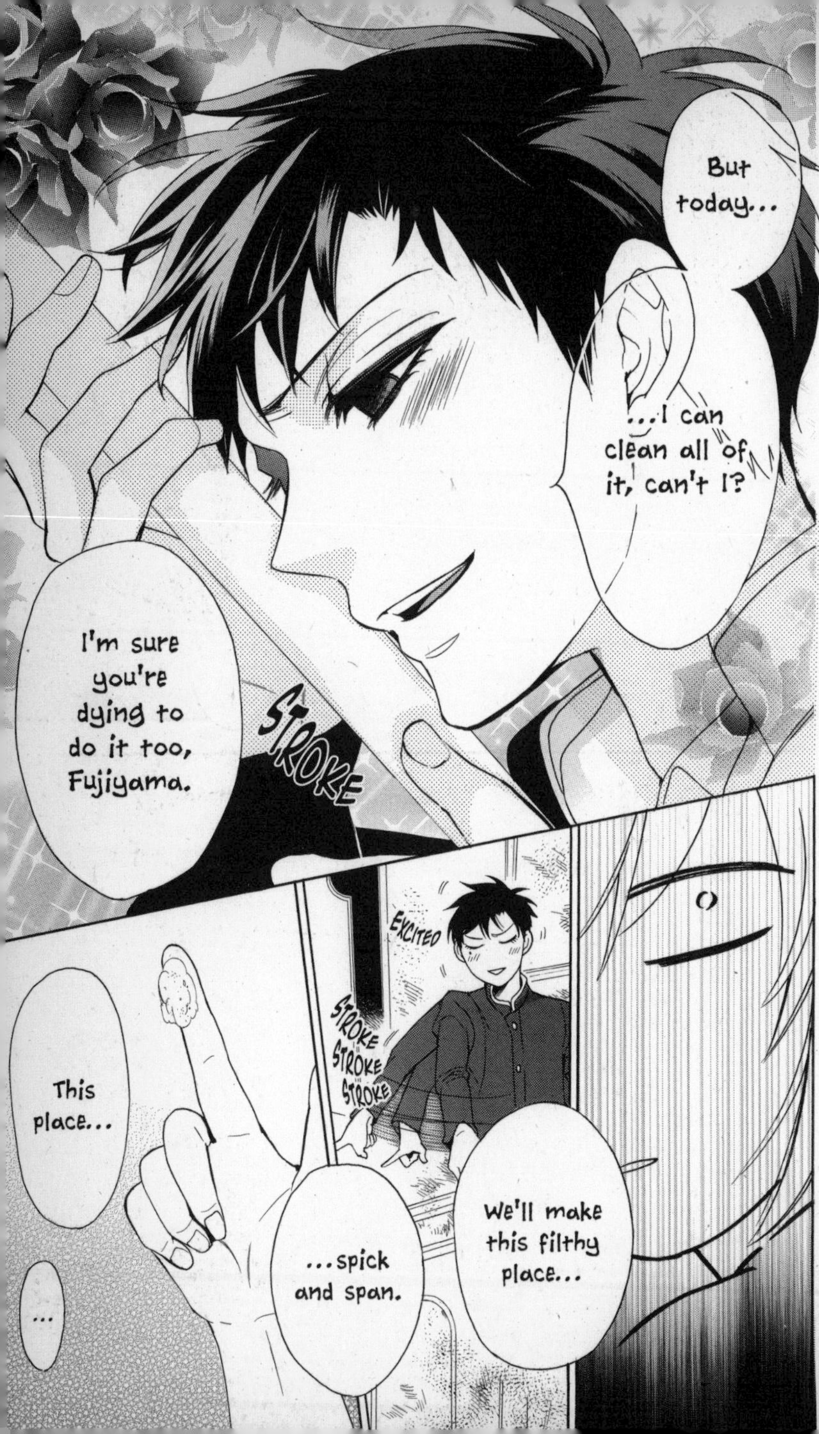
But today...
...I can clean all of it, can't I?
I'm sure you're dying to do it too, Fujiyama.
STROKE
We'll make this filthy place...
...spick and span.
EXCITED
STROKE STROKE STROKE
This place...
...

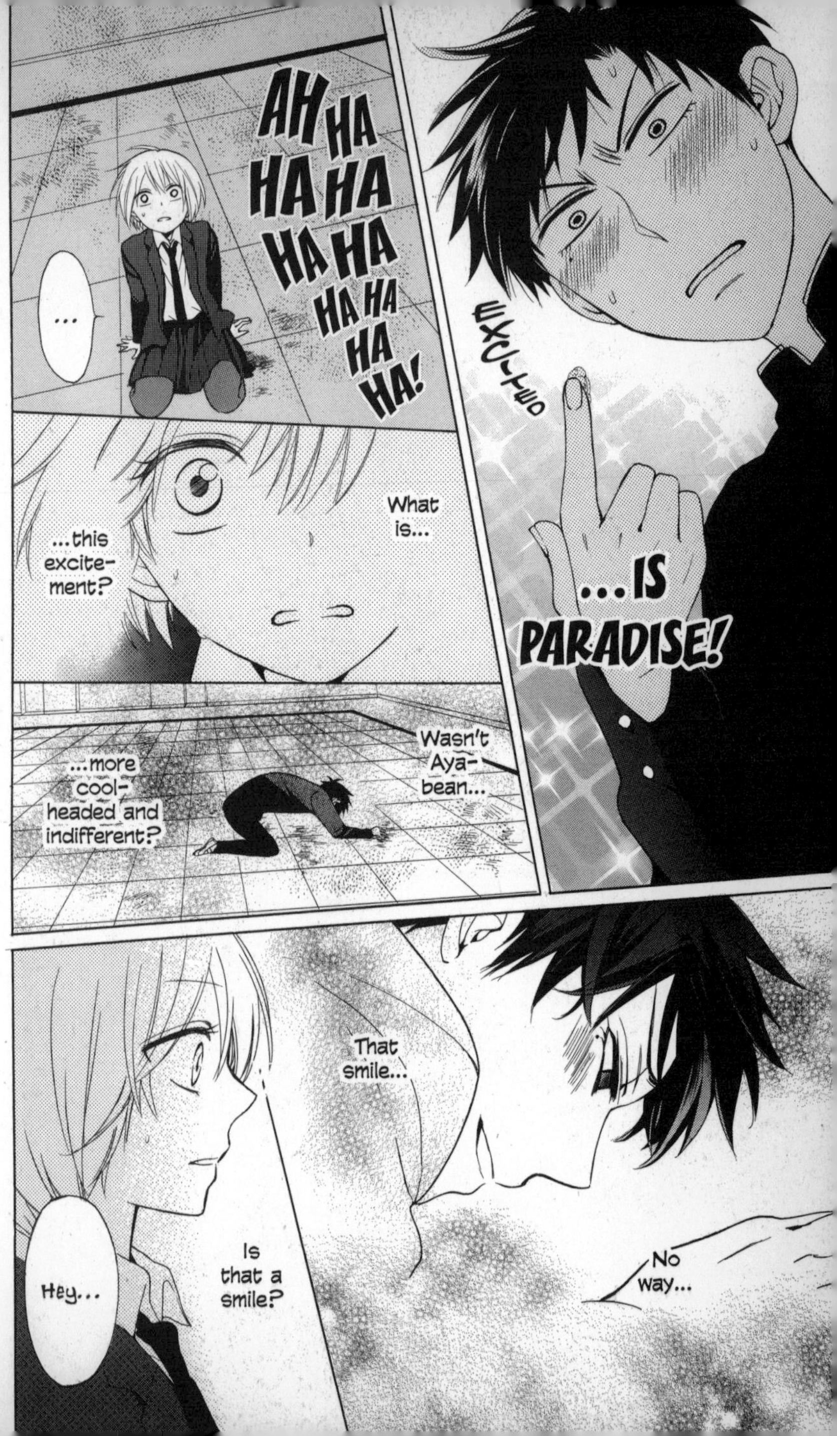
EXCITED
...IS PARADISE!
AH HA HA HA HA HA HA HA HA HA!
...
What is...
...this excitement?
Wasn't Aya-bean...
...more cool-headed and indifferent?
No way...
That smile...
Is that a smile?
Hey...

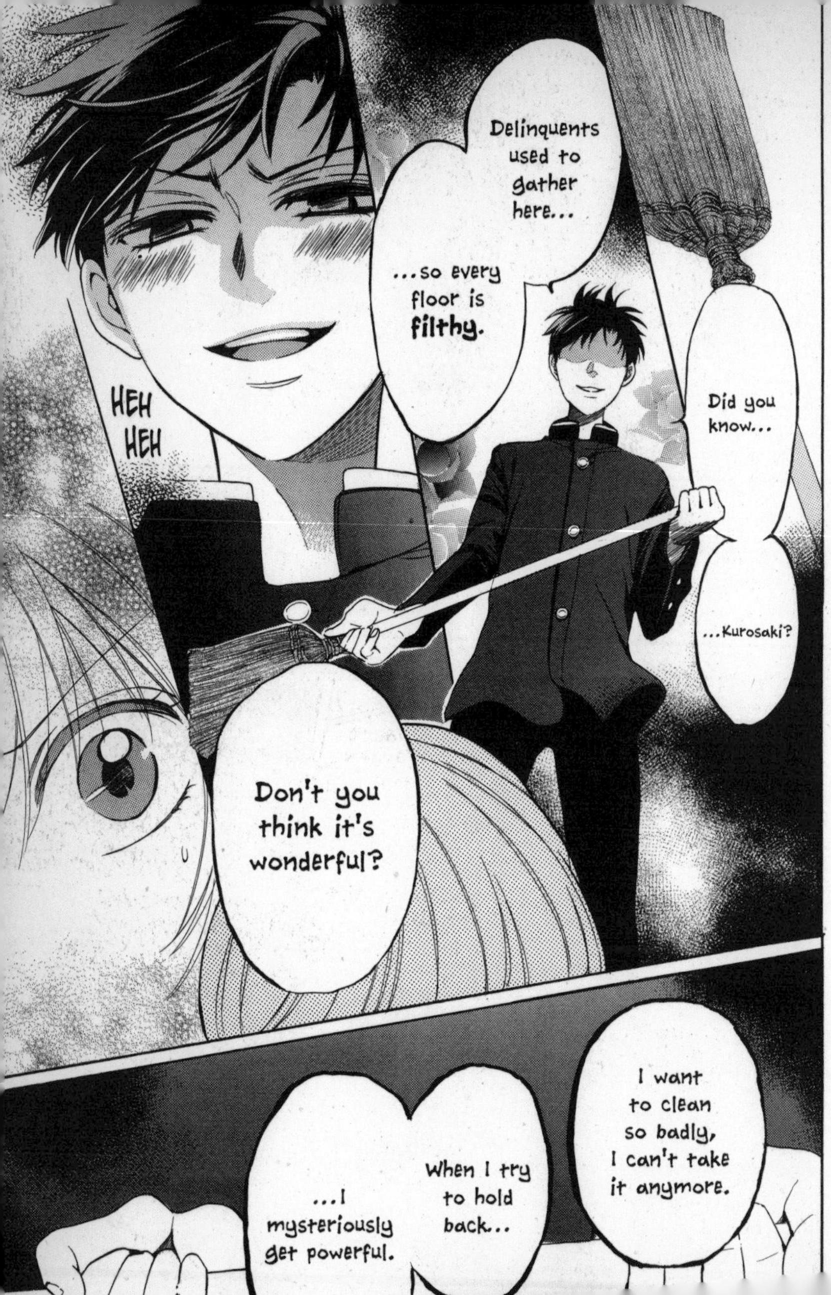
Delinquents used to gather here...
...so every floor is filthy.
Did you know...
...Kurosaki?
HEH HEH
Don't you think it's wonderful?
I want to clean so badly, I can't take it anymore.
When I try to hold back...
...I mysteriously get powerful.

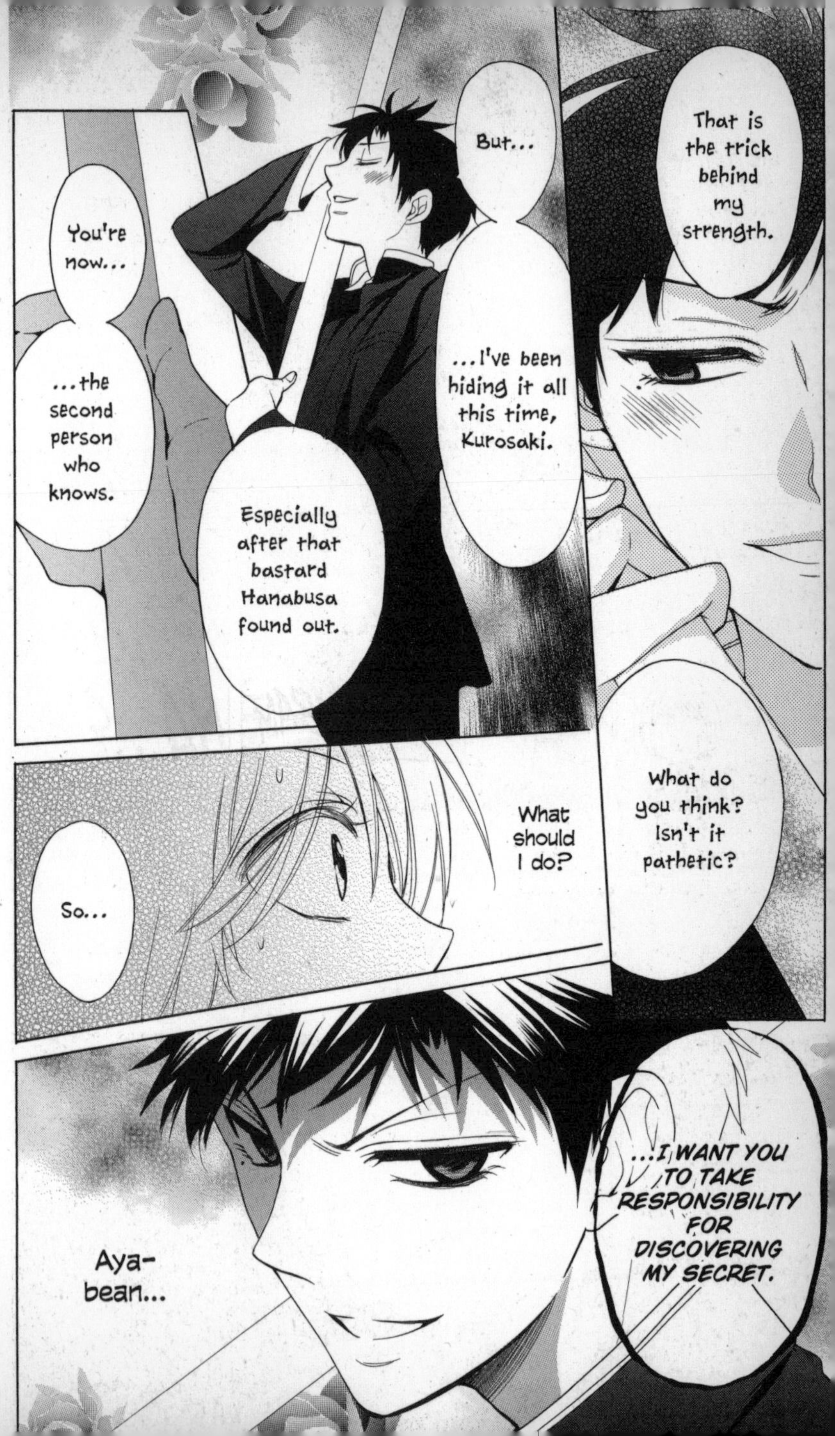
That is the trick behind my strength.
What do you think? Isn't it pathetic?
But...
...I've been hiding it all this time, Kurosaki.
Especially after that bastard Hanabusa found out.
You're now...
...the second person who knows.
What should I do?
So...
...I WANT YOU TO TAKE RESPONSIBILITY FOR DISCOVERING MY SECRET.
Aya-bean...

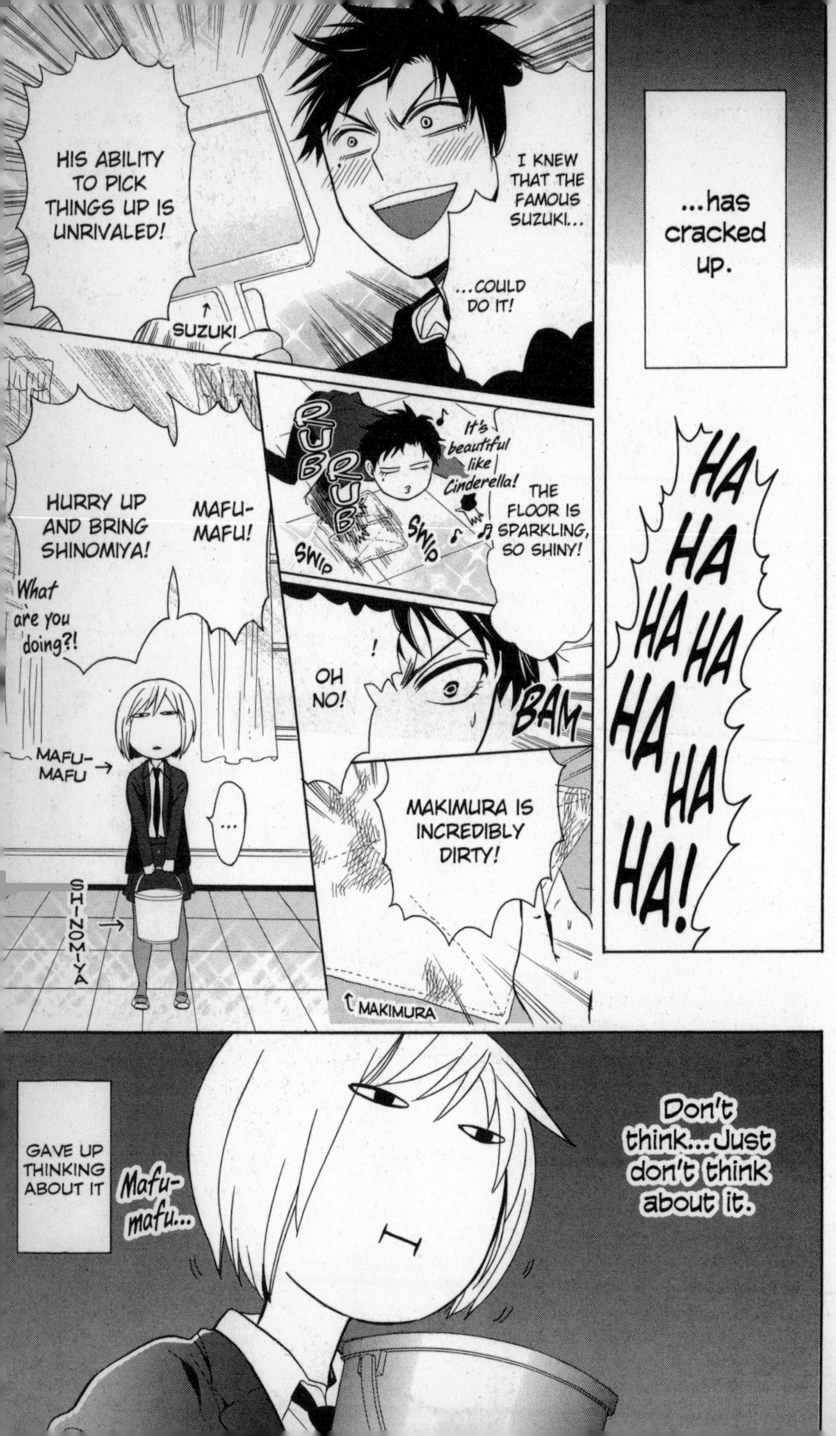
...has cracked up.
HA HA HA HA HA HA HA HA HA!
I KNEW THAT THE FAMOUS SUZUKI...
...COULD DO IT!
HIS ABILITY TO PICK THINGS UP IS UNRIVALED!
SUZUKI
It's beautiful like Cinderella!
THE FLOOR IS SPARKLING, SO SHINY!
RUB RUB
SWIP SWIP
!
OH NO!
BAM
MAKIMURA IS INCREDIBLY DIRTY!
MAKIMURA
MAFU-MAFU!
HURRY UP AND BRING SHINOMIYA!
What are you doing?!
...
MAFU-MAFU
SHINOMIYA
Don't think...Just don't think about it.
Mafu-mafu...
GAVE UP THINKING ABOUT IT

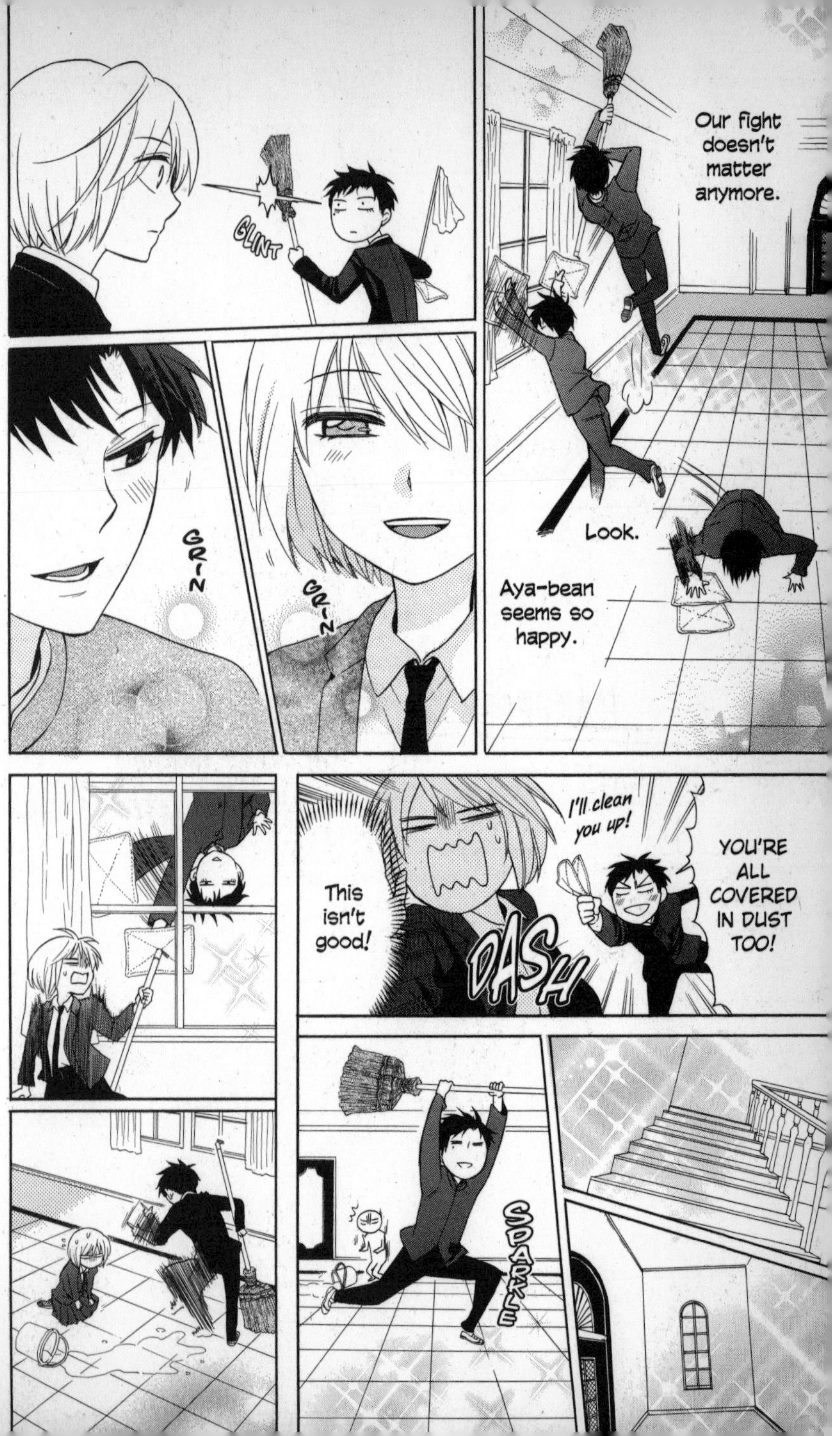
Our fight doesn't matter anymore.
Look.
Aya-bean seems so happy.
GLINT
GRIN
GRIN
I'll clean you up!
YOU'RE ALL COVERED IN DUST TOO!
This isn't good!
DASH
SPARKLE

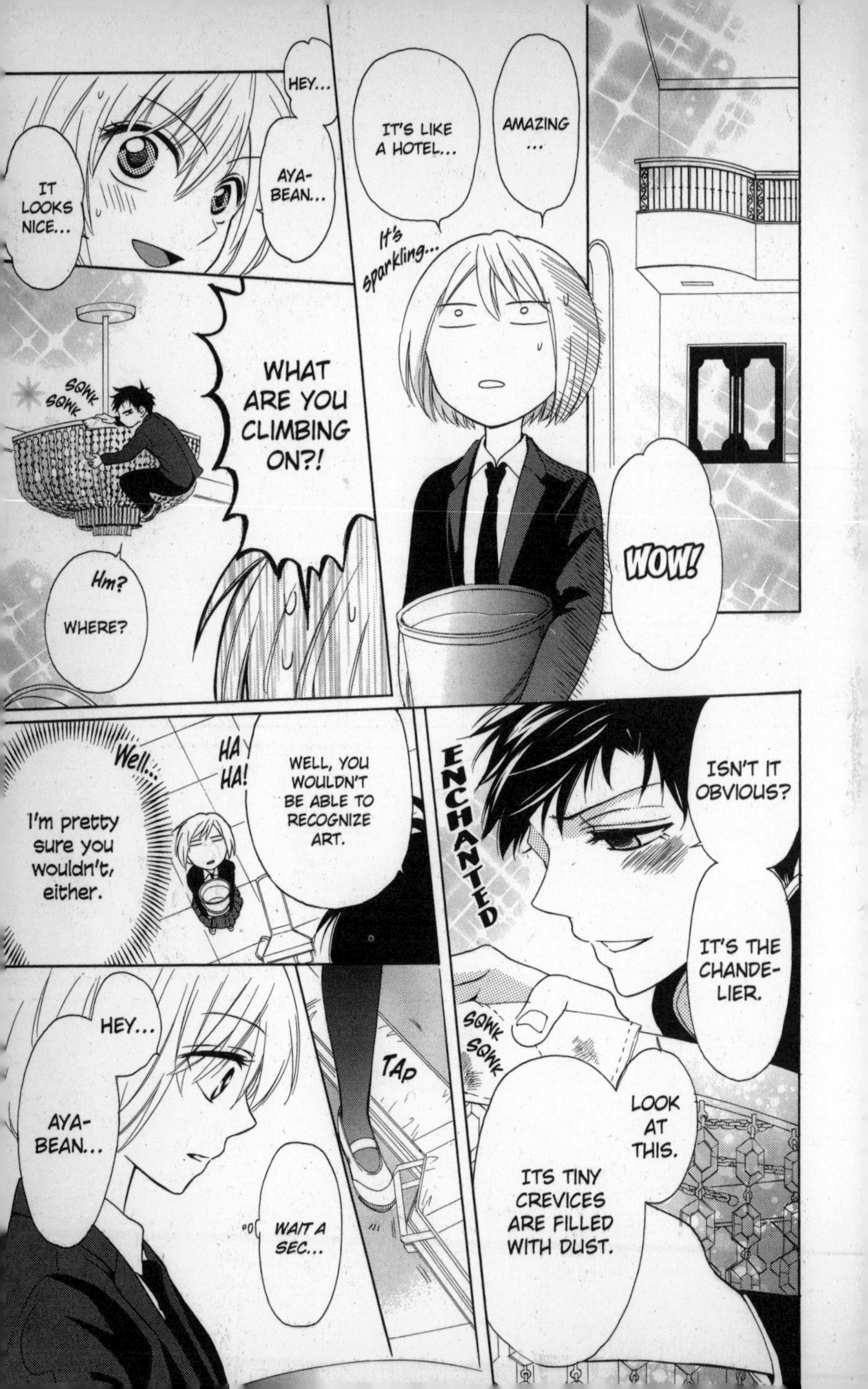

WOW!
AMAZING...
IT'S LIKE A HOTEL...
It's sparkling...
HEY... AYA-BEAN...
IT LOOKS NICE...
WHAT ARE YOU CLIMBING ON?!
SQWK SQWK
Hm? WHERE?
ENCHANTED
ISN'T IT OBVIOUS?
IT'S THE CHANDELIER.
WELL, YOU WOULDN'T BE ABLE TO RECOGNIZE ART.
HA HA!
Well... I'm pretty sure you wouldn't, either.
SQWK SQWK
LOOK AT THIS.
ITS TINY CREVICES ARE FILLED WITH DUST.
TAP
WAIT A SEC...
HEY... AYA-BEAN...

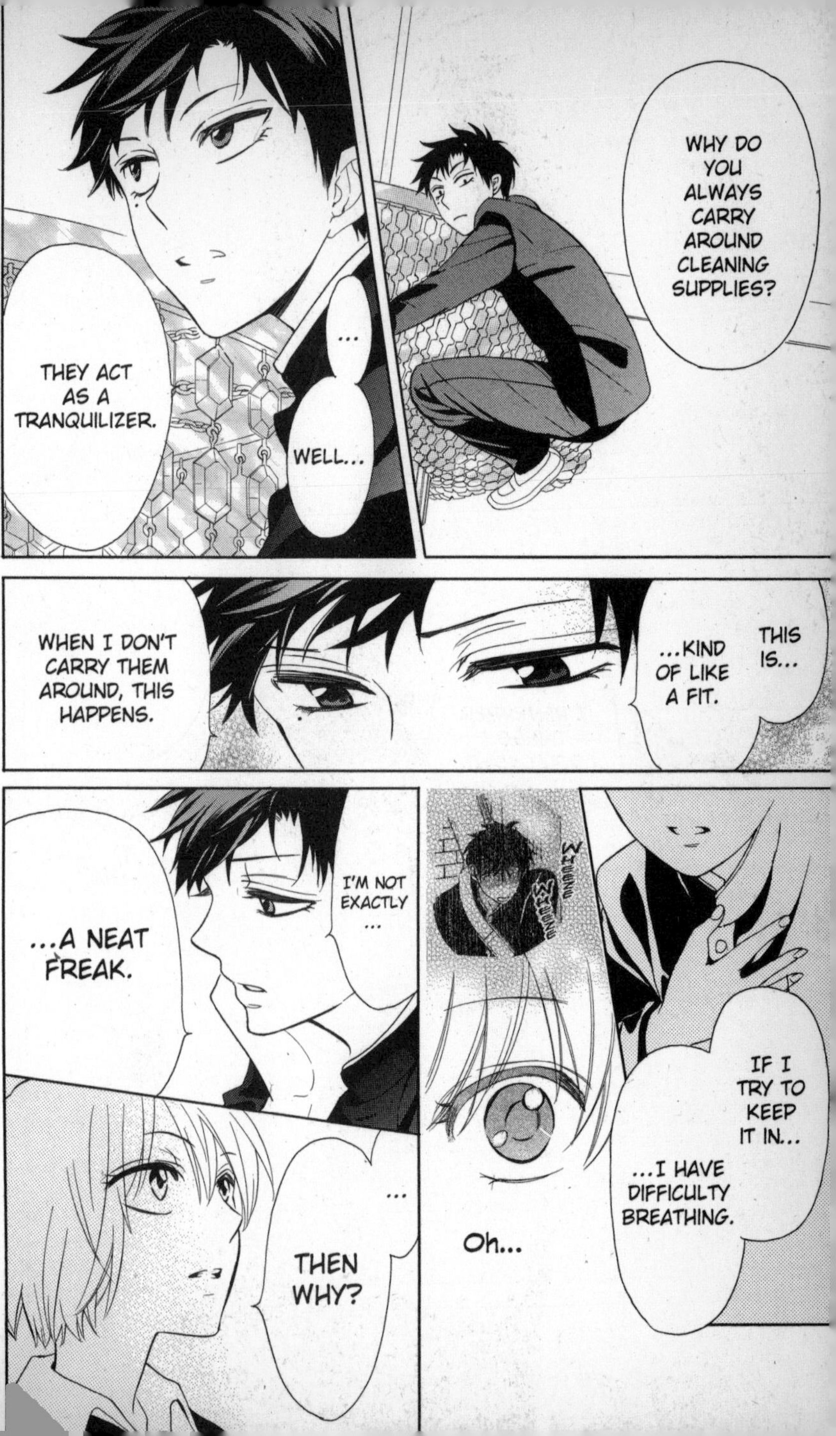
WHY DO YOU ALWAYS CARRY AROUND CLEANING SUPPLIES?
...
WELL...
THEY ACT AS A TRANQUILIZER.
THIS IS...
...KIND OF LIKE A FIT.
WHEN I DON'T CARRY THEM AROUND, THIS HAPPENS.
WHEEZE
WHEEZE
IF I TRY TO KEEP IT IN...
...I HAVE DIFFICULTY BREATHING.
Oh...
I'M NOT EXACTLY ...
...A NEAT FREAK.
...
THEN WHY?

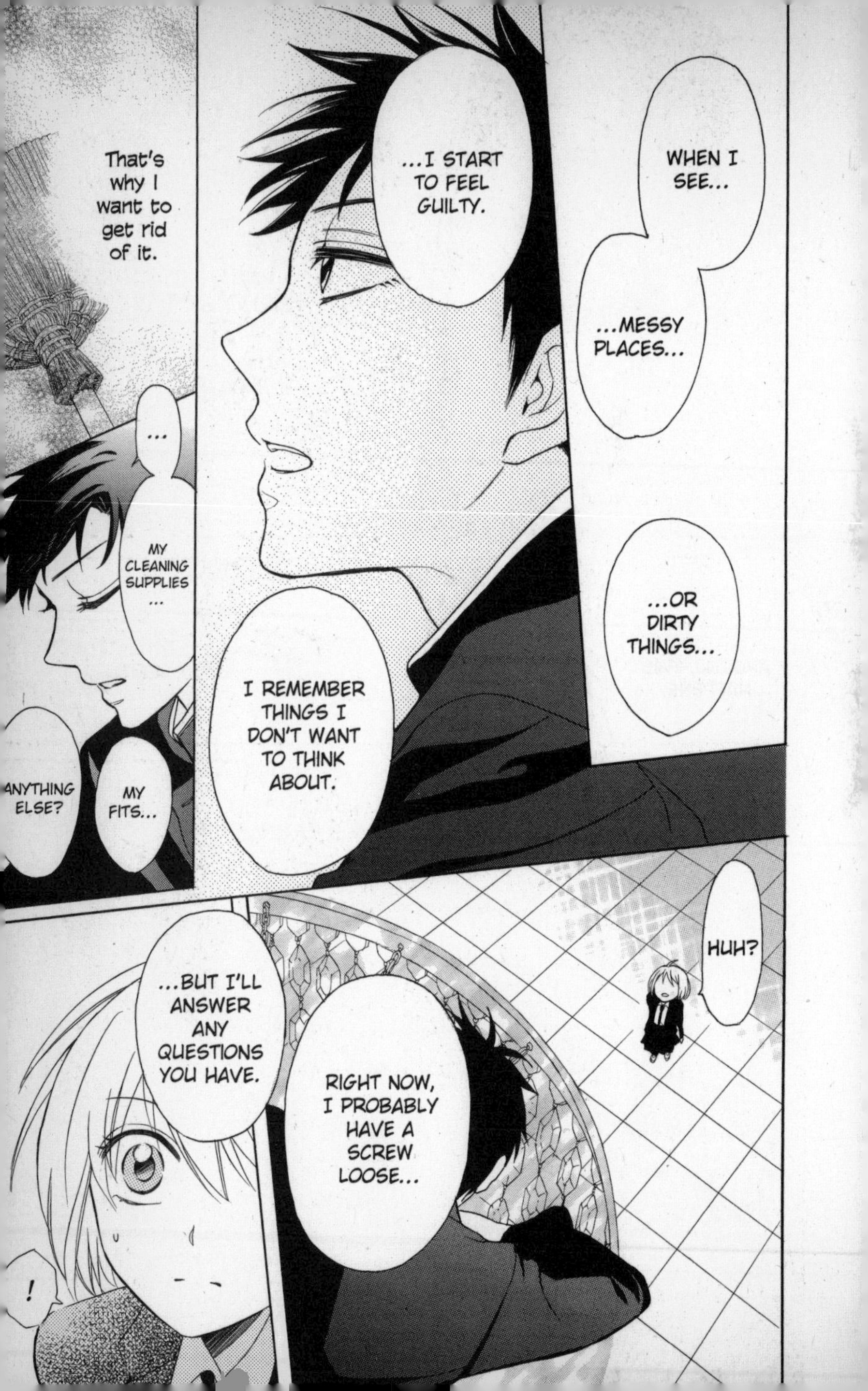
WHEN I SEE...
...MESSY PLACES...
...OR DIRTY THINGS...
...I START TO FEEL GUILTY.
I REMEMBER THINGS I DON'T WANT TO THINK ABOUT.
That's why I want to get rid of it.
...
MY CLEANING SUPPLIES...
MY FITS...
ANYTHING ELSE?
HUH?
RIGHT NOW, I PROBABLY HAVE A SCREW LOOSE...
...BUT I'LL ANSWER ANY QUESTIONS YOU HAVE.
!

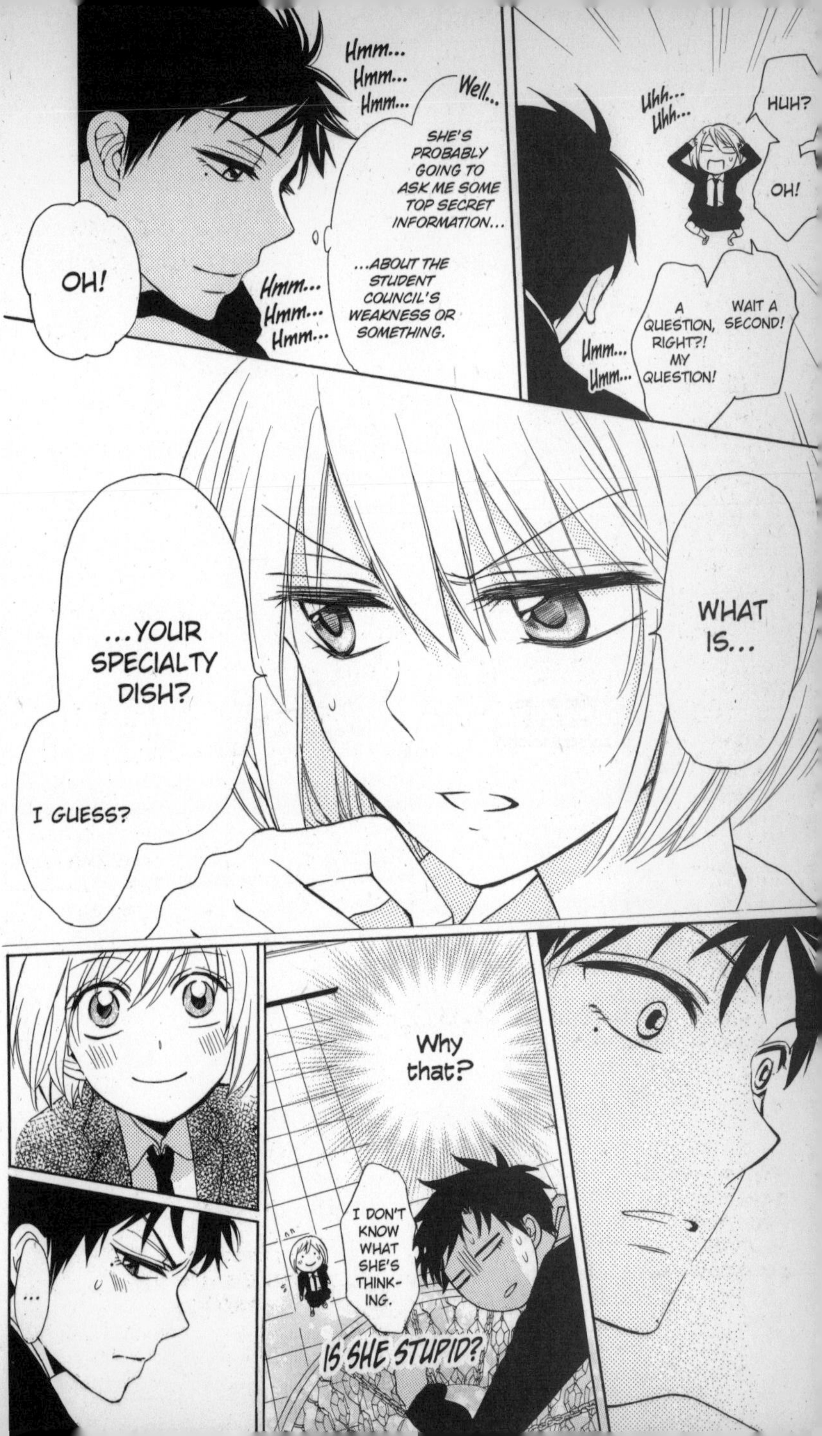
HUH?
OH!
Uhh... Uhh...
WAIT A SECOND!
A QUESTION, RIGHT?! MY QUESTION!
Umm... Umm...
Hmm... Hmm... Hmm...
Well...
SHE'S PROBABLY GOING TO ASK ME SOME TOP SECRET INFORMATION...
...ABOUT THE STUDENT COUNCIL'S WEAKNESS OR SOMETHING.
Hmm... Hmm... Hmm...
OH!
WHAT IS...
...YOUR SPECIALTY DISH?
I GUESS?
Why that?
I DON'T KNOW WHAT SHE'S THINK-ING.
IS SHE STUPID?
...

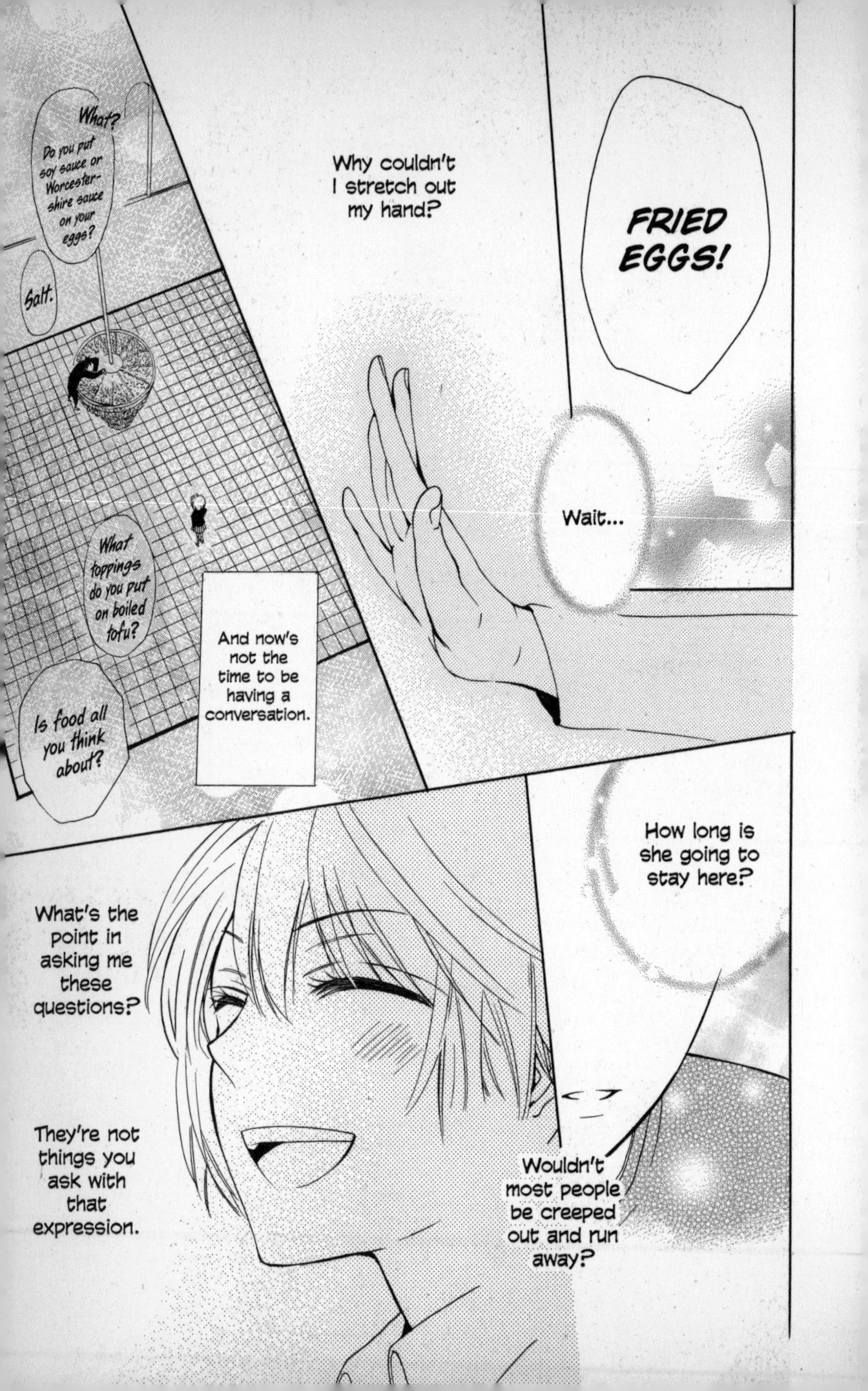
FRIED EGGS!
Wait...
Why couldn't I stretch out my hand?
What?
Do you put soy sauce or Worcester-shire sauce on your eggs?
Salt.
What toppings do you put on boiled tofu?
Is food all you think about?
And now's not the time to be having a conversation.
How long is she going to stay here?
Wouldn't most people be creeped out and run away?
What's the point in asking me these questions?
They're not things you ask with that expression.

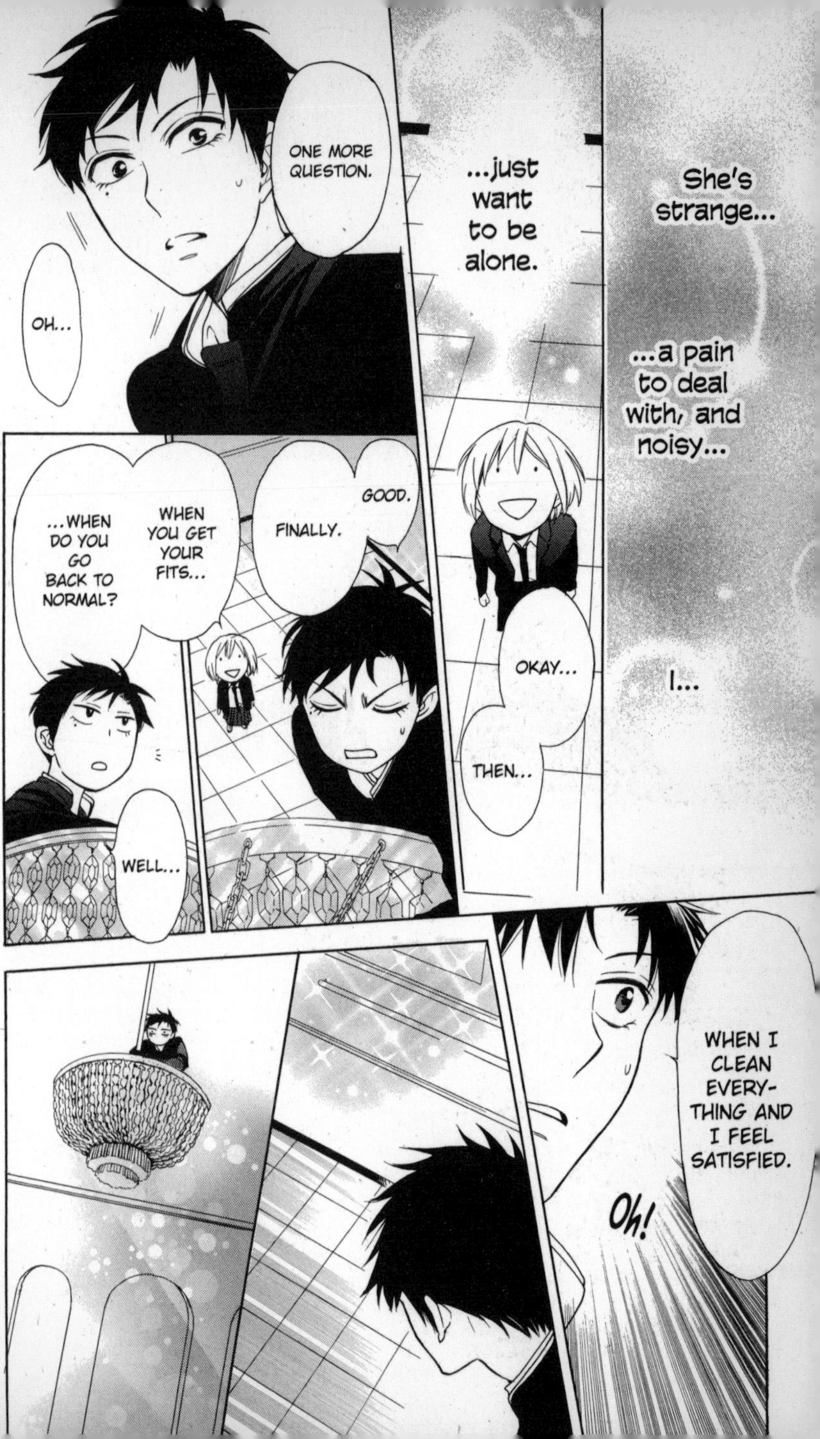
She's strange...
...a pain to deal with, and noisy...
I...
...just want to be alone.
OKAY...
THEN...
ONE MORE QUESTION.
OH...
GOOD.
FINALLY.
WHEN YOU GET YOUR FITS...
...WHEN DO YOU GO BACK TO NORMAL?
WELL...
WHEN I CLEAN EVERYTHING AND I FEEL SATISFIED.
Oh!

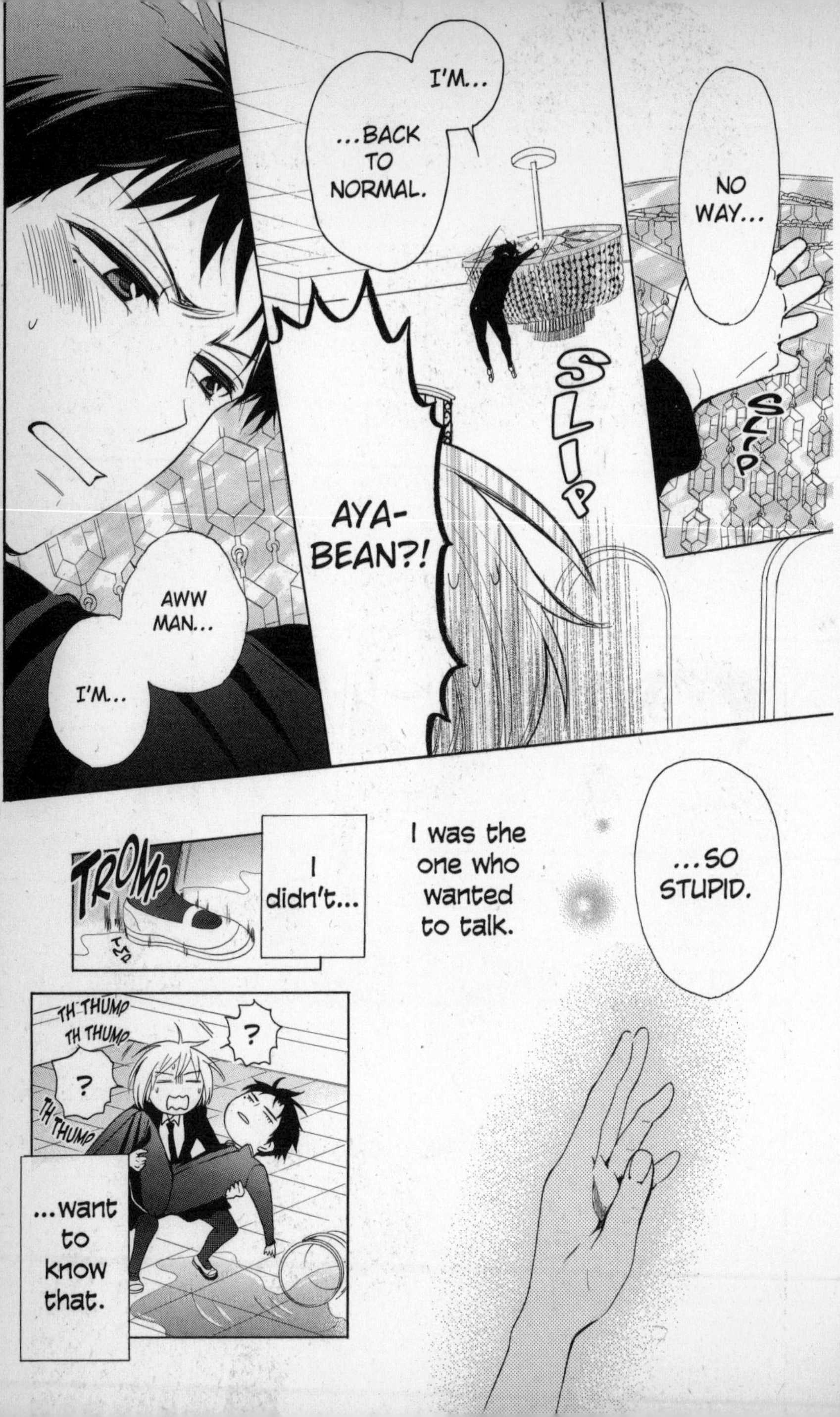
NO WAY...
SLIP
I'M...
...BACK TO NORMAL.
SLIP
AYA-BEAN?!
AWW MAN...
I'M...
...SO STUPID.
I was the one who wanted to talk.
I didn't...
TROMP
TH THUMP
TH THUMP
TH THUMP
?
?
...want to know that.

TOGETHER WITH AYA-BEAN 1

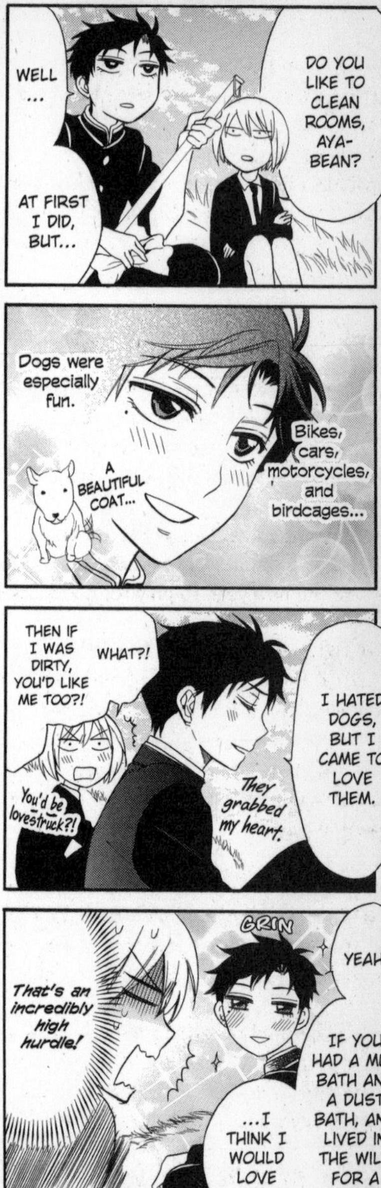
DO YOU LIKE TO CLEAN ROOMS, AYA-BEAN?
WELL...
AT FIRST I DID, BUT...
Bikes, cars, motorcycles, and birdcages...
Dogs were especially fun.
A BEAUTIFUL COAT...
I HATED DOGS, BUT I CAME TO LOVE THEM.
They grabbed my heart.
WHAT?!
THEN IF I WAS DIRTY, YOU'D LIKE ME TOO?!
You'd be lovestruck?!
GRIN
YEAH.
IF YOU HAD A MUD BATH AND A DUST BATH, AND LIVED IN THE WILD FOR A WEEK...
...I THINK I WOULD LOVE YOU.
That's an incredibly high hurdle!

TOGETHER WITH AYA-BEAN 2

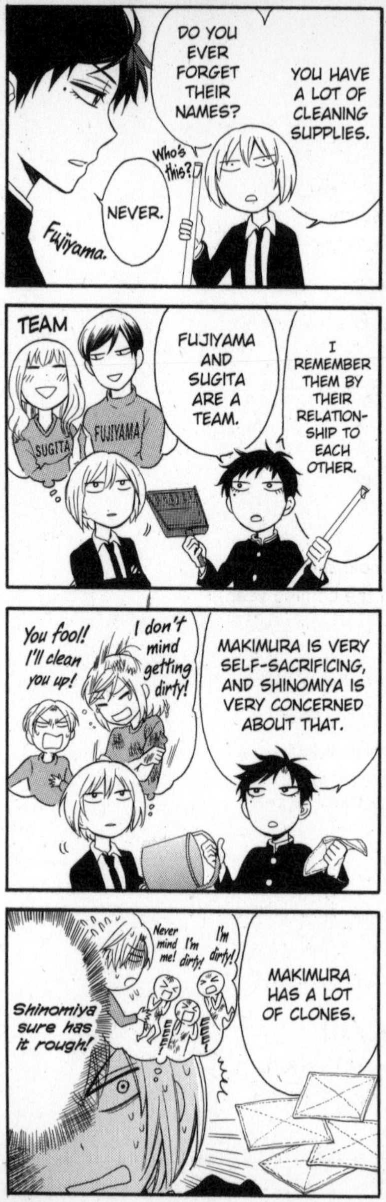
YOU HAVE A LOT OF CLEANING SUPPLIES.
DO YOU EVER FORGET THEIR NAMES?
NEVER.
Who's this?
Fujiyama.
I REMEMBER THEM BY THEIR RELATIONSHIP TO EACH OTHER.
FUJIYAMA AND SUGITA ARE A TEAM.
TEAM
FUJIYAMA
SUGITA
MAKIMURA IS VERY SELF-SACRIFICING, AND SHINOMIYA IS VERY CONCERNED ABOUT THAT.
I don't mind getting dirty!
You fool! I'll clean you up!
MAKIMURA HAS A LOT OF CLONES.
I'm dirty!
I'm dirty!
Never mind me!
Shinomiya sure has it rough!

End Notes

Page 3, panel 2: Hordes of couples
Christmas Eve is a popular date night in Japan.

Page 9, panel 3: Cake, chicken
Christmas cake in Japan is traditionally a sponge cake with whipped cream and strawberries. Chicken is also considered a Christmas food in Japan, much the way turkey or goose are holiday fare in the United States.

Page 43, panel 1: Osechi
Osechi is a traditional Japanese meal eaten during the New Year's holidays. It includes such foods as fish cakes, sweet potato mashed with chestnuts, black beans, tuna fish wrapped in seaweed, herring roe, omelets with fish paste or mashed shrimp, and vegetable soup with sticky rice cakes.

Page 43, panel 6: Go to the shrine
In Japan it is traditional to visit a shrine or temple the first week of the new year, to pray for good luck in the coming year.

Page 53, panel 6: Mochi kinchaku
A rice cake in a deep-fried tofu pouch held together with either toothpicks or dried gourd shavings.

Page 54, panel 1: Bondage knots
These are examples of *kikkoushibari*, a tying pattern used in Japanese bondage.

Page 56, panel 3: Secret Stew
A version of the hot pot dish *yaminabe* where everyone brings a secret ingredient and adds it to the hot pot while the lights are off. Each participant has to have a bite of the resulting dish.

Page 59, panel 4: Choco pies and mame daifuku
Choco pies are a popular snack food in Korea and Japan. *Mame daifuku* are sticky rice cakes filled with a paste of red beans or soybeans, azuki beans, and mochi.

Page 71, panel 3: 235 yen
Around $3.00 U.S.

Page 71, panel 5: Croquette bread
Japanese croquettes are breaded, deep-fried patties of various mashed ingredients like meat, seafood, vegetable and potatoes. Croquette bread is either a sandwich with the croquette as the filling, or a bun with the croquette baked in.

Page 104 panel 1: Mafuyu's face mask
In Japan it is normal to see people wearing masks like this. They are worn to protect others from your germs if you are feeling unwell.

Page 109, panel 1: Shogi
A Japanese board game similar to chess where the object of the game is to capture the opponent's king. Each player has twenty pieces.

Page 161, panel 7: Shoe cupboard
In Japan, shoes are removed inside most buildings. In schools, a cubby for your outdoor shoes and your indoor shoes are provided to students.

Izumi Tsubaki began drawing manga in her first year of high school. She was soon selected to be in the top ten of *Hana to Yume's* HMC (*Hana to Yume* Mangaka Course), and subsequently won *Hana to Yume's* Big Challenge contest. Her debut title, *Chijimete Distance* (Shrink the Distance), ran in 2002 in *Hana to Yume* magazine, issue 17. Her other works include *The Magic Touch* (*Oyayubi kara Romance*) and *Oresama Teacher*, which she is currently working on.

ORESAMA TEACHER
Vol. 11
Shojo Beat Edition

STORY AND ART BY
Izumi Tsubaki

English Translation & Adaptation/JN Productions
Touch-up Art & Lettering/Eric Erbes
Design/Yukiko Whitley
Editor/Pancha Diaz

ORESAMA TEACHER by Izumi Tsubaki © Izumi Tsubaki 2011
All rights reserved. First published in Japan in 2011 by HAKUSENSHA, Inc., Tokyo.
English language translation rights arranged with HAKUSENSHA, Inc., Tokyo.

Printed in Canada

Published by VIZ Media, LLC
P.O. Box 77010
San Francisco, CA 94107

10 9 8 7 6 5 4 3 2 1
First printing, November 2012

www.viz.com   www.shojobeat.com

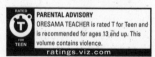

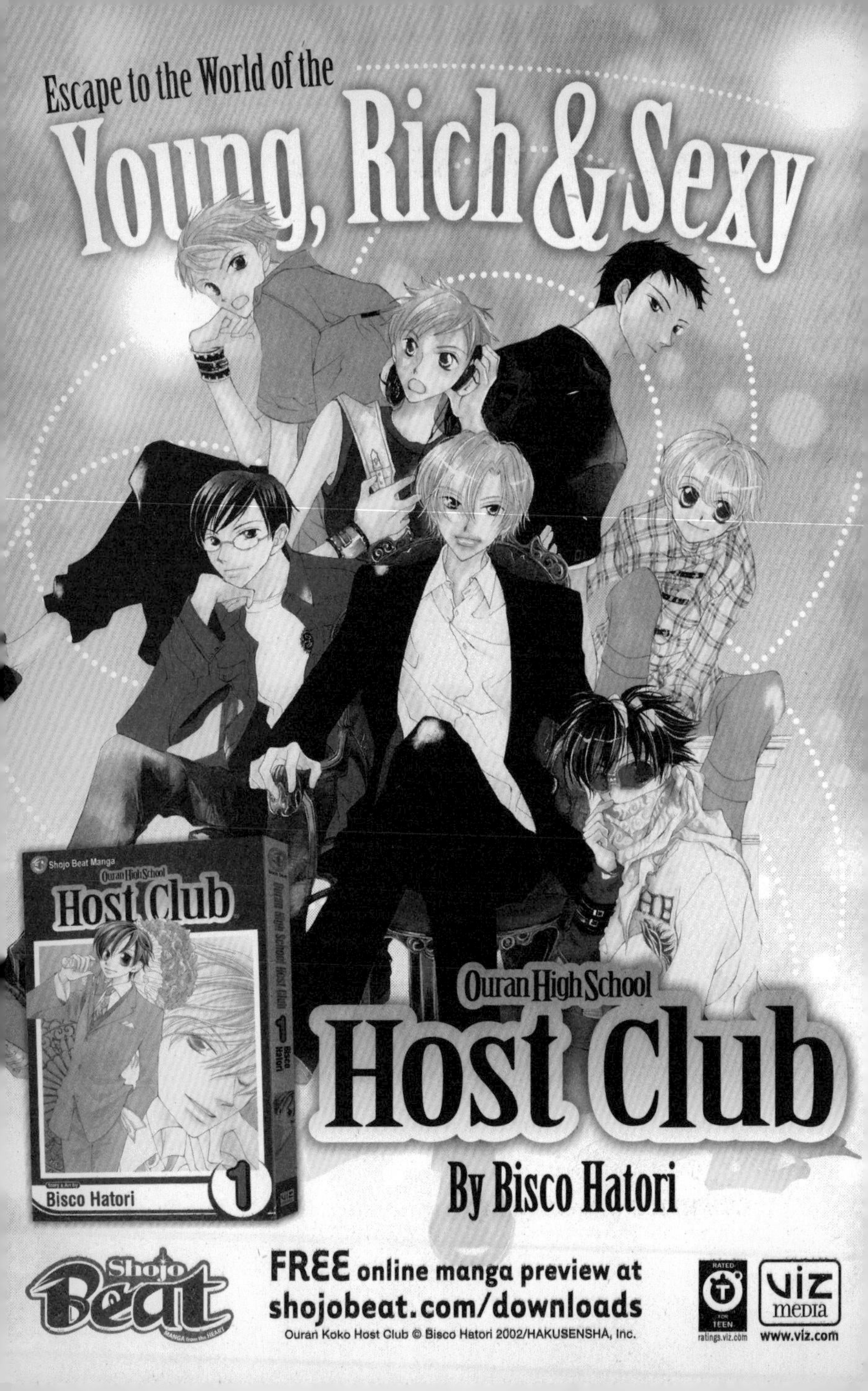

Can love trump a cursed life?

Sawako's a shy, lonely, pure-hearted student who just happens to look like the scary girl in a famous horror movie! But when she manages to befriend the most popular boy in school, will her frightful reputation scare off her best chance for love?

kimi ni todoke
From Me to You

By Karuho Shiina

Find out in the *Kimi ni Todoke* manga—
BUY YOURS TODAY!

Winner of the 2008 Kodansha Manga Award
(shojo category)

On sale at **www.shojobeat.com**
Also available at your local bookstore or comic store.

KIMI NI TODOKE © 2005 Karuho Shiina/SHUEISHA Inc.

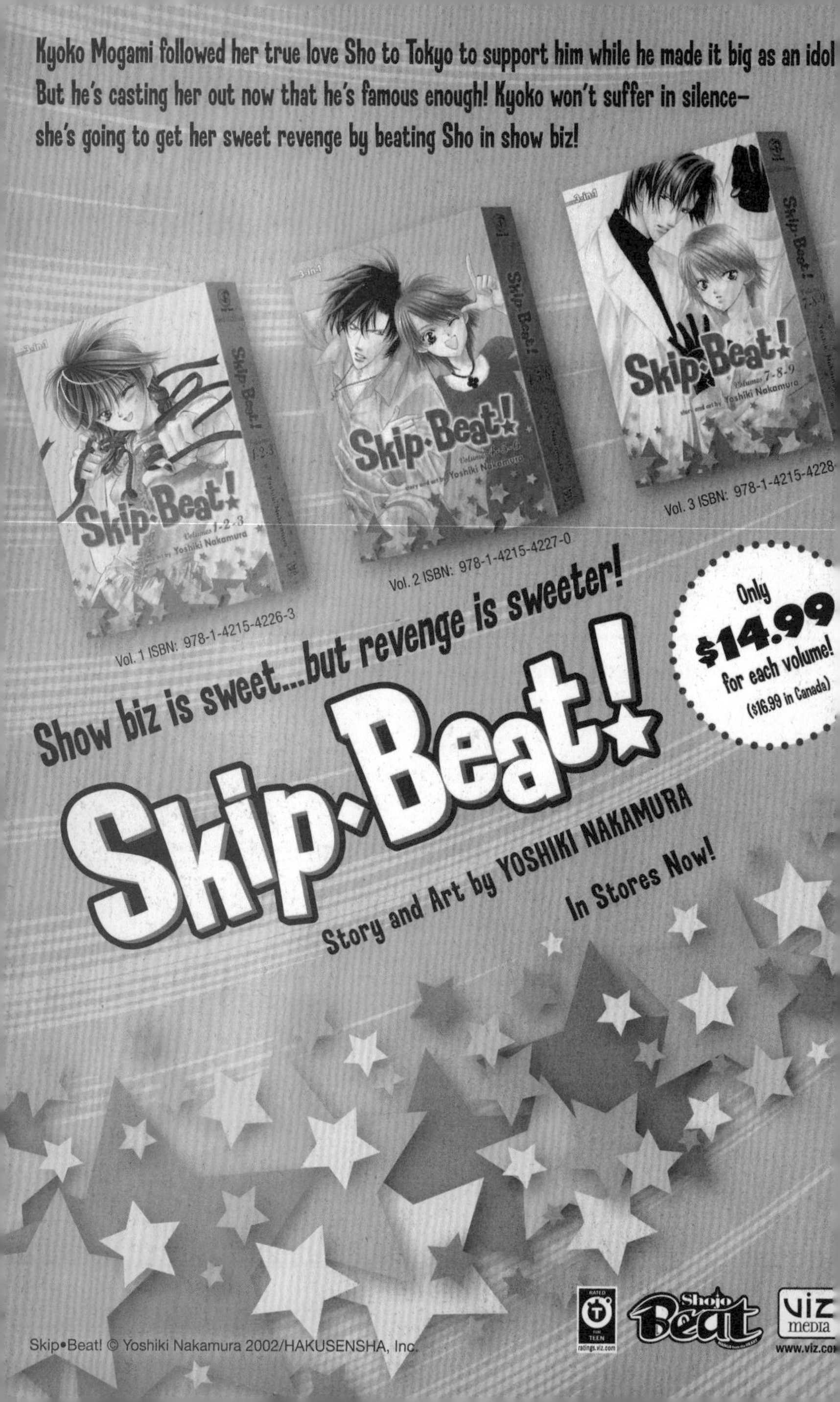
Kyoko Mogami followed her true love Sho to Tokyo to support him while he made it big as an idol
But he's casting her out now that he's famous enough! Kyoko won't suffer in silence–
she's going to get her sweet revenge by beating Sho in show biz!
Skip·Beat!
Yoshiki Nakamura
Skip·Beat!
Yoshiki Nakamura
Skip·Beat!
Volumes 7-8-9
Yoshiki Nakamura
Vol. 1 ISBN: 978-1-4215-4226-3
Vol. 2 ISBN: 978-1-4215-4227-0
Vol. 3 ISBN: 978-1-4215-4228-
Only
$14.99
for each volume!
($16.99 in Canada)
Show biz is sweet...but revenge is sweeter!
Skip·Beat!
Story and Art by YOSHIKI NAKAMURA
In Stores Now!
Skip•Beat! © Yoshiki Nakamura 2002/HAKUSENSHA, Inc.
RATED T TEEN
ratings.viz.com
Shojo Beat
VIZ media
www.viz.co

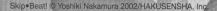

Surprise!

You may be reading the wrong way!

It's true: In keeping with the original Japanese comic format, this book reads from right to left—so action, sound effects, and word balloons are completely reversed. This preserves the orientation of the original artwork—plus, it's fun! Check out the diagram shown here to get the hang of things, and then turn to the other side of the book to get started!

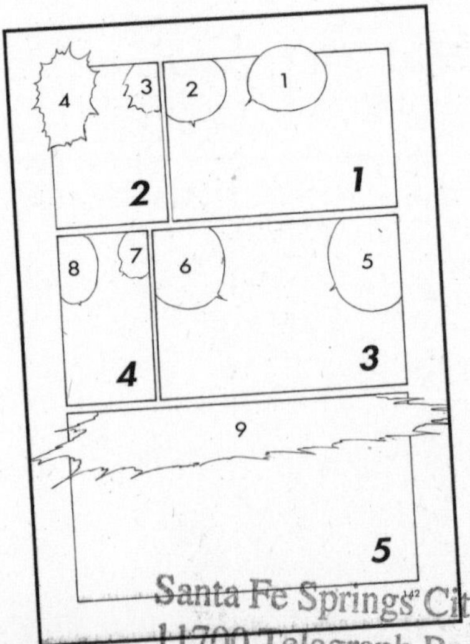

1
2
1
3
4
2
5
6
3
7
8
4
9
5

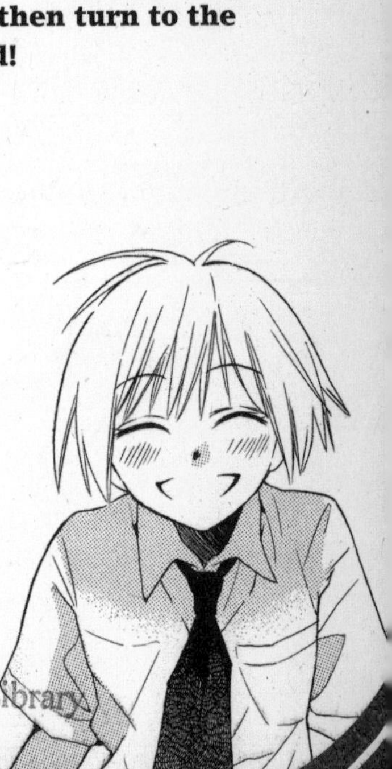